Colonial al-Andalus

Colonial al-Andalus

SPAIN AND THE MAKING OF MODERN MOROCCAN CULTURE

Eric Calderwood

THE BELKNAP PRESS OF HARVARD UNIVERSITY PRESS

Cambridge, Massachusetts   London, England

2018

Copyright © 2018 by the President and Fellows of Harvard College
All rights reserved

First printing

LIBRARY OF CONGRESS CATALOGING-IN-PUBLICATION
DATA Names: Calderwood, Eric, 1979– author.
Title: Colonial al-Andalus : Spain and the making of modern
Moroccan culture / Eric Calderwood.
Description: Cambridge, Massachusetts : The Belknap Press of Harvard
University Press, 2018. | Includes bibliographical references and index. Identifiers:
LCCN 2017041941 | ISBN 9780674980327 (alk. paper)
Subjects: LCSH: National characteristics, Moroccan. | Morocco—
Civilization. | Andalusia (Spain)—Civilization—Islamic influences. |
Spain—Colonies—Africa.|Spain— Foreignrelations— Morocco.|
Morocco—Foreignrelations— Spain.
Classification: LCC DT312 .C35 2018 | DDC 964—dc23 LC record available
athttps:// lccn.loc.gov/2017041941

CONTENTS

	Note on Transliteration	*vii*
	Introduction	1
1	Tetouan Is Granada	30
2	Al-Andalus and Moroccan Literary History	74
3	Al-Andalus, Andalucía, and Morocco	116
4	Franco's Hajj	142
5	The Invention of Hispano-Arab Culture	167
6	Moroccan Alhambras	208
7	The Daughter of Granada and Fez	251
	Epilogue: The Afterlife of Colonial al-Andalus in Contemporary Morocco	286
	Notes	*301*
	Bibliography	*349*
	Acknowledgments	*377*
	Index	*383*

NOTE ON TRANSLITERATION

FOR ARABIC WORDS, I have followed, in general, the transliteration system of the *International Journal of Middle East Studies*. There are, however, some exceptions to this rule. Many of the Moroccan authors I discuss in this book write in multiple languages, including Arabic and one or many European languages. If I am referring exclusively or primarily to an author's Arabic-language body of work, then I transliterate his or her name according to the *IJMES* system. In the case of authors whose work is primarily in European languages, I default to the spelling preferred by the author in question—which, in the case of Maghribi authors, often follows French orthographic conventions. Thus, for example, I write "Abdelmajid Benjelloun" rather than "'Abd al-Majid bin Jallun." For place names, such as Tangier and Tetouan, I give the standard transliterations that are in common use in English-language maps and guides.

INTRODUCTION

TETOUAN, THE FORMER CAPITAL of the Spanish Protectorate in Morocco (1912–1956), sits in the Martil River valley, a few kilometers from Morocco's Mediterranean coast and just south of the Strait of Gibraltar. The city is divided into an old city (the Medina), which dates back to the fifteenth century, and a colonial annex (the Ensanche) built by the Spanish in the early twentieth century.[1] If you exit the old city through the Cemetery Gate (Bab al-Maqabir), you will come across the main Muslim cemetery, which straddles the road and creeps up neighboring Mount Dersa. The cemetery affords a panoramic view of Tetouan, whose sand-colored walls and whitewashed buildings accentuate the many shades of green that color the river valley and the face of Mount Ghurghiz, on the other side of the valley (Figure 1). The gulls that float and screech overhead are reminders of the proximity of the Mediterranean Sea, which appears in the distance. The bird calls mingle with the sound of hammering that wafts in from the nearby carpentry workshops. Tetouan's cemetery is a point of transit that connects the artisanal quarters of the old city with the poor neighborhoods that abut the cemetery. Old men in djellabas and young men in tracksuits plow along the cemetery's narrow paths, without having much time to notice the tombs that they pass. Throughout the cemetery, goats graze among the clumps of overgrown grass and under the shade of palm, cedar, and fig trees.

The cemetery's most prominent feature is a whitewashed mausoleum, with green tile trim, that houses the remains of two men who died five centuries apart: Abu al-Hasan 'Ali al-Manzari, the city's

Figure 1. Panorama of Tetouan's cemetery and surrounding valley, May 2016. Photograph © Eric Calderwood.

fifteenth-century founder, and ʿAbd al-Khaliq al-Turris (1910–1970), the leader of the Moroccan nationalist movement in northern Morocco (Figure 2).[2] I first noticed the mausoleum in 2008. Amid the quiet abandonment of Tetouan's main cemetery, the large and faded mausoleum caught my eye. Who was al-Manzari? Who was al-Turris? Why were they buried together? The first two questions were easy to answer, but the third one turned out to be an enigma that has kept me thinking for the past several years. The surprising union of al-Manzari and al-Turris, whose lives were separated by five hundred years, illustrates a larger story about Moroccan history that this book seeks to tell. Through this story, I hope to change the way that we imagine the relationship between Spain and Morocco, the medieval and the modern, as well as between colonialism and anticolonial resistance in North Africa and the Middle East.

Figure 2. Mausoleum of al-Manzari and al-Turris in Tetouan, May 2016. Photograph © Eric Calderwood.

Al-Manzari, Tetouan's founder, hailed from Granada, the last Muslim kingdom in al-Andalus (medieval Muslim Iberia). The son of a wealthy Granadan family, al-Manzari served as the commander of the military outpost at Píñar, between Granada and its northern border with the Christian kingdom of Castile. Píñar fell to Castilian forces in 1485. Its loss was a prelude to the Christian occupation of Granada in 1492, which concluded the Christian Reconquest of al-Andalus and brought to a close nearly eight centuries of Muslim rule in Iberia. Al-Manzari did not remain in his native al-Andalus to see the Catholic Monarchs enter Granada on January 2, 1492. Rather than submitting to Christian rule, al-Manzari preferred exile in a new country. In 1484 or 1485, around the time of the conquest of Píñar, al-Manzari emigrated to northern Morocco with a band of a few dozen followers.[3] There, he oversaw the rebuilding of Tetouan on top of the remains of an older settlement.

Tetouan would eventually emerge as the cultural capital of northern Morocco and as a point of contact and exchange between Europe and Africa, but the city that al-Manzari and his followers built was essentially a garrison town: a heavily fortified citadel whose walls enclosed a mosque and a public bath (both still standing today), and a handful of houses.[4] Al-Manzari probably conceived of Tetouan as a provisional base for taking back Granada and the other conquered cities of al-Andalus. Instead, Tetouan became a permanent settlement, which grew quickly over the next two decades. In 1492, with the Christian conquest of Granada, waves of Andalusis, including some Granadan Jews, left the Iberian Peninsula and settled in Tetouan and other Moroccan cities. While many Andalusi Muslims emigrated from the Iberian Peninsula in 1492, many also chose to remain in Granada. The Capitulations of Granada, the peace treaty signed with the Catholic Monarchs, guaranteed that the new rulers would respect the Muslims' religious practices, private property, and right to emigrate.[5] In 1500, however, the Spanish began a brutal campaign to force Spanish Muslims to convert to Christianity.[6] In response, many Muslims fled Spain for North Africa, never to return. In the first decade of the sixteenth century, Tetouan's population jumped from two thousand to over ten thousand, swelled by the massive arrival of refugees from Spain.[7]

Al-Manzari continued to rule Tetouan until his death in late 1540 or early 1541. He died without fulfilling his dream of returning to al-Andalus, but the city that he and his followers built included a few echoes of the Granada that they had left behind. For example, near the remains of al-Manzari's Casbah stands a covered gateway that was modeled on the Gate of Justice in Granada's Alhambra.[8] In the neighborhoods clustered around al-Manzari's Casbah, the doors of the oldest houses are decorated with iron pomegranates, in order to signal their owners' descent from Granada (which means "pomegranate" in Spanish). Outside the city walls, Tetouan's cemetery is punctuated with domed cubical structures, known as *qubbas,* which were a common architectural feature in Andalusi cemeteries. These domed cubes were built in the late fifteenth or early sixteenth century as mausoleums for the Granadan mujahidin who accompanied al-Manzari across the Strait of Gibraltar.[9]

Al-Manzari's mausoleum, in contrast, was not built in the sixteenth century. In fact, al-Manzari's final resting place underwent an important transformation in the second half of the twentieth century. Up until Moroccan independence in 1956, al-Manzari had his own grave in Tetouan's cemetery. It was a modest tomb surrounded by four low walls. A picture of al-Manzari's original tomb appears in the first volume of Muhammad Dawud's encyclopedic *History of Tetouan* (*Tarikh Titwan*), published in 1959 (Figure 3). Dawud was part of a generation of Moroccan nationalist intellectuals who contributed to the revival of Morocco's Andalusi heritage, from cultural practices like Andalusi music to foundational figures like al-Manzari. In the 1960s, a group of Tetouani civic leaders formed a committee to design a new mausoleum for Tetouan's Andalusi founder.[10] The committee commissioned the architect Sa'd Binnuna to design the mausoleum. The architect was the youngest son of 'Abd al-Salam Binnuna, often hailed as the father of the Moroccan nationalist movement.[11] The committee that oversaw the mausoleum project also included several prominent Moroccan nationalists from the north, such as 'Abd al-Khaliq al-Turris.

Al-Turris's interest in Tetouan's Andalusi founder is not surprising. Throughout his career, al-Turris closely aligned himself with the cultural memory of al-Andalus. Like many leaders of the Moroccan nationalist movement, he claimed descent from al-Andalus.[12] In fact, his last name comes from the Spanish surname *Torres*, which is the spelling that al-Turris adopted when writing his name in Latin script. In a 1936 speech in support of Franco's military uprising in the Spanish Civil War, al-Turris asserted that Moroccans enjoy a "spiritual union" with the Spanish because they all descend from "a single family" that traces its roots back to al-Andalus.[13] After Moroccan independence, al-Turris served as Morocco's first ambassador to Spain. In the 1960s, he remained active in several political and cultural projects, including the committee that oversaw the building of the mausoleum for al-Manzari. Al-Turris and his colleagues decided to build the new mausoleum on top of al-Manzari's original tomb. The project was in its final stages when al-Turris died suddenly of a heart attack in May of 1970. He was buried in the mausoleum that he helped to design.

Al-Manzari's shared mausoleum with al-Turris elides a temporal gap of five centuries. It unites, under one roof, the history of Tetouan's Andalusi foundation, embodied by al-Manzari, and the history of the Moroccan nationalist movement, embodied by al-Turris. The building thus

Figure 3. Al-Manzari's original tomb in Tetouan. Image from Muhammad Dawud, *Tarikh Titwan*, vol. 1 (Tetouan: Matba'at Maktabat "Cremades," 1959), between pages 96 and 97. Reproduction courtesy of the Mohamed Daoud Foundation for History and Culture, Tetouan, Morocco.

draws a direct line between the Andalusi migration to Morocco in the fifteenth century and the struggle for Moroccan independence in the twentieth century. It epitomizes an idea that I will be calling, in this book, the "Andalus-centric" narrative of Moroccan history. According to this narrative, the culture of al-Andalus did not disappear in 1492, with the Christian Reconquest of Muslim Granada; rather, Andalusi culture migrated from the Iberian Peninsula to Morocco, where it has continued to thrive until the present day.

Celebrations of Morocco's Andalusi identity abound in contemporary Moroccan literature, historiography, and political discourse. For instance, the Moroccan historian M'hammad Benaboud has argued:

> The footprints of al-Andalus in Morocco remain deeply rooted, both in cities and in the countryside, and they constitute an integral part of the Moroccan sociocultural fabric. The profound integration of the Andalusi heritage into daily life, at a collective and individual level, is so important that it is even reflected in the behavior and consciousness of the Moroccan, whose identity would not be comprehensible without it.[14]

Many Moroccan, European, and American scholars echo Benaboud's assertion that the legacy of al-Andalus is an essential component of Moroccan identity and culture.[15] Such assertions are not limited to scholarly writings. Al-Andalus also figures prominently in contemporary Moroccan artistic production. In literature, some of Morocco's most eminent novelists and poets, such as Bin Salim Himmish and Ahmad Tribaq, have written important works with Andalusi themes.[16] Andalusi music is Morocco's national music and is commonly featured on national television, at official functions, and at weddings and other celebrations.[17] Al-Andalus has even made the leap to the big screen, where it has served as the setting for popular Moroccan films, such as Said Naciri's *Abdou in the Time of the Almohads* (2006).[18] Finally, al-Andalus is one of the drivers behind tourism to Morocco, the country's second largest source of income.[19] Since 1992, the fifth centennial of the fall of Granada, Morocco and Spain have collaborated on a number of tourism initiatives and traveling exhibitions that promote the two countries' shared Andalusi heritage.[20]

While several cities compete for the mantle of Morocco's most Andalusi city, Tetouan, the former capital of the Spanish Protectorate in Morocco, has emerged in the past two decades as a major hub for the celebration of al-Andalus in contemporary Morocco. Tetouan's cultural scene and tourism industry revolve around the memory of al-Andalus. Its annual Festival of Andalusi Music brings together the leading Andalusi orchestras from Tetouan, Tangier, Fez, and Rabat. Dozens of local businesses are named after places or people from Andalusi history, including a cafe, a hair salon, and a jewelry store that all share the name "Granada." Historians from both sides of the Mediterranean extol Tetouan's connection to al-Andalus—and, in particular, to Granada. In fact, many scholars refer to Tetouan as "the daughter of Granada," a nickname for Tetouan that was coined by the nationalist M'hammad Binnuna in the 1950s.[21] When UNESCO declared Tetouan's old city a World Heritage Site in 1997, its report called Tetouan "a true synthesis of Moroccan and Andalusian cultures," and it praised the "clear Andalusian influence" of Tetouan's art and architecture.[22] For many Moroccan writers, al-Andalus's influence on Tetouan goes far beyond architecture and encompasses domains as diverse as cuisine, clothing, handicrafts, dialect, and even temperament.[23] In 1999, Muhammad al-Sabbagh, Tetouan's most famous contemporary poet, published a book called *I Am al-Andalus* (*Ana al-Andalus*). The title indicates the intense sense of identification that many Tetouanis feel with al-Andalus.

This phenomenon is not limited, however, to Tetouan. Morocco's Andalusi identity has become a matter of national doctrine. Even the most recent Moroccan constitution, ratified in 2011, propagates the idea that modern Moroccan culture descends directly from al-Andalus. The constitution's preamble highlights the influence of al-Andalus on Moroccan national identity and affirms "the Moroccan people's attachment to the values of openness, moderation, tolerance, and dialogue."[24] The constitution thus aligns Morocco with one of the most potent modern myths associated with al-Andalus: the idea that al-Andalus was an exceptionally tolerant place, where Muslims, Christians, and Jews peacefully coexisted. This idea is known, in Spanish, as *convivencia* ("coexistence"). Many scholars have warned that it is anachronistic to use the modern concept of tolerance to describe interfaith relations in the Middle Ages.[25] Despite this objection, the myth of Andalusi tolerance has become quite powerful in the post-9/11 era, when it has served as a counterweight to the "clash of civilizations" mentality that underwrote the Bush-era "war on terror."[26] Since 2001, Morocco has leveraged its historical connection to al-Andalus in order to present itself as a model of interfaith tolerance and as an intermediary between the Muslim world and the West.[27] Al-Andalus is not only a means of articulating Morocco's relationship with the West; it also functions as a sign of prestige and power within Moroccan domestic politics. During the colonial period, many of the leaders of the Moroccan nationalist movement emphasized their Andalusi ancestry. Today, Moroccans of Andalusi descent are still a political elite that enjoys close ties to the royal family.[28] In short, al-Andalus is a powerful tool for understanding social relations in Morocco and also for mapping Morocco's understanding of its place in the world.

Colonial al-Andalus argues that Morocco's Andalusi identity is not a medieval legacy, but is, instead, a modern invention that emerged from the colonial encounter between Spain and Morocco in the nineteenth and twentieth centuries. Starting with the Spanish-Moroccan War of 1859–1860, Spanish writers revived the memory of al-Andalus in order to emphasize Spain's historical connection to North Africa and to justify Spain's colonial presence in Morocco.[29] The exploitation of Spain's Muslim past reached its apogee in the Spanish Civil War (1936–1939), when Francisco Franco led a military uprising that toppled the Spanish Republic. During the Civil War, Franco and his collaborators used the memory of al-Andalus as a tool to recruit approximately eighty thousand Moroccan soldiers to fight in their rebel army.[30] To ensure Moroccan support for the rebel cause, Franco also granted unprecedented freedoms to the Moroccan nationalist movement, including the creation of an Arabic-language nationalist press and the legalization of nationalist parties. From these institutions of Moroccan nationalist politics, forged in the opening months of the Spanish Civil War, emerged a widespread call for the creation of a Moroccan national culture, whose cornerstone would be Morocco's Andalusi heritage. Thus, in one of the eloquent ironies of colonial history, the Spanish insistence on Morocco's Andalusi heritage, which had served as a justification for Spanish colonialism, galvanized the Moroccan national culture that would supplant colonial rule. A Spanish way of talking about Morocco became a Moroccan way of talking about Morocco.

This book advances the claim that Morocco's Andalusi identity is a product of the colonial encounter between Spain and Morocco. Until now, it has been difficult to see this argument clearly because it runs counter to many common assumptions about Morocco, Spain, and the relationship between Europe and North Africa. First of all, my argument exposes some uncomfortable alliances between people and projects that we do not normally place side by side: Spanish fascists and Moroccan nationalists, Catholics and Muslims, and colonizing and colonized subjects. Acknowledging these alliances may provoke cognitive dissonance, and even some pain, especially for Moroccan political elites and cultural luminaries, who have invested significant energy in promoting their country's Andalusi identity. This book's story also cuts against the grain of the existing scholarship on Morocco and North Africa, which has focused, almost exclusively, on the history of French colonialism in North Africa. This focus has not only marginalized modern Spanish-Moroccan relations, but it has also limited the conceptual categories that we use to understand colonialism and its long-term impact on colonized societies. Rather than conceiving of colonialism and anticolonial nationalism as two opposing forces, this book, instead, shows how they often work as two sides of the same coin, reinforcing each other and reproducing each other's logic. Finally, my study attempts to distinguish rigorously between the history of medieval al-Andalus and the various meanings and uses that that history has accrued in modern times. This approach might encounter some resistance from scholars and writers who have wanted to find in the memory of al-Andalus a symbol of intercultural tolerance and a roadmap for peaceful relations between Europe and the Muslim world. In my account, the modern memory of al-Andalus is inseparable from the legacy of colonialism, and it entangles in its confusing web a surprising cast of characters, including Spanish fascists and Moroccan nationalists.

There are some important caveats to my argument. First, I am not contesting the well-documented fact that tens of thousands of Andalusis migrated from the Iberian Peninsula to Morocco from the end of the fifteenth century to the beginning of the seventeenth century, and that the Andalusi migration had a profound impact on social and cultural life in Morocco.[31] It is also important to acknowledge that there were previous articulations of a distinct Andalusi identity before the period of Spanish colonialism in Morocco. Both Alexander Elinson and Camilo Gómez-Rivas have persuasively argued that a distinct idea of Andalusiness came into focus in the thirteenth and fourteenth centuries, when Andalusi writers, such as al-Shaqundi (d. 1231/2) and Ibn al-Khatib (d. 1375), were pushed into North African exile on account of the political turmoil on the Iberian Peninsula and the rapid advance of the Christian Reconquest of al-Andalus.[32] While in exile, both al-Shaqundi and Ibn al-Khatib penned influential works in praise of al-Andalus, emphasizing their homeland's cultural superiority over the Maghrib. Thus, the Maghrib originally served as a foil against which elite Andalusi writers defined their superiority. The assertion of Andalusi supremacy often had ethnic overtones. The writings of al-Shaqundi and Ibn al-Khatib exalt Arab culture in al-Andalus while downplaying the contributions of Berbers, the indigenous peoples of North Africa. The anti-Berber sentiment in medieval Andalusi literary culture continues to have ramifications in contemporary Morocco, where celebrations of al-Andalus are sometimes seen as a way of marking distance from an indigenous Berber culture and identity.[33]

In other words, Spanish colonialism did not invent al-Andalus, nor did it offer the first articulation of Andalusi identity in North Africa. What it did was inaugurate a certain set of ideas about how Morocco became Andalusi and how Morocco's Andalusi culture manifests in the modern period. A powerful synthesis of these ideas appears in the work of Rodolfo Gil Benumeya (1901–1975), an influential theoretician of Spanish colonialism under Franco:

> In 1492 and in 1610, the majority of Muslims from Andalucía and Murcia went to Morocco. There, they founded neighborhoods and cities, where they faithfully preserved and reproduced all of the customs of their land of origin. Fez, Tetouan, and Rabat are the three great Andalusian capitals. . . . They gave a Hispano-Muslim organization to the Moroccan state and government, and, to Moroccan Islam, they gave a local air that does not exist in the countries of the East because it originates on the shores of the Guadalquivir. Thanks to Fez, Tetouan, and Rabat, Morocco eventually became a living museum, where the Andalucía of the Middle Ages remains intact.[34]

Gil Benumeya's passage, written in 1942, crystallizes the main components of a historical narrative that will appear, in different forms and in different languages, throughout this book: from 1492 on, Andalusi Muslims left the Iberian Peninsula and immigrated to Morocco, where they rebuilt their civilization, especially in Fez, Tetouan, and Rabat. Morocco's Andalusi cities serve today as a "living museum," where Moroccans have preserved Andalusi culture. Gil Benumeya goes on to catalog a series of cultural practices that, he claims, have descended from al-Andalus to modern Morocco, including music, architecture, crafts, clothing, dialect, and religion.[35]

Today, scholarly and popular Moroccan representations of al-Andalus bear a striking resemblance to Gil Benumeya's text, or to other Spanish colonial texts from the 1930s, 1940s, and 1950s. For example, in a 1992 lecture, Muhammad Binsharifa, the director of the Moroccan National Library, said:

> To this day, we still see in Morocco the manifestations of the continuity that existed between Morocco and al-Andalus, despite the passage of many centuries since the end of al-Andalus. . . . The heritage of al-Andalus is still preserved and uninterrupted in Morocco, as exemplified by the families of Andalusi origin in many cities and villages. We see it in architecture, music, cuisine, and other refinements of civilization.[36]

More recently, in a 2013 book about Tetouan, the historian Muhammad al-Sharif wrote that Tetouan "still preserves Andalusi architecture inside its walls, and Tetouan's residents still preserve the dialect, music, fashion, and the traditional crafts of al-Andalus. [Tetouan] truly resembles, to a great extent, Granada with its narrow streets and the manner of its buildings."[37] Like the shared mausoleum of al-Manzari and al-Turris, Binsharifa and al-Sharif emphasize the uninterrupted transmission of Andalusi identity from fifteenth-century Iberia to contemporary Morocco. Their remarks point to medieval roots, but they reproduce ideas that first emerged under the auspices of Spanish colonialism, as I hope to show over the following chapters.

The key difference in the contemporary Moroccan iteration of this narrative of Moroccan history is that Spanish colonialism has been expunged from it. Spanish colonial writers imagined themselves as the saviors of Morocco's Andalusi heritage. In 1939, Tomás García Figueras, a leading Francoist in Morocco, wrote: "Millions of Muslims scattered around the whole world . . . follow with enthusiastic attention the spiritual and human work that is the Spanish Protectorate in Morocco, and through it, they witness the renaissance of that splendid cultural coexistence [*convivencia*] of both peoples in al-Andalus."[38] For García Figueras, Spanish colonialism marked the renaissance of al-Andalus in Morocco. Indeed, renaissance was a central trope of Francoist writings about Morocco. In contemporary Moroccan culture, the trope of renaissance has been replaced by the trope of continuity. Contemporary Moroccan intellectuals share with Spanish colonial writers a set of ideas about how Andalusi culture was transmitted to Morocco and what Morocco's Andalusi culture looks like. Today, though, these ideas have shed any association with colonial ideology. A narrative that was forged in the service of colonialism has taken on a life of its own as a centerpiece of Moroccan national identity.

Colonial al-Andalus in Modern Spanish and Moroccan Studies

This story is a cautionary tale about colonialism's capacity to generate the tools of its own destruction. But it is not just that. It also confounds the dominant understanding of modern Spanish and Moroccan history. The historical scholarship on modern Spain has generally treated the Spanish Civil War (1936–1939) as a rupture that separates two irreconcilable views of Spain. On the one hand are the Republicans, who advocate for a pluralistic Spain that is tolerant of regional, linguistic, and cultural difference; on the other hand are the Francoists, who fight for a Catholic, monolingual (Castilian-speaking), and imperial nation.[39] The tendency to cast the Civil War as a complete rupture in Spanish history has obfuscated the unexpected ways in which Republicans and Francoists shared interests and discourses in Morocco. Spanish colonialism made strange bedfellows of liberals and fascists. Spanish colonial writers of all ideological stripes justified Spain's role as a colonizer in the Muslim world by celebrating the idea of *convivencia,* the harmonious coexistence of the Abrahamic faiths in al-Andalus. This particular view of medieval Iberian history has largely been associated with the Republican cause and, more broadly, with liberal and progressive views of Spanish history.[40] In contrast, I argue that Spain's claim to a tradition of exemplary tolerance, grounded in its Muslim past, underpins diverse ideological projects, including fascism.

This study also contributes to an ongoing revision of modern Moroccan history. Until recently, the historiography of twentieth-century Morocco, like Spanish historiography, was structured around a great rupture: Moroccan independence from Spanish and French colonial rule in 1956. Early Moroccan nationalist historiography, written during the 1950s and 1960s, tended to depict the colonial period as an aberration that temporarily severed the historical unity of the Moroccan nation.[41] My book challenges this alleged continuity between precolonial and postcolonial Morocco. It thus joins a growing body of scholarship that aims to show how the colonial experience continues to shape and define political and cultural debates in post-independence Morocco. Recent scholarship on Morocco has elucidated how European colonialism fundamentally altered Moroccan discourses about religion, national and ethnic identity, gender, science, music, and the arts. Edmund Burke III, for example, argues that French colonial ethnography invented the idea that Morocco has its own distinctive form of Islam, "Moroccan Islam," and that the discourse on Moroccan Islam has become a source of legitimacy for the Moroccan monarchy in the post-independence era.[42]

Burke's work exemplifies a recent shift in North African studies toward analyzing North African national cultures as discursive constructs rather than ontological essences.[43] This new trend in North African studies takes inspiration from the scholarship on nationalism—and, in particular, from Hobsbawm's insight that national traditions are often "invented." Theorists of nationalism have emphasized the anachronistic nature of nationalist imaginaries, which often legitimize the nation by projecting it back onto a distant and venerated past.[44] What is unique about my study is that it analyzes the simultaneous use of the same mythic past, al-Andalus, by two ideological projects that were deeply in conflict with each other: Spanish colonialism and Moroccan nationalism.

The other major contribution that this book makes to Moroccan and North African studies is that it reinserts Spanish colonialism into Moroccan colonial history. Between 1912 and 1956, Morocco was divided into a French Protectorate and a Spanish Protectorate. The French Protectorate, whose capital was Rabat, occupied central Morocco, including the historic cities of Fez and Marrakesh.[45] The Spanish Protectorate was divided into a northern and a southern zone (Figures 4 and 5). The northern zone of the Spanish Protectorate, whose capital was Tetouan, covered Morocco's Mediterranean coast (except for Tangier, which was an international zone) and the northern part of Morocco's Atlantic coast.[46] The southern zone of the Spanish Protectorate included the city of Sidi Ifni, which was ceded to Spain in 1860, and vast swaths of the

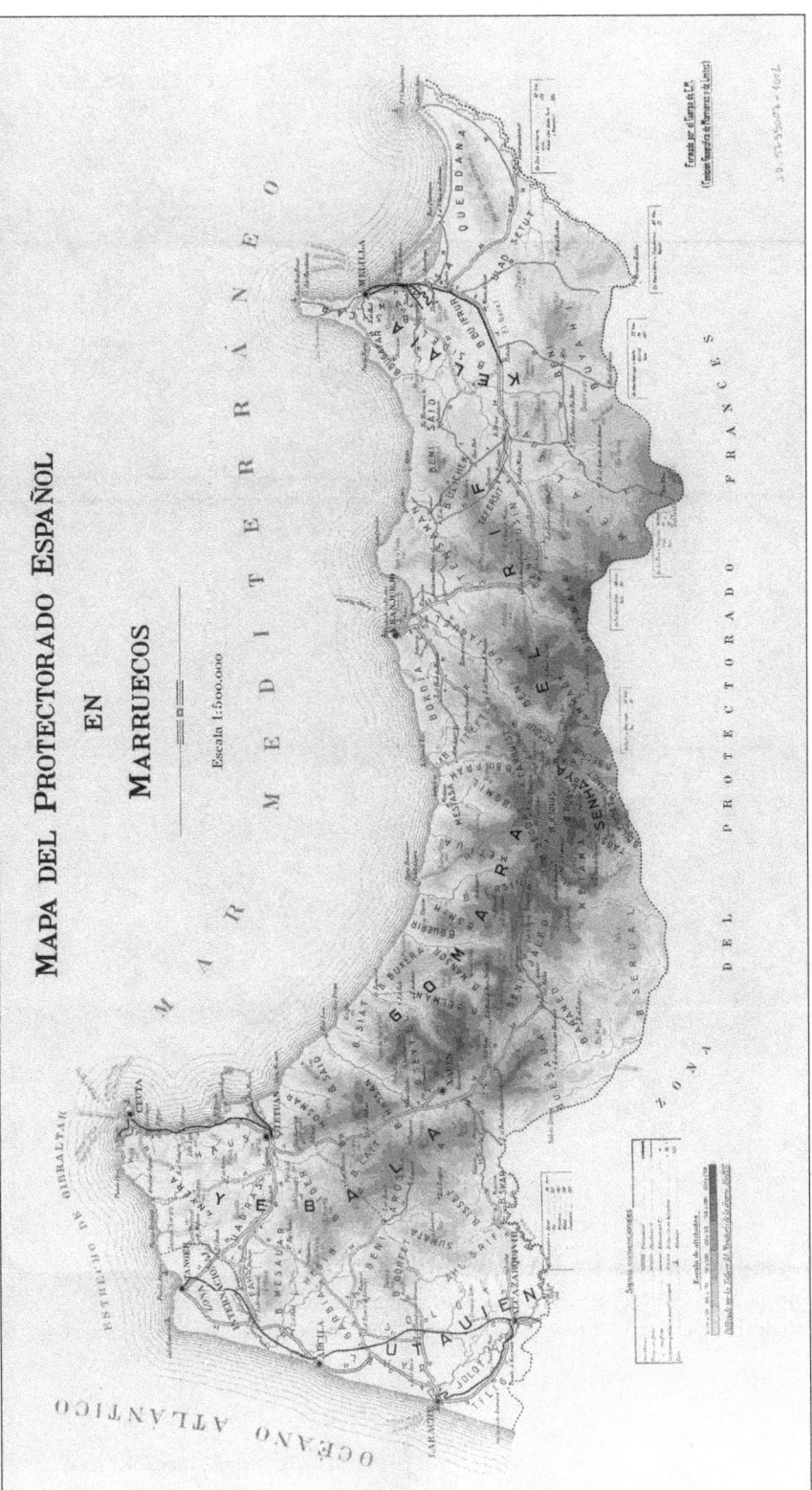

Figure 4. "Mapa del Protectorado Español en Marruecos," España Comisión Geográfica de Marruecos, Sección de Límites Comité Oficial de Turismo—Tetuán, *Ketama y el Rif* (Madrid: Talleres del Ministerio de la Guerra, 1932). Spanish National Library, MR/33-41/1748.

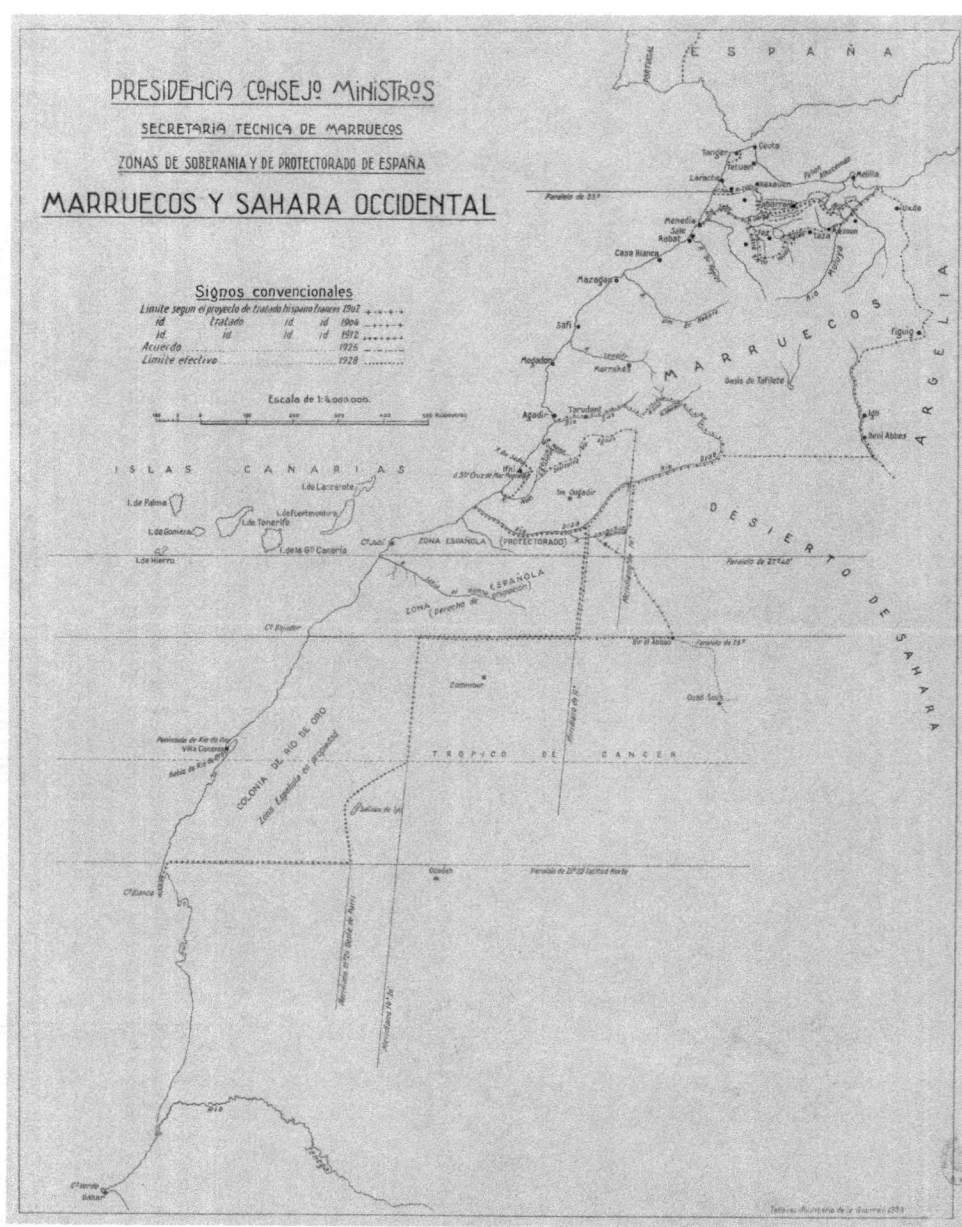

Figure 5. "Marruecos y Sahara Occidental: Zonas de Soberanía y de Protectorado de España," Presidencia Consejo Ministros, España Secretaría Técnica de Marruecos (Madrid: Talleres del Ministerio de la Guerra, 1935). Spanish National Library, AFRMPS/3/20.

Sahara desert, from the Dra'a River in the north down to the present-day border with Mauritania.⁴⁷ Throughout the Protectorate period, Morocco was governed by a complicated cast of Moroccan and European authorities. The sultan, while based in the French zone, remained the figurehead of the Moroccan state in all of the territories that came under French and Spanish rule. His representative in the Spanish zone was the caliph, who also came from the ruling 'Alawi dynasty. Although the sultan and the caliph were formally recognized as the highest Moroccan authorities in the French and Spanish zones respectively, their powers were undermined by the European colonial governments that grew up around them. The French and Spanish Protectorates officially ended in 1956 with the declaration of Moroccan independence. Spain, however, did not withdraw from its Saharan territories until 1976, and it continues to occupy the enclaves of Ceuta and Melilla on Morocco's Mediterranean coast. Indeed, Ceuta and Melilla have become flashpoints in Europe's ongoing migration crisis, since they serve as the political boundary between Africa and the European Union and as major points of entry for undocumented migrants from North and West Africa.⁴⁸

Up until now, Moroccan colonial history has largely been narrated from the perspective of French colonialism and the various reactions it elicited among Moroccans living in the French zone. Spanish colonialism in Morocco, when it is considered at all, is often treated as a sideshow to French colonialism; by extension, Moroccan nationalist culture under Spanish colonial rule is seen as an appendix to the nationalist movement that developed in the French zone. A number of historical factors have conspired to relegate Spanish colonialism to the margins of Moroccan colonial history. Since independence, Moroccan political power and state research institutions have concentrated in the capital city of Rabat, which was also the capital of the French Protectorate.⁴⁹ French has remained one of the major languages of higher education, commerce, and diplomacy in Morocco, despite the emphasis that Moroccan nationalists put on the need to Arabize the entire Moroccan educational system.⁵⁰ As a result of these historical and institutional processes, the scholarship on colonial Morocco has been biased toward French and Arabic sources that emphasize the histories of the major cities from the former French zone, including Rabat and Fez.

The historical formation of academic disciplines in Europe and the United States has also played an important role in marginalizing the history of Spanish colonialism in Morocco. In the Anglo-American academy, Morocco and the Maghrib have largely been studied and taught under the rubric of Francophone studies, whereas the field of modern Arabic studies in the Anglo-American academy has focused on Egypt and, to a lesser extent, the Levant.[51] In Spain, there is a rich tradition of scholarship on Hispano-Arab cultural relations, but this scholarship has focused, almost exclusively, on the medieval period. Over the past two decades, scholars in Spain and the United States have shown a renewed interest in Spanish colonialism in Morocco.[52] Yet, none of the existing studies analyzes the extensive corpus of Moroccan writings about Spanish colonialism or examines the impact of Spanish colonialism on modern Moroccan culture. Therefore, the cultural history of Spanish colonial Morocco, as represented by Arabic and Spanish sources, has existed in an academic no-man's-land, in the interstices between disciplinary and colonial legacies.

This book does not attempt to provide a comprehensive history of Spanish colonialism in Morocco. Instead, it seeks to trace the genealogy of Morocco's Andalusi identity by examining Spanish and Moroccan representations of al-Andalus from the beginning of the colonial period in 1859 until the period of Moroccan independence in 1956.[53] In pursuit of this story, I will draw upon a diverse array of sources in Spanish, Arabic, French, and Catalan, spanning several genres and media. The sources that I examine in this book have either been ignored or studied in isolation, without consideration for how they reverberate across national, cultural, and linguistic lines. Reinserting Spanish colonialism into the history of modern Morocco is not just a matter of getting a more complete and accurate account of European colonialism in Morocco. Rather, I contend that both European colonialism and Moroccan responses to it take on new meanings when they are seen in this comparative and multilingual perspective.

Colonial al-Andalus offers new transnational frameworks for examining Moroccan colonial history. Rather than locating Spanish colonialism on the periphery of French colonialism, this study sketches an alternative map, one that crisscrosses the Mediterranean and links

Spanish colonial Morocco to movements of peoples and ideas between Morocco, Madrid, Seville, Geneva, Mecca, Lebanon, and Egypt. This book therefore responds to the recent call, in postcolonial studies, to move beyond the colonizer-colonized binary and toward frameworks that emphasize lateral connections between colonized subjects and spaces.[54] Along these lines, Olivia C. Harrison has called "for a repositioning of the field of Maghrebi studies along an East-West, rather than North-South, axis."[55] Extending Harrison's proposal one step further, my analysis of Spanish colonialism in Morocco deploys a circum-Mediterranean approach, which positions Morocco within transnational flows that encompass Europe, North Africa, and the Middle East.

Colonial al-Andalus in Mediterranean Perspective

Colonial al-Andalus departs from the existing scholarship on European colonialism in the Arab-Islamic world, which has largely taken for granted a whole set of binary oppositions: Islam and the West, colonizer and colonized, as well as colonialism and nationalism. This study exposes the limits of these simplistic oppositions by examining Spanish and Moroccan discourses built on the multidirectional use of a shared past. It illustrates the unexpected ways in which colonial discourses migrate across geographic and cultural lines, taking on new ideological contours along the way. My comparative and multilingual approach brings into relief the surprising intersections between Spanish colonial culture and Moroccan nationalist culture. I believe that this story has broad implications for postcolonial studies and for the study of Mediterranean cultural history because it challenges our understanding of the conceptual borders between Europe and Islam, and between colonialism and anticolonial resistance.

Edward Said's classic *Orientalism* (1978) has long served as the dominant paradigm for analyzing European colonialism in the Arab and Muslim worlds. Said's brilliant study demonstrates how Western representations of "the Orient" helped to consolidate Europe's colonial power in Arab and Muslim countries. Said offers three interrelated definitions of the key term "Orientalism." First, Orientalism is an academic discipline that emerged in the nineteenth century as a space for studying the languages and cultures of the Orient.[56] Second, Orientalism is a "style of thought based upon an ontological and epistemological distinction made between 'the Orient' and (most of the time) 'the Occident.'"[57] That is, Orientalism is a style of Western thought based upon the total alterity of the Orient (whence the ontological distinction) and the total superiority of Western modes of knowing (whence the epistemological distinction). Building on the previous two definitions of Orientalism, Said posits his third and most historically specific definition of the term:

> Taking the late eighteenth century as a very roughly defined starting point Orientalism can be discussed and analyzed as the corporate institution for dealing with the Orient—dealing with it by making statements about it, authorizing views of it, describing it, by teaching it, settling it, ruling over it: in short, Orientalism as a Western style for dominating, restructuring, and having authority over the Orient.[58]

This final definition, which is the motor behind Said's book, takes inspiration from Foucault's idea that power is not only repressive but also "productive," in the sense that it often produces the very categories that it seeks to regulate.[59] Building on this idea, Said argues that the academic discipline of Orientalism produced the category of "the Orient," which it then sought to dominate by regulating the boundaries of what could be known or said about the Orient. For Said, Orientalism is not only a powerful discursive tool that the West used to exercise its mastery over other parts of the world; it is also the image against which the West defines itself. Orientalism is, in Said's words, "premised upon exteriority."[60] It defines a strategic location that is always outside the West, and that the West has used to calibrate its identity—an identity that is defined as distant from and superior to the Orient.

My book revises Said's account by showing how Islamic history shaped European colonialism, and how European colonialism shaped national identity in a postcolonial Muslim context. In so doing, this book addresses two shortcomings that scholars have noted in Said's work. First, scholars have criticized Said for basing his argument on a monolithic view of the "West" and the "East."[61] Second, they have criticized Said for his failure to examine Orientalism's relationship to its inverse image: non-Western representations of the West (what some have called "Occidentalism").[62]

As scholars have pushed the study of European colonialism in the Arab-Islamic world beyond the geographic contexts studied by Said, they have noticed significant wrinkles and variations in European discourses about Arabs and Muslims. Although Said speaks broadly of "Orient" and "Occident," he actually paints on a much smaller geographic canvas: for Said, the "West" means France and Britain, and the "Orient" means Egypt and the Levant.[63] One of the nineteenth-century figures who exemplifies Said's notion of Orientalism is the French Orientalist Ernest Renan. In a lecture delivered at the Collège de France in 1862, Renan famously asserted that "Islam is the most complete negation of Europe."[64] This virulent prejudice against Islam might, as Said argues, have been one of the defining features of French Orientalist scholarship. Nevertheless, as Karla Mallette has shown, southern European Orientalists did not share Renan's belief that there is an irreconcilable difference between Islam and Europe.[65] Mallette surveys the evolution of Orientalist philology in Italy, Spain, and Malta, which were all ruled by Muslims in the Middle Ages. In these southern European contexts, Orientalists often celebrated the Arab and Muslim contributions to modern European culture and emphasized the cultural unity of the Mediterranean world. This tradition of southern Orientalism is not, to borrow Said's phrase, "premised upon exteriority." Instead, it locates the Orient within Europe, emphasizing the connectivity between the two.

In both Spain and Morocco, the memory of al-Andalus throws into question any neat distinction between East and West. Spain, which is conspicuously absent from Said's *Orientalism,* has often stood as Europe's internal other. In European culture, especially from France and England, Spain has been imagined as a fuzzy border between East and West and between Europe and Africa, a place where cultural and racial distinctions become murky. This idea is summed up in the nineteenth-century French quip that "Africa begins in the Pyrenees."[66] The adage points to Spain's liminal position on the fringes of Europe, but also to the country's deep historical and cultural connections to North Africa. In the eyes of many Europeans, eight centuries of Muslim rule in Iberia made

Spain exotic, different, and potentially suspect. Starting in the nineteenth century, Spaniards took advantage of this accusation of otherness and used it to justify their colonial aspirations in North Africa. By highlighting Spain's Muslim past, Spanish writers claimed a cultural and even biological affinity with their neighbors to the south. Thus, Spanish colonial thinkers turned a supposed weakness into a strength by making the legacy of al-Andalus the main justification for Spain's expansion into North Africa and the Muslim world. The colonial myth of al-Andalus was, in turn, taken up by Moroccans and used to craft a national identity, one that emphasized Morocco's place at the crossroads of Europe and the Muslim world. Thus, the idea of al-Andalus has served to approximate Spaniards to Africa while distancing Moroccans from it.

In one of the best studies to date on Spanish colonialism in Africa, Susan Martin-Márquez has coined the term "disorientation" to describe how Spanish colonial writers both produce Orientalist discourse and, simultaneously, make themselves the object of it by reveling in their nation's Muslim past.[67] Spain's "disorienting" position on both sides of Orientalism profoundly altered the nature of Spanish colonial discourse. The dominant trope of Spanish colonialism in Morocco was "brotherhood," a discourse that emphasized the geographic, cultural, and racial proximity between Spaniards and Moroccans.[68] In contrast, the dominant trope of French colonialism in Africa was the "civilizing mission," a discourse premised on the total superiority of the colonizer and the total alterity of the colonized.[69] As the French notion of a "civilizing mission" illustrates, European colonial power was often predicated on the idea that colonized peoples were inferior and radically different.[70] Yet Spanish colonialism confounds this idea, since its justification was similarity, not difference. To be clear, I am not suggesting that Spanish colonialism, with its rhetorical emphasis on "brotherhood," was a more benevolent form of colonialism than the French variety. Instead, I want to highlight the diverse rhetorical strategies that different European nations used to justify their colonial projects, and then to trace, through the Moroccan example, some of the long-term consequences of those rhetorical strategies.

By replacing the binary opposition between Europe and Islam with a focus on cultural connections across and around the Mediterranean,

Colonial al-Andalus also engages recent developments in the field of Mediterranean studies.[71] In this reemerging field, the Mediterranean serves as the conceptual antagonist to the nation. The buzzwords in the field of Mediterranean studies are "bridges" and "connectivities."[72] Scholars have adopted the Mediterranean paradigm as a way of transcending the constraints of nationalist thinking and also as a way of undermining binaries that have long plagued the study of the region, such as the binary of "Islam and the West." Indeed, the "Mediterranean" has become a shorthand for a defense of interfaith and cross-cultural tolerance in the face of nationalism, xenophobia, and religious extremism. In this light, the Spanish discourse of *convivencia* can be seen as one instance of a larger constellation of discourses that circulate in (and about) the Mediterranean. The race to Mediterraneanism is not limited to the academic sphere, but rather has poured out into political and civic life. In 2008, forty-three heads of state from the Mediterranean region came together to create the Union for the Mediterranean, whose goals, in the words of its website, are "the creation of an area of peace, stability, security and shared economic prosperity" and also the "promotion of understanding between cultures and civilizations in the Euro-Mediterranean region."[73] Mediterranean projects, be they academic or intergovernmental, tend to emphasize flows over borders, connections over exceptions, and affiliations over separations.

This book has a vexed relationship with the field of Mediterranean studies. It shares the field's emphasis on transnational analysis but complicates the ideological valence of that emphasis. Discourses of exemplary tolerance, be they Andalusi or Mediterranean, can be put to the service of projects that are anything but tolerant, such as fascism. I therefore want to open up the study of colonial Moroccan history to transnational flows of peoples and ideas that crisscross the Mediterranean, without investing those flows, a priori, with a positive valence.

The other major shortcoming of the Mediterranean paradigm for this project is that Moroccan writers, during the colonial period, did not talk about themselves as "Mediterraneans." That is, they did not identify themselves vis-à-vis the Mediterranean as a cultural or geographic category.[74] Even Spanish writers of the colonial period did not emphasize the Mediterranean (as geography or identity), preferring instead to emphasize the

Strait of Gibraltar as the narrow "river" that connects the Iberian Peninsula and North Africa.[75] To be sure, being in and of the Mediterranean has become a significant part of how contemporary Spain and Morocco present themselves to the world.[76] Nevertheless, I would venture that Spain and Morocco both "became Mediterranean" after the colonial period.

Indeed, it often seems that the Mediterranean is an asymmetrical category, foisted by some "Mediterranean" (often European) cultures on others. In recent years, Moroccan politicians and writers have willingly adopted the Mediterranean label, perhaps because it allows them to signal Morocco's proximity to Europe. This move is paradoxical, since the Mediterranean has also served, in the not too distant past, to mark a cultural divide between "advanced" northern Europe and "backward" southern Europe.[77] Today, though, the symbolism of the Mediterranean has evolved. The Middle Sea now evokes fluidity, connectivity, and a commitment to unity across difference. Thus, "being Mediterranean" allows some European countries, such as Spain, to claim a culture of tolerance and openness to Europe's neighbors to the south, while it allows other non-European countries, such as Morocco and Turkey, to signal their proximity to a multicultural Europe—and, potentially, their distance from other Muslims.

I insist, however, that this web of meaning was not fully in place during the period that is the object of this study. The characters in this book move across the space of the Mediterranean, but they do not engage the Mediterranean as a key symbol of identity or as a unit of analysis. Instead, it is al-Andalus that informs the colonial encounter between Spain and Morocco and the way that Spanish and Moroccan writers imagine their place in the world.

Like the Mediterranean, al-Andalus is a malleable site of meaning, one that shifts and adapts to different cultural and political needs. My goal, in this book, will be to trace those shifts and to show how a certain set of ideas about al-Andalus served to justify Spain's colonization of Morocco and then, surprisingly, to define the Moroccan national culture that supplanted colonial rule. For the writers and politicians at the heart of this study, al-Andalus functions as both history and poetry. That is, al-Andalus is both a specific time and place and also an idea that transcends time and place.⁷⁸ Al-Andalus expands and contracts. It is a living present grounded in a lost past. It resides in the Iberian Peninsula, in North Africa, and in the space in between. It is a specific chapter in medieval Mediterranean history, and it is a universal heritage that bridges seemingly irreconcilable divisions between East and West. If this book is a study of how Morocco became Andalusi, then it is also a study of how al-Andalus came to signify many things to many people. I intend to historicize Morocco's modern claim to an Andalusi identity, but in order to do so, I need to show how al-Andalus broke free from its original referential meaning and morphed into an idea that floats in between Muslims and Christians, North Africans and Europeans, and past and present.

Overview

The book is organized chronologically, tracing Spanish and Moroccan representations of al-Andalus through the vicissitudes of the colonial period (1859–1955). In each chapter, I isolate a figure, text, or concept that allows me to reconstruct a key moment in the Spanish and Moroccan negotiation of the cultural memory of al-Andalus. The chapters thus operate on two parallel levels: close textual analysis and broad cultural framing.

Chapter 1 explores the rhetorical uses of al-Andalus in Spanish writings from the period around the Spanish-Moroccan War of 1859–1860. It shows how Spanish writers mobilized the memory of Spain's Muslim past in order to assert a historical and natural connection between Spain and Morocco. I draw on a diverse array of literary, journalistic, and visual sources, but I focus on Pedro Antonio de Alarcón's *Diary of a Witness of the War of Africa* (1860), the most famous Spanish account of the war. I track two of the main motifs in Alarcón's *Diary*: first, the idea that modern Tetouan is a continuation of Muslim Granada; and second, the idea that the Spanish-Moroccan War is a continuation of the Christian Reconquest of Granada in 1492. Alarcón's *Diary* anticipates the historical and genealogical imaginaries that will animate Spanish colonial discourse for the next century.

Chapter 2 explores the place of al-Andalus in modern Moroccan literary history. At the center of this chapter is the Moroccan poet, scholar, and visual artist Mufaddal Afaylal (1824–1887). Afaylal produced two contradictory texts about the Spanish-Moroccan War: a famous elegy and a heretofore unstudied manuscript chronicle. For the elegy, Afaylal adopted an Andalusi literary genre, the city elegy, in order to emphasize the parallel between the Spanish occupation of Tetouan in 1860 and the Christian Reconquest of al-Andalus. In the chronicle, Afaylal avoids comparison to al-Andalus and instead mounts a vicious critique of the Moroccan army. The elegy illustrates the appeal of al-Andalus as a discursive model for making sense of the colonial encounter; the chronicle signals the limits of what al-Andalus can say in (and about) nineteenth-century Morocco. My reading of Afaylal thus highlights the tension between poetry and history, the universal and the particular.

Chapter 3 examines the elision of three related geohistorical concepts: al-Andalus (medieval Muslim Iberia), Andalucía (a region in southern Spain), and Morocco. I trace this elision back to early twentieth-century Spanish writers, especially Blas Infante (1885–1936), who is hailed today as the father of Andalusian nationalism. Infante's writings celebrated the role of cultural and ethnic diversity in the making of the southern Spanish region of Andalucía. In post-Franco Spain, Infante's work has become linked with the myth of *convivencia*. Yet Infante's reputation as a champion of intercultural tolerance masks two understudied aspects of his work and its afterlife: his repudiation of Catalan nationalism and his influence on the discourse of Spanish colonialism in Morocco. In this chapter, I analyze Andalusian nationalism's clash with Catalan nationalism in order to show how Spain's peripheral identities shaped and were shaped by debates about al-Andalus and colonial Morocco. This chapter also questions the ideological valence of *convivencia*, a concept often associated with Republican intellectuals like Infante. Although Infante was killed by rebel troops at the beginning of the Spanish Civil War, his work nonetheless exerted significant influence over Francoist writings about Morocco. This chapter thus illuminates the surprising overlaps between Republican and Francoist discourses about Morocco and about Spain's Muslim past.

Chapter 4 examines Franco's sponsorship of the Moroccan hajj, the Muslim pilgrimage to Mecca. Franco's support for the Moroccan hajj began during the Spanish Civil War and continued intermittently through the 1950s. This chapter centers on an important but unstudied Arabic account of the first Moroccan hajj sponsored by Franco: Ahmad al-Rahuni's *Journey to Mecca* (1941). The text narrates the pilgrimage to Mecca and also two separate visits to Spain, which bookended the author's pilgrimage. Al-Rahuni depicts Franco as a defender of Islam and of the cultural heritage of al-Andalus. He also blurs the line between Mecca and Spain by casting Spain's Islamic heritage sites as a metaphorical Mecca to which Muslims should make pilgrimage. *Journey to Mecca* thus highlights the collaboration between Spanish fascism and the Moroccan intellectual elite. It also offers insight into how an educated Moroccan viewed Spanish colonialism and, in particular, the Francoist celebration of al-Andalus.

Chapters 5 and 6 work together to trace the origins and political uses of the concept of "Hispano-Arab culture," which was invented by Francoists as a discursive strategy for justifying Spanish colonialism and for distinguishing it from French colonialism. At first, Hispano-Arab culture was a cultural ideal grounded in the myth of *convivencia*. Over the course of Francoist rule in Morocco (1936–1956), Hispano-Arabism evolved from being a cultural ideal to being a specific set of cultural practices that defined Spain and Morocco's shared Andalusi heritage. This shift can also be thought of as the shift from Cordoba to Granada. In the historical imaginary of Hispano-Arabism, Cordoba represented the ideal of interfaith tolerance, whereas Granada stood in for the music and decorative arts that Andalusi exiles supposedly brought to Morocco. In Chapter 5, I focus on the Cordoba portion of this story—that is, on the Francoist promotion of a Hispano-Arab cultural ideal that supposedly tied together interfaith life in al-Andalus and Spanish colonialism in Morocco. The motor behind this project was the General Franco Institute, whose publications codified the concept of Hispano-Arab culture. The institute also facilitated cultural exchange between Spain, Morocco, and the Arab world. Arab intellectuals who visited Morocco as guests of the General Franco Institute produced Arabic texts that helped to propagate, to a broad Arab readership, the idea that Franco's aim in Morocco was to resurrect al-Andalus. In the second half of the chapter, I analyze the most famous of these Arabic texts, Amin al-Rihani's *Morocco* (1940).

Chapter 6 continues to investigate the Francoist promotion of Morocco's Andalusi culture, while shifting focus from the Hispano-Arab cultural ideal to a set of Andalusi cultural practices symbolized by Granada. In particular, I examine Spanish colonial efforts to define, preserve, and administer two aspects of Moroccan culture that the Spanish associated with Muslim Granada and the Alhambra: crafts and music. My analysis centers on the careers of two Spaniards: Mariano Bertuchi (1884–1955), a Granadan artist who trained a generation of Moroccan artisans and artists; and Patrocinio García Barriuso (1909–1997), who played an important role in the revival of Andalusi music in Morocco. Bertuchi and García Barriuso helped to codify a canon of Andalusi arts, which, today, are upheld as essential components of Morocco's Andalusi identity.

Chapter 7 explores the emergence of the "Andalus-centric" narrative in Moroccan historiography and scholarship at the end of the colonial period and the beginning of the independence period. The chapter opens with the story of Shakib Arslan's visit to Tetouan in August of 1930. Arslan, a Lebanese Druze prince, was one of the most famous writers and politicians in the Arab and Muslim worlds, and the author of influential works that popularized a view of al-Andalus as a "lost paradise." Arslan's visit to Tetouan helped launch the careers of several young Moroccan nationalist intellectuals, such as Muhammad Dawud, M'hammad Binnuna, and ʿAbd al-Khaliq al-Turris. In this chapter, I trace how Moroccan nationalists adopted and eventually overcame Arslan's ideas about al-Andalus. This process unfolded in two waves. In the first wave, Moroccan nationalists, especially Muhammad Dawud, adopted Arslan's idiom of "the lost paradise" and used it to insert their nationalist struggle within broader reform movements in the Arab-Islamic world. In a second wave of responses to Arslan's work, Moroccan nationalists, especially those trained at Spanish colonial academic institutions, asserted that al-Andalus was not lost, but rather was alive and well in Morocco. They also claimed al-Andalus as a Moroccan national heritage, rather than a pan-Arab one. This chapter thus maps out the genealogy of Moroccan nationalist representations of al-Andalus, showing how Moroccans adapted ideas taken from Spanish colonial culture, while also engaging cultural and political movements from other parts of the Arab world.

The epilogue addresses the afterlife of colonial al-Andalus in contemporary Moroccan culture. I approach this topic through brief narrative explorations of spaces in Tangier and Rabat. I dwell, in particular, on a monument complex in the capital city of Rabat. In the decades since Moroccan independence, Rabat's most famous Andalusi structure, the twelfth-century Hassan Minaret, has been incorporated into a monument complex celebrating the ruling ʿAlawi dynasty. I use the monument complex as a springboard to discuss how Spanish colonial discourses about al-Andalus have made their way into many aspects of Moroccan life, including the official discourse of the Moroccan monarchy in the twenty-first century.

1

TETOUAN IS GRANADA

IN APRIL OF 1861, the Spanish writer Pedro Antonio de Alarcón (1833–1891) posed for a series of portraits in the photography studio of his friend José Martínez Sánchez, located in Madrid's central Puerta del Sol.¹ In one of these portraits, Alarcón gazes intently at the viewer from underneath the tasseled hood of an embroidered djellaba, the tunic traditionally worn by Moroccans (Figure 6).² On his feet, he wears leather slippers. From his wrist hang the prayer beads used by Moroccan Muslims to count prayers and perform *dhikr* (invocations of God's name). The clothes that Alarcón donned for the photo shoot were a reminder of the writer's recent return from northern Morocco, where he was sent by the Spanish newspaper *El Museo Universal* to cover the Spanish-Moroccan War of 1859–1860. Alarcón wrote the most famous Spanish account of the war, the *Diary of a Witness of the War of Africa* (*Diario de un testigo de la guerra de África,* hereafter the *Diary*). The *Diary* was published serially throughout the war, and then as a book in 1860. It was a huge commercial success in Spain, selling more than fifty thousand copies and launching Alarcón to literary fame.³

On the back of one of Alarcón's portraits from 1861, there is a brief inscription that explains the occasion for his Moroccan drag: "Pedro Antonio de Alarcón (writer and poet) with the costume that he wore to

Figure 6. Portrait of Pedro Antonio de Alarcón, dressed in a Moroccan djellaba, 1861. Photograph by José Martínez Sánchez. *Fotografías Recogidas por el Pintor Manuel Castellano: Tomo 6*, Spanish National Library, 17/LF/51, page 41r, 4.

the ball of the Duchess of Medinaceli in 1861." The note refers to the glamorous costume ball that the Duchess of Medinaceli threw on the night of April 1, 1861.[4] The event had been the talk of Madrid's society gossip for the preceding two months. The guests, numbering over a thousand, vied with each other to produce the most elegant and surprising costumes. The numerous newspaper accounts of the ball gave top billing to the hostess, the Duchess of Medinaceli, who wore a shimmering mermaid costume designed in Paris. The newspapers *La Época* and *El Contemporáneo* also singled out Alarcón, who went to the ball dressed as Mulay al-'Abbas, the general of the defeated Moroccan army in the Spanish-Moroccan War.[5]

Two days after the ball, on April 3, 1861, *La Época* published an account of the event written in the form of a fictitious letter from Mulay al-'Abbas to "the poet Chorby," one of the Moroccans who appear in Alarcón's *Diary*.[6] The article was presumably penned by Alarcón himself, who frequently published chronicles of Madrid society in *La Época*.[7] The article is written in the breathless and impassioned style of the *Diary*. Its pseudo-Moroccan narrator describes the ball as the Prophet Muhammad's "paradise, populated by the elite of his *houris*."[8] He hails the Duchess of Medinaceli as a "great sultana" and says that her mermaid dress "deserves and requires a longer commentary than all those that have been written about the Koran."[9] The apocryphal Mulay al-'Abbas also alludes to his encounters at the ball with guests who reminded him of Spain's Muslim past and its recent war with Morocco. "I saw," he writes, "some of the generals and leaders who defeated me last winter and many descendants of all those people connected to us during the war of the eight centuries."[10] In the space of one brief sentence, the pseudo-Moroccan narrator leaps from the nineteenth-century Spanish-Moroccan War to the medieval struggle between Christians and Muslims for control of the Iberian Peninsula. The participants of one conflict mix and mingle with the descendants of the other on the duchess's dance floor.

After the ball, the Duchess of Medinaceli put out a call, through the Madrid newspapers, asking her guests to have their portraits taken in the costumes they wore to the party. She intended to gather all of the portraits together in an album commemorating the ball.[11] Her request was probably the catalyst for Alarcón's photo session in Martínez Sánchez's studio. It is not clear whether Alarcón's portraits ever made it back to the duchess for her album. Today, though, they belong to the Spanish National Library, where they appear in an album containing a motley collection of portraits, whose subjects range from the Duke of Medinaceli, dressed in a seventeenth-century costume, to circus performers and zarzuela chorus girls (Figure 7). The placement of Alarcón's Moroccan portraits within a gallery of circus performers and masquerading aristocrats underlines their performative nature. Alarcón's portraits suggest that cultural identity is like a costume that can be put on or taken off at one's will, and that becoming Moroccan is as simple as slipping on a djellaba and a pair of leather sandals.

Throughout his career, Alarcón made much of his personal connection to Spain's Muslim past. He was born in the city of Guadix, which was one of the last bastions of the Muslim kingdom of Granada and later became a focal point for the crypto-Muslim (Morisco) resistance against Christian rule in the Alpujarras Rebellion of 1568–1570.[12] From his early Orientalist writings to the end of his life, Alarcón brandished Granada's Muslim heritage as a sign of identity and a badge of honor. In one of the most oft repeated anecdotes from his life, Alarcón ran into the writer Emilia Pardo Bazán in the manuscripts room of the Spanish National Library in May of 1887. According to Pardo Bazán's account of the meeting, she expressed concern for Alarcón's health after noting his obesity, yellowish complexion, and laborious breathing. Alarcón stoically replied: "You know well that I'm a Moor . . . and, therefore, fatalist. Allah is great, and He will do with me whatever he wishes."[13] The term "Moor," which Alarcón uses to describe himself, is one of the most vexed terms in the cultural representation of Spanish-Moroccan relations. In modern usage, the term can refer to many distinct categories, including Muslims (a religious category), Arabs or Berbers (ethnic categories), inhabitants of al-Andalus (a historical designation), and the people of North Africa or Morocco (regional or national categories). Like the term "Oriental," the word "Moor" tells us more about the person who uses it than it does about the thing it supposedly describes. It is thus best understood as a category of the Spanish imagination, rather than as a descriptor of peoples or cultures. The semantic

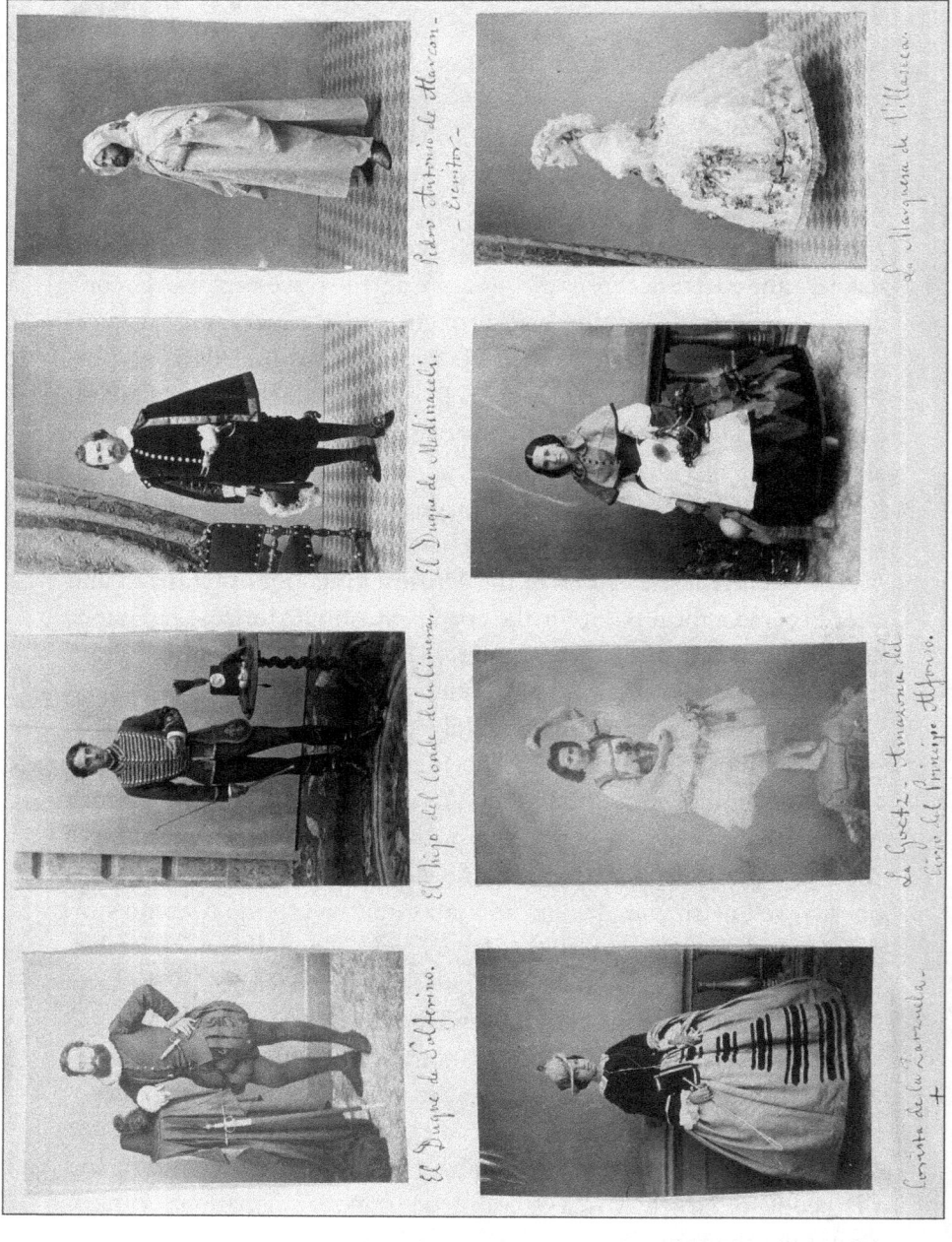

Figure 7. Reproduction of a page from an archival photography album. *Fotografías Recogidas por el Pintor Manuel Castellano: Tomo 6*, Spanish National Library, 17/LF/51, page 41.

slippage built into the term "Moor" mirrors the shifts in time and place that characterize Alarcón's self-fashioning in his literary oeuvre—and especially in his *Diary*.

Alarcón was hardly the first European to try to play the part of an "Oriental." The British Orientalist Sir Richard Burton famously adopted a Muslim alter ego, Abdullah, in order to make the pilgrimage to Mecca in disguise in 1853.[14] Moreover, portraits of European subjects in exotic attire were an important subgenre of European Orientalist photography.[15] Nevertheless, Alarcón's repeated performances and poses as a "Moor" point to the unique place of the Orient in the Spanish imagination and in Spanish colonial discourse. Susan Martin-Márquez has coined the term "disorientation" to describe Spanish writers' ambiguous position inside and outside of Orientalist discourse.[16] Alarcón, like many of his Spanish contemporaries, both produces Orientalist tropes and also strategically makes himself the object of them. Martin-Márquez notes Alarcón's fascination with al-Andalus, but she argues that the Spanish writer maintains a clear distinction between Spain's Muslim past and its European and Catholic present.[17] In contrast, I do not see, in Alarcón's work, such a clear distinction between past and present, and between North Africa and Europe. Instead, I believe that Alarcón foreshadows a key trope in twentieth-century Spanish colonial discourse: the idea that Spain is "neither Orient, nor Occident," but is, instead, a point of union and exchange between Europe and the Arab-Islamic world.[18] Alarcón strategically ties his identity to Granada and, thus, to Spain's ambiguous cultural location between East and West.

In what follows, I will explore the rhetorical uses of al-Andalus in Spanish writings from the period around the Spanish-Moroccan War of 1859–1860. I will track how Spanish writers such as Alarcón mobilized the memory of Spain's Muslim past in order to assert a historical and genealogical connection between Spain and Morocco. This strategic use of the memory of al-Andalus served to naturalize Spain's colonial claims on Morocco. Its implicit logic was that Spain was not colonizing Morocco, but rather was returning to Morocco, which had always been part of Spain. To illustrate this idea, I will draw on a diverse array of literary and journalistic sources, but I will focus on Alarcón's *Diary*, the most famous account of the war that marked the beginning of Spanish colonialism in Morocco. I will track, in particular, two of the main motifs in Alarcón's *Diary:* first, the idea that modern Tetouan is a continuation of Muslim Granada; and second, the idea that the Spanish-Moroccan War is a continuation of the Christian Reconquest of Granada in 1492. Both of these ideas would exert significant influence over later Spanish colonial representations of Morocco. They would also resonate, in surprising ways, in twentieth-century Moroccan responses to Spanish colonialism.

The main objective for this chapter will, thus, be to trace the origins of colonial al-Andalus; that is, to show how the revival of interest in al-Andalus in nineteenth-century Spain became a rhetorical tool for justifying Spain's colonial presence in North Africa. Alarcón was a pioneer in this discursive project. His *Diary* anticipates the genealogical, geographical, and racial metaphors that would become central to Spanish colonial discourse in the twentieth century. Alarcón also contributed to the formation of a new historical narrative about the transmission of Andalusi culture from medieval Granada to modern Tetouan. In particular, he locates Tetouan's Andalusi heritage in its architecture and music, two arenas of Moroccan culture that would be of special interest to Spanish colonial thinkers in the 1930s, 1940s, and 1950s. This narrative of cultural transmission linking medieval Granada to modern Tetouan would also prove useful to Moroccan nationalists fighting against Spanish colonialism in the middle of the twentieth century. Therefore, Alarcón's *Diary* not only illustrates the origins of Spanish colonial discourse but also foreshadows the paradoxical ways in which al-Andalus would be put to the service of diverse and contradictory ideological projects in both Spain and Morocco.

Origin Stories

The Spanish-Moroccan War of 1859–1860 was, in part, a conflict over where Spain ends and Morocco begins. The incident that sparked the war was a dispute over the border separating Ceuta, the Spanish enclave on the Moroccan coast, and the surrounding Moroccan territories.[19] Ceuta has been under Iberian control since 1415 and has long been a point of contention between Spain and Morocco.[20] On August 10, 1859, a group of men from the neighboring Anjara clan tore down a border post that the Spanish had set up beyond the limits of Ceuta. According to the Moroccan historian al-Nasiri, the Anjara also "defiled" a Spanish flag with excrement.[21] The incident led to a diplomatic crisis between Spain and Morocco. The Spanish public, stoked by a warmongering press, called for an armed response to the incident, which became known as "the affront to our pavilion in Ceuta."[22] Amid the public fury, the journalist and novelist Manuel Ibo Alfaro wrote, in a comment that reflected the bellicose spirit of the times: "Our pavilion is stained; this stain can only be washed away with blood."[23] Led by Leopoldo O'Donnell, the president of the Spanish government, Spain declared war on Morocco on October 22, 1859.

The ensuing war is known, in Spanish historiography, as the War of Africa; in Moroccan historiography, it is known as the War of Tetouan. The two disparate names give a sense of the competing geographic imaginaries that were at play. In nineteenth-century Spain, "Africa" was a common metonymy for Morocco, Spain's closest African neighbor. There was more at stake, however, in the Spanish name for the war. Under the grandiose label "the War of Africa" lurked the conviction that Spain was destined, by geography and history, to lead Europe's colonial expansion into the neighboring continent.

This destiny was a common theme in the Spanish press's coverage of the war. On October 12, the editors of *La Discusión*, an important Madrid daily, wrote that the war with Morocco "is, for us, a providential issue because God's finger has, since the beginning of modern history, signaled to us the path of Africa."[24] The remark implied that Spain had a providential duty to follow in the path of the Christian Reconquest of al-Andalus and to carry its historical struggle against Muslims across the Strait of Gibraltar to Morocco. Other writers asserted that Spain should not limit its ambitions to Morocco. In February of 1860, Gabino Tejado, writing for the newspaper *El Pensamiento Español*, envisioned a Spanish conquest of the entire African continent: "We signal as the space of our conquests in the African continent all of the area stretching from Ceuta to the Cape of Good Hope, and from the western border of Egypt to the Atlantic.... Our duty as a race and our interest as a nation call us to conquer in Africa as much as we can, as often as we can."[25]

Tejado's vision of a vast Spanish empire in Africa never came to fruition. Nevertheless, by calling the conflict "the War of Africa," Spanish writers invested the military campaign in Morocco with the continental ambitions that electrified Spanish society during the war.

On December 12, 1859, Pedro Antonio de Alarcón sailed into Ceuta as a special correspondent for the newspaper *El Museo Universal* and as a volunteer soldier in the Third Corps of the Army of Africa.[26] Alarcón's employer, *El Museo Universal,* published a steady stream of articles on Moroccan and "Moorish" themes in the months leading up to the declaration of war and throughout the campaign. The newspaper's coverage of the war bolstered the idea that Spain had a "natural" place in Morocco, based on the geographic and historical proximity between the two countries. In November of 1859, *El Museo Universal* published a two-part series on Moroccan history and geography. The series concluded with a bold declaration about Spain's geographic destiny: "Spain has finally understood that its border must be the Atlas [Mountains]."[27] The statement anticipated one of the key tropes of the geographic imaginary that drove Spanish colonialism. From the middle of the nineteenth century through the middle of the twentieth century, numerous Spanish colonial apologists would emphasize that Spain and Morocco form a single geographic unit, bordered by the twin mountain chains of the Pyrenees to the north and the Atlas to the south.[28]

El Museo Universal's coverage also helped to frame the War of Africa as a continuation of the Christian Reconquest of al-Andalus. Several articles published in the fall of 1859 hint at the parallels between the fifteenth-century conquest of Granada and the nineteenth-century campaign in Morocco. These parallels boil to the surface in a bombastic poem that graced the cover of the December 1 issue. The poem, titled "To Spain: Memories and Hopes," was written by Manuel Fernández y González, a Granadan author of popular historical fiction on Orientalist themes and a close friend and collaborator of Alarcón.[29] The "memories" of the poem's title are remembrances of Spain's lost imperial splendor, and the "hopes" are the poet's call for a revival of Spain's imperial glory through the war against Morocco. The parallel between the Spanish-Moroccan War and the Reconquest of al-Andalus is especially emphatic in the poem's final stanzas. In them, the speaker observes that the Moroccan adversary is not "an unknown enemy," but rather the same "ferocious people" who "fought with you / for centuries and centuries."[30] The speaker then enumerates the most famous battles of the Christian Reconquest, starting with Covadonga (c. 718) and ending with the Catholic Monarchs' occupation of Granada: "And your queen Isabel, your beloved queen, / Unmatched in faith and grandeur, / In God's name donned / on her head, the crown of her Granada. / In God's name, go against the Moor!"[31] These verses deftly perform a temporal elision. In the gap between the penultimate line and the last line, the speaker jumps from 1492 to the present, entreating his compatriots to follow Isabel the Catholic's example and to "go against the Moor!" The temporal elision is bolstered by the lucky coincidence that Queen Isabel II (r. 1833–1868), whose reign coincided with the Spanish-Moroccan War, was named after the queen who had led the Christian Reconquest of Granada.

Indeed, the conflation of the two Isabels was a common trope in Spanish writings about the war.[32] In another instance of this trope, Antonio Ros de Olano, a Spanish general and Romantic poet, envisions a massive triumphal arch connecting Isabel I to Isabel II, and Granada to Tetouan: "Granada and Tetouan, in which Isabel of Castilla and Isabel of Spain have established their throne through arms, are the majestic pillars of an immense triumphal arch. . . . Isabel I takes Granada from the Arabs who came from Damascus; Isabel II takes Tetouan from the Arabs who came from Granada."[33] These lines come from Ros de Olano's *Legends of Africa* (*Leyendas de África*), which was written during the Moroccan campaign and published by the same editors who published Alarcón's *Diary*. Alarcón and Ros de Olano shared more than just editors. Alarcón served under Ros de Olano during the Moroccan campaign, and he copied, in the *Diary*, a chapter from the *Legends of Africa*, in which Ros de Olano narrates Tetouan's fifteenth-century foundation by Muslim exiles from Granada.[34]

For my purposes, the most significant text that appeared in *El Museo Universal* during the buildup to the Spanish-Moroccan War was Alarcón's short story, "A Conversation in the Alhambra" ("Una conversación en la Alhambra"), published on October 15, 1859.[35] In the story, a Moroccan descendant of Muslim Granada returns to the city of his forefathers and visits the Alhambra, where he reveals his identity to a Spanish narrator. The action takes place in the present, but Granada's medieval past sits close beneath the surface. In the story's opening sentence, the narrator calls Granada "the city of Isabel the Catholic," and he later describes it as "the city of Boabdil," in reference to the last Muslim ruler of Granada, Abu ʿAbd Allah Muhammad b. ʿAli ("Boabdil" in European sources).[36] The narrator also calls Granada "the Jerusalem of the West," thus highlighting its symbolic place between Orient and Occident.[37]

The story's plot mirrors its setting, probing the limits between Spain and Morocco, Christianity and Islam. At the beginning of the story, the Spanish first-person narrator travels to Granada for the Corpus Christi celebration. Along the way, he shares a stagecoach with an enigmatic stranger, whose features evoke the Orient of Romantic literature: "His well-groomed beard, extremely black, was, by nature, of a Nazarene style. His large and expressive eyes, of a velvety black, reminded me of the pirates described by Lord Byron."[38] When the stagecoach arrives in Granada, the two men part ways before the narrator has a chance to uncover the identity of his mysterious travel companion. The following afternoon, though, they run into each other in the Alhambra. The narrator describes the palace by citing José Zorrilla, another Romantic Orientalist: "That palace, made by fairies, according to Zorrilla, was in the saddest solitude and deepest silence."[39] Alarcón's frequent literary allusions reveal a problem that is common to this story and to his *Diary* of the Spanish-Moroccan War: his representations of Muslims and even of his native Granada are heavily mediated by Romantic literary depictions of the Orient.[40] That is, Orientalist tropes structure the way Alarcón sees Granada, Morocco, and Muslims in general.

The narrator approaches the stranger in the Patio of the Lions, where they observe signs of construction work. The stranger believes that the Spanish workers are tearing down the Alhambra, but the narrator assures him that the Spanish are restoring, not destroying, the country's most famous Islamic monument:

> "They aren't tearing it down," I replied. "Rather, they're reconstructing it.... Mr. Contreras, the intelligent artist commissioned by our government to restore this casbah, discovered

underneath the crass Christian work the pure lineaments of the primitive Arab construction. Now, he is working to remediate the ravages of time and poor taste, reconstructing these buildings to the same way that they were four centuries ago."[41]

The narrator's language evokes the image of the palimpsest: to reconstruct the Alhambra, the Spanish must peel away one "crass" layer of cultural history in order to discover, underneath it, the "pure lineaments" of the Arab-Islamic culture that was lost in 1492. The narrator thus casts himself and his countrymen as the defenders and restorers of the cultural legacy of al-Andalus, which hides underneath the surface of modern Granada.

The conversation about the restoration of the Alhambra inspires the mysterious stranger to reveal his identity: he is the last descendant of the Zegrí clan of Granada. The Zegrís rose to posthumous fame through a late-sixteenth-century Spanish retelling of the final years of the Muslim kingdom of Granada, Ginés Pérez de Hita's *Historia de los bandos de Zegríes y Abencerrajes* (1595).[42] Pérez de Hita's work inaugurated a seminal theme in modern representations of Muslim Granada: the rivalry between the Zegrí and the Abencerraje families, a rivalry that culminated in the (potentially legendary) massacre of the Abencerraje family in one of the Alhambra's rooms, today known as the "Sala de los Abencerrajes." The violent fate of the Abencerraje clan kindled the imagination of many Romantic writers and painters, including Chateaubriand.[43] Indeed, the plot of Alarcón's story clearly mirrors Chateaubriand's classic *Les aventures du dernier Abencérage* (c. 1826), which recounts the journey of the last surviving member of the Abencerraje clan to Granada, his ancestor's lost home.[44] Despite the clear parallels between the two texts, Alarcón's story is also presented as an alternative and corrective to Chateaubriand's novella. "Chateaubriand himself," the narrator wryly comments, "would have given his Abencerraje in exchange for my Zegrí!"[45] The narrator implies that the French can merely fantasize about Muslim Granada, while he, a Spaniard and a Granadan, can have living contact with its descendants and its culture.

After the stranger reveals his identity, he leads the narrator to the nearby Hall of Ambassadors, which overlooks the city of Granada.

There, the last Zegrí asserts that he and the other exiles from al-Andalus belong to Spain, not North Africa:

> Yes, I am African, I am Aben-Adul, the last of the Zegrís! . . . I misspeak: I am as Spanish as you are! I am an exiled Granadan! I am of a banished race. It has not even been three centuries since my forefathers . . . were thrown out of the houses that they had constructed, from the lands that they had worked. . . . *"You are African,"* you said to them, when they had been living in Spain for seven centuries![46]

Aben-Adul insists that North Africans of Andalusi descent are Spanish, not Moroccan. To emphasize this point, he explains that when his ancestors arrived in North Africa, they were treated as suspicious outsiders: "We arrived there, and the kings of the Atlas and of the desert said: *'You are Spaniards . . . return to the sea!'* "[47] Aben-Adul thus depicts the Andalusis as a people in perpetual exile, stuck in limbo between the two shores of the Mediterranean.

The exchange between Aben-Adul and the narrator illustrates a broader process of historical revision that took place in Spain in the nineteenth century. As Martin-Márquez has noted, nineteenth-century Spanish liberals reclaimed Spain's Muslim past as an integral part of the national story rather than as an aberrational challenge to it.[48] In this rethinking of national history, a North African of Andalusi descent, like Aben-Adul, is not an outsider; rather, he is "as Spanish as" the Granadan narrator. Toward the end of the story, Aben-Adul tells the narrator that he learned about the history of al-Andalus from "a generous Christian," who also taught him Spanish and convinced him to convert to Christianity.[49] This detail reaffirms Spain's role as the defender of the Andalusi heritage. Indeed, it suggests that al-Andalus resides within, not against, Christian Spain.

"A Conversation in the Alhambra" ends with another nod to Spain and Morocco's shared cultural heritage. As the narrator and Aben-Adul look out over Granada from the Alhambra, the sound of a fandango wafts up from the city streets. The fandango is a popular song and dance form, which, in the nineteenth century, became closely associated with flamenco.⁵⁰ Aben-Adul calls the fandango "the echoes of Africa" and "the caravan's prayer."⁵¹ Likewise, the narrator associates the fandango with North Africa and with the memory of Granada's Muslim past, calling the music "that Berber song, that mysterious guitar . . . that lost memory of the Arabs, that exiles' grief that we feel, that hope of new fatherlands [*patrias*] that inspires us."⁵² In this final scene of the short story, the fandango is depicted as something both distant and near, mysterious and familiar. It is "the echoes of Africa," but, at the same time, those echoes point back to earlier songs and earlier memories, whose origin is in Muslim Granada. Woven into this moment of cultural recovery and intercultural recognition is a subtle reminder of Spain's colonial mission in Morocco. The fandango contains, as the narrator remarks, "the hope of new fatherlands that inspires us." The music reminds Spaniards of their lost Arab-Islamic past, but it also pushes them toward their future in Morocco.

This intermingling of past and present, of Muslim Granada and modern Morocco, is a central theme in Alarcón's account of the Spanish-Moroccan War. The *Diary* opens with a prologue that powerfully condenses the historical and genealogical metaphors underpinning Alarcón's understanding of Spain's place in Morocco. The prologue is addressed to Ros de Olano, Alarcón's general and comrade in letters:

> It was several years ago, my respected and dear General, when the desire to travel through the empire of Morocco first moved my heart. Born, as I was, in the Sierra Nevada, from whose summits you can just make out the beaches where Moordom [*la morisma*] sleeps its historical death; the son of a city that preserves the footprints of Arab domination, and that was one of their last trenches in the fifteenth century, and was later the epicenter of the Morisco rebellion; breast-fed with the traditions, chronicles, and legends of that race that, like the waters of the flood, submerged Spain and then later departed, but left behind, in mountains and plains, indelible signs of the cataclysm; having spent my youth in the ruins of mosques and casbahs, and caressed the dreams of my adolescence to the sound of the Moors' songs, in the light of their poetry, perhaps

under the very same roofs that sheltered their last pleasures, it was natural that, upon abandoning my paternal home and casting through the world a gaze avid for poetic impressions, I felt seduced by the nearness of Africa, and I yearned to cross the Mediterranean in order to touch, so to speak, in that marvelous continent, the living reality of the past.[53]

I have quoted the *Diary*'s opening paragraph in its entirety because it foreshadows many of the text's central themes. The entire paragraph consists of two sentences, both concerned with origins: the origin of the author's interest in Morocco, the origin of his life story, and the origins of Spain's entanglement with Morocco.

The first clause of the long second sentence places an individual speaking subject in opposition to a North African collective subject: the first-person narrator ("Born, as I was . . .") looks down from the privileged perspective of the Sierra Nevada (the mountains outside Granada) to the beaches of nearby Morocco, where "Moordom sleeps its historical death."[54] The unusual term "Moordom" evokes the Orientalist idea that the peoples of the Orient are an indistinguishable and unchanging collective mass, devoid of individual subjectivity. I am reminded, here, of Delacroix's famous painting *The Fanatics of Tangier* (1837–1838), which depicts a crowd of "fanatical" Muslims as a confusing mass of flailing limbs. In Delacroix's painting, as in Alarcón's text, it is difficult to know where one Moroccan ends and another one begins. The ontological collectivity of all Moroccans is not the only motif that Alarcón's passage shares with other Orientalist texts. By evoking "Moordom's historical death," the narrator also draws upon the idea that Western temporality does not apply to the Orient, and that Oriental peoples exist outside of historical time.[55] In Orientalist writings, as Martin-Márquez has observed, "Travel through space is also conceived of as travel through time."[56] Alarcón's text exemplifies this trope of anachronistic time travel: the narrator imagines that the impending journey to Morocco will allow him "to touch . . . the living reality of the past."[57] Alarcón's language here is tactile, desirous, as if he saw travel to Morocco as a form of sexual union with the past.

Up until this point, Alarcón's prologue might appear to be a textbook case of Orientalism, but Alarcón deploys biological metaphors that complicate his relationship with standard Orientalist discourses. According to Said, Orientalism is a "style of thought based upon an ontological and epistemological distinction made between 'the Orient' and (most of the time) 'the Occident.'"[58] In contrast with Said's formulation, Alarcón's *Diary* blurs the ontological distinction between Orient and Occident. In the *Diary*'s opening paragraph, Alarcón casts himself as the son of two related cultural forces: Muslim Granada is figured as his symbolic mother, and Christian Spain is figured as his symbolic father. Family metaphors are, perhaps, the most common feature of nationalist discourses.[59] What is curious about Alarcón's *Diary* is that it envisions a national "family" that is not ethnically or religiously homogeneous; it traces a family tree with roots in Muslim Granada and branches that stretch from Spain to Morocco.

In the opening paragraph of the prologue, Alarcón gives short shrift to his "paternal home," Spain. Instead, he focuses on his return to his symbolic mother, al-Andalus, which he hopes to "touch" in Morocco. Alarcón describes himself as "the son of a city that preserves the footprints of Arab domination, and that was one of their last trenches in the fifteenth century, and was later the epicenter of the Morisco rebellion."[60] He thus highlights the Muslim heritage of his native Guadix and stresses that the city was not only one of the last territories to fall to the Christian Reconquest but also a major site of resistance when the Morisco (crypto-Muslim) communities near Granada rose up against Spanish Christian rule in the Alpujarras Rebellion of 1568–1570. Although it is a commonplace to call oneself a "son" of a city, Alarcón accentuates the maternal metaphor by saying that he was "breastfed [*amamantado*] with the traditions, chronicles, and legends" of the Arabs who once populated Guadix.[61] He also claims that the "indelible signs" of Spain's Muslim past nourished his youth, spent "in the ruins of mosques and casbahs."[62] Ruins, often a site for nostalgic reflection in Romantic art and literature, do not merely function here as abstract signs of loss or abandon; they are also the monuments, the material reminders, of a past that is not external to Alarcón but rather is claimed as his own.

Alarcón's prologue not only marks a departure from conventional Orientalist practice; it also signals a shift in Spanish national historiography. In the narrative of Spanish national history that was hegemonic until the mid-nineteenth century (and that continued to shape historiographic debates in the twentieth century), 1492 is defined as a moment of national consolidation: with the Reconquest of Granada, the expulsion of the Jews, and the so-called "discovery" of the New World, Spain comes into being as a Christian, white, Castilian-speaking, and expansionist nation.[63] This historiographic narrative excised Muslims and Jews from the nation, as if al-Andalus were a parenthesis that had no impact on Spain's national character.

In Alarcón's *Diary*, 1492 marks a moment of national disintegration, not consolidation. The prologue offers an alternative narrative of Spanish history, in which the expulsion of the Muslims and the Jews sets in motion a process of national decline. By traveling to Morocco, Alarcón hopes to remedy this error in Spanish national history:

> What carried my gaze anew to the nearby al-Gharb was not the desire to perform a poetic pilgrimage; it was the certainty that there was the treasure of grandeur that we, the Spanish, lost nearly three centuries ago, and that we have sought out, in vain, in other places; it was the thought that the empire of the Catholic Monarchs and of Philip II began to decline the day that Philip III expelled from Spain the Moriscos and the Jews, who, we could say, took with them the talisman of our fortune; it was seeing, as clear as the light of day, that Spain must go to Africa to recover that talisman, or (to say it another way) that Spain must understand that the most natural function of its existence is a constant expansion to the South.[64]

In this quick summary of Spanish imperial history, Alarcón plays fast and loose with dates and facts: he appears to conflate the expulsion of the Moriscos in 1609–1614, under the reign of Philip III, with the expulsion of the Jews in 1492, under the Catholic Monarchs. It is clear, though, that Alarcón is less interested in hard historical facts than in large, providential movements of Spanish destiny.

Decades before the so-called "Disaster" of 1898, in which Spain lost its last colonies in the Americas, Alarcón advocates for a reorientation of Spanish history along a North-South axis: Spain must expand to the south in order to recover the "talisman" of its fortune. It is curious to note that Alarcón's revision of Spain's post-1492 history revolves around the repeated use of the word "talisman," itself a lexical marker of East-West encounters. The word entered the Romance languages from the Arabic *ṭilasm* ("seal" or "charm"), which, in turn, came from Greek.[65] Alarcón advocates for a Spanish nation that, like the word "talisman," traverses the Mediterranean. In so doing, he revives the ideological legacy of Isabel the Catholic, whose final will (1504) famously exhorted Spaniards "not to cease in the conquest of Africa."[66] For Alarcón, Spain's place in Africa is not only necessary and providential; it is also, to use his word, "natural." The adjective resonates with the biological metaphors that proliferate in the prologue's opening paragraph. Alarcón figures his trip to Morocco as a return to his "nature" as the offspring of a mixed marriage between a Muslim mother and a Christian father. Likewise, he encourages the Spanish nation to return to its "nature" by expanding south to Morocco.

Alarcón's desire to reclaim Spain's Muslim past coexists uneasily with his desire to revive Spain's transhistorical struggle against Islam. He observes: "The War of Africa's significance is also religious, insofar as Spain, eternal vanguard of Christianity, returns to the breach against the infidels; . . . insofar as it accelerates the death of Islamism in Europe."[67] This comment, taken from the prologue, forecasts the *Diary*'s frequent depiction of the Spanish-Moroccan War as an extension of the medieval Christian Reconquest of al-Andalus. For instance, when Alarcón first lays eyes on Ceuta, he immediately associates the city with the great battles of Andalusi history: "Ceuta is a monument of our past power and a pledge made to Moordom to continue the uninterrupted combat that we have sustained with them since Muhammad's times; a combat whose magnificent episodes, of varying fortune for our cause, are Guadalete, Salado, las Navas, Alarcos, Clavijo, and Granada."[68] Looking at Ceuta, Alarcón summarizes the entire history of al-Andalus through a quick survey of its battles, from Guadalete, the decisive victory of the Muslim forces over the Visigoths in 711, to the conquest of Granada. Yet, for Alarcón, the history of al-Andalus does not end with Granada. The slippery term "Moordom" allows Alarcón to elide the historical distance between the period of early Islam ("Muhammad's times"), the period of Muslim rule in the Iberian Peninsula, and the period of the Spanish-Moroccan War of 1859–1860.

The *Diary*'s prologue thus casts Alarcón as both a descendant of al-Andalus and an heir to the Reconquest, the son of a Moorish mother and the eternal enemy of the Moor. In my reading of the text, I insist on the importance of not resolving these paradoxes and tensions. Reading Spanish colonial texts requires a certain degree of negative capability—an ability to keep in mind multiple contradictory positions. Spanish colonial discourse—like the ideas of the "Orient" and the "Moor"—does not have any ontological stability. Rather, it is best understood as a series of shifting poses, like the costumes that Alarcón donned to pose as a Moroccan in the portraits that I discussed at the beginning of this chapter. One of the recurring themes of this book will be that of strange bedfellows—people and projects that should stand at odds with each other, but instead mutually support each other. It is in this spirit of paradoxical ideological fluidity that Alarcón can present himself, simultaneously, as a proud descendant of Muslim Granada and as a representative of the Christian Reconquest of al-Andalus.

Seeing Granada in Morocco

Alarcón's *Diary* is an emphatically visual text. Alarcón constantly reminds the reader of his status as an eyewitness observer to the war. This theme first emerges in the prologue, in which Alarcón describes his plan for the *Diary*:

> Then, the idea for the book that I intend to write emerged in my imagination; a book that will be the diary of my impressions and thoughts during the war; the chronicle of whatever I see and contemplate; the description of whatever places I explore and of whatever events I attend. Lacking the historian's talents, I will be content to be an exact narrator.... What history does not say, what military reports do not narrate, what newspapers do not perceive; the personal, private, profane history of the war—all this will make up the miscellaneous, unadorned, improvised, and heterogeneous book that I have envisioned ever since I made up my mind to accompany our soldiers to Africa.[69]

Alarcón defines his "diary" in opposition to history: it will say "what history does not say." Alarcón returns to this idea several times throughout the *Diary*, such as when he prefaces his first description of a battle with the following caveat: "I will only speak to you of what I personally witness and understand, and as it will be impossible for me to be in all parts at the same time, I will, naturally, be obliged to omit many deeds that are worthy of mention. I am truly sorry, but, fortunately, this book is not the *History of the Campaign* but rather the *Diary of a Witness*."[70] In both of the quoted passages, the diary, as a genre, is defined by its sole reliance on eyewitness testimony. In contrast, history, for Alarcón, exists at one remove from visual experience. According to Alarcón, a diary is a direct transmission of empirical observation, whereas a history is a polished narrative based on a reconstruction of data from several sources. There is a paradox at the center of Alarcón's definition of his *Diary*: he acknowledges that it omits many things, and yet for that very reason, he insists that it allows the reader to "see" more directly.

For all of its emphasis on vision, the *Diary* is actually a very opaque text. Like Alarcón's portraits, the *Diary* draws attention to the limits of the visible—to the fact that things are not always what they appear to be. It demonstrates how vision itself is a culturally constructed category, densely mediated, and interpolated by existing discourses and representations. That is, the eye only sees what it has been taught to see.[71] I will return to the problem of eyewitness testimony in Chapter 2, when I analyze the work of Mufaddal Afaylal, another self-proclaimed eyewitness to the Spanish-Moroccan War. For now, I would like to signal a tension in Alarcón's representation of Morocco. He joins the war effort in order to see Morocco, but in the end, what he "sees" is Granada—and, in particular, the Granada that was constructed by Spanish and French literary representations of Granada's Muslim past. Al-Andalus is, then, the lens through which Alarcón sees Morocco—and not just any al-Andalus, but specifically the literary Granada constructed by a European textual tradition that stretches from Ginés Pérez de Hita, in the late sixteenth century, to the European Romantics in the nineteenth century. Al-Andalus serves as a framework that makes Morocco legible to Alarcón, and also as an obstacle that blocks his ability to see Morocco.

Alarcón frequently compares Moroccan architecture to monuments from al-Andalus, such as the Alhambra. One of the first examples of this tendency comes when Alarcón describes the Serrallo, a fortified palace complex built by the governor of Tetouan, Ahmad b. ʻAli al-Rifi, during his siege of Ceuta in the early eighteenth century.[72] Alarcón compares the eighteenth-century Moroccan palace to famous buildings from medieval Iberia: "The dominant type of orientalism that is found in its galleries and balconies is the same one that is in the Cathedral of Cordoba. However, in its most run-down section, which doubtlessly was the most sumptuous, you can still see some vestiges of that other pure and elegant taste that predominates in the Alcázar of Seville and in the Alhambra of Granada."[73] In this description, the Serrallo offers the Spanish visitor an architectural tour of the entire sweep of Andalusi history, from the Umayyad-era Mosque of Cordoba (later turned into the Cathedral of Cordoba) to Granada's Alhambra, which dates back to the thirteenth century. The three Andalusi monuments mentioned by Alarcón underwent significant transformations and restorations between the time of their construction and the time of the Spanish-Moroccan War.[74] Nevertheless, Alarcón takes their styles to be discrete, inalienable, and unchanging models of Muslim aesthetics. He also upends the standard account of Andalusi history, which tends to depict tenth-century Cordoba as the apex of Andalusi culture. In this standard account, the dissolution of the Umayyad caliphate of Cordoba in 1031 marks the beginning of a long decline that ends in the conquest of Granada.[75] Alarcón does not subscribe to this "rise-and-fall" model of Andalusi history. Instead, his al-Andalus becomes condensed and purified over time, until it culminates in the "pure and elegant taste" of Granada's Alhambra.

For Alarcón, nostalgia for Granada and al-Andalus cuts across cultural lines, shaping both Spanish and Moroccan desires. In his description of the Serrallo, the palace is not only an architectural homage to al-Andalus; it is also a vantage point from which Moroccans can contemplate their enduring relationship with the Iberian Peninsula. In his mind's eye, he restores the Serrallo to its former splendor and imagines the view that the palace afforded to its former inhabitants:

> With a little bit of knowledge about the Moors' palaces and with some patience and attention, the mind can reconstruct that fan-

tastic palace [*alcázar*], located in a delightful spot, from which you can glimpse . . . Spain's coasts, which are seen in the distance, like a golden dream or like a sweet memory for the Arabs, and the African coast, which fades from view in the direction of the prophet's tomb.[76]

Despite his much-vaunted commitment to eyewitness testimony, Alarcón releases himself to a vision that moves across time and space. Placing himself in the position of one of the palace's former Moroccan inhabitants, Alarcón looks out at the Spanish coast, which evokes the "sweet memory" of the Muslim presence there in the Middle Ages. His vision also stretches eastward toward Medina, where the Prophet Muhammad is buried. Alarcón's eye thus brings together al-Andalus and Islam's holiest sites in one imagined frame, as if both places were sites of Muslim pilgrimage.[77]

Al-Andalus structures Alarcón's view not only of Moroccan buildings but also of Moroccans themselves. The Spanish writer's first face-to-face encounter with a Moroccan took place in Ceuta on January 5, 1860. Alarcón was in Ceuta to recover from an injury that he had suffered in the Battle of Castillejos on January 1, 1860. While in Ceuta, Alarcón went to visit some wounded Moroccan soldiers who were receiving treatment in a Spanish hospital. With the help of a French journalist, who had learned Arabic in Algeria, Alarcón struck up a conversation with a wounded Moroccan, "Omar-Ben-Mohammed," who hailed from the capital city of Meknes. Alarcón calls his Moroccan interlocutor "a veritable Arab of legend."[78] As the phrase suggests, Alarcón's description of the Moroccan is deeply indebted to literary legend—and, in particular, to the literary genre known as the *novela morisca*. The genre emerged in sixteenth-century Spain, with such classics as Pérez de Hita's *Guerras civiles de Granada*, and it later provided much of the source material and tropes for nineteenth-century Romantic representations of Granada, such as Chateaubriand's *Dernier Abencérage*.[79]

Alarcón's exchange with Omar resembles a miniature *novela morisca*, tucked inside his account of the war. After discussing the Moroccan soldier's participation in military campaigns against the French and the Spanish, Alarcón turns the conversation to Granada:

> "You will not deny to me that the Moors abhor us because they remember that they were in Spain for eight centuries, and they believe that they were dispossessed of it unjustly, even though all we did was recover what was ours."
>
> "Oh! *Garnata!*" Omar said, in the manner that I write it.
>
> "*Garnata!* That is where we come from."
>
> "That is where I was born."
>
> "Ah!" the kaïd murmured, and he looked at me melancholically.[80]

The scene stages a moment of intercultural recognition, a common motif in the *novela morisca*. Like the two characters in Alarcón's "A Conversation in the Alhambra," these two soldiers in the Spanish-Moroccan War are drawn together by their joint affiliation with Granada. They are two Granadans who meet to reenact, several centuries later, the dramatic struggle for al-Andalus. Omar sighs for the loss of Granada, and Alarcón, perhaps to give the scene an air of authenticity, transcribes the city's name in a way that approximates its Arabic pronunciation: "*Gharnāṭa*." Omar's lament for the fall of Granada evokes the famous (and probably apocryphal) scene of Boabdil, the last Muslim ruler of Granada, looking down at his city from the Sierra Nevada for the last time and crying for its loss. The oft-repeated scene, known as "the Moor's last sigh," has long been a mainstay of European representations of Muslim Granada.[81] In fact, Chateaubriand's *Last Abencerrage* opens with a retelling of the story of "the Moor's last sigh." Chateaubriand's narrator goes on to explain that the Muslim Granadans went into exile in North Africa, where they "carried in their new homeland the remembrance of their old homeland. The *Paradise of Granada* was always alive in their memory."[82] Like Chateaubriand's last Abencerrage, Alarcón's Moroccan interlocutor keeps alive the memory of *Garnata*, despite the passage of several centuries. As we will see in Chapter 7, the Edenic view of al-Andalus as "lost paradise" will play an important role in modern Arabic letters after Shakib Arslan's Arabic translation of Chateaubriand's novella in 1897.

Chateaubriand's Granada is also the lens through which Alarcón first describes Tetouan. Crossing over the mountainous terrain near Cabo

Negro, Alarcón catches his first glimpse of Tetouan, which sends him searching for a way to describe it. The search leads him to Chateaubriand and then to a series of comparisons between Granada and Tetouan:

> Tetouan! I don't tire of looking at it.... I don't know how to describe it to you so that you may see it, so that you may imagine it as it is...
>
> But why do I doubt? Have you seen Granada from the heights of Fajalanza? Have you read, at least, *The Last Abencerrage* and the description that Chateaubriand gives of the Damascus of the West?
>
> Well, Tetouan is Granada! That is, the plain, the limits of its horizon, its coloring, its air, its light, its region in its entirety, completely recall the plain of Granada.
>
> The same dark green, the same abundance of fruit trees, identical houses in the field... Ah! The illusion is complete. Why not? Although it might be a delirium, don't take me out of it. The Atlas is Sierra Nevada; Cabo Negro, Sierra Elvira; Sierra Bermeja and the Tower of Geleli represent the heights of the Alhambra. These three rivers are the Darro, the Genil, and the Beiro.[83]

Tetouan is Granada—here, in one phrase, is Alarcón's Moroccan imaginary. In order to describe Tetouan, Alarcón alludes to the passage in Chateaubriand's novella in which the last Abencerrage, Aben-Hamet, first sees Granada from the heights of the surrounding hills.[84] Alarcón implies that to see Tetouan one only needs to have seen Granada, or even to have read Chateaubriand's description of Granada. Alarcón then offers a laundry list of similarities between the two cities, encompassing their natural setting, their architecture, and even their light and air.

In this passage, Tetouan is not only Granada's twin; it is an allegory—that is, a text that must be read in relation to another parallel text. Thus, Tetouan's every component can be rewritten to summon Granada and its environs: Morocco's Atlas Mountains become Granada's Sierra Nevada; Tetouan's Tower of Geleli (in Arabic, *Burj al-Qalalin*) becomes the Alhambra; Tetouan's rivers become Granada's Darro, Genil, and Beiro.

Curiously, the equivalences run across space, time, and media of representation. Not only is Tetouan interchangeable with Granada, but Granada itself is interchangeable with "the description that Chateaubriand gives" of it. The Romantic representation of Nasrid Granada structures Alarcón's vision of Tetouan, and it also supplants his vision of his native Andalucía.

As Alarcón approaches Tetouan with the Spanish army, European representations of Muslim Granada continue to overtake his descriptions of Morocco and Moroccans. After the Spanish army defeats the Moroccan forces in the Battle of Tetouan (February 4, 1860), setting the stage for the Spanish occupation of the city, Alarcón imagines Mulay al-'Abbas, the general of the defeated Moroccan army, as Boabdil, the last Muslim ruler of Granada. Looking up at the mountain to which the Moroccan army retreated, Alarcón comments: "I imagine Muley-el-Abbas [sic] on top of that mountain, fixing his eyes on Tetouan and sighing like Boabdil when, from the summit of the Veleta, he looked at his Granada for the last time. Heroic and hapless prince! Worthy, perhaps, of better fortune!"[85] In Alarcón's eyes, Mulay al-'Abbas reenacts the scene of "the Moor's last sigh." The Moroccan general's sigh for Tetouan collapses with Boabdil's sigh for Granada, and the two figures converge into one figure, whose fate stretches from 1492 to 1859. Indeed, Alarcón refers to the "prince" in the singular, as if the distinction between the fifteenth-century Granadan and the nineteenth-century Moroccan were immaterial. Even though Alarcón casts himself as an heir to the Spanish Reconquest, he also evinces sympathy for Boabdil and Mulay al-'Abbas, both of whom are "worthy, perhaps, of better fortune!" It is easy to imagine the jump from this parenthetical comment to the costume ball in 1861, when Alarcón dressed up as Mulay al-'Abbas.

Alarcón's identification with Mulay al-'Abbas intensifies when he sees the Moroccan general in person for the first time. On February 23, 1860, Mulay al-'Abbas met with Leopoldo O'Donnell, the commander of the Spanish army, in order to discuss the terms of Morocco's surrender. Alarcón attended the meeting, along with a few other Spanish journalists and several officials from the Spanish army. He offers the following description of Mulay al-'Abbas:

> When I saw him caress his beard with that naked, fine, and correctly formed hand... I experienced a lively sympathy toward that enemy of my God and of my fatherland.
>
> And it was, perhaps, that I saw him with the eyes of an artist and that I personified in him the unfortunate and valiant Muza, who is still loved in Granada by the great-grandsons of the conquerors of the Alhambra.[86]

Alarcón compares the Moroccan general to Muza, a fictional figure from the sixteenth-century Spanish ballad tradition who was developed by Pérez de Hita into one of the main characters of the *Historia de los bandos de Zegríes y Abencerrajes* (1595).[87] In Pérez de Hita's novel, Muza is Boabdil's half brother, the son of a Nasrid sultan and a Christian mother. At the end of the novel, Muza converts to Christianity. In Carrasco Urgoiti's interpretation of the novel, the character Muza allows Pérez de Hita to reconcile his idealization of Muslim Granada with his defense of the superiority of the Christian faith.[88] A similar dynamic might be at play in Alarcón's description of Mulay al-'Abbas. The Moroccan foe may be idealized and celebrated, but only insofar as he can be contained within Spanish culture. Alarcón appropriates and domesticates Mulay al-'Abbas by translating him into a Spanish literary figure, Muza.

Alarcón's description of the meeting between Mulay al-'Abbas and Leopoldo O'Donnell highlights the tension between his literary imagination and his proclaimed status as an eyewitness. Of the meeting between the two generals, Alarcón writes: "This solemn and picturesque scene—which I have been lucky enough to witness [*presenciar*]—marvelously rounds out the gallery of grand pictures [*cuadros*] that the romantic war of Morocco has offered for the consideration of poets and artists."[89] Alarcón calls attention to his role as a witness, using a verb, *presenciar*, which suggests both physical presence and eyewitness authority. In the same sentence, however, he deploys words that suggest that his representational strategy owes less to eyewitness testimony than it does to performance and painting: the meeting between the two generals is, in Alarcón's words, a "picturesque scene," and the entire *Diary* is a "gallery of grand pictures." Alarcón's diction is both pictorial and theatrical: *cuadros* can refer to "paintings" hanging in a gallery, but it can also refer to theatrical tableaus, where actors hold a pose to represent a scene. In fact, a tableau is a helpful metaphor for thinking about Alarcón's representation of Morocco, since he represents the country as a place where time stands still and where actors pose for the consideration of a Western audience.

Given Alarcón's emphasis on Morocco's anachronism, its location outside of Western time, it is fitting that he offers his first extended description of Tetouan from the vantage point of the city's cemetery. On February 6, 1860, Alarcón and the Spanish army entered Tetouan from the direction of the Muslim cemetery outside the city's Cemetery Gate. As Alarcón narrates the approach to the city, he imagines the Andalusi exiles whose graves are underfoot: "At this rumbling of foreign arms, of Christian swords, the former Tetouani generations must have shuddered in their eternal resting places, the noble Moors who were born in Granada and came to die in this land."[90] In other words, the Spanish enter Tetouan by, quite literally, trampling on the remains of the exiles from Muslim Granada. In this passage, the history of al-Andalus is "buried"—literally and figuratively—underneath the events of the Spanish-Moroccan War.

Alarcón and his companions ride to the cemetery's highest point atop Mount Dersa. The setting recalls the *Diary*'s prologue, in which Alarcón imagines himself at the top of the Sierra Nevada, looking down on Morocco. Likewise, in the cemetery passage, Alarcón places himself at a strategic height from which his vision can take in all of Tetouan and its history. From his perch at the top of the cemetery, he envisions Tetouan as an extension of his native Andalucía. Tetouan's dazzling whitewashed houses remind him of Cádiz.[91] He remarks that the only thing interrupting the "severe uniformity" of Tetouan's whitewashed houses are "the high minarets of the mosques, some of which are not completely white but rather are covered with mosaics of vivid colors. The one belonging to the great mosque is extremely elegant, and it recalls the Giralda of Sevilla."[92] The Giralda, the bell tower of Seville's cathedral, was originally the minaret of a mosque built by the Moroccan Almohad dynasty in the twelfth century. The Almohad mosque was transformed into a cathedral after the Christian conquest of Seville in 1248. As I will discuss in later chapters, the Giralda would become, in the twentieth century, an important symbol of Spain and Morocco's shared Andalusi heritage. In the case of Alarcón's text, it is striking that he compares Tetouan's mosque to a Spanish monument with a transnational and layered genealogy: a mosque that was built by a Moroccan dynasty and was later converted to a Spanish church. Like the literary figure of Muza, the Giralda represents a Muslim other that is incorporated into Spanish culture; it is an alterity that can be contained through appropriation.

Alarcón's descriptions of Tetouan, written during his sojourn in the city, illustrate the assumption that Morocco is part of an immutable Oriental essence. Looking down at Tetouan from the elevated perspective of the cemetery, Alarcón muses:

> I would have gladly spent hours and hours contemplating Tetouan from those heights. Certainly, I would not have seen anything new that I had not observed at first glance. . . . The city that I was looking at was no longer the city that spread out beneath me . . . It was the city of my memories, the one from my dreaming fantasy, the one from my poetic loves. It was the Oriental city, the Arab city, whichever one it might be, called by this name or that name. It was the mysterious refuge of a race that has been separated from the world; it was the secret of a forgotten history; it was the reality of my childhood illusions; it was the Granada of the fourteenth century; it was Damascus; it was Medina; it was Isfahan . . . ; it was the disobedient Mahometan civilization that no longer goes to visit us in Europe; that wants to pass for dead; that lives here hidden and solitary . . . All of this was what I saw with the eyes of imagination as I contemplated Tetouan from the height of the cemetery.[93]

Alarcón both revels in his contemplation of Tetouan and also acknowledges that he has seen everything that he needs to see upon first glance. In fact, Alarcón goes so far as to suggest that he is not seeing Tetouan at all, but rather is examining a fantastical city that he has been constructing in his mind since childhood. According to Alarcón, Tetouan is interchangeable with any other Muslim city from any period of

Islamic history, be it Muslim Granada, Damascus, or Isfahan (in today's Iran). This passage, then, begs an important question about Alarcón's project of "eyewitness" testimony: if Tetouan is interchangeable with any other Muslim city (past or present), then why is it necessary for Alarcón to make the journey to Tetouan in the first place? The ocular authority that supposedly gives legitimacy to Alarcón's *Diary* bumps up against an epistemological crisis: can Alarcón be an "eyewitness" if he only sees through what he calls "the eyes of imagination"? It is, at least, interesting to note how little the experience of seeing Tetouan changes Alarcón's view of the place.

Alarcón's commentary from Tetouan's cemetery carries the hallmark of European Orientalist thought—in particular, the Orientalist tendency to view the Orient in essentialist terms. Amid this performance of textbook Orientalism, however, Alarcón still manages to sneak in the idea that differentiates Spanish colonial discourse from other European discourses in the Arab and Islamic worlds. His Tetouan is part of an immutable Oriental essence that resists the forces of Western time, and yet that essence is not entirely alien to Alarcón. Rather, it is part of him and his homeland: Tetouan is, among other places, "the Granada of the fourteenth century."[94] While Tetouan's connection to Muslim Granada is not the main note that Alarcón strikes in the cemetery passage, it insinuates itself throughout Alarcón's diary entries written in Tetouan. Every time that Alarcón seems to signal Tetouan's total alterity, he complicates the claim by asserting Tetouan's historical connection to Spain. For instance, in the entry from his first day in Tetouan, Alarcón writes: "Tetouan is what it had to be, what I wished it to be: a completely Arab city, a town dissimilar in everything from those in Europe, a nest of Moors, a resurrection of the run-down Albayzín of Granada."[95] The sentence underlines Tetouan's representativeness as an Arab city (one might say, in the singular, *the* Arab city), but then, the sentence takes a surprise turn and calls Tetouan the "resurrection" of Granada's Albayzín neighborhood, known for its connection to Granada's Muslim past. In other words, Tetouan is both totally dissimilar to Europe and, at the same time, similar to Granada (or, at least, Granada's past). Alarcón stakes out an ambiguous position between Orient and Occident in which Tetouan's history collides with Granada's history, and he places himself at the center of that collision.

For Alarcón, the relationship between Tetouan and al-Andalus is reciprocal, moving backward and forward in time: that is, Tetouan allows him to visit Granada's past, and Spain's Islamic heritage allows him to see and understand Tetouan. Alarcón's *Diary* thus outlines a paradox of origins: al-Andalus is at the origin of Alarcón's vision of Tetouan, but Tetouan is at the origin of his vision of al-Andalus. Alarcón's attempt to describe Tetouan's material culture exemplifies this paradox of origins:

> The scant furniture, the curtains, the rugs, the armoires, the tableware; everything that I examined was authentic and artistic; it has an extremely marked Oriental character; it is full of inscriptions and allegorical geometric figures, and it matches perfectly all of the Morisco objects that are conserved in our Spain, the remains of the long Hagarene domination. Thus, the arts, the crafts, the customs, everything that is related to the Moors' life, continues in the *status quo* that characterizes the essence of their civilization. Nothing has varied, nothing has progressed, nothing has changed in style or substance. Visiting Tetouan today is the same as seeing Cordoba in the thirteenth century.[96]

Alarcón considers Tetouan's furniture and material objects "authentic" insofar as they resemble the Muslim art and artifacts found in Spain. As often happens with claims of authenticity, there is no stable point of origin for Alarcón's claim. The resemblance between objects found in Spain and Morocco authenticates both the Moroccan objects and the Andalusi objects. In this circular logic, the point of origin continually loops back on itself: Alarcón draws on Andalusi culture to explicate Tetouani culture, but he also uses Tetouani culture to explicate Andalusi culture. Alarcón's text illustrates a logical quandary that would dog Spanish cultural policies in Morocco throughout the colonial period. In the twentieth century, many Spanish writers would assert the need to preserve Morocco's Andalusi heritage, and, at the same time, Spanish architects and artists would look to Morocco as the basis upon which to restore Spain's Islamic heritage sites, such as the Alhambra. Preservation would be an enduring concern and trope for Spanish colonial thinkers, but the historical basis for preservation efforts would remain in constant flux.

Alarcón eschews this problem of flux. His assessment of Moroccan culture is built on the premise that it is unchanging and also that it is interchangeable with the culture of al-Andalus. Morocco becomes, in Alarcón's account, a time capsule or a museum that can transport Spanish travelers to earlier moments in Iberian history. For that reason, Alarcón can say: "Visiting Tetouan today is the same as seeing Cordoba in the thirteenth century."[97] Presumably, Alarcón is referring to Cordoba's life as a Muslim city before 1236, the date of the Christian conquest of the city. To some extent, though, dates are insignificant when analyzing Alarcón's *Diary*, not only because Alarcón cites them haphazardly, but also (more importantly) because Alarcón believes that Muslim culture never changes or varies. His view of a static, immutable Moroccan culture is deeply indebted to the European Orientalist tradition. Nevertheless, subsequent Spanish colonial thinkers would break from this static view and propose, instead, a narrative of historical decline, in which Spain must intervene in Morocco in order to rescue Andalusi culture from a process of degeneration that began with the Andalusi migration to North Africa.

After Alarcón equates nineteenth-century Tetouan with thirteenth-century al-Andalus, he concludes the chapter by reproducing, word for word, the entire first paragraph of the *Diary*'s prologue:

> Visiting Tetouan today is the same as seeing Cordoba in the thirteenth century. I have, therefore, fulfilled the desire that moved me when I wrote these phrases in the introduction to the present book:
> "Born, as I was, in the Sierra Nevada, from whose summits you can just make out the beaches where Moordom sleeps its historical death; the son of a city that preserves the footprints of Arab domination. . . . I felt seduced by the nearness of Africa, and I yearned to cross the Mediterranean in order to touch, so to speak, in that marvelous continent, the living reality of the past."[98]

Alarcón's dramatic act of self-citation is a wonderful illustration of Derrida's concept of *différance*. Derrida uses this term to play on the two meanings of the French verb *différer,* "to differ" and "to defer."⁹⁹ Derrida's wordplay is helpful for thinking about Alarcón's self-citation. Alarcón's repeated paragraph points to the difference that is produced by deferral. The first iteration of the paragraph, in the prologue, is a declaration of individual origins ("Born as I was . . .") in opposition to the collective stasis of "Moordom." The same paragraph then returns, after a lapse of two months, in Alarcón's first entry about Tetouan.

The return of the *Diary*'s first paragraph offers a few possible readings, which are not mutually exclusive. One reading would treat this gesture as conventional Orientalism. In this reading, Alarcón's repetition of a paragraph written before his arrival to Morocco serves as an implicit confirmation that a European does not need to travel to Morocco in order to see Morocco. The repetition thus implies that Morocco is exactly the country that Alarcón had envisioned from his perch on Granada's Sierra Nevada. The *Diary* is, then, the chronicle of a journey foretold, the story of a representation whose parameters were set in place before the journey began. Alarcón's Morocco is immutable, internally consistent, and entirely legible. This reading of Alarcón's self-citation closely aligns the *Diary* with Orientalism's essentialist views of the Orient. It also undermines the significance that Alarcón gives to his experience as an eyewitness to the War of Africa. Finally, the Orientalist reading of the *Diary* locates Alarcón outside of Morocco and inside of Western historical time: he is a historically situated subject looking down on an undifferentiated mass of Moroccans who live in a "historical death."

Alarcón's self-citation can also be read as a more ambivalent act of cultural appropriation. It could be an attempt to mimic the stasis that he attributes to Morocco. Alarcón stresses that, in Morocco, "Nothing has varied, nothing has progressed, nothing has changed in style or substance."¹⁰⁰ In this light, repetition could be Alarcón's way of "passing" as Moroccan: the first iteration of the paragraph, in the prologue, signals a desire to transcend space and time in order to reconnect with a lost part of his self, and the second iteration of the paragraph signals the fulfilment of that desire. Between the prologue, written in Spain, and the diary entries, written in Tetouan, "Nothing has varied, nothing has progressed." Through repetition, Alarcón takes himself and the reader out of the linear progression of time. His self-citation performs the stasis that he ascribes to Tetouan, and that makes the city indistinguishable from al-Andalus.

The self-citation might also help us to interrogate the meaning of Alarcón's Moroccan portraits, which I discussed at the beginning of this chapter. In the scholarship on Alarcón, there has been a tendency to take at face value the "Moorish" identity that Alarcón claims for himself.[101] Nevertheless, Alarcón's portraits demonstrate that—at least in the context of Spanish colonialism in Morocco—things should not be taken at face value. The Moroccan clothes that Alarcón wears in the portraits are, like his repeated paragraph in the *Diary*, a text whose meaning shifts when it is deferred to a new context. In both the portraits and the *Diary*, the exercise of Spanish power over Morocco is routed through the assertion that Spain and Morocco are similar. In the next section, I will take up another instance of cross-cultural appropriation through similarity: Alarcón's Moroccan alter ego, Chorby.

Alarcón and Chorby: Colonial Ventriloquism

Alarcón spent six weeks in Tetouan, from February 6 to March 22, 1860. While there, he sought out Moroccan interlocutors in order to understand, in his words, "the present history in reverse"—that is, in order to see how Moroccans experienced and viewed the war, leading up to the occupation of Tetouan.[102] Alarcón's attempt to reconstruct the Moroccan version of the war exposes one of the tensions at the heart of his *Diary*: he claims to have unfettered access to Moroccan subjectivity, but his representation of Moroccan voices makes them sound suspiciously similar to his own. The *Diary* thus serves as an exercise in colonial ventriloquism. Alarcón appears to valorize Moroccan perspectives, but he projects his own voice onto his Moroccan interlocutors. In this sense, Alarcón's insistence on the importance of Moroccan perspectives is similar to his emphasis on his status as an eyewitness. In both cases, Alarcón legitimizes his account of the war by tying it to evidence that, on closer inspection, reveals itself to be dubious and illusory.

One of the few Moroccan characters whose direct speech is recorded in the *Diary* is a poet named Chorby, whom Alarcón met during his stay in Tetouan. Alarcón introduces Chorby in a diary entry from March of 1860, in which he describes the Moroccan poet as "an opulent Moor, devoted to the *belles-lettres* since his early years and one of the most learned men of this empire, according to his compatriots."[103] Although Chorby only speaks limited and broken Spanish, Alarcón overcomes the linguistic barrier and engages the Moroccan in "a very deep and transcendental conference on the arts, science, politics, and literature."[104] Through this conversation, Alarcón learns about Chorby's education and literary career. According to Alarcón, Chorby has memorized the Qur'an and more than a hundred Qur'anic commentaries.[105] "He knows," Alarcón observes, "the history of the Arab domination in Spain, albeit roughly."[106] Alarcón also hails Chorby as a fellow writer, calling him "my brother in Apollo."[107] The phrase mixes a reference to the Greek god of poetry with a fraternal metaphor that highlights Alarcón's efforts to imagine a Hispano-Moroccan family. Alarcón attributes several literary works to Chorby, including a hagiographic account of a Muslim saint from Fez, a book of Islamic jurisprudence, a commentary on the Qur'an, and verses in praise of God, the Prophet Muhammad, and the Moroccan sultan.[108]

Alarcón describes Chorby as one of the most learned and accomplished writers in Morocco, but it is actually very difficult to identify the Chorby in question—or even to know for certain whether he existed. "Chorby" must be Alarcón's transliteration of "Shurbi," the name of a prominent family in Tetouan. Yet, none of the major sources on Tetouani history mention a single writer or scholar from the Shurbi family. Ahmad al-Rahuni (1878–1953) does not mention any writers or scholars from the Shurbi family in his ten-volume history of Tetouan, *'Umdat al-rawin fi tarikh Tittawin*.[109] Muhammad Dawud's three-volume work *Families of Tetouan* (*'A'ilat Titwan*, c. 1960s–1970s) has an entry about the Shurbis, but it does not mention any poets or writers from the family.[110] Alarcón might be referring to Muhammad b. Ahmad al-Shurbi, who was married to a member of the Erzini (al-Razini) family, whose house Alarcón visited and compared to "a patio of the Alhambra in Granada."[111] This Shurbi, however, is not known to have written anything. In short, Alarcón might very well have met a Moroccan named Chorby in 1860, but his Moroccan acquaintance certainly was not "one of the most learned men" in Morocco, as Alarcón claims.

Regardless of the historical identity of Chorby, he is perhaps best understood as a literary alter ego for Alarcón. It is, thus, fitting that Chorby left a trace in Spanish sources but not, apparently, in Moroccan ones. Like the tunic and slippers that Alarcón wore to the Duchess of Medinaceli's ball in 1861, Chorby is a costume that Alarcón dons to claim a pseudo-Moroccan identity. In fact, it is worth recalling that Chorby (or the figure of Chorby) played a role in the duchess's ball. As I previously discussed, Alarcón published an account of the ball in the form of a fictitious letter from Mulay al-'Abbas "to the poet Chorby, in Tetouan."[112] Chorby serves, therefore, as the addressee for Alarcón's account of the costume ball, written from an apocryphal Moroccan perspective. As the fictional audience for Alarcón's newspaper piece, Chorby helps to authenticate Alarcón's performance as a Moor.

Chorby plays a similar role in the poem "To Chorby, Moroccan Poet" ("A Chorby, poeta marroquí"), which Alarcón wrote in Tetouan in 1860.[113] Despite the poem's interesting parallels with Alarcón's *Diary*, it has not received any scholarly scrutiny, nor has it been translated into English. I will, therefore, offer a translation of the poem, and then I will analyze it in light of Alarcón's colonial ideology:

> *I*
> You ask me who I am, oh Mahometan!
> And you tell me that you are the inheritor
> of those Moors who on Hispanic soil
> erected to their god and to their women
> the superhuman palace of the Alhambra.
>
> You ask me who I am . . . and, meanwhile, you cry,
> calling yourself a foreigner and a pilgrim
> in this house where you were born and where you reside,
> and you announce to me that to the Granadan sky
> the Moorish moons will return again.
>
> *II*
> I no longer know who I am, oh Mahometan!
> I was born where you want to die;

> I dreamed about your race on Hispanic soil,
> and today, when my feet first touch African soil,
> I think that I am ... the same person as you!
>
> A foreigner in Africa, you cry ...
> I have cried in Spain as a pilgrim;
> and today, a guest in the house where you reside,
> I think that I see the Granadan sky
> crowned again with Moorish moons.[114]

The poem is a monologue dressed up as a dialogue. A first-person speaker, born in Granada, apostrophizes a Muslim interlocutor ("Oh Mahometan!") who is invoked but never speaks. The poem is a study in mirrors, of a singular speaker who divides himself in two, and of two cultural identities that merge into one. It stages the marriage of a Spanish "I" and a Moroccan "you" through a shared link to Muslim Granada.

The poem's structural balance reinforces its emphasis on mirroring and doubling. The twenty-line poem is divided into two sections, each of which consists of two five-line stanzas. The rhyme scheme of ABABA is repeated in both sections of the poem, with a slight variation (ABAAB) in the third stanza. In fact, the poem's two sections not only share the same rhyme scheme, but they even share the same rhyme words: *Mahometano* ("Mahometan"), *hispano* ("Hispanic"), and *africano* ("African"); *lloras* ("you cry"), *moras* ("you reside"), and *moras* ("Moorish"); *peregrino* ("pilgrim," "wanderer") and *granadino* ("Granadan"). These repeated rhymes not only interweave the poem's sections but also highlight the merged identities that are at the poem's core.

The poem's first line highlights the question of identity: "You ask me who I am, oh Mahometan!" The poem is, thus, framed as a response to a Muslim interlocutor, Chorby, who has asked a question that antecedes the temporality of the poem. Chorby is, thus, both present and absent: his question is the occasion for the poem, and yet the poem speaks *for* Chorby, rather than registering his speech. The speaker calls Chorby a "Mahometan," a term that Alarcón occasionally uses to refer to Muslims.

Unlike the more common term "Moor," the adjective "Mahometan" (*mahometano*) rhymes with "Hispanic" (*hispano*). The rhyme of *mahometano* and *hispano* appears in the first stanza and then is repeated in the third stanza, where it is joined with *africano* ("African"). Thus, through rhyme, the poem draws together Spain, Islam, and Africa. Granada is the point at which Spain, Islam, and Africa come together, and it is also the point of union between the speaker and his Moroccan interlocutor, Chorby. The speaker evokes his native city through the adjectival form *granadino* ("Granadan"), which is twice rhymed with the adjective *peregrino,* meaning "pilgrim," "wanderer," and "foreigner." This rhyming pair emphasizes the theme that Muslim Granada is a heritage that wanders between Spain and Morocco. Both the speaker and his interlocutor are pilgrims in search of their homeland, Granada, and they are also both wandering subjects who recognize themselves in the other.

The tension between where you are and who you are is present in the repeated rhyme of *moras* ("you reside") and *moras* ("Moorish"), which appears in the second stanza and then again in the last lines of the poem. This rich rhyme is a variation on the rhetorical figure of polyptoton because it entails the repetition of two homonyms that are different parts of speech: in the first usage, *moras* is the second-person singular form of the literary verb *morar* ("to reside"); in the second usage, *moras* is the plural, feminine adjective form of *moro* ("Moorish"). The polyptoton highlights the gradual merging of the speaker's abode, Granada, with Chorby's abode, Tetouan. In the second stanza, Tetouan is figured as the house where Chorby "resides" (*mora*) while he is waiting for "Moorish moons" (*lunas moras*) to return to the Granadan sky. In the final stanza, the speaker repeats this play on *moras/moras*. He says that being a guest in Tetouan ("huésped de la casa donde moras") makes him imagine that he is seeing the return of Moorish Granada.

The poem's structure is chiastic: a Spanish speaker becomes Moroccan, and a Moroccan city becomes Spanish. The poem thus mirrors the process through which the speaker (Alarcón) becomes Chorby and Tetouan becomes Granada. In the first stanza, the speaker addresses his Moroccan interlocutor, Chorby. In the second stanza, the speaker transmits Chorby's voice through indirect discourse. In the third stanza, the speaker imagines that his identity has merged with the identity of his Moroccan interlocutor: "I think that I am . . . the same person as you!" (v. 15). In the fourth stanza, as the Spanish guest merges with the Moroccan host, Tetouan merges with Muslim Granada.

The poem illustrates Alarcón's colonial ventriloquism—that is, his ability to throw his voice onto Moroccan subjects, who then become mouthpieces for Spanish colonial discourses. The poem also reinforces a central theme from Alarcón's *Diary:* the cultural and historical similarity between nineteenth-century Tetouan and medieval Granada. Alarcón's writings about Morocco inaugurate a long tradition of Spanish colonial literature in which Spanish writers—especially writers from the southern region of Andalucía—claim to have a special understanding of Moroccan culture because of Spain's Muslim heritage.

Conclusion: The Legacy of the Spanish-Moroccan War

On March 23, 1860, the Spanish army defeated the Moroccan army in the decisive Battle of Wad Ras, marking the end of combat in the Spanish-Moroccan War. On March 25, O'Donnell and Mulay al-'Abbas agreed to a preliminary peace agreement, which was officially ratified by both sides on May 26.[115] The peace agreement sparked a backlash in Spain. The Spanish public had assumed that Spain would, at the very least, keep Tetouan and the other territories that its army had occupied during the Moroccan campaign. Instead, the peace treaty did not offer any territorial concessions to Spain. In response, the Spanish press coined a sardonic motto that summed up the public's widespread disappointment with the war's outcome: "A mighty war, a puny peace" ("Una guerra grande, una paz chica").[116]

Despite the Spanish public's bitter response, the peace treaty had long-lasting and devastating consequences for Morocco. Among other concessions, Morocco agreed to pay Spain a huge war indemnity of twenty million Spanish duros, which was more than double the total wealth of the Moroccan state at the time.[117] The peace treaty authorized the Spanish army to continue occupying Tetouan until the Moroccan government had paid off the indemnity. Eager to bring the unpopular

Spanish occupation to an end, the Moroccan government struggled to piece together the money required to pay off the onerous war indemnity. The sultan attempted to raise taxes and asked for voluntary contributions to the state's coffers, but neither initiative brought in much money, and both aggravated popular discontent. Moroccan and European diplomatic agents participated in failed attempts to secure loans from Great Britain and France in 1861. The Spanish government then announced its intention to annex Tetouan because of Morocco's failure to pay the war indemnity. Fearing another war between Spain and Morocco, the British government decided to intervene in order to protect its commercial interests in Morocco and to solidify its political influence there. The British representative in Tangier, John Drummond Hay, helped convince English capitalists in London to offer the Moroccan government a high-interest loan. In October of 1861, Spain and Morocco reached an agreement that stipulated that Spain would withdraw from Tetouan once Morocco had paid off a portion of the promised war indemnity. In order to pay off the rest of the Spanish indemnity and the cost of the British loan, Morocco agreed to forfeit the majority of its customs revenues to the two European countries.

The Spanish army evacuated Tetouan on May 2, 1862, but the European presence in Morocco was just beginning. Spanish and British agents were installed in Morocco's primary ports in order to levy customs duties. For the next twenty years, Morocco forfeited the majority of its customs revenues (one of the country's primary sources of income) to Spain and Britain. The arrangement devastated the Moroccan economy and weakened the country's political institutions, while at the same time consolidating European influence in Morocco.[118] In many ways, the Spanish-Moroccan War generated the economic and political conditions that enabled European colonialism in Morocco. Reflecting on the war's consequences at the end of the nineteenth century, the Moroccan historian al-Nasiri wrote: "This war of Tetouan is what pulled off the veil of respect from Morocco. Christians lorded over it, and Muslims were broken as they had never been before."[119] The Spanish and French Protectorates in Morocco were not officially established until 1912, but the writing was already on the wall for the Moroccans who lived through the aftermath of the Spanish-Moroccan War.

Curiously, Pedro Antonio de Alarcón, the most famous Spanish advocate for the war, became an opponent of Spanish colonialism in Morocco. When news of the occupation of Tetouan reached Spain, the Spanish public erupted in euphoria. Many journalists and politicians called for the army to take Tangier, and some even advocated for the Spanish conquest to extend to the rest of Morocco and beyond.[120] On February 11, 1860, five days after the Spanish army entered Tetouan, the troops received a large shipment of mail, including newspapers. In the *Diary,* Alarcón describes the satisfaction with which he and his fellow soldiers read the correspondence from home and learned of the enthusiastic response to the taking of Tetouan.[121] He expresses concern, however, over the growing calls, in the Spanish press, for the expansion of the army's campaign beyond Tetouan:

> Those words spoke about conquest, about colonization, about how we ought to go to Tangier, to Fez, and even to Tafilalt [*Tafilete*]; about uprooting Islam in Africa; about improvising a new Spain on this side of the Strait [of Gibraltar]; about planting the cross on top of the Atlas and converting to Christianity ten million fanatical Muslims or about annihilating them with the thirty or forty thousand men that make up our army . . . about reproducing, in short, the Austrian policy [*la política austríaca*], which is so brilliant, so poetic, so heroic, but so fatal for Spain; as brash in its origins as it is devastating in its development and useless in its results.[122]

Alarcón alludes to a press that speaks recklessly of sending the Spanish army to the Tafilalt, a large oasis in the southeast of Morocco. In contrast with these grandiose plans, Alarcón outlines the case against Spanish colonialism in Morocco—or, at least, against a colonial enterprise based on territorial occupation and violent evangelism.

In particular, he warns against reproducing "the Austrian policy," by which he means the politics of the Hapsburg dynasty, whose rule (1516–1700) coincided with Spain's apogee as an imperial power. Alarcón's critique of Hapsburg-like expansionism—which he calls both "brilliant" and "fatal"—contradicts other moments in the *Diary,* where he extols the military exploits of the Hapsburg period. For instance, in his first entry from Tetouan, Alarcón greets the Spanish occupation of the city as a "magnificent resurrection" of such episodes in Spanish imperial history as the conquest of Mexico (1519–1521) and Charles V's victory in the Battle of Pavia (1525).[123] Alarcón's *Diary* is saturated with such contradictory impulses. Throughout the text, the Spanish eyewitness and soldier vacillates between exalting Spain's imperial history and distancing Spain's modern mission in Morocco from the errors of the past and from the imperialist ambitions of France and Great Britain.

On March 22, 1860, the day before the Battle of Wad Ras, Alarcón left Morocco for Spain. In the last diary entry written in Morocco, Alarcón declares: "I believe that our mission in Africa is finished for now; that the continuation of the war has no purpose; that it will be a calamity for my country . . . that the press in the capital, a powerful lever that moves public opinion at will, is pushing our army toward an abyss, inspired by error, by ignorance, by a misunderstood patriotism."[124] In this way, Alarcón announces his departure from Morocco, telling his readers that he is returning to Madrid to be a "soldier in the combats of the press," fighting for an end to the Spanish campaign in Morocco.[125] Critics have had trouble explaining Alarcón's apparent change of heart about Spain's mission in Morocco.[126] Perhaps Alarcón felt that he had an obligation to return home to serve as a representative of the Spanish soldiers, who, according to him, were unanimous in their opposition to a continuation of the war.[127] Perhaps he was just tired after a long and wet campaign in which more Spanish soldiers died of cholera than in combat.[128] Unlike other scholars, I will not offer an interpretation that explains (or explains away) the apparent contradictions in Alarcón's *Diary*. In fact, I think that the productive power of contradiction is one of Alarcón's primary contributions to Spanish colonial discourse. His self-fashioning as a Moor and as a torchbearer for the Christian Reconquest anticipates some of the discursive and ideological paradoxes that would characterize Spanish (and eventually Moroccan) writings about Spanish colonialism in Morocco. Despite Alarcón's enigmatic desire to prevent the Spanish colonization of Morocco, his *Diary* had a significant impact on the colonial discourses that the Spanish would develop in Morocco over the next century.

Like many subsequent colonial Spanish writers, Alarcón emphasizes the geographic and historical continuity between northern Morocco and southern Spain. This rhetorical move not only shapes his representation of Morocco but also inflects his understanding of Spain. Indeed, for Alarcón, the continuity between Spain and Morocco penetrates to the level of race. Noting the ease with which a Spaniard can pass as a Moroccan, Alarcón comments: "For a while now, I have marveled on a daily basis at the perfect resemblance that exists between the truly Moorish types and the vast majority of our Andalusians and Valencians."[129] Alarcón anticipates, here, a major trope in Spanish colonial discourse: the idea that Spaniards and Moroccans are "blood brothers," linked by a racial bond.[130] This trope is often attributed to Joaquín Costa, who famously declared, in a speech delivered at Madrid's Alhambra Theater in 1884: "There exists between Spaniards and Moroccans a certain secret powerful attraction, which can only be explained by some ethnic relationship that unites them, fortified and confirmed by age-old influences from their natural milieu.... Moors and Spaniards are brothers who belong to the same Mediterranean race."[131] Costa, like Alarcón, imagines a racial bond between Spain and Morocco, fortified by natural and historic circumstances.

While Costa's metaphor of a "Hispano-Moroccan brotherhood" played a more central role in subsequent Spanish colonial texts, I find Alarcón's genealogical imaginary to be more supple and multifarious. In Alarcón's *Diary*, Spaniards and Moroccans are brothers, but they are also sons of the same "mother," al-Andalus, whose daughters are Granada and Tetouan. Such malleable metaphors of family and filiation underwrite the Spanish colonial understanding of Morocco—and, later, Moroccan responses to Spanish colonialism. In the mid-twentieth century, Moroccan nationalists coined Tetouan's nickname as "the daughter of Granada and Fez."[132] They thus cast Tetouan as a member of a Hispano-Moroccan family with roots on both sides of the Strait of

Gibraltar. As Spanish and Moroccan writers compete (and, at times, collaborate) to tell the story of where Moroccan culture comes from, family metaphors and origin stories form the narrative frameworks in which their stories unfold.

Perhaps Alarcón's most important contribution to Spanish colonial discourse is his insistence on Tetouan's connection with Granada. Alarcón is a pioneer in the discursive and ideological process that I call "colonial al-Andalus" because his writings wed a vision of intercultural affiliation with a project of interstate domination. Despite Alarcón's repeated insistence on his status as an eyewitness, he has difficulty seeing Morocco. His Tetouan is largely a product of nineteenth-century European Romantic representations of Muslim Granada, particularly Chateaubriand's *Last Abencerrage*. Nevertheless, Alarcón's simple formulation, "Tetouan is Granada," blossomed, in subsequent colonial texts, into increasingly sophisticated historical narratives that interweave Spanish and Moroccan culture. The discovery, preservation, codification, and promotion of Morocco's Granadan heritage would become a cultural mission shared by Spanish colonial actors from across the political spectrum—including, notably, Spanish fascists. (It is not a coincidence that Alarcón enjoyed a revival in the 1940s, under Francoism.) Indeed, "Tetouan is Granada" might be taken as a motto for Spanish colonialism in Morocco.

In Chapter 2, I will discuss the life and work of a Moroccan contemporary to Alarcón, Mufaddal Afaylal (1824–1887), who was also an "eyewitness" to the Spanish-Moroccan War. By juxtaposing Alarcón and Afaylal, I hope to illuminate the divergent ways in which Spaniards and Moroccans thought and wrote about al-Andalus in the early days of Spanish colonialism in Morocco. Both Alarcón and Afaylal espouse views of the Spanish-Moroccan War that are predetermined and structured by pre-existing literary representations of Christian-Muslim relations in al-Andalus. Yet, the two writers do not share the same literary baggage, and the differences in their literary educations lead to different visions of the war. Despite the differences between Alarcón and his contemporary Afaylal, Spanish and Moroccan writings about al-Andalus draw closer over the course of the colonial period. In a surprising turn, Alarcón's Romantic Granada played a significant role in twentieth-century Moroccan representations of Tetouan and its Andalusi heritage, particularly in the literature and historiography of the 1950s. Alarcón might easily be confused for a conventional Orientalist or imperialist, but his writings foreshadow the surprising convergence of Spanish and Moroccan culture that unfolded over the following century.

2

AL-ANDALUS AND MOROCCAN LITERARY HISTORY

IN 1992, MAHMUD DARWISH (1941–2008), arguably the most famous Palestinian poet, published the book *Eleven Stars* (*Ahad 'ashar kawkaban*), whose title poem elegizes the fall of al-Andalus in 1492. The book's title alludes to a well-known verse in the Qur'anic telling of the story of Joseph, an archetypal figure of emigration and exile in the Abrahamic traditions.[1] Through the allusion, Darwish ties the story of al-Andalus to an older story of loss and eventual redemption. Yet his allusions move both forward and backward in time, linking al-Andalus to an older Islamic paradigm (the Joseph story) and also to contemporary events. Indeed, Darwish's lament for al-Andalus has most often been interpreted as an allegory for the loss of Palestine, the central theme of the poet's oeuvre.[2] Throughout the title poem, the speaker deploys oxymorons that conflate past and present, and time and space, as when he fears "a present that is no longer / present."[3] Oxymorons abound in Darwish's writings, perhaps because they allow the poet to probe the political and existential contradictions of the Palestinian people, a nation without a nation-state.[4]

Like Palestine, al-Andalus has been an absence that is very present in modern Arabic poetry, inspiring works by such canonical poets as the Egyptian Ahmad Shawqi (1868–1932) and the Syrian Nizar Qabbani (1923–1998).[5] By the time Darwish published *Eleven Stars* in 1992, al-Andalus had become not only a celebrated chapter in Arab and Islamic history, but also a topos within modern Arabic letters for reflecting on the past, present, and future of the Arab and Muslim worlds.[6] That is, al-Andalus is not only a place in history but also a place in discourse.[7] Darwish signals as much in the last lines of *Eleven Star*'s opening poem: "And in the end, we'll ask ourselves: was al-Andalus / here or there? On earth . . . or in poems?"[8]

In this chapter, I will take up Darwish's question: where and how does al-Andalus exist? In history—in place and time—or in poems? To frame this problem in different terms, I mean to explore the tension between the specificity of al-Andalus as a particular place and time in Islamic and Iberian history and the plasticity of al-Andalus as an idea that travels across time and performs useful work for writers living in different historical and cultural contexts. This chapter will thus probe the border between the specific and the general, the historical and the atemporal—and between history and poetry, a distinction as old as Aristotle. In the *Poetics* (which, as luck would have it, was transmitted to Europe through the work of the Andalusi philosopher Ibn Rushd), Aristotle famously claimed that the difference between the historian and the poet "is that the former relates things that have happened, the latter things that may happen. . . . Poetry tends to speak of universals, history of particulars."[9] Aristotle's dictum will provide both a guide and a foil for this chapter, in which I will illuminate the limits of poetry's ability to express the universal and also the limits of history's ability to express the particular.

Modern representations of al-Andalus, such as Darwish's *Eleven Stars*, endow it with a sort of universality, an ability to transcend historical specificity. Al-Andalus travels well. It *translates*, in the etymological sense of "crossing over." Yet something is always gained and lost in that process of translation, and these modulations are what I hope to track. What happens to al-Andalus when it is translated into new historical and cultural contexts?

The question of the translatability of al-Andalus has broad relevance for the study of modern Mediterranean cultures, as evidenced by the popularity of al-Andalus in recent literature and film from Spain, Morocco, Egypt, Syria, Palestine, and beyond. What interests me in this chapter, though, is the trajectory of modern Moroccan appropriations of al-Andalus. That is, what is the specific cultural work that al-Andalus performs in modern Morocco, and how does that work evolve over time? In the introduction, I have already outlined this book's argument, which is that the idea that Moroccan culture descends from the culture of al-Andalus is a modern invention that emerges from the colonial encounter between Spain and Morocco. This chapter's aim will be to trace the Moroccan origins of that process of invention. I will argue that, in the middle of the nineteenth century, al-Andalus offered Moroccan writers a wellspring of poetic topoi and tropes for thinking about the origins of European colonialism in Morocco and, more broadly, for representing conflict between Islam and Christianity. Although a powerful and pervasive source of poetry, al-Andalus had not yet hardened into what it would become in the twentieth century: a keystone of Moroccan national identity linked to a specific narrative of cultural transmission, manifested in architecture, music, and other cultural practices that Moroccans inherited directly from medieval Iberia.

At the center of this chapter will be the Moroccan poet, scholar, and visual artist Mufaddal Afaylal (1824–1887), whose life spanned the beginning of European colonialism in North Africa—including the French invasion of Algeria in 1830 and the Spanish occupation of his native city of Tetouan in 1860. During the Spanish occupation of Tetouan (1860–1862), Afaylal went into nomadic exile. He settled his family in Chefchaouen, another city whose history is tied to the post-1492 Andalusi migration to Morocco.[10] From 1860 to 1862, Afaylal spent long periods in Chefchaouen, but he also traveled widely across Morocco, with excursions to Tangier, Fez, and Rabat, as well as frequent visits to the tomb of 'Abd al-Salam b. Mashish (known as "Mulay 'Abd al-Salam"), an important Sufi pilgrimage site in northern Morocco.[11] During this period, Afaylal also produced two of the most important Moroccan texts about the Spanish-Moroccan War of 1859–1860. The first was an elegy for Tetouan written in the style of the city elegy genre that was popular in al-Andalus.[12] The second was a chronicle that described life in Tetouan during the months leading up to the Spanish occupation of the city. The chronicle also includes Afaylal's description of his visit to the Moroccan army's camp near Tetouan and his pointed criticism of the Moroccan army's leaders, whom he represents as both incompetent and immoral.

Read together, Afaylal's elegy and chronicle paint a profoundly contradictory picture of the war that marked the beginning of Spanish colonialism in Morocco. The elegy uses an Andalusi literary genre to establish a parallel between the Spanish occupation of Tetouan in 1860 and the Christian Reconquest of the Muslim cities of al-Andalus. Afaylal thus writes Tetouan's history into the broader categories of Andalusi history, Islamic history, and Arabic literary history. The chronicle, in contrast, avoids such transhistorical comparisons and focuses, instead, on Afaylal's status as an eyewitness to the war's events and consequences. Thus, the elegy and the chronicle seem to set up the classic opposition between poetry and history, the universal and the particular.

Yet this facile opposition breaks down easily. Afaylal's elegy evokes the literary conventions of the Andalusi city elegy, but it also subverts them in significant ways. In so doing, it signals both the appeal of al-Andalus as a discursive model for making sense of the colonial encounter and also the limits of that model. Indeed, I will argue that Afaylal's exercise in literary history leads to a mimetic and hermeneutic impasse: Afaylal's elegy attempts to represent and interpret Moroccan colonial experience through an Andalusi literary model and yet ultimately signals al-Andalus's inability to represent or interpret the colonial encounter. It would be tempting to read Afaylal's chronicle of the war as the solution to this impasse. Instead, the chronicle highlights the problems of eyewitness testimony and the limits of what history can say. It is therefore fitting that the conclusion of Afaylal's chronicle draws upon the rhetorical conventions of the city elegy genre. History converges on poetry, even as it attempts to escape its orbit.

This chapter, then, will advance arguments on two fronts. First, I will demonstrate the cultural work that al-Andalus—and, specifically, Andalusi literary history—performs in nineteenth-century Morocco. Second, I will examine poetry and history as two (ultimately insufficient) modes of talking about a traumatic experience of loss—in this case, the violent military occupation of Afaylal's home city, Tetouan.

Thick Reading: A Methodological Excursus

This chapter will be the most philological one in the book, and, at the outset, I feel compelled to give a brief justification for this methodological approach. In turning to philology, I mean to invoke a critical practice whose modern genealogy connects Nietzsche to de Man to Said.[13] While philology has, in recent times, been dismissed as a detached, sterile, and even reactionary form of humanistic inquiry, Said defends its worldliness in his essay "The Return to Philology." To read philologically, Said argues, is to attend to the unresolved dialectical relationship between literary texts and the historical, social, political, and economic forces that shape them. Philology thus places the literary text, to quote Said, "in a position that obviously depends on history but is not reducible to it."[14] In Said's formulation, philology is both a method and an ethos. As a method, philology relies on the patient scrutiny of words deployed in specific historical circumstances. As an ethical stance, it entails both an openness to what a text says and an ability to detect the text's silences. Said describes these contrasting movements as "reception and resistance," which he sees as the twin motors behind philological inquiry.[15]

Building on Said, my methodology for this chapter will be what I call "thick reading," a combination of "close reading," a practice that remains central to Said's philology, and "thick description," Geertz's famous description of what ethnography does. For Geertz, "thick description" entails placing an anecdote within a network of signifying structures that give the anecdote social and cultural meaning. Thus, to describe an anecdote or a social ritual "thickly" is to reconstruct the cultural context in which the described phenomenon is intelligible and meaningful.[16] In describing my methodology as "thick reading," I hope to gesture toward the two parallel scales on which this chapter will unfold: close textual analysis and large cultural framing. My goal will be to offer compelling readings of Afaylal's elegy and chronicle, the most important Moroccan literary representations of the Spanish-Moroccan War. At the same time, I hope to reconstruct the cultural framework in which these texts circulated.

My desire to "thick read" Afaylal's work responds to my belief that Afaylal's cultural world has largely been lost to scholars outside of Morocco. Put simply, the literary history of nineteenth-century Morocco, of which Afaylal is a prime example, has still not been written. The study of nineteenth-century Moroccan literature has faced both material and epistemic obstacles.[17] The material limitations stem from the relatively late introduction of the printing press in Morocco. Lithographic printing was not introduced in Morocco until 1864, and it did not become widespread until the 1880s. The use of movable type for Arabic texts did not take off in Morocco until the beginning of the twentieth century.[18] Thus, nineteenth-century Morocco, particularly during Afaylal's lifetime, was primarily a manuscript culture. While Moroccan scholars have made admirable strides, in recent decades, in publishing critical editions of nineteenth-century manuscript works, there are still many important nineteenth-century authors whose work remains in manuscript form—and must, therefore, be read on site in Moroccan archives. Mufaddal Afaylal is one of them.

Much of Afaylal's extant literary oeuvre is collected in a manuscript held at the Dawud Library in Tetouan.[19] The manuscript is known as *Kunnash Afaylal* (hereafter, the *Kunnash*), which could be translated as "Afaylal's Notebook." Excerpts from Afaylal's *Kunnash,* including his elegy and chronicle about the Spanish-Moroccan War of 1859–1860, have been published by Moroccan historians, but the manuscript has never been published in its entirety.[20] Although Afaylal is widely recognized as one of the leading cultural figures of nineteenth-century Morocco, his *Kunnash* has received very little scholarly attention—particularly outside Morocco.[21] This neglect cannot be explained alone by the material constraints that limit the circulation of manuscripts. Rather, Afaylal's *Kunnash,* a hybrid of genres and discourses, exemplifies the epistemic limitations that have plagued the study of nineteenth-century Moroccan literature—and, indeed, all Arabic writing that does not easily fit into the existing literary-historical narratives.

For the past century, both Western and Middle Eastern scholars have dismissed and derided the Arabic literature produced between roughly 1150 and 1850. According to the standard literary-historical narrative, Arabic literature enjoyed a "golden age" of creativity around the tenth century, when talented poets and writers vied for the patronage of Muslim rulers from Baghdad to Cordoba. Around 1150, Arabic literature entered a long period of decline, which scholars have dubbed "the period of decadence."[22] During this supposed period of decline, Arabic literature lost, in the words of Salma Khadra Jayyusi, "its former zest and spirit" and became repetitive, conventional, sterile, and affected.[23] The long "period of decadence" came to an end with the advent of European imperialism in the nineteenth century, which sparked a cultural renaissance in the Arab world known as the *Nahḍa* (literally, "the rising"). During the *Nahḍa,* Arab writers, mostly in Egypt and Beirut, translated European literary works into Arabic and began to adopt European literary genres, such as the novel. Thus, in the dominant scholarly narrative, the emergence of modern Arabic literature is cast as a liberation from the burden of a moribund tradition, which is often (implicitly or explicitly) associated with Islamic institutions of learning.[24]

This standard account of Arabic literary history has had a deleterious effect on the study of modern Moroccan literature. Many scholars of Arabic literature have simply ignored all Moroccan literary production between, roughly, the sixteenth century and the middle of the twentieth century, when the first Moroccan novels started to appear.[25] Moroccans were relatively late in adopting European literary genres compared to their counterparts in other parts of the Arab world. For that reason, nineteenth-century Moroccan literary culture does not fit easily into a Eurocentric notion of "literature." Moreover, nineteenth-century Moroccan literature (however broadly we might construe that category) does not tend to embody the post-Romantic aesthetic values of originality and individuality, which have been the guiding principles in scholarly accounts of the rise, fall, and modern rebirth of Arabic literature. Where, for example, in the standard narrative of modern Arabic literature, would we place seminal Moroccan works such as al-Kattani's *Salwat al-anfas* (1887), a biographical dictionary of scholars and saints buried in Fez?

Likewise, Mufaddal Afaylal's *Kunnash* exemplifies nineteenth-century Moroccan literature's vexed place within Arabic literary historiography. It is precisely the sort of literary text that scholars of Arabic literature have sidestepped in their eagerness to chart the triumph of rationalist "modernity" over moribund "tradition."[26] The *Kunnash* moves between literary genres and linguistic registers. It can be read neither as straightforward narrative, nor as devotional text, nor as a work of poetic originality. Its organization is thematic rather than chronological. It opens with a brief introduction in which Afaylal presents his family tree, going all the way back to Adam, and then cites several Sufi invocations. After the introduction, the *Kunnash* is divided into three large thematic sections of varying lengths. The first narrates Afaylal's studies in Tetouan and Fez. The second contains his chronicle of the Spanish-Moroccan War of 1859–1860. The third consists of Afaylal's descriptions of his travels in Morocco, particularly his visits to the mausoleums of Muslim saints. Throughout the text, Afaylal intersperses his poems and also his commentary on the books that he reads and the conversations that he has with other Moroccan scholars. Roughly 150 pages long, the manuscript is written in Afaylal's attractive Maghribi script. It is worth noting that Afaylal was an accomplished calligrapher, who also produced a beautiful illustrated manuscript of Ibn al-Tayyib's *al-Anis al-mutrib*, an eighteenth-century biographical dictionary of Moroccan literary figures (Figure 8).[27] The *Kunnash* is written in black, red, and blue ink and features occasional geometric designs.

Memoir, objet d'art, reading journal, travelogue, poetic anthology, Afaylal's *Kunnash* defies easy categorization. Like Afaylal himself, the *Kunnash* is a border creature, the product of a literary imagination that straddles different periods of Moroccan cultural history and attests to Morocco's long-standing relationship with the Iberian Peninsula. In the pages that follow, my goal will be to read Afaylal's *Kunnash* on its own terms rather than trying to assimilate the text to a Romantic notion of "literature" or to cultural processes that happened in other parts of the Arab world. In so doing, I hope to contribute to what Jeffrey Sacks has called "the critique of the domesticating force of legibility in the disciplines of the humanities."[28] I want to make Afaylal and his world legible without domesticating them—that is, without squeezing them into a teleological narrative of rationalist modernity or a Eurocentric notion of literature. I will attempt to reconstruct the cultural framework within which Afaylal lived and wrote. To that end, I will offer, in the next section, a brief intellectual biography of Afaylal, emphasizing his education, his colleagues and companions, his travels, and his readings.

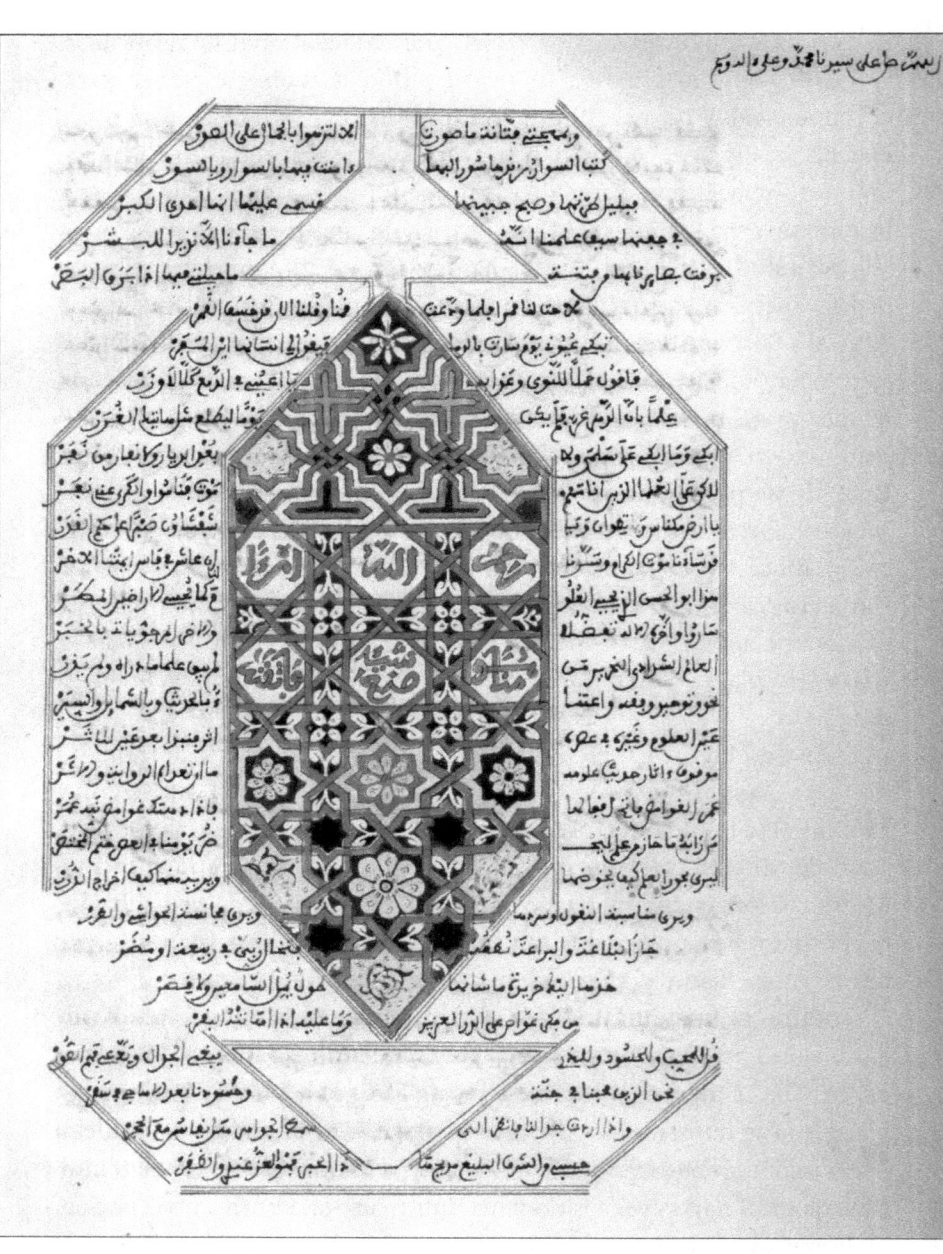

Figure 8. Calligraphy by Mufaddal Afaylal (second half of the nineteenth century).
Courtesy of the Tétouan-Asmir Association, Morocco.

In particular, I will examine how Andalusi literature and the cultural memory of al-Andalus informed Afaylal's upbringing and education. Then, in the final two sections of the chapter, I will read Afaylal's elegy and chronicle within the cultural framework that I build in the next section.

A Portrait of a Nineteenth-Century Moroccan Scholar: Mufaddal Afaylal

Afaylal's life and work offer an illustrative portrait of nineteenth-century Moroccan intellectual life. Afaylal hailed from an educated Tetouani family, as evidenced by the fact that his father, Muhammad b. al-Hashimi Afaylal, was one of his first teachers. Afaylal studied logic with his father in the Qasba Mosque, Tetouan's oldest mosque.[29] As a young student in Tetouan, Afaylal also studied under two of the leading intellectual figures of nineteenth-century Morocco: Muhammad al-Harraq (d. 1845), a Sufi scholar and poet, and Muhammad al-Saffar (d. 1881), a legal scholar who wrote one of the most influential Moroccan travel narratives about Europe from the precolonial period.[30]

Afaylal attended al-Saffar's classes on Islamic law and Arabic grammar at Tetouan's Mosque of al-Saqiya al-Fawqiyya (literally, "the Mosque of the Upper Fountain") from 1842 to 1849.[31] During these years, al-Saffar went from being a local teacher of Islamic law to being a central figure in Moroccan diplomacy and politics. Al-Saffar was born in Tetouan to a family that traced its roots back to the town of Jaén (*Jayyan*) in al-Andalus.[32] His ancestors came to Tetouan at the end of the fifteenth century with the wave of migrants who left al-Andalus after the Christian Reconquest of Granada.[33] The recipient of an elite religious education at the Qarawiyyin Mosque in Fez, al-Saffar returned to his native Tetouan in 1836 to work as a notary and to teach Islamic sciences at the Mosque of al-Saqiya al-Fawqiyya, where Afaylal first encountered him.[34] In 1845, al-Saffar was thrust into the public spotlight when Tetouan's governor, 'Abd al-Qadir Ash'ash, picked him to serve as his secretary on a royal embassy to France. Al-Saffar accompanied Ash'ash to France in December of 1845, spent ten weeks there, and returned to Tetouan in early March of 1846.[35] Later that year, al-Saffar penned a detailed account of the journey to France, which he sent to Sultan ʿAbd al-Rahman (r. 1822–1859).[36] Al-Saffar went on to become a close adviser to the sultan, eventually rising to the rank of first minister, the highest position in the sultan's court.[37]

Afaylal's studies with al-Saffar coincided with the period in which al-Saffar went to France and wrote his influential travel narrative. Al-Saffar taught Arabic grammar to Afaylal through the works of the Andalusi grammarian Ibn Malik (d. 1274), who, like al-Saffar's ancestors, was from the town of Jaén on the Iberian Peninsula.[38] Under al-Saffar, Afaylal also studied *Khalil's Summary* (*Mukhtasar Khalil*), a fourteenth-century summary of the Maliki school of Islamic law.[39] Afaylal and al-Saffar were not only pupil and teacher; they were also friends and travel companions. Al-Saffar accompanied Afaylal on several excursions, including a pilgrimage to the tomb of Mulay ʿAbd al-Salam.[40] They also traveled together as part of a delegation of Tetouani notables who went to Meknes in September of 1859 to pledge their allegiance to the new sultan, Muhammad IV (r. 1859–1873), who ascended to the throne on the eve of the Spanish-Moroccan War of 1859–1860.[41] Around that time, Afaylal wrote two of the most important Moroccan texts about the Spanish-Moroccan War. More broadly, he and his contemporary al-Saffar were witnesses to the dramatic cultural and political transformations that Morocco experienced in the nineteenth century, when the European powers vied for control of Morocco.[42]

Both al-Saffar and his disciple Afaylal were products of a border culture. With this assertion, I mean to counter the long-standing tendency of scholars to view nineteenth-century Morocco (and, in particular, pre-1860 Morocco) as an isolated backwater, shielded from meaningful contact with Europe.[43] In contrast with this view, I believe that al-Saffar and Afaylal's writings indicate a keen awareness of Tetouan's proximity to Christian Europe and of northern Morocco's historical relationship with the Iberian Peninsula. Perhaps the clearest manifestation of the border culture that al-Saffar and Afaylal inhabited is the frequency with which both writers use terms borrowed from the Romance languages—and, in particular, from Spanish. Al-Saffar peppers his travelogue with Hispanisms, such as *kudshī* (from the Spanish *coche*, "coach"), *qashīna* (from the Spanish *cocina*, "kitchen"), and *bāshādūr* (from the

Spanish *embajador,* "ambassador").⁴⁴ Afaylal, unlike his teacher, never left Morocco. Yet his chronicle of the Spanish-Moroccan War also offers a diverse array of Arabized Spanish loanwords, such as *garra* (from the Spanish *guerra,* "war"), *bābūr* (from the Spanish *vapor,* "steamship"), and *bunba* (from the Spanish *bomba,* "bomb").⁴⁵ It is not a coincidence that these Hispanisms relate to war and transport. In mid-nineteenth century Morocco, one need not have traveled to Europe to know the language of Europe's increasing military presence in North Africa.

For residents of nineteenth-century Tetouan, proximity to Europe was a matter of lived experience, not just linguistic hybridity. Tetouan is one corner of a triangle connected to Ceuta and Tangier, Morocco's main points of contact with Europe in the mid-nineteenth century. Despite Tangier's growing importance as a diplomatic and commercial hub, Ceuta had an even stronger symbolic resonance for Afaylal and his contemporaries: it was the primary symbol of Tetouan's proximity to Spain and al-Andalus. From the eleventh to the fourteenth century, Ceuta was a major point of intellectual exchange between al-Andalus and North Africa. After falling to Portuguese control in 1415, Ceuta became the front line for conflict between Muslim Morocco and the Iberian powers. It was still a Spanish military stronghold in Afaylal's lifetime, so it is not surprising that Afaylal did not make many trips there. His *Kunnash* does, however, include one account of a trip to Ceuta.⁴⁶ The account illustrates how Afaylal associated Ceuta with the history of al-Andalus and with the long-standing struggle between Christians and Muslims on both sides of the Mediterranean.

In March of 1858, Afaylal set out from Tetouan to visit the mausoleum of a local saint from Ceuta, Sidi al-Mubarak.⁴⁷ He traveled in the company of his spiritual master (*shaykh*) 'Abd al-Salam b. Raysun (d. 1882) and a group of Tetouan's notables and merchants. Two days after leaving Tetouan, the group of Tetouani pilgrims arrived in Fnideq, the Moroccan town on the border of Ceuta.⁴⁸ They set up camp on a spot that was thick with historical significance. In his description of the place, Afaylal notes the tombs for Ceuta's scholars and mujahidin, testaments to Ceuta's past as a beacon of Islamic learning and its present as a contested border between Morocco and Spain.⁴⁹ Indeed, the struggle for Ceuta was not just a distant cultural memory. As Afaylal and his companions approached Ceuta, they passed by vestiges of recent Moroccan attempts to take the city, including "a mountain of cannon balls and bombs [al-bunba]" left behind by Sultan Mulay al-Yazid during his siege of Ceuta in 1790–1791.[50]

Upon reaching the mausoleum of Sidi al-Mubarak, Afaylal and his companions took in a view that brought together, in a single frame, twelve centuries of Moroccan-Iberian relations. Afaylal writes: "We prayed the noon prayer at the mausoleum of Sidi al-Mubarak, and we alighted in a place that overlooked the two seas [i.e., the Mediterranean and the Atlantic]. The mausoleum was to the right, Ceuta was in front of us, Gibraltar was to the left, and Dar al-Bayda' was behind us."[51] Afaylal describes a vantage point that encompasses two seas (the Mediterranean and the Atlantic), two continents (Africa and Europe), and two temporalities (past and present). To Afaylal's left was Gibraltar, whose Arabic name, *Jabal Ṭāriq*, alludes to Tariq b. Ziyad, the Berber commander who led the Muslim invasion of the Iberian Peninsula in 711. In front of him was Ceuta, the front line in Morocco's long-standing conflict with the Iberian Peninsula. Behind Afaylal was Dar al-Bayda', a palace complex built by Ahmad b. ʿAli al-Rifi, the governor of Tetouan, during his long siege of Ceuta (1713–1727).[52] As Afaylal's description illustrates, the walk from Tetouan to Ceuta, with its views across the Strait of Gibraltar, offers a condensed history lesson in the shifting relations between Morocco and Spain, and between the medieval and the modern periods.

Afaylal's pilgrimage to the tomb of Sidi al-Mubarak also afforded him an unexpected and rare visit inside Ceuta's fortified walls. Afaylal's description of Ceuta (which I will quote at length) illustrates how Andalusi poetry shapes, and even supplants, his observations about Spain and the Spanish:

> On Sunday, Christian notables from Ceuta (may God destroy them!) came out to us to ask us to enter Ceuta. And they sent to us all that we needed in the way of sweets and the like.... When the afternoon prayer drew near, they brought out their soldiers, accompanied by music. Some of the people entered Ceuta, and I was among the group that entered. I found it to be extremely

fortified. From the land side, the moat surrounds it. After it, there is a surrounding trench. Then, there is a wall whose cannons fire at the feet. Then, a wall whose cannons fire above that. Then, more walls on top, and more walls on top, all of them with cannons. Between each wall, is a path. Then, there is a gap in the sea and on top of it is an iron bridge, which is the gate to the city. If the city closes, the sea comes between it and the mainland. If it opens, it becomes a bridge for crossing. After that, an extremely high wall, on which there are also cannons.

Then, I began to contemplate its buildings, houses, and its atmosphere, and I remembered what Ibn al-Murahhal said about it:

> Behold Ceuta and look at its beauty,
>   and you will desire its charm.
> As if it were a lute
>   lying upside down in the sea.

On its mountain is a long tomb that is known as the tomb of Sabt b. Ham b. Nuh [Noah] (peace be upon him!). The city derives its name from him. The minister Ibn al-Khatib the Granadan signaled that [fact] with what he said in his poem:

> Salutations, oh planner Sabt, son of Noah,
>   from each cloud that comes and goes!
> Residence of Abu al-Fadl 'Iyad,
>   whose fragrance gardens exhaled.

Then, we returned to our place. The next day, we were informed that the Christians were starting a sort of fun and entertainment. They came out to us, men and women. Our master ['Abd al-Salam b. Raysun] felt disgust at encountering them, and he ordered us to depart at once. We didn't eat breakfast until we were back in Fnideq.[53]

Perhaps the most striking trait of Afaylal's description of Ceuta is the almost total lack of ethnographic detail. This is the only moment in the *Kunnash* in which Afaylal describes a face-to-face encounter with the Christian Spaniards who lived near his native Tetouan. Yet he does not individualize the inhabitants of Ceuta; rather, he refers to them, in the collective, as "the Christians." It is also noteworthy that the collective identity that Afaylal ascribes to the people of Ceuta is religious ("the Christians") rather than ethno-national ("the Spanish"). Indeed, the categories of "Spain" and "Morocco" are practically absent in Afaylal's writings. Only later, in the twentieth century, would the Moroccan relationship with al-Andalus be framed in national, rather than religious, terms.

While Morocco and Spain are absent from Afaylal's account, al-Andalus is very present; indeed, it takes the place of ethnographic observation. Afaylal relies on poems from two Andalusi writers, Ibn al-Murahhal (1207–1300) and Ibn al-Khatib (1313–1375), to stand in as descriptions of the city. In fact, upon closer scrutiny, a gap emerges at the center of Afaylal's account. The Moroccan describes Ceuta's walls, cannons, moat, trenches, and drawbridge gate. But then his description falters, and literary allusion takes its place. "I began to contemplate," Afaylal writes, "its buildings, houses, and its atmosphere, and I remembered what Ibn al-Murahhal said about it."[54] Thus, what Ibn Murahhal said about Ceuta takes the place of what Afaylal saw there. I am underlining this tension between empirical observation and literary allusion because several scholars have celebrated Afaylal's status as an "eyewitness" to the origins of Spanish colonialism in Morocco.[55] Yet Afaylal suffers the same predicament as the Spanish eyewitness Alarcón: there are limits to what his eye can see. For Afaylal, Andalusi literary history performs two contradictory functions: it provides a cultural code that makes Spain legible, and it delimits what can be known and said about Spanish-Moroccan relations.

Afaylal's citations of Ibn al-Murahhal and Ibn al-Khatib not only demonstrate his familiarity with Andalusi poetry but also map out a cultural landscape that connects nineteenth-century Morocco to a long chain of literary luminaries whose lives and works spanned the Strait of Gibraltar. Ibn al-Murahhal, whose short poem about Ceuta serves as Afaylal's description of the city, was born in Málaga in 1207.[56] He later moved to Granada, where he served in the court of the first Nasrid sultan, Muhammad I. Throughout his career, Ibn al-Murahhal moved between al-Andalus and the Maghrib, but he spent most of his life in his adopted city of Ceuta, to which he dedicated many poems. In addition to his notable accomplishments as a poet, he also played an important political role as an intermediary between Nasrid Granada and the Maghrib. Ibn al-Murahhal's efforts to unite al-Andalus and the Maghrib have led the modern editor of his collected works to bestow on him the epithet "the writer of the two shores," referring to the northern and southern shores of the Strait of Gibraltar.[57]

Ibn al-Khatib, the second Andalusi poet cited by Afaylal, also lived and wrote between "the two shores." Born in Loja in 1313, Ibn al-Khatib grew up in Granada, where he rose through the ranks of court positions under the Nasrid sultans Yusuf I (r. 1333–1354) and Muhammad V (r. 1354–1391).[58] Political turmoil in Granada pushed Ibn al-Khatib into exile in the Maghrib in 1359. While in exile, he traveled extensively and wrote several famous works in *saj'* (rhymed and cadenced prose) describing the geography and customs of the Maghrib and comparing them, at times unfavorably, to those of his native al-Andalus.[59] Ibn al-Khatib's life and work contributed to the political and cultural interweaving of Granada and North Africa. Not only did he steer Granada's foreign policy toward a closer cooperation with the Maghrib, but his place in the pantheon of Andalusi literary history was secured through the intervention of a North African admirer, Ahmad b. Muhammad al-Maqqari (d. 1632). Al-Maqqari canonized Ibn al-Khatib's work in a monumental encyclopedia of Andalusi literature, *Nafh al-tib*, which preserved and popularized Andalusi poetry for subsequent generations of Arabic readers.[60]

Ibn al-Khatib's short poem about Ceuta, quoted by Afaylal, provides an Islamic origin story for Ceuta. The etymology of the city's name is often traced to the Latin *septem*, in reference to the seven nearby hills. In contrast, most of the Arabic chronicles attribute the city's name to Sabt, a descendant of the prophet Noah.[61] Ibn al-Khatib salutes Sabt as Ceuta's "planner" and thus places Ceuta within Islamic, rather than Latinate, history. He further emphasizes Ceuta's Islamic heritage in the next line, also quoted by Afaylal: "Residence of Abu al-Fadl 'Iyad, / whose fragrance gardens exhaled." The allusion here is to Abu al-Fadl 'Iyad b. Musa (d. 1149), one of the most important figures of Maliki scholarship in the Islamic West. Born in Ceuta, 'Iyad studied in al-Andalus and subsequently served as head judge in Ceuta and Granada.⁶² Centuries after his death, 'Iyad's biography was popularized by none other than al-Maqqari, the same compiler who canonized Ibn al-Khatib's writings. Al-Maqqari's *Azhar al-riyad fi akhbar 'Iyad* (*The Flowers of the Gardens: On the News of 'Iyad*, c. 1617) details 'Iyad's life and work, and it also contains information about scholars and poets from al-Andalus. In fact, the two Andalusi poems cited by Afaylal in his description of Ceuta appear side by side in al-Maqqari's *Azhar al-riyad*, which is probably where Afaylal found them.⁶³

Thus, what Afaylal's narration lacks in ethnographic detail is made up for by a dense network of citations linking Morocco to al-Andalus. In this network, the quotations of Ibn al-Murahhal and Ibn al-Khatib wrest control of Ceuta from the Spanish occupier by placing the city within currents of people and culture that weave together Ceuta and Granada, North Africa and al-Andalus. Ibn al-Murahhal and Ibn al-Khatib embody the generations of Andalusi scholars who unified the intellectual life of "the two shores." They also conjure the phantom presence of al-Maqqari, the North African compiler who defined the Andalusi literary canon and preserved it for future generations of Arabic readers.

This citational relationship with al-Andalus runs through Afaylal's *Kunnash*, which evokes a literary almanac of Andalusi representations of Morocco. Afaylal took a particular interest in Ibn al-Khatib's travel narratives, and he borrowed from them to describe nineteenth-century Morocco. During the two-year Spanish occupation of Tetouan, in 1860–1862, Afaylal went into nomadic exile, visiting several cities with Andalusi roots, including al-Qasr al-Kabir, Rabat, and Salé. His descriptions of these cities are written in rhyming prose that evokes Ibn al-Khatib's elegant style. Furthermore, Afaylal reproduces long passages from Ibn al-Khatib's descriptions of Salé and al-Qasr al-Kabir.⁶⁴ Thus, in Afaylal's travel narratives about Morocco, as in his description of Ceuta, the authority of Andalusi texts trumps the authority of the author's empirical observation. Al-Andalus as a place in discourse displaces Morocco as a place.

Ibn al-Khatib was not the only Andalusi author who left an indelible mark on Afaylal. In 1855, when Afaylal was twenty-one, he read *al-Wafi fi nazm al-qawafi*, a treatise about poetry by the famous Andalusi poet al-Rundi (d. 1285).⁶⁵ Like Ibn al-Khatib and Ibn al-Murahhal, al-Rundi was an Andalusi writer whose life spanned the two shores of the Mediterranean. His poetry and his treatise on poetry were well known in the Maghrib during the thirteenth century, and several manuscripts of *al-Wafi* continue to exist in North African archives, including a manuscript in Tetouan's General Library.⁶⁶ Al-Rundi's treatise offered Afaylal an erudite survey of the genres, rhetorical figures, and prosody of Arabic poetry. Yet al-Rundi's *Wafi* is far more than a technical manual for composing verse. It is also a literary history of Arabic poetry, which illustrates the literary tastes of the thirteenth-century Andalusi cultural elite. In this literary history, al-Rundi gives pride of place to the poets of his native al-Andalus, citing verses from some of the most famous Andalusi poets, including Ibn Zaydun (d. 1070), al-Muʻtamid b. ʻAbbad (d. 1095), and his contemporary Ibn al-Murahhal.⁶⁷ He also frequently cites his own poetry, of which he clearly had a high opinion. Al-Rundi's literary tastes surely rubbed off on the young Afaylal. In fact, Afaylal indicates that he memorized some of al-Rundi's poems. In a description of a trip made to Fez in 1857, Afaylal mentions that he entertained one of the city's literary luminaries by reciting, from memory, one of al-Rundi's love poems.⁶⁸

Al-Rundi's most famous poem is an elegy, rhymed in the letter *nūn*, for Seville and the other Muslim Andalusi cities that were conquered by Christian forces in the middle of the thirteenth century. Al-Rundi's elegy reflects the political upheavals that rocked al-Andalus in the thirteenth century. By the time al-Rundi died in 1285, al-Andalus, which had once stretched into today's France, had been reduced to the kingdom of Granada. The poets of al-Andalus cultivated a special genre, the city elegy, to mourn the loss of their cities to the Christian Reconquest. Today, al-Rundi's elegy is considered the most famous exemplar of the city elegy genre. It is reproduced in both of al-Maqqari's influential anthologies of Andalusi literature, which helped to spread its fame among North African readers—a fame that has continued until the present day.⁶⁹ In the next section, I will read Afaylal's elegy for the occupation of Tetouan as an example of the Andalusi city elegy genre. In particular, I will compare Afaylal's elegy with al-Rundi's famous elegy for Seville in order to show how Afaylal productively uses an Andalusi genre in order to establish an affective and literary relationship between nineteenth-century Morocco and al-Andalus.

Tetouan as Seville: Afaylal and the Andalusi City Elegy

In February of 1861, a year after going into exile from Tetouan, Mufaddal Afaylal wrote an elegy lamenting the Spanish occupation of his hometown.[70] He composed the poem in the style of a city elegy. This genre originated in the Arab East and migrated to al-Andalus, where it became one of the most popular poetic genres.[71] City elegies lament the destruction of a cherished urban space by combining rhetorical elements from two different Arabic poetic traditions: the pre-Islamic ode and the elegy for a deceased loved one. Thus, the city elegy is, as Elinson observes, "curiously poised between the reality of a tangible loss acutely felt by the individual, and a highly conventional language that is used to understand and express it."[72] Andalusi city elegies offer a poetic record of specific episodes in the turbulent history of al-Andalus, but they do so in a conventional language that associates those episodes with earlier moments in Arabic literary history, harkening back to Abbasid Baghdad and pre-Islamic Arabia. In other words, the Andalusi city elegy was always already a palimpsest—celebrating al-Andalus but also tracing the cultural imprint of classical Arabic literary culture on al-Andalus.

Elinson has argued that the city elegy rose to prominence in al-Andalus in the early eleventh century, in the waning years of the Umayyad caliphate, as a literary tool for asserting the superiority of Arab culture over North African Berber culture.[73] Nevertheless, by the thirteenth century, when al-Rundi wrote his famous elegy for Seville, the genre had pivoted to address the conflict between Islam and Christianity. Al-Rundi's elegy distinguishes not between Arabs and Berbers but rather between Muslims and Christians. It dramatizes the destruction of a Muslim Andalusi city at the hands of a Christian "barbarian." The opposition between a Muslim city and a Christian foe is also what animated Afaylal's elegy for Tetouan in 1861. The nineteenth-century Moroccan poem echoes al-Rundi's elegy and other thirteenth-century Andalusi poems that dramatize the conflict between Muslims and

Christians. Afaylal thus ties the Spanish-Moroccan War of 1859–1860 to the Christian Reconquest of al-Andalus. In so doing, the Moroccan poet adds another layer to the palimpsestic quality of the city elegy genre: Afaylal's city elegy evokes thirteenth-century al-Andalus, just as the Andalusi city elegies evoke Abbasid Baghdad and pre-Islamic Arabia.

In what follows, I will offer a full translation of Afaylal's elegy for Tetouan, and then I will analyze it in light of its intertextual relations with Andalusi literary history:

(1) Oh Fate! Tell me: why did you destroy all peace
(2) And expose it to tragedies without fearing reproach?
(3) You debased the fate of a place that was a symbol of greatness
(4) And handed it over to enemies who are not worth a nail clipping.
(5) And Religion cries with tears that resemble the outpouring of clouds
(6) Over mosques where wine has come to be sold.
(7) On how many saints' mausoleums, from which miracles emerge,
(8) Have monks hung their cross and bridle!
(9) And how many houses of descendants of the Prophet and virtuous scholars
(10) Have become urinals for a barbarian who doesn't show them respect!
(11) And over how many—how many!—things, which do injustice to Religion,
(12) Do the eyes of depression and remorse cry!
(13) Tetouan, you were but a dove among cities,
(14) Or like a preacher who fell down after donning his turban.
(15) Or rather, you were a splendid garden whose flowers flashed a smile,
(16) Or like the face of a bride, above whose cheeks there is a beauty mark.
(17) You surpassed in beauty and excellence Fez, Egypt, and the Levant.
(18) Fate cast its eye on you, just like the fate of Zarqa al-Yamama,[74]
(19) And dispersed the people until nothing was left but a trace.
(20) What a beautiful time, what sweet passion,
(21) We spent with powerful and grand luminaries
(22) Reciting poetry and composing *maqāmāt*.[75]
(23) Together we were united because happiness requires union.
(24) Joy yearned for it longingly and desired to kiss it lightly.
(25) Good fortune helped it to fulfill its wishes and desires.
(26) Oh, what beautiful nights, if only they hadn't become like a dream!
(27) Tetouan, oh abode of intimacy and den of leaders!
(28) Is there a path to union with you? For our separation has completed a year,
(29) And the heart has melted in longing, grief, and sadness,
(30) And passion has weakened the body until it has almost emaciated its bones.
(31) Oh people of Tetouan, have patience! For every event will pass.

(32) Nothing is eternal... Does a shadow linger?
(33) If the lucky star disappeared and the star of misfortune shines,
(34) A full moon will rise, and its brilliance will obliterate the darkness.
(35) So cling to hope and adhere faithfully to the truth.
(36) Think better thoughts, and you will be saved in this life and on the Day of Judgment.
(37) Entrust the matter to God. He will not inflict His vengeance upon us.
(38) Victory will only come to the judicious man who performs good deeds.
(39) Wherever he ends up, he will be satisfied, even if it were in Qasr Kutama![76]
(40) And he continuously awaits his end at any moment,
(41) Always observing God in his heart and openly.
(42) He seeks a good ending and a residence in the everlasting Home.[77]

Afaylal's elegy consists of forty-two lines, each ending in the monorhyme -āma, and each divided into two hemistiches. It opens with a customary gnomic introduction (vv. 1–4) on the vicissitudes of Fate (al-dahr), a common motif in the classical Arabic ode.[78] The poem is then divided into three interrelated but distinct thematic units. The first is the elegy proper (vv. 5–12), where the speaker laments the destruction of Tetouan at the hands of the Spanish army. The second is a panegyric (vv. 13–30) in praise of the city that existed before the Spanish occupation. The third and final section is a stoic conclusion (vv. 31–42), in which the speaker counsels the people of Tetouan to have patience and to entrust their well-being to God. The transitions between the gnomic introduction and the three thematic units are demarcated by the use of apostrophe or a change in grammatical subject: in the first line, the speaker apostrophizes "Fate" (v. 1); in the first section (elegy), the speaker personifies "Religion" (v. 5); in the second section (praise), he addresses "Tetouan" (v. 13); in the final section (stoic conclusion), he addresses the "people of Tetouan" (v. 31). Each section is thus marked by a change in addressee and grammatical subject.

Afaylal's poem clearly deploys the rhetorical conventions of the city elegy genre, thereby asserting the relationship between al-Andalus and nineteenth-century Morocco, and between the Christian Reconquest and Spanish colonialism. Yet, the poem's stoic conclusion, which calls for patient endurance and faith in God, subverts one of the city elegy's central functions: the incitement to vengeance or armed resistance. Thus, my goal here will be to trace Afaylal's use of Andalusi literary history and also his strategic departure from it. There are two things at stake in this literary-historical exercise. First, I hope to show how Andalusi poetry mediated the cultural encounter between a nineteenth-century Moroccan and the onset of Spanish colonialism. Second, I want to problematize the dichotomy between literary "tradition" and literary "modernity" by showing how Afaylal is not merely recycling Andalusi poetry but rather is adapting and molding it to a new cultural context. I will begin by drawing intertextual connections between Afaylal's elegy for Tetouan and al-Rundi's elegy for the Andalusi cities conquered in the thirteenth century. Then, I will show how Afaylal's elegy deviates from its Andalusi predecessors. My analysis will thus illuminate how al-Andalus served Afaylal as a discursive model for understanding and representing Spanish colonialism in Morocco, but it will also highlight the insufficiency of the Andalusi model.

Afaylal's elegy for Tetouan shares with the Andalusi city elegy tradition a common repertoire of images and rhetorical strategies. Like its Andalusi predecessors, Afaylal's elegy relies heavily on water imagery and on the depiction of the occupied city as a lost paradise or a raped virgin.[79] It also draws upon rhetorical figures that the Andalusi city elegy borrowed from the pre-Islamic ode and from the Arabic elegiac tradition, such as antithesis, repetition (anaphora), paronomasia, and apostrophe.[80] Afaylal uses this shared repertoire of images and tropes to establish connections between Tetouan's plight and the plight of al-Andalus. These intertextual connections would be apparent to an educated nineteenth-century Moroccan reader, who, like Afaylal, would be deeply steeped in Andalusi literary history. In my analysis of Afaylal's elegy, I will focus on its use of water imagery and the figures of antithesis, repetition, and paronomasia.

Antithesis structures Afaylal's poem, particularly in the opening elegiac section (vv. 5–12). The conflict between Islam and Christianity is represented by the opposition between a personified "Religion" (v. 5) and "a barbarian" (‘ilj) (v. 10), who desecrates Religion's abode by drinking wine in mosques and urinating in the houses of pious Muslims. The opposition between "Religion" (who represents Islam) and the "barbarian" (who represents the Christian invader) bookends a series of related oppositions between tears and wine (vv. 5–6), a Muslim saint and a Christian monk (vv. 7–8), as well as between the house of a descendant of the Prophet and a urinal (vv. 9–10). The poem's rhyme scheme accentuates these antitheses: in the original Arabic, the rhyme scheme alternates between the barbarian's "wine" (*al-mudāma*, v. 6), the Muslim saint's "miracles" (*al-karāma*, v. 7), the Christian monk's "bridle" (*lijāma*, v. 8), and the Muslim scholar's "virtue" (*istiqāma*, v. 9).[81]

Water metaphors flow through this edifice of antitheses, dramatizing the transformations that Tetouan has suffered on account of the Spanish occupation. The elegiac section begins and ends with tears. In the opening line, "Religion cries with tears that resemble the outpouring of clouds" (v. 5), and in the last line of the section, "the eyes of depression and remorse cry" (v. 12). In between the two sets of tears are other liquid metaphors that highlight water's ambivalence as a fluid symbol of cleansing, abundance, renewal, and grief. The section's first two lines illustrate this symbolic ambivalence: "Religion cries with tears that resemble the outpouring of clouds / Over mosques where wine has come to be sold" (vv. 5–6). The couplet moves from tears to rain to wine. It is worth noting that Afaylal foresakes the common Arabic word for wine, *khamr*, in favor of a more obscure one: *al-mudāma*. The word choice is more than a mere flash of erudition. The three root letters of *al-mudāma* (*d-w-m*) denote perpetuity or permanence—as in the adjective *dāʾim* ("perpetual," "eternal"). The rare word *al-mudāma* stands in juxtaposition to the verb that ends the first hemistich, *aḍḥat* ("to begin, to come to"), which denotes change and transformation. Thus, the couplet places wine's ominous permanence in opposition to the turbulent transformations affecting Tetouan. This opposition between permanence and transformation foreshadows the wordplay that Afaylal performs at the end of the poem (to which I will return later).

Afaylal couches his representation of the Spanish occupation of Tetouan in a highly conventional language borrowed from the city elegy tradition. A brief comparison between Afaylal's elegy (1861) and al-Rundi's elegy (c. 1248) will demonstrate the extent to which the nineteenth-century Moroccan poet was drawing upon an older Andalusi literary idiom. Like Afaylal, al-Rundi opens his elegy with a gnomic introduction on the vicissitudes of Fate. He then elegizes several conquered Andalusi cities through the use of anaphora, antithesis, and water imagery:

> Therefore ask Valencia what is the state of Murcia; and where
> is Játiva, and where is Jaén?
> Where is Córdoba, the home of the sciences, and many a
> scholar whose rank was once lofty in it?
> Where is Seville and the pleasures it contains, as well as its
> sweet river overflowing and brimming full? . . .
> The tap of the white ablution fount weeps in despair, like a
> passionate lover weeping at the departure of the beloved,
> Over dwellings emptied of Islam that were first vacated and
> are now inhabited by unbelief;
> In which the mosques have become churches wherein only
> bells and crosses may be found.
> Even the mihrabs weep though they are solid; even the pulpits
> mourn though they are wooden! (vv. 17–19, 21–24)[82]

Al-Rundi's emphatic repetition of the interrogative *ayna* ("where?") lends rhythm to verses 17 through 19, as if these verses were a refrain or a chant: "*Where* is Játiva, and *where* is Jaén? / *Where* is Córdoba . . . / *Where* is Seville . . . ?" (my italics). Afaylal creates a similar sonic effect through his use of the exclamatory particle *kam* ("How many . . . !"): "*How many* saints' mausoleums . . . / *How many* houses . . . / *How many—how many!*—things . . ." (vv. 7–11; my italics). Repetition is the most common rhetorical device in the Arabic elegiac tradition. It was also a prominent feature in the Andalusi city elegy, where Andalusi poets used repetition to invoke and keep alive, through language, the memory of a conquered city.[83]

Another striking similarity between Afaylal's elegy and al-Rundi's elegy is their shared reliance on antithesis. Afaylal's elegy opposes personified "Religion" to a profane Christian "barbarian" (vv. 5–10). Likewise, al-Rundi juxtaposes "Islam" and "unbelief" (v. 22), and "mosques" and "churches wherein only bells and crosses may be found" (v. 23). Both elegies, though separated by six centuries, dramatize the destruction of a Muslim city through the image of a desecrated mosque: in al-Rundi, the mosque becomes a church; in Afaylal, it becomes a tavern. The irreverence toward Muslim sacred spaces is embodied in the figure of the "barbarian" (*'ilj*), a derogatory term for Christians that appears in both elegies. At the end of al-Rundi's elegy, the Christian "barbarian" rapes a Muslim virgin, another common motif in city elegies.[84] Afaylal hints at this threat in the second section of his elegy, when he compares Tetouan, before the Spanish occupation, to "a splendid garden" and "the face of a bride" (vv. 15–16). These virginal images of Tetouan as a garden and a bride come after the speaker has lamented the Christian profanation of the city. In this context, they suggest not only innocent beauty but also the imminent danger of its destruction.

In al-Rundi's elegy, as in Afaylal's elegy, the antithetical opposition between Islam and Christianity is harnessed to a rich repertoire of water images, which exemplify water's fluid and ambivalent symbolism. Al-Rundi associates Seville's former splendor with "its sweet river overflowing and brimming full" (v. 19). The vision of Seville's sweet and flowing water evokes the Qur'anic description of the heavenly paradise as "gardens graced with flowing streams."[85] Yet, water is not a stable signifier in al-Rundi's elegy. In the ensuing lines, Seville's "sweet river" morphs into the tears of a mosque's ablution fount (v. 21) and prayer niche (v. 24). The transformation from flowing streams to flowing tears evidences, yet again, water's symbolic ambivalence. Water purifies the body, as when Muslims perform ablutions before prayer, but it also signals grief and devastation. In a similar fashion, Afaylal's elegy uses shifting liquid imagery—tears, rain, wine, and urine—to depict the Spanish conquest of Tetouan. Both Afaylal and al-Rundi are drawing upon water's deep resonance in the Arabic poetic tradition. Indeed, the most conventional topos in the pre-Islamic ode is the image of weeping over an abandoned campsite. Water metaphors thus link Afaylal to Andalusi poetry, which, in turn, echoes poetic motifs dating back to pre-Islamic Arabia.[86]

Another significant link between Afaylal and the Andalusi city elegy is the Moroccan poet's reliance on the figure of paronomasia. Most Arabic words are built around three consonant roots, which can be manipulated to create different meanings and parts of speech. In Arabic poetics, paronomasia (*jinās*) entails the juxtaposition of words that share the same three consonant roots in order to draw out surprising connections of meaning and sound. Since paronomasia relies on the sounds and structure of the Arabic language, it is notoriously difficult to render in English translation. Yet the figure is enormously important for understanding Afaylal's poetic practice. Heinrichs calls paronomasia "the most popular rhetorical figure" in Arabic poetics, and the figure abounds in Andalusi city elegies.[87] In Afaylal's elegy, paronomasia performs two roles. First, it highlights the contrast between permanence and change, which is one of the thematic axes of the poem. Second, it connects, through sound and etymology, the poem's elegiac section (vv. 5–12) with its stoic conclusion (vv. 31–42), in which the speaker counsels the people of Tetouan to find solace in God.

Afaylal's elegy emphasizes three sets of trilateral roots: *d-w-m*, which connotes permanence and continuity; *h-w-l*, which connotes transformation and change; and *q-w-m*, which connotes rising or getting up, but can also connote taking up residence or being honest (like the English word "upright"). Afaylal combines these three root systems to create unexpected chains of meaning, highlighting the contrast between stability and change. All three root systems converge in the first two lines of the elegy's concluding section. Along with a literal translation of these lines, I am providing a transliteration of the original Arabic so that English readers can appreciate the sound structure:

> Oh people of Tetouan, have patience! For every event will pass.
> *[yā ahla tiṭwāna ṣabran fa-mā li-khaṭbin idāma]*
> Nothing is eternal. Does a shadow linger?
> *[dawāmu ḥālin muḥālun wa-hal li-ẓillin iqāma?]* (vv. 31–32)

In a virtuosic display of paronomasia, Afaylal strings together two words with the roots *d-w-m*, immediately followed by two words with the roots *h-w-l*: "*idāma / dawāmu ḥālin muḥālun.*" On the levels of sound and sense, Afaylal evokes the alternation between the contrasting forces of continuity and change. The word play also links these verses to the beginning of the poem, where the speaker laments the "wine" (*al-mudāma*) that is being sold in Tetouan's mosques, and the end of the poem, where he calls on the people of Tetouan to look to the afterlife "continuously" (*bi-istidāma*). Thus, the etymological chain of words that share the trilateral root *d-w-m* charts the elegy's movement from lament to stoic endurance.

Alongside the conflict between permanence and change, emerges the theme that Muslims will rise and find reward in the afterlife. Through paronomasia with words that share the roots *q-w-m,* the following images form another etymological chain and come into relation with each other: the "upright" scholar (*'ālim dhī istiqāma,* v. 9); the shadow that does not linger (literally, the shadow that has no "residence," *iqāma,* v. 32); the Day of Judgment (*yawm al-qiyāma,* v. 36); and "the everlasting Home" (*dār al-muqāma,* v. 41). Afaylal's emphatic use of paronomasia thus maps out the poem's thematic movements, from the upheaval of Christian occupation to the constancy of the Islamic faith, which offers solace and a reward in the afterlife. Afaylal's etymological pyrotechnics also pay homage to al-Rundi and the poets of al-Andalus, who prized such wordplay.

Thus far, I have attempted to demonstrate Afaylal's reliance on the rhetorical conventions of the Andalusi city elegy genre, especially antithesis, water imagery, repetition, and paronomasia. I have largely relied on a comparison between Afaylal's elegy and al-Rundi's elegy. While I believe that it is likely that Afaylal knew al-Rundi's famous elegy, my argument does not depend on a direct relationship of transmission and imitation. Instead, I argue that both Afaylal and al-Rundi participate in generic conventions that a nineteenth-century Moroccan audience would have strongly associated with Andalusi poetry. Through the literary idiom of the city elegy, Afaylal approximates Morocco to al-Andalus, Tetouan to Seville, and the Spanish army to the Christian "barbarian" of the Andalusi Muslim imaginary. Nevertheless, Afaylal's elegy, for all of its clear similarities to the Andalusi city elegy genre, also subverts the genre in a significant and surprising way: it does not incite the Muslim reader to take back the conquered city.

In a motif commonly known as *taḥrīḍ* (incitement), city elegies often end with a call for the audience to take back the conquered city.[88] For example, in the conclusion of al-Rundi's elegy, the speaker apostrophizes North African Muslims and urges them to join their Andalusi brothers in the fight against the Christian Reconquest of al-Andalus:

> And you who are living in luxury beyond the sea enjoying life,
>   you who have strength and power in your homelands,
> Have you no news of the people of Andalus, for riders have
>   carried forth what men have said [about them]?

How often have the weak, who were being killed and captured
while no man stirred, asked our help?
What means this severing of the bonds of Islam on your
behalf, when you, O worshippers of God, are [our]
brethren? (vv. 30–33)

As these lines indicate, al-Rundi's elegy not only laments the fall of Andalusi cities but also highlights the solidarity between all Muslims and incites North African Muslims to fight against the Christian Reconquest of al-Andalus. A similar call to arms appears in the conclusion of an elegy by Ibn al-Murahhal, al-Rundi's contemporary. Ibn al-Murahhal's poem exhorts North Africans to join forces with Muslim Granada in the fight against the Christian Reconquest of al-Andalus.[89] The *taḥrīḍ* motif did not disappear after the fall of al-Andalus. It remained a defining feature of the city elegy until the twentieth century, when it appeared in works such as Ahmad Shawqi's lament for the French bombardment of Damascus in 1925.[90]

Given the centrality of *taḥrīḍ* for the city elegy, its absence in Afaylal's elegy is resounding. Why would the Moroccan poet painstakingly perform his familiarity with an Andalusi literary genre, only to subvert the genre with a surprise ending? My interpretation is that Afaylal's emphatic departure from the Andalusi intertext signals the crisis of al-Andalus as a mode of transhistorical interpretation and representation. That is, Afaylal's elegy for Tetouan demands to be read transhistorically and intertextually—alongside al-Andalus and Andalusi poetry. Yet, the elegy also dramatically illustrates the shortcomings of the transhistorical imagination. It deploys Andalusi literary history to address the present, but the exercise spawns a hermeneutic and mimetic crisis. In this case, al-Andalus is not sufficient to understand or to represent the nineteenth-century colonial encounter between Spain and Morocco. Afaylal's chronicle of the Spanish-Moroccan War, which is much less famous than his elegy, illustrates another mode of interpreting and representing the beginning of Spanish colonialism, but the chronicle will not resolve the hermeneutic and mimetic problems outlined by the elegy.

Seeing and Speaking in Afaylal's Chronicle (c. 1859–1860)

Afaylal's elegy might be the most famous poem ever written about Tetouan, but there is actually little in the poem to indicate that it is talking about Tetouan. In the poem's most cited verse, Afaylal coins Tetouan's epithet, "the dove," by which the city is still known today: "Tetouan, you were but a dove among cities" (v. 13).[91] The line might be an allusion to the stunning whiteness of Tetouan's whitewashed medina, which contrasts with the lush green of the surrounding valley. Yet the dove has also functioned as a conventional symbol of mourning in Arabic elegies going back to pre-Islamic times.[92] Indeed, poetic conventions seem to overwhelm historical specificity in Afaylal's elegy. Were it not for the allusions to Tetouan and Qasr Kutama (today's al-Qasr al-Kabir), the poem could just as easily be about Morocco or al-Andalus, the nineteenth century or the thirteenth century. At first glance, then, Afaylal's elegy seems to conform to the Aristotelian notion that poetry should speak of universals, not particulars.

Afaylal's chronicle, in contrast, offers a more particular, historically rooted vision of the Spanish-Moroccan War. The chronicle is written in the first-person singular, and it emphasizes Afaylal's authority as an eyewitness to the events of the war. The chronicle's authority, therefore, relies not on a transhistorical connection to al-Andalus but rather on the prestige of eyewitness testimony. Yet, as I have already intimated, things are not as simple as they appear. Afaylal's poem manipulates the conventions of the city elegy in order to signal both proximity to and distance from al-Andalus. It therefore stages a universality *manquée*—an Andalus that tries but fails to serve as an explanation for Moroccan colonial history. Likewise, Afaylal's chronicle, for all of its emphasis on eyewitness testimony, ultimately points toward what the eye cannot see and what the eyewitness cannot say.

Like the elegy, the chronicle generally casts the Spanish-Moroccan War as a clash between religions, not nation-states. In it, Afaylal usually refers to the Spanish as "the Christians" and the Moroccans as "the Muslims." Other terms that he uses to refer to the Spanish are "the enemy" (*al-ʿadū*) and "the infidels" (*al-kuffār*).[93] Thus, the chronicle appears, at first blush, to be governed by the same dichotomous world view that structured the elegy. Yet, the chronicle also opens up significant fissures in this dichotomy, signaling tensions and variations within the categories of "Christian" and "Muslim." While Afaylal never refers to "Moroccans," he does identify different European nationalities that intervened in nineteenth-century Morocco. Relying on Hispanisms, Afaylal occasionally refers to the Spanish as "the *sbanyūl*" (from *español*, "Spanish"), and he calls the French "the *franṣīṣ*" (from *francés*, "French"). He also gestures toward fissures within the Moroccan Muslim community. In fact, the chronicle inverts one of the elegy's core themes, the unity of the Muslim community in the face of a common enemy, the Christian "barbarian." In the chronicle, the Moroccans are defeated not by a profane Christian enemy or by fickle Fate but rather by themselves. Afaylal attributes the Moroccan defeat to the incompetence and moral lassitude of the Moroccan leaders, especially Mulay al-ʿAbbas, the general of the Moroccan army and the brother of Sultan Muhammad IV.

Afaylal's acerbic critique of a representative of the ruling ʿAlawi dynasty is striking within the context of nineteenth-century Moroccan historiography. Sahar Bazzaz has argued that the field of Moroccan studies has tended to privilege a state-centered paradigm and has shown little interest in "the ways non-state actors articulated and negotiated the social, political, and intellectual/epistemological transitions that characterized the Moroccan nineteenth century."[94] If, as Bazzaz argues, Moroccan historiography has positioned the Moroccan state as the sole representative of the Moroccan nation, then Afaylal's chronicle offers an alternative historical narrative, one that allows us to read Moroccan history beyond the state. This alternative narrative emphasizes the tensions between the national and the local, and between the political and the religious.

The chronicle's first allusion to the Spanish-Moroccan War indicates the shift from a transhistorical perspective—centered on al-Andalus and the unity of Muslim peoples—to a local, contingent perspective, centered on nineteenth-century Tetouan. Afaylal writes: "On Sunday, the 26th of Rabiʿ al-Awwal 1276 [23 October 1859], *garra* with the *sbanyūl* was announced in Tetouan's markets."[95] The sentence's meaning hinges upon the reader's comprehension of two Hispanisms: *garra*, from the Spanish *guerra* ("war"), and *sbanyūl* ("Spanish"). Elsewhere, Afaylal refers to the conflict with the Spanish as *qitāl* ("combat") or, more often, *jihād* (a notoriously vexed term, which, in this context, means something akin to "holy war"). Given the diversity of terms with which Afaylal designates the war, we might translate his Hispanism *garra* not as "war" (its Spanish meaning) but rather as "war with the Spanish." That is, *garra* is a term that locates the war within a specific geography (Spanish-Moroccan) and within a specific linguistic position: that of a nineteenth-century Moroccan exposed to words and peoples from Europe.

Indeed, European loanwords abound in Afaylal's chronicle, where they attest to Morocco's position between continents, languages, and cultures. An illustrative example is the following passage, in which Afaylal describes fighting that took place near Tetouan in November of 1859:

> At the end of the day, the Muslims were defeated, and they fled before the Christians, leaving behind the killed and the injured to the enemy.
>
> On the 28th of Rabiʿ al-Thani 1276 [23 November 1859], the two sides fought a big battle with gunpowder alone, not with swords. A large number were killed and wounded on both sides. The Muslims were defeated at the end of the day, and six of them were captured. On that day, a big steamship [*bābūr*] came to the port of Tetouan, belonging to the *Fransīs*, who was at peace with the Muslims. Then it went. The following day, it came with three big *fragatas* ["*frāgat*," frigates]. They began to attack the fort with cannonballs, bombs [*al-bunba*], and the *kunbra,* which is shaped like a sugarloaf and filled with gunpowder and mercury. On its head, there is a wick filled with spirits [*isbirṭū*, i.e., alcohol]. If it happens to fall inside a wall and explode, it will demolish the wall. [The ship] hurled four thousand [of these bombs] upon them on that day, and it demolished the fort of Martin. Two men died in it, and six were injured. The walls of the city shook from the sound of their cannons.[96]

The passage captures the terror and cacophony of war, but it also represents the Spanish-Moroccan War as a moment of linguistic, technological, and epistemic flux. In the first sentence, Afaylal calls the Moroccans "the Muslims" and positions them in a fight with "the Christians" or "the enemy." These categories of religious identity are familiar. The next paragraph, however, introduces a new player, the *Franṣīṣ*, whose position within the Muslim-Christian framework is uncertain. The *Franṣīṣ* is "at peace with the Muslims," but he also bombards them. Afaylal uses a dialectal word to describe the French people: *Franṣīṣ*, an Arabicized version of the Spanish *francés*. He then hits the reader with a dizzying stream of neologisms and Arabicized European loanwords. He glosses one of them, *al-kunbra*, but he apparently assumes that his readership will understand the others: *bābūr* (steamship), *frāgat* (frigates), *al-bunba* (bombs), and so on.

The use of Hispanisms and other European loanwords is not the only manifestation of the chronicle's linguistic hybridity. While Afaylal's elegy demonstrates his command of literary standard Arabic (*al-fuṣḥā*), his chronicle often approximates oral speech. The chronicle's orality manifests itself on several levels, from the transcription of everyday dialogue to the incorporation of Moroccan dialectal words, such as the noun *al-ghawth*, meaning "outcry" or "hubbub," or the verb *yatakayyaf*, meaning "he smokes pot."[97] Just as the chronicle exerts pressure on the elegy's religious dichotomies, it also exerts pressure on the Arabic language's diglossia by mixing together standard and dialectal usages. Afaylal's elegy approximates the language of al-Andalus, whereas his chronicle very much speaks the language of mid-nineteenth-century Tetouan.

The text's narrative voice also exemplifies the shift from a transhistorical perspective to a local and historically rooted one. The chronicle is an emphatically first-person narrative, which repeatedly underlines the authority of the narrator's personal experience and eyewitness testimony. A few days after news of the declaration of war reached Tetouan, in October of 1859, the city council received a letter from the sultan's representative in Tangier, informing them that the Spanish army was planning to march on Tetouan.[98] Afaylal describes the city's frantic preparations for war, emphasizing his role as an eyewitness: "Equipment and gunpowder were distributed to the people, and about half of the people of the city were left without equipment. And when I saw that with my own eyes [*'āyantu*], I took my family out of the city, and I brought them to a village near Tetouan, which is called Bani Salih."[99] The verb that Afaylal uses to describe his observation is ʿāyantu ("I saw with my own eyes"), which is built on the noun "eye" (ʿayn). The word choice here is not neutral. Afaylal had much more common words at his disposal, such as shāhadtu ("I witnessed"), which he uses in other parts of the *Kunnash*.[100] In his war chronicle, however, Afaylal stresses the verb ʿāyantu, which evokes the eye and the eyewitness (shāhid al-ʿayn). Indeed, "seeing with one's own eyes" is a recurring trope in the text. Afaylal's chronicle is autoptic in the ancient rhetorical sense: it rests its authority on eyewitness testimony.[101]

As Afaylal describes a meeting of Tetouan's notables, he emphasizes again his role as eyewitness:

> On the 15th of Rabiʿ al-Thani [10 November 1859], the town's notables gathered together in the council, and with them were the scholars. A terrible fear of the Christians had overcome them. They advised each other on the matter. They came to an agreement that if the Christians came, the mountain people would combat them. Either the Muslims would defeat them, or, if not, they would negotiate for peace on their town, and they would enter under the Christians' rule. When *I saw that with my own eyes* [ʿāyantu], I said: "Now it is necessary to remove our families and children from this town." And I reminded them of the Prophet's saying (peace be upon him!): "Whoever believes in God and Judgment Day does not expose his children to the polytheists."[102] I left with my family for Chefchaouen on Monday, the 16th of Rabiʿ al-Thani 1276 [11 November 1859],[103] and I got there on the following day in the afternoon. I alighted in a house near its Great Mosque. Then I left them there and returned to Tetouan, with the intent of fighting jihad and inciting [taḥrīḍ] believers to combat.[104]

According to Afaylal, Tetouan's leader opted to use the people of the surrounding mountain region as human shields between them and the advancing Spanish army. If the mountain people could not stop the Spanish army, then the Tetouani leaders would submit to Christian rule. In this scene, Afaylal represents himself as a sole voice of moral dissent. He "sees with his own eyes" the council's cowardly actions and invokes a Prophetic tradition to remind his countrymen of the importance of protecting their family and children from the "polytheists," another Islamic term for Christians.[105] Afaylal implies that his vision is both physical and moral. He sees the impending danger that looms over Tetouan, and he witnesses the moral incapacity of the city's leaders to face it.

In Afaylal's account, the divisions among Moroccan Muslims overshadow the division between Muslims and Christians. Witnessing these divisions, Afaylal decides to evacuate his family from Tetouan and move them to the nearby city of Chefchaouen. He then returns to Tetouan "with the intent," he says, "of fighting jihad and inciting believers to combat."[106] It is worth drawing attention to the use of the word *taḥrīḍ* ("inciting") at the conclusion of the passage. The absence of *taḥrīḍ* is, as I have argued, the main point of divergence between Afaylal's elegy for Tetouan and the Andalusi city elegy tradition. The chronicle's narrator thus stands in implicit opposition to the elegy's speaker: the elegy advocates for stoic patience, while the chronicle advocates for jihad. Yet Afaylal's zeal for combat against the Spanish army diminishes as he continues to witness "with his own eyes" his countrymen's behavior.

Afaylal reserves his sharpest criticism for Moroccan political and military leaders, but the common people of Tetouan and the soldiers in the Moroccan army are not spared from his jabs. In one passage, he mockingly records the speech of illiterate Tetouanis who mispronounce classical Arabic words: "Since the *guerra* [*garra*] broke out, the people of Tetouan would say with a single tongue: 'God will provide faiath' (with an extra *a*)."[107] In the same passage, Afaylal suggests that his countrymen suffer not only from ignorance but also from delusional confidence. Their contempt for the Spanish leads them to underestimate the Spanish threat and even to envision an imminent Moroccan takeover of the Spanish enclave of Ceuta:

> They used to say: "The *español* [*sbanyūl*] is the worst of the races, and he's in no position to come our way." And they swear that with a mistaken faith, and then they even began to swear . . .

that they—that is, the Muslims—would enter Ceuta. They also swear in each battle that the Muslims who show up for battle are braver than the Prophet's Companions, and one of them even said: "better than the Prophet's Companions." And if I forbid them from [saying] that, they would say: "This guy debases Islam." . . . The greatest calamity is their bad judgment and their lack of planning. The only person they put in charge of the business of jihad is he who has no intellect and no religion.[108]

Afaylal accuses his countrymen of heretical behavior. He claims that they compared themselves to the ṣaḥāba, the Companions of the Prophet Muhammad. By emphasizing the political and moral shortcomings in the Moroccan camp, Afaylal's chronicle destabilizes the antithetical opposition between religion and unbelief around which his elegy for Tetouan is structured. The chronicle suggests that Islam was eroded from within rather than destroyed by an external foe.

Curiously, Afaylal uses poetry to signal his distance from the city elegy genre. After complaining that the Moroccan leaders have "no intellect and no religion," Afaylal inserts a witty couplet:

> The Christians want to shoot their cannon
>   on Tetouan (which has no defender),
> And those in charge are defective,
>   and their minds are crazy and immature.[109]

This couplet, like the city elegy, deploys figures of sound, but it uses them to deflate, rather than bolster, the Moroccan Muslim cause. The first line contains two instances of ingenious paronomasia. The line opens with three words that play on the consonants r-w-m and r-m-y: "yarūmu al-rūmu ramiyan" ("the Christians want to shoot"). In addition, each hemistich of the line ends with a homograph—that is, with words that are visually identical but are pronounced differently: madāfiʿ ("cannons") and mudāfiʿ ("defender"). The sound play associates the Christians and their desire to shoot (as if one were an extension of the other), and it also juxtaposes the Christian cannons and the lack of a

Muslim defender. Likewise, the rhyme scheme highlights the incompetence of the Moroccan leadership by drawing together the words "defender" (*mudāfiʿ*) and "immature" (*yāfiʿ*, literally "adolescent"). The couplet thus parodies the rhetorical conventions of the city elegy, using them for subversive ends.

Afaylal's chronicle gradually inverts the binaries that structure his elegy: religion and infidelity, the mosque and the tavern, the lost paradise and the barbarian's urinal. This process of symbolic inversion becomes clear when Afaylal describes the Moroccan army, led by the caliph Mulay al-ʿAbbas.[110] Afaylal calls the caliph's advisers "the enemies of God" and claims that their goal is "to hand over the country to the enemy."[111] Furthermore, his description of the Moroccan army's camp approximates the army to the barbarian who defiles Tetouan in his elegy:

> By chance, I camped near the caliph's tent. . . . [112] The call to prayer was heard, and he and three others prayed: his imam, his muezzin, and his Qurʾanic reciter. And the soldiers surrounded him. One of them was smoking kif [*yatakayyaf*], and one of them was singing verses. I did not see a collective prayer performed in that camp, despite its vastness, neither at night nor during the day, nor did I see a reader of a *ḥizb*[113] from the Holy Qurʾan. And there was not, among them, anyone with the knowledge to lead them in prayer. On the contrary, they never pray at all. You would find a man sitting, and while you were there watching, he would urinate and defecate, and then change his clothes. And despite this situation, they are eager to defeat the enemy, and they say, "The Prophet's religion will vanquish!" But they have lost his religion. And when I saw that with my own eyes [*ʿāyantu*], I left them and returned to Tetouan, waiting to see what the Maker of all beings would do.[114]

The description of the army's camp echoes some of the conventional images of the occupied Muslim city in the city elegy genre. In Afaylal's elegy, "Religion cries . . . / Over mosques where wine is now sold" (vv. 5–6). In the chronicle, the Moroccan soldiers smoke marijuana, sing, urinate, and defecate while the caliph prays. In al-Rundi's thirteenth-century city elegy, "The tap of the white ablution fount weeps . . . / Over dwellings emptied of Islam that . . . are now inhabited by unbelief" (vv. 21–22). In Afaylal's nineteenth-century chronicle, the Moroccan soldiers boastfully invoke the protection of "the Prophet's religion," but they do not pray or read from the Qur'an. Indeed, Afaylal asserts that the Moroccans "have lost [the Prophet's] religion." Afaylal stresses that he is narrating what he has "seen with his own eyes." But what Afaylal's eyes see begins to converge with what literary history has taught them to see. His eyewitness account of the war deploys some of the same rhetorical strategies that are found in his elegy about the war.

In the city elegy tradition, the barbarian figure not only destroys the city; he defiles it. He is a source of ritual impurity or pollution (najāsa): he turns the cleansing power of the ablution fount into the sullying force of wine and urine.[115] It is therefore noteworthy that Afaylal's chronicle resorts to the language of ritual impurity to describe the Moroccan army's presence near Tetouan. Here, the Moroccans, rather than the Spanish, play the role of the profane "barbarian" of the city elegy imaginary:

> [Mulay al-'Abbas] pitched his tents in the Qalalin Fort, and his camp spread through those gardens until it reached the Cemetery Gate. They tied their horses to the tombs of the Muslims, and they defiled them [najjasūhum] and disgraced their sanctity. That day, the people of Tetouan went out for jihad from the Cemetery Gate. When they looked at the Christians, they were struck with fear, and they returned to Tetouan, entering through Bab al-'Uqla without having fought.[116]

The scene takes place in Tetouan's Muslim cemetery, in which al-Manzari's mausoleum stands today. In Afaylal's telling, the Moroccan army not only occupied the cemetery; it defiled it. The verb that Afaylal uses, najjasa, is usually reserved for polluting substances (such as urine, feces, and wine) that require ritual ablutions. The passage's paratactic structure implies a causal relationship between two seemingly unrelated events: the Moroccan army sullies the Muslims' tombs, and then the people of Tetouan are too afraid to face the Spanish army in battle. Afaylal's descriptions of the Moroccan army foreshadow the chronicle's conclusion, in which Tetouan's putative saviors become its worst looters.

On February 4, 1860, the Moroccan army was routed in the Battle of Tetouan.[117] While the Spanish-Moroccan War would continue until April of 1860, the Battle of Tetouan dealt a mortal blow to the Moroccan army and paved the way for the Spanish occupation of Tetouan on February 6, 1860. In between the battle and the Spanish occupation of the city, Tetouan endured thirty-six hours of looting. This episode constitutes the conclusion of Afaylal's chronicle of the war. After the Moroccan army's disastrous defeat, "the vanquished Muslims," Afaylal writes, "entered the city crying."[118] The caliph, Mulay al-'Abbas, ordered to have all of his money and property removed from the city. His decision to abandon the city unleashed panic and chaos in Tetouan, as Afaylal describes:

> When the people of the city saw that with their own eyes [*āyana*], they removed their children that night, and they smashed the city gates. The most shameless among them began to pillage the Jews. Then, the news reached the caliph's camp, outside the city. They entered the city and started plundering the Muslims who were fleeing to preserve their religion. And that night there was corruption as had never before been seen in all of time. *How many* pregnant women miscarried! *How much* blood was spilled! *How much* furniture was stolen! People left that night with the dearest things, which are money and children, and they left behind their houses, including whatever rare treasures they had. They scattered to the villages.[119]

The passage's opening sentence features the final instance of the autoptic motif: the people of Tetouan "see with their own eyes" and thus join Afaylal in vision and insight. The act of bearing witness shifts from the individual to the collective, from the narrator to the townspeople.

Despite this emphasis on sight, Afaylal's description of the looting in Tetouan is quite opaque. Like the city elegy, it relies on rhetorical questions, anaphora, paronomasia, and metonymy to represent a tragedy that challenges representation. Indeed, this passage is the place where Afaylal's chronicle and his city elegy collide with greatest force. In both texts, the repetition of the exclamatory particle *kam* ("How many . . . !" or "How much . . . !") emphasizes and augments the sense of loss. Both texts also play on words with the trilateral roots *f-r-q* ("to separate") in order to evoke a classic motif that the Andalusi city elegy adopted from pre-Islamic poetry: the separation of the elegist from a beloved city, which is like the separation of the lovers at the abandoned desert campsite.[120] In Afaylal's elegy for Tetouan, the speaker laments that Fate "dispersed [*farraqa*] the people until nothing was left but a trace." And in the chronicle, the people of Tetouan "scattered [*taffaraqū*] to the villages" in order to escape the looting and pillaging of their hometown. Thus, the mass exodus from Tetouan is associated with an archetypal separation from home, from a lover, or from paradise. Finally, both the chronicle and the elegy use trauma suffered by women—rape and miscarriage—as a metonymy that stands in for a collective experience of trauma.

Indeed, the elegiac conclusion to Afaylal's chronicle could be read as an example of the repeating and "working through" that is often associated with representations of traumatic experience.[121] Dominick LaCapra has defined trauma as "a shattering break or cesura in experience" that poses specific problems for representation and writing.[122] Afaylal's chronicle seems to point to such a "break" in experience—one that disrupts representation. The chronicle's concluding section offers not a linear description of the looting of Tetouan but rather a series of fragmented snapshots, such as the scene of two Moroccan soldiers stripping naked a fleeing woman.[123] "Such deeds," Afaylal exclaims, "originated from many people, going beyond what this sheet of paper can contain!"[124] The text thus points to an experience that exceeds representation, that goes beyond what discourse "can contain." Although Afaylal's chronicle insists on the primacy of eyewitness observation, it concludes with a gesture toward what cannot be seen, said, or comprehended.

I would describe Afaylal's attempts to represent the Spanish-Moroccan War as asymptotic: that is, always approaching, but never arriving to, an adequate representation. Both the elegy and the chronicle stage, in different ways, a mimetic impasse. The elegy evokes Andalusi literary history but also underlines the inadequacy of Andalusi literary conventions for representing nineteenth-century Moroccan history. The chronicle asserts the authority of eyewitness evidence but also probes the limits of this evidence. As Joan Scott has argued, personal experience is not a transparent category that can serve as the unassailable bedrock for historical explanation; rather, it is discursive in nature.[125] That is, experience works within—indeed, it is produced by—historically situated categories of representation. Transferring Scott's insights to the case of Mufaddal Afaylal, we could say that his eyewitness experience does not offer us a transparent window into what "really happened" in Tetouan before the Spanish occupation of the city. Instead, Afaylal's eyewitness testimony allows us to track and interrogate the discourses that shape and, to a certain extent, produce Afaylal's vision. In other words, I am refusing to distinguish between Afaylal's "experience" and the discourses that structure it. Much like Alarcón, Afaylal ends up seeing what his eyes have been trained to see. The chronicle appears to offer a corrective to the city elegy, with experience trumping analogy and vision supplanting literary history. In the end, though, the chronicle reinforces, rather than subverts, the rhetorical conventions through which the city elegy makes the occupation of Tetouan legible and visible.

Conclusion

Afaylal's chronicle does not make any explicit allusions to al-Andalus, though the conventions of the Andalusi city elegy lurk, like a phantom, in the background of the text. In this brief conclusion, I would like to return to the issue of al-Andalus in order to consider what kind of cultural work it does and does not perform in nineteenth-century Morocco. For Afaylal and his contemporaries, al-Andalus is, first and foremost, a source of poetry. Moreover, it is a source of poetry that ties together the histories of the "two shores," the Iberian Peninsula and the Maghrib, and that provides a template for thinking and writing about conflict between Muslims and Christians. That is, al-Andalus entails poetry that is useful for thinking about religious and cultural difference. Notably, Afaylal neither trumpets the Andalusi heritage of his native

Tetouan nor calls himself or his culture "Andalusi." He neither evokes the mass migration of Andalusi Muslims to Tetouan and other Moroccan cities nor underlines the traces of Andalusi civilization that are preserved in Moroccan music, architecture, and ethics.

In retrospect, these absences are quite striking. To illustrate this point, I would like to turn, briefly, to a twentieth-century Moroccan description of Afaylal's contemporary and spiritual master, 'Abd al-Salam b. Raysun. The historian Muhammad Dawud (1901–1984), writing in the early years of Moroccan independence, claimed that Ibn Raysun

> had, from a young age, a great love of music.... The music that he used to study, relish, and know masterfully was the refined Andalusi music that the emigrants from al-Andalus brought with them from their first city, Granada the Andalusi, to their second city, Tetouan the Moroccan. They would still memorize it by heart and sing it with its various instruments and master its different rhythms. And they would pass it down in a traditional way from generation to generation for hundreds of years until this age of ours.[126]

In Dawud's biography of Ibn Raysun, Andalusi music is part of a continuous chain of cultural transmission from fifteenth-century Granada to twentieth-century Morocco. In the *Kunnash*, Afaylal frequently alludes to the musical sessions that he enjoyed alongside his master, Ibn Raysun. For example, in a note from October of 1867, Afaylal writes: "I attended an evening of music [*laylat ṭarab*] with our master and blessing Sidi 'Abd al-Salam b. Raysun. Among what the singers said was the famous *tawshīḥ*, which begins..."[127] Afaylal then reproduces a few lines from the lyrics of *Nubat al-Isbahan,* one of the eleven suites that make up the Moroccan Andalusi music repertoire. The lyrics are from a *tawshīḥ,* a strophic poetic form that has roots in medieval Iberia.[128]

In later chapters, I will discuss the revival of Moroccan Andalusi music under European colonialism in the twentieth century. For now, I would merely like to draw attention to Afaylal's fleeting reference to "an evening of music" in October of 1867. What kind of music were Afaylal and his companions listening to, and, more importantly, what did the music mean to them? Afaylal uses the term *ṭarab*, which can mean "music," but whose original meaning denotes ecstasy or the pleasurable feeling induced by music.[129] In the twentieth century, the North African musical tradition to which Afaylal refers has come to be known under the umbrella term "Andalusi music" (*al-mūsīqā al-andalusiyya*), and in Morocco, it is often known as *al-āla* ("instrument") or *al-ṭarab al-andalusī* ("Andalusi music/pleasure").[130] Unlike Muhammad Dawud, though, Afaylal does not draw an explicit connection between this music and al-Andalus. Perhaps, for Afaylal, the connection was too obvious to be stated.

My contention, however, is that between Afaylal's lifetime and Dawud's lifetime, there is a significant shift in how Moroccans think and write about their connection to al-Andalus. Al-Andalus is both present and malleable for a nineteenth-century Moroccan scholar such as Mufaddal Afaylal. Indeed, it is one of the primary discursive models through which Afaylal makes sense of the Spanish-Moroccan War. Nevertheless, in Afaylal's writings, al-Andalus has not yet consolidated into a defined narrative of identity, transmission, and heritage. That is, there is still not a clear narrative about how Morocco became Andalusi, and how Morocco's Andalusi-ness manifests in music, architecture, crafts, and a specific way of practicing Islam. Thus, Afaylal engages al-Andalus, but not the "Andalus-centric" narrative of Moroccan history to which I referred in my introduction. The "Andalus-centric" narrative of Moroccan history would not emerge until the early twentieth century, when Spanish colonial discourse developed a specific repertoire of ideas about Morocco's Andalusi heritage and Spain's connection to it. I will turn to this process in Chapter 3.

3

AL-ANDALUS, ANDALUCÍA, AND MOROCCO

IN 1924, THE WRITER and politician Blas Infante (1885–1936), hailed today as the "Father of the Andalusian Fatherland" ("Padre de la Patria Andaluza"), boarded a rickety boat in Lisbon, setting off for Casablanca.[1] The conventional route for a Spanish traveler headed to North Africa, through the Spanish Protectorate zone in northern Morocco, was closed due to the Rif War (1921–1927), in which the Spanish army brutally suppressed an armed resistance led by the Riffian leader Muhammad ʿAbd al-Karim al-Khattabi.[2] Infante was not, however, headed for a destination in the Spanish zone. Rather, he had set his sights on Aghmat, a small town in southern Morocco whose most famous attraction is the tomb of al-Muʿtamid Ibn ʿAbbad (1040–1095), the eleventh-century poet-king of Seville. After the Moroccan Almoravid dynasty conquered Seville in 1090, they took al-Muʿtamid as a prisoner and brought him to the desolate town of Aghmat, where he died in exile in 1095. Today, al-Muʿtamid is perhaps best known for the mournful poetry he wrote in his Moroccan exile, poetry that has served as inspiration and ornamentation for many modern adaptations of Andalusi history in Arabic and Spanish—including, notably, Blas Infante's 1920 play *Motamid*.[3]

In a manuscript account of his sojourn in Morocco, Infante described the impetus for his visit to far-flung Aghmat: "In 1924, I resolved to resume the pilgrimages that our fathers made, for some time, to the tomb of one of the most representative men of the spirit of our land, Abu al-Qasim ibn 'Abbad [i.e., al-Mu'tamid], the true king of Seville, Cordoba, Malaga, and the Algarve. The last pilgrim had been a son from my Hills of Ronda, al-Khatib, minister to the Sultan of Granada in the fourteenth century."[4] For Infante, the journey to Aghmat was not a mere exercise in intrepid cultural tourism; rather, it was a "pilgrimage" to the spiritual Mecca of Andalusian culture. Referring in the first-person plural to "the spirit of our land," Infante strategically conflates Andalucía (the modern region in Spain) and al-Andalus (medieval Muslim Iberia) in order to draw a direct line between himself and al-Mu'tamid. Infante's Moroccan travelogue abounds in references to the hajj, the Muslim pilgrimage to Mecca. Yet the primary model upon which Infante fashions his visit to Aghmat is not the religious pilgrimage to Mecca but rather the cultural pilgrimage that literary luminaries from al-Andalus, whom Infante hails as "our fathers," made to Aghmat to pay their respects to the deceased poet-king of Seville.[5] The last of these Andalusi literary pilgrims in Aghmat was Ibn al-Khatib (1313–1375), with whom Infante signals a common place of origin, calling him "a son from my Hills of Ronda [mi Serranía de Ronda]." Infante thus places himself in a cultural genealogy that runs from al-Mu'tamid's Seville to Ibn al-Khatib's Granada to modern-day Andalucía.

Motamid, Infante's play on the life and death of the eponymous king, ends with an epilogue that recreates the scene of Ibn al-Khatib's fourteenth-century visit to Aghmat. In the epilogue, the fictional Ibn al-Khatib scandalizes the inhabitants of Aghmat by performing in front of al-Mu'tamid's tomb the rituals that are normally reserved for the pilgrimage to Mecca. Infante's Ibn al-Khatib says:

> The Muslim pilgrims that go to Mecca circle around the Kasba [*sic*] seven times.
> This cemetery is Mecca. The stones of this tomb are the Kasba for the pilgrim of true royalty's Religion, which is the Religion of liberty, of Beauty, and of Love.[6]

The ensuing stage direction describes Ibn al-Khatib circumambulating the tomb as if it were the Kaʿba in Mecca.[7] *Motamid*'s epilogue thus stages and presages the "pilgrimage" that Infante would perform in Aghmat in 1924. It also casts al-Muʿtamid's tomb—and the mythic al-Andalus it metonymically represents—as an elegiac monument to an alternate theology: one that is neither Muslim nor Christian, but rather is based on the universal principles of "liberty, Beauty, and Love."

In Infante's notes about his trip to Morocco, he treats al-Andalus as a passport that facilitates his passage and introduces him into Moroccan society. He even suggests that al-Andalus allows him to "pass" as a native Moroccan. On his journey to Aghmat, Infante alighted in nearby Marrakesh, where he imagined that he had gone native, writing:

> I am not an outsider [*forastero*] in Marrakesh. The Andalusian Moors predominate in the ethnic make-up of the Muslim *medina*. Presiding over the buried psychic construction that my memory now excavates [are] the spirits of the illustrious Andalusians who inspired the most learned caliphs of the Maghrib, who had their imperial center here.... Marrakesh is, for my pilgrimage, the border of the Holy Land, of the Temple.... I perform an ablution in the fountain of history, with fecund values born of a culture that they tried to obscure and that went underground.[8]

This passage weaves together metaphors of pilgrimage, archaeology, and genealogy. Like Alarcón, who saw Tetouan as a palimpsest, Infante represents Marrakesh as a palimpsest, where the Andalusi past coexists with the Moroccan present. The city carries the racial trace of al-Andalus through the descendants of the exiled Andalusis, "the Andalusian Moors," who predominate in the city's "ethnic make-up." Yet the spirit of al-Andalus only becomes visible through Infante's archaeological gaze. His memory "excavates" the "spirits of illustrious Andalusians." These sons of al-Andalus bestowed upon Morocco cultural values that are also metaphorical "sons" of the Andalusian family tree: "fecund values born of [literally, 'sons of'] a culture that they tried to obscure and that went underground." Thus, in traveling to Morocco, Infante aspires to visit not only al-Muʿtamid's tomb but also the tomb of al-Andalus itself. For Infante, Morocco is a monument that pays homage to al-Andalus, whose culture was driven underground but will be revived by the heroic intervention of modern Andalusians such as himself.

Infante's celebration of Spain's Muslim past and of Andalucía's geographic and cultural proximity to Morocco has played a fundamental role in his posthumous recognition as the "Father of the Andalusian Fatherland." In post-Franco Spain, Infante's legacy of political *andalucismo* (or Andalusian nationalism) has become inexorably linked with the myth of *convivencia,* the supposedly harmonious coexistence of Christians, Muslims, and Jews in al-Andalus. For instance, the Parliament of Andalucía's online homage to Blas Infante emphasizes that, "Another basic axis of his thought was to accomplish a 'pro-African' foreign policy, in an attempt to revive the al-Andalus in which Arabs, Jews, and Christians cohabited in open tolerance."[9] In a similar vein, the preamble to Andalucía's Statute of Autonomy (2007) formally recognizes Blas Infante as the "Padre de la Patria Andaluza" and describes Andalucía as an "example of human mixture [*mestizaje*]" and "a border space that has facilitated contacts and dialogue between North and South."[10] Such invocations of Andalucía's exemplary tolerance are not limited to government publications; they also permeate the discourses of contemporary Andalucía's tourism industry and of the region's growing population of Spanish converts to Islam, who often represent their conversion as a "return" to Andalucía's Muslim origins.[11]

While Infante's love of al-Andalus and his professed desire to strengthen the ties between Spain and Morocco could be construed as admirable examples of multiculturalism *avant la lettre,* they should nonetheless raise red flags for scholars of modern Spanish history. After all, it was precisely Spain's claims to a "Hispano-Moroccan brotherhood" that underwrote the country's colonial projects in Morocco.[12] Although Blas Infante was a victim of Francoist violence, his writings helped to shape the discourse of Spanish colonialism in Morocco under Franco. Several Andalusian writers from the 1940s and 1950s used *andalucismo* as an argument to naturalize Spain's colonial claims in Morocco. Contemporary scholars of *andalucismo* have tended to downplay its crucial role in the formation of Francoist colonial discourse, in an effort to whitewash Infante's ideological legacy of any connection with Francoism or with Spanish colonialism in Morocco.[13] This chapter will examine Blas Infante's contradictory legacy as a champion of intercultural tolerance and as an apologist for Spanish colonialism in Morocco.

At the center of this chapter is the elision between three related geohistorical concepts: al-Andalus (medieval Muslim Iberia), Andalucía (a region in southern Spain), and Morocco (the North African nation-state). The key rhetorical move that Blas Infante perfected was the elision of these three concepts in time, space, and culture. This elision, while strategic, rested on some sturdy foundations. For one, al-Andalus has always been a porous geographic concept. The historical al-Andalus expanded and contracted over time, and Andalusi rulers often had North African territories under their control—just as al-Andalus itself was under North African control during the Almoravid and Almohad periods (eleventh to thirteenth centuries). Furthermore, as we have seen, several Andalusi luminaries, such as Ibn al-Khatib, had careers that spanned the two shores of the Strait of Gibraltar. Finally, there is an obvious etymological and geographic relationship between Andalucía and al-Andalus. The modern Spanish region takes its name from the Arabic name for Iberia, and several of the cultural capitals of medieval al-Andalus—including Cordoba, Granada, and Seville—are located within the borders of today's Andalucía.

For all these reasons, it is tempting to overlook Blas Infante's breezy movements across space and time. I argue, though, that it is crucial for us to scrutinize his efforts to conflate al-Andalus, Andalucía, and Morocco into a single idea and culture, stretching across time and space. This conflation is the driving force behind Spanish colonialism in Morocco from the 1930s to the 1950s. It is also a point of convergence between Spanish liberals, like Blas Infante, and Spanish fascists, who will take up the banner of his ideas after the Spanish Civil War. Indeed, in the historical arc of this book, Blas Infante's life and work serve as a pivot to illuminate the migration of ideas from the Republican imaginary to the fascist imaginary. The surprise that this chapter reveals is that Blas Infante, a Republican martyr, helped sow the seeds of the colonial ideology that would guide Francoism in Morocco. This story of strange bedfellows throws into doubt the common understanding of the Spanish Civil War as a conflict that divided two irreconcilable views of Spain.

At stake here are not only Spanish ideas about Morocco but also long-standing debates about Spain itself. Infante saw Andalucía as the antithesis and repudiation of Catalonia, often considered Spain's most European region.[14] Indeed, Infante's brand of *andalucismo*—and its Francoist adaptations—entails a wholesale reorientation of Spanish culture and politics toward Africa and away from Europe. The long-standing French quip about Spain, dating back to the nineteenth century, is that "Africa begins in the Pyrenees."[15] The quip barely conceals a claim of white supremacy; it implies that Spain was "tainted"— both racially and culturally—by the eight centuries of Muslim rule on the Iberian Peninsula. Infante associates this idea with Europe and with Catalonia, which he treats as a synecdoche of Europe. For Infante, Catalonia is monoracial, monocultural, and exclusionary, and it stands in contrast with a multiracial and radically open Andalucía. Infante's writings invoke interracial and interfaith tolerance, but they also proved surprisingly useful for establishing Spanish hegemony in northern Morocco. My goal in this chapter will thus be to track Blas Infante's ideological legacy in multiple geographical and historical directions— backward in time to al-Andalus, southward to Morocco, and eastward to Catalonia and Europe. Infante's *andalucismo* bolstered Spain's claims on Morocco while exerting pressure on competing efforts to pull Spain toward Europe.

Andalucía and Catalonia: Spain around the Periphery

Andalusian nationalism is rarely considered in dialogue with other Iberian peripheral nationalisms.[16] Although Infante's *The Andalusian Ideal* (*El ideal andaluz*, 1915) is today considered the paradigmatic text of Andalusian nationalism, the political movement actually emerged in the nineteenth century, at the same time as the more well-known peripheral nationalisms in Catalonia and the Basque Country. Starting with the Junta de Andújar of 1835, Andalusian liberals clamored for more political autonomy.[17] These efforts culminated in the Constitution of Antequera (1883), whose first article declared: "Andalucía is sovereign and autonomous; it is organized in a representative republican democracy, and it does not receive its power from any external authority."[18] The calls for Andalusian autonomy, which would reach their apogee under the Second Spanish Republic, have often been considered in the context of what Acosta Sánchez has called "the struggle against centralization."[19] Indeed, scholars of modern Spanish history and politics have a tendency to approach the study of Iberian nationalisms from the lens of a "center-periphery" binary, in which each periphery is understood in relation to Madrid and Castile. Nevertheless, Infante developed his *andalucista* ideology in implicit and sometimes explicit dialogue with Catalan nationalism. Scholars have been reluctant to consider the transversal relations between Andalusian nationalism and other peripheral nationalisms and have tended to focus, instead, on Andalusian nationalism's place within the "center-periphery" paradigm. In this section, I will build on recent work in Hispanic and postcolonial studies in order to propose a different model for understanding lateral relations between peripheral-nationalist discourses, which sometimes bypass the "center" altogether.

Joan Ramon Resina has recently advocated for the creation of a new academic discipline, Iberian studies, which would serve as an alternative to a centripetal Hispanism that has privileged Castilian culture to the detriment of the other cultural and linguistic identities of the Iberian Peninsula. The field of Iberian studies would, in Resina's words, consider Castilian culture "in relation rather than in opposition to the other languages of the same geocultural space."[20] Iberian studies is first and foremost a critique of what Resina has called "Hispanism's cozy monolingualism."[21] The dominant criterion of Resina's Iberian studies is language, which Resina opposes to state-centric disciplines (e.g., Spain and Portugal). Multilingual Iberian studies could therefore serve as an intellectual and political counterweight to what Resina calls "Castilianization," the privileging of Castilian language and culture that accompanied the rise of a centralized Spanish nation-state in the nineteenth century.[22]

While the Iberian studies model is a welcome response to Hispanism's excessive emphasis on Castilian culture, it nonetheless has limited usefulness for the study of Andalusian nationalism. I share Resina's commitment to multilingualism (Iberian and otherwise), but I would add that it is important not to conflate linguistic pluralism and all other forms of cultural diversity. In asserting the significance of the Iberian Peninsula's linguistic pluralism, Resina paradoxically masks other forms of resistant or nonhegemonic identity. After all, as the case of Blas Infante demonstrates, not all writing in Castilian is Castile-centric. Andalusian nationalism opens a space for what we might call, following Deleuze and Guattari, a "minor" use of the Castilian language.[23]

One of the unintended consequences of the recent turn to Iberian studies might therefore be to reify the very cultural relations that it hopes to illuminate and problematize. In other words, focusing exclusively on Castilian culture's relationship with its linguistic others (Catalan, Basque, and Galician culture) might only serve to reinforce Castilian culture's status as "center" and might also obfuscate the fissures and differences that lie within this seemingly homogeneous and hegemonic "center."[24] The importance of "minor" Iberian nationalisms, such as *andalucismo*, resides in their role as political Trojan horses, eroding the dominant center from within. And yet, their subversive power moves in both directions: decentering Castilian as the language of power and also questioning Catalan, Basque, and Galician's status as the sole languages of resistance. I have elsewhere coined the term "transperipheral" to describe critical approaches that highlight relations between Spain's peripheries.[25] In such approaches, peripheral subjects identify themselves vis-à-vis each other rather than in relation to a dominant center. Put simply, the path from Seville to Barcelona need not pass through Madrid.

From the early part of the twentieth century to the onset of the Second Spanish Republic in 1931, *andalucismo* evolved from an implicit debate with Catalan nationalism to an explicit repudiation of it. The key Catalan intertext in this evolving polemic between Andalusian nationalism and Catalan nationalism is Prat de la Riba's classic *Catalan Nationality* (*La nacionalitat catalana*, 1906). The book asserts Catalonia's status as a nation and establishes a contrast between Catalonia and Spain—or, at least, a Spain that is primarily identified with Castile and Castilian culture. The primary grounds upon which Prat de la Riba defends Catalonia's claim to nationhood are the region's distinctive language, art, legal system, and "national spirit" (*l'esperit nacional*), a concept that Prat de la Riba derives from the German philosophical term *Volksgeist*.²⁶ Of these traits of national identity, Prat de la Riba privileges the importance of language, saying: "Great, total, [and] irreducible are the differences that separate Castile and Catalonia, Catalonia and Galicia, Andalucía and the Basque Country. They are separated—to look no further—by that which most separates, that which makes men foreign from each other.... Language separates them."²⁷ Prat de la Riba treats language as the defining category of national (and even human) identity. Language is "what makes men foreign from each other." To contextualize this stance, it bears remembering that the revival of the cultural uses of the Catalan language was a key element of the nineteenth-century Catalan cultural renaissance known as the *Renaixença*.²⁸

While Prat de la Riba's definition of Catalan nationality draws upon the nineteenth-century revival of Catalan language and culture, it also masks a highly racialized conception of national identity. Brad Epps has argued that Catalan nationalists purchase Catalonia's much-vaunted modernity by way of the Africanization of the rest of Spain.²⁹ Susan Martin-Márquez has traced this phenomenon back to the nineteenth century, when the rise of scientific racism in Spain allowed Catalan anthropologists to argue that the Catalan race had maintained a superior Aryan Gothic character because it had barely mixed with the Muslim inhabitants of medieval Iberia.³⁰ Prat de la Riba's race-baiting is not quite as explicit as that of his nineteenth-century Catalanist counterparts; he nonetheless stresses the region's geographic and cultural distance from Spain's Semitic past.

Prat de la Riba refers to his mother tongue as "Limousin" (*llemosí*), thereby linking the Catalan language to the French region of Limousin and to the Occitan languages spoken in southern France.³¹ He also asserts that Catalonia's national art, like its language, comes from across the Pyrenees, rather than from the other side of the Strait of Gibraltar: "The unity of the artistic ideal of our nationality was also incarnated in ... Gothic architecture, which, having come from the lands of the North, did not peak among us until it had molded itself to the demands of our race's genius."³² Prat de la Riba celebrates Gothic architecture as a Nordic inheritance that reached its fullest expression when it came into contact with the "genius" of the Catalan "race." Elsewhere, he is even more explicit in distancing Catalan art from Spain's Muslim past, writing: "How were the truly Spanish people to believe that ... giving ourselves over to the Gothic and the Romanesque of our monuments, we would feel a more intense devotion toward the Alhambra or the Giralda?"[33] This rhetorical question hinges upon a clear distinction between "the truly Spanish people" and the first-person plural "we," indicating the Catalan people. Prat de la Riba associates the famous monuments of Muslim Spain, the Alhambra and the Giralda, with "the truly Spanish people," whereas he associates the Catalans with architectural styles that come, in his words, "from the lands of the North." The contrast between architectural styles and tastes is, of course, saturated with cultural and political meaning. It serves to approximate Catalonia to Europe and to push the rest of Spain toward North Africa.

While Catalan nationalist thought was constructed on the notions of linguistic and racial difference, Andalusian nationalism defended the importance of racial and cultural mixing. 1914 was a watershed year in the formulation of Andalusian nationalist doctrine, as it saw the publication of two of the foundational texts of *andalucismo,* each of which celebrated Andalucía's racial and cultural hybridity and contested, explicitly and implicitly, Prat de la Riba's theories of Catalan nationality. The first of the two texts is Infante's *The Andalusian Ideal,* which was initially a lecture that Infante delivered at the Ateneo de Sevilla on March 23, 1914, and was later published in book form in 1915. The Ateneo de Sevilla was also the motor behind the second foundational *andalucista* text from 1914. That year, the Ateneo organized a contest for the best work on Andalusian regionalism. (I will return, in a moment, to the difference between "regionalism" and "nationalism.") The Ateneo's contest was convened under the motto, "Sólo Dios es vencedor," the Spanish translation of the motto of Nasrid Granada: "There is no victor but God" (*Wa-lā ghālib illā Allah*). The prize went to Isidro de las Cagigas's "Notes for a Study of Andalusian Regionalism," which was subsequently published in a three-part series in the magazine *Bética,* a major incubator for early *andalucista* thought.

Without naming Prat de la Riba directly, De las Cagigas defines Andalusian regionalism *against* the criteria of race, language, and law, which had formed the basis of Prat de la Riba's definition of Catalan nationality. De las Cagigas writes: "Andalucía does not seek separatism; Andalucía still has not intensively marked its borders in order to close them to outsiders; Andalucía does not boast of a privileged race, a private language, or an exclusive law; Andalucía does not dream of turning into a concrete and homogeneous unit."[34] This defense of Andalucía, framed in terms of what Andalucía is not, is also an implicit critique of Catalanist thought. De las Cagigas implies that Catalan nationalism is "exclusive" and "homogeneous." In contrast, he affirms that Andalusians constitute "an infinite mix of heterogeneous elements, brought from all over, and principally from the Orient."[35] He thus presents Andalusian culture as open, universal, and heterogeneous, and he ties these traits to the "mix" (*mezcla*) of cultures and races that have passed through the region.

Like De las Cagigas, Infante locates Andalucía's strength in its history of cultural and racial mixing. Indeed, the importance of admixture, both racial and cultural, is the underlying theme of Infante's *Andalusian Ideal,* which has enjoyed more posthumous fame than De las Cagigas's essay. In the *Ideal,* Infante argues that miscegenation is a necessary ingredient for cultural vitality:

> With regards to the mixture of so many races, there are those who say that the antagonistic physiological elements will destroy each other, producing a weak compound. To combat this amusing theory, I merely have to say that homogeneity and infecundity, which are synonyms in zoology, appear to be so in anthropology, too. The Toba and the Eskimo, homogeneous races, are dying races.[36]

Infante argues, here, against the grain of a century's worth of European racial biology, which had upheld racial boundaries between Europeans and Africans by promoting the theory that improper racial mixing resulted in degeneracy.[37] Countering his contemporaries' fears of racial mixture, Infante sets out to rebut those who believe that Andalucía is naturally predisposed to backwardness, due to its Semitic and African past. Ventriloquizing his opponents, Infante writes: "'They have African blood in their veins!,' say those who believe that being African is a stigma."[38] Countering the "stigma" of Andalucía's "African blood," Infante instead represents the Muslim invasion of Iberia in 711 as an invigorating infusion of blood: "The Arab invasion nourished Andalusians, principally with Arab and Berber blood."[39] From here, Infante draws a line of causality between the "infusion" of Arab and Berber blood in the eighth century, and the cultural splendor that the Iberian Peninsula witnessed in the following centuries.

In particular, Infante underlines the spirit of *convivencia* that characterized the tenth-century Umayyad caliphate in Cordoba: "There has not been—either in the centuries in which it developed, or even long afterward—a more tolerant or more free civilization than the Arab-Andalusian one."[40] In Infante's telling, al-Andalus's culture of freedom and interfaith tolerance was reinforced by the eagerness with which the Andalusis studied the science of the ancient Greeks. Al-Andalus was to become, in Infante's words, "the refuge for Greek genius during the medieval barbarism in the rest of the world."[41] Indeed, Infante muses that Europe might never have emerged from its "medieval barbarism" into the Renaissance had it not been for the civilizing presence of al-Andalus. Along these lines, he writes: "And here's how the Semitic ancestry that is thrown in our face as a stigma . . . is our greatest claim to glory. It is glorious Andalucía to whom Europe and the world owe the nourishment . . . of the roots of the Renaissance."[42] Thus, Infante generates strength from a perceived weakness: not only is Andalucía's "Semitic ancestry" not a stigma; rather, it is precisely what has driven Andalucía's contribution to the formation of modern Europe.

In *The Andalusian Ideal*, Infante's response to Catalan nationalism is oblique. His celebration of Andalucía's Semitic heritage presents an implicit critique of the Catalanist emphasis on Catalonia's Nordic heritage. Like his colleague De las Cagigas, Infante also asserts that Andalucía does not need its own language or its own legal tradition to celebrate its unique cultural heritage.[43] Perhaps the most radical point of divergence between Prat de la Riba and Infante is the terminology that they employ to describe their proposed collective identities: for Prat de la Riba, Catalonia is, unquestionably, a "nation," whereas for the early Infante, Andalucía is a "region." In fact, in *The Andalusian Ideal*, Infante goes so far as to refute the very existence of Iberian peripheral nationalities, writing: "In Spain, then, there are only regions. There can only be regions."[44] This position has led many scholars to refer to *andalucismo* as a "regionalism," rather than a "nationalism." However, starting with the Cordoba Manifesto of 1919, Blas Infante and his *andalucista* partisans would change lexical tracks and would begin referring to Andalucía as a "nationality." The Cordoba Manifesto, written in the heyday of the Wilsonian emphasis on national self-determination, proclaims: "Andalusians: Andalucía is a nationality."[45] Surprisingly, this new emphasis on Andalucía's status as a nation did not serve to approximate *andalucismo* to Catalan nationalism. On the contrary, Infante would increasingly frame Andalusian nationalism as a repudiation of Catalan nationalism, which he viewed as an inauthentic and dangerously European influence on Spain.

This line of critique emerges most clearly in Infante's 1931 polemic, *The Truth about the Tablada Plot and the Free State of Andalucía* (*La verdad sobre el complot de Tablada y el estado libre de Andalucía*). Written in the early months of the Second Spanish Republic, the work revolves around an antagonistic opposition between Andalucía and Europe. In it, Infante claims that Andalucía is "the most Spanish Spain among the Spains, the one from which was always condensed the authentic and original energy of Spain, diluted in the Europeanism of the country's center and north."[46] Infante resorts, here, to the language of authenticity and dilution—so common in theories of scientific racism. Yet in this case, the danger of dilution and degeneracy comes from Europe, not from Africa. For this reason, Infante advocates for the symbolic separation of Spain from Europe, observing: "Spain has a dilemma: Europe or Andalucía. Europe is broken. Spain no longer needs to be the instrument of Europe, against us, who conserve the most original part of Spain.... The cry of *free Andalucía:* might it not be the same as *free Spain... from Europe?*"[47] Playing on Andalusian electoral slogans from the early 1930s, Infante envisions a Spain that is detached from Europe and oriented toward a southern center of gravity.

In calling for Spain's "freedom" from Europe, Infante is also advocating for its separation from Catalonia. Indeed, throughout his 1931 polemic, Infante treats Catalonia as a synonym for Europe, such as when he observes: "Catalonia, it is more Europe than Andalucía. We cannot be, we don't want to be, we will never become Europeans.... We have never stopped being what we truly are: that is, *Andalusians;* Euro-Africans, Euro-Orientals, universalist men, harmonious syntheses of men.... We have not been able to become Europeans, despite the barbarous colonization."[48] In this passage, Infante associates Catalonia with Europe and also with the Christian Reconquest of al-Andalus. Indeed, he implies that the invaders of Spain were not the Muslims who entered Iberia in 711, but rather the Christian Europeans who kicked them out in 1492. He emphasizes this inversion of the standard historical narrative by calling the post-1492 consolidation of Spain a period of "colonization" (*coloniaje*). Likewise, he refers to Europeans as "barbarians," a word that is usually reserved for subaltern Others. This dismissal of Europe is echoed in the prologue to Infante's text, which is attributed to the Junta Liberalista de Andalucía, the primary Andalusian nationalist organization during the Second Spanish Republic. The organization's prologue calls for a Spain that is "free from the colonial influence of a foreign, barbarous, and failed continent, like Europe."[49] Europe is thus depicted as a "barbarous" and "colonial influence," whose cultural encroachment on Spain represents a dangerous threat to Andalucía's "Euro-African" character.

Catalonia stands in as the representative of "barbarous" Europe and as the adversary to the "universalist" identity that Infante wants to stake out for Andalucía. Infante contends that Catalan nationalism is predicated on an attitude of ethnic and social exclusion. As evidence, he reminds his readers of a famous Catalanist motto: "Catalonia, for and by the Catalans."[50] The source that Infante is paraphrasing is Prat de la Riba and Pere Muntañola's *Compendium of the Catalanist Doctrine* (*Compendi de la doctrina catalanista,* 1894), a popular primer for Catalan nationalist thought. The *Compendium* is organized as a series of questions and responses, one of which is:

> Question: What famous phrase summarizes our aspirations and is going to constitute the motto of our flag?
> Answer: Catalonia for the Catalans![51]

In contrast with the Catalan nationalist motto, Infante asserts that the motto of Andalusian nationalism is: "In Andalucía, there are no foreigners."[52] He thus presents *andalucismo* as a nationalism that is open to everyone—a nationalism without foreigners.

In fact, Infante argues that Andalusian nationalism is a rebuke not only of Catalan nationalism but also of the notion of nationalism itself. Of the Andalusian nationalists' agenda, he says: "It was an *internationalist, universalist* nationalism, the opposite of all those nationalisms inspired by the European principle of nationalities. To be even clearer, it was a paradox: the Andalusian nationalists decided to defend an *anti-nationalist nationalism*."[53] Infante thus establishes a contrast between the supposedly "universalist" nature of Andalusian nationalism and what he calls "the European principle of nationalities," which is embodied by Catalan nationalism. He attempts to resolve the apparent contradiction between nationalism and universalism by proposing a paradoxical "internationalist nationalism" or "anti-nationalist nationalism."

What are we to make of this call for an "anti-nationalist nationalism"? It is a paradox that sets up a similar tension in Infante's thinking about Morocco. Infante claims all Moroccans as "Andalusians," but he insists that doing so is neither colonial nor imperial, since the idea of Andalucía is, for him, universal. He thus outlines a discourse that we might call "cosmopolitan imperialism," an expansionist ideology whose power is masked by claims of equality and tolerance. In what remains of this chapter, I will show how Infante's cosmopolitan imperialism has survived the trials and tribulations of Spain's turbulent twentieth century, serving diverse ideological causes, including Francoism.

Andalucismo as Cosmopolitan Imperialism

On August 10, 1936, just a few weeks after the outbreak of the Spanish Civil War, Blas Infante was shot dead by rebel troops on the highway outside of Carmona. Considering that the "Father of the Andalusian Fatherland" was one of the many victims of Francoist violence, it is a cruel irony of history that his ideas made their way into several facets of Francoist culture. For instance, Infante's celebration of racial mixing anticipated the Francoist conception of race, which, as Goode has argued, was based on the belief that racial strength emanated from mixture and hybridity.[54] Another example of Infante's contradictory ideological legacy is that his *andalucista* discourse was appropriated by Francoist intellectuals to justify Spain's colonial projects in Morocco.

Infante's writings carried inscribed upon them the seeds of colonial domination. His belief in the universality of Andalusian culture shaped his view of Andalucía's role in the world—and, specifically, of Andalucía's historical claims over Morocco. In what follows, I will examine Infante's efforts to justify Spanish colonialism in Morocco, and then I will trace the migration of Infante's ideas into the work of Rodolfo Gil Benumeya (1901–1975), one of the most prominent apologists for Spanish colonialism under Franco.

Starting in 1931, Catalan nationalists began to clamor for a new homeland, known as the *Països Catalans,* whose borders would exceed Catalonia and even Spain, encompassing the Catalan-speaking regions of Valencia, the Balearic Islands, France, and Italy.[55] In response to this expansionist view of the Catalan nation, Infante offered the competing notion of "*pan-andalucismo.*"[56] Through it, he envisioned an Andalucía that spanned the Mediterranean: "Knowledge of our History ... also justifies our aspiration of getting to reestablish our cultural unity with the Orient.... Here are the facts: one million two hundred thousand Muslim and Mosaic Andalusians stretch from Tangier to Damascus."[57] Infante thus imagines a vast, trans-Mediterranean network of Andalusians, stretching south to Morocco and east to Damascus. To support this imagined geography, he expands the borders of Andalucía and broadens the definition of Andalusian. His census of the Andalusian people transcends Spain and includes "Muslim and Mosaic Andalusians"—that is, the descendants of the Muslims and Jews ("Mosaics") who were expelled from the Iberian Peninsula.

Infante first encountered the Andalusi diaspora during his 1924 trip to Morocco, when he met several Moroccans who claimed to be of Andalusi descent. In the journal from his trip, Infante wrote that Andalusian nationalism's role in colonial Morocco should be to unite Peninsular Andalusians with the exiled Andalusians in North Africa. "It is necessary," he wrote, "to unite one with the other.... In this sense, there is an *andalucismo* like there is a Zionism. We, too, need to reconstruct a Zion."[58] Infante compares *andalucismo* to Zionism by suggesting that both are aimed at returning an exiled community to its mythic homeland. The comparison highlights the wide-ranging and incongruous contexts with which al-Andalus has been associated in modern times.

Ironically, al-Andalus has also served, in modern Arabic literature, as a metaphor for Palestine, another lost homeland.[59]

Upon his return from Morocco, Infante pledged to help the country's Andalusi diaspora return home to Andalucía, writing: "Your return to Andalucía is, for us, not only a fraternal problem, but also a human and sentimental one, and a matter of just historical reparation."[60] Infante would make the utopian dream of reconstructing al-Andalus in the present a central piece of the *andalucista* political platform. In 1931, he called on his compatriots to "restore al-Andalus in Andalucía, bringing its essential inspirations up to date."[61] This call exhibits, again, the slippage between al-Andalus and Andalucía, past and present—and between ideas and places. Infante frames *andalucismo* as the political program through which the idea of al-Andalus takes material form in the modern place of Andalucía.

In 1931, Infante also called on the newly formed Spanish Republic to delegate to Andalucía the control of the Protectorate in Morocco and to make Morocco "an autonomous state in federation with the other Andalusians, within the great Amphictyony [*Anfictionado*] of Andalucía."[62] Infante uses an obscure Hellenism, *Anfictionado,* to imagine an Andalusian federation that is united in its plurality. He thus reinforces Andalucía's association with classical Greek culture, while positing a geopolitical framework that links modern Andalucía and Morocco. Despite his territorial aspirations in Morocco, Infante insists that the *andalucista* program is not comparable to other forms of European imperialism: "It is not imperialism, such as the one that emanates from the principle of nationalities. It is a recognition and defense of brotherhood."[63] Infante's insistence that Andalusians share a bond of "brotherhood" with Moroccans draws on a constellation of family metaphors that had circulated in Spanish colonial thought since the nineteenth century.[64] In this case, Infante uses the fraternal metaphor to distance *andalucismo* from European imperialism. In fact, he goes so far as to assert that Andalucía's desire to annex northern Morocco actually responds to Moroccan desires: "The Moors, culturally directed by the Andalusian families (both Muslims and the Sephardic Hebrews), feel the yearning for a social and political expression of our brotherhood."[65] Here, as usual, the term "Moors" is ambiguous, but it appears to refer to the indigenous Berbers of North Africa, or to North Africans in the collective. Infante depicts Moroccan Andalusians as an ecumenical elite within Moroccan society, and he implies that Moroccan Andalusians will accept and endorse Spain's fraternal claims on North Africa.

Infante's attempts to parse out the ethnic and religious differences within Moroccan society point to a broader theme in his writings about Morocco, al-Andalus, and Andalucía. Throughout his work, Infante only celebrates Moroccan history and culture insofar as they can be considered subordinate categories of Andalusian history and culture. For this reason, Infante repudiates the Almoravids and the Almohads, the two Moroccan Berber dynasties who ruled al-Andalus from 1086 to 1248. Infante's contempt for the Almoravids and the Almohads goes back to his earliest writings. In *The Andalusian Ideal,* Infante remarks that the people of al-Andalus felt "an invincible repugnance toward the Moors."[66] Similarly, the play *Motamid* stages a confrontation between the "barbarous rudeness" of the Almoravids and the "delicacy and spiritual power" of al-Andalus.[67] In the play, the Andalusi characters denigrate the Almoravids as "fanatical tribes," "barbarous Africans," and "those terrifying black Moors."[68] Such virulent racism discords with Infante's present-day fame as a champion of intercultural tolerance, but it foreshadows his attempts, in the early 1930s, to reimagine Morocco as a geographic, cultural, and political extension of Andalucía. Just as Infante tries to detach Spain from Europe, so too does he try to detach Morocco from North Africa. In both cases, his political and geographic imaginaries converge on Andalucía, which he depicts as the spiritual capital of a trans-Mediterranean empire. This imperial and expansionist view of Andalucía would eventually make its way into Francoist culture.

After the Spanish Civil War, Rodolfo Gil Benumeya emerged as the standard-bearer of *andalucismo* and also as a leading theoretician of Spanish colonialism in Morocco.[69] Born Rodolfo Gil Torres, Gil Benumeya adopted a pen name that indicated his fascination with al-Andalus. His pseudonym Benumeya means, in macaronic Arabic, "son of the Umayyads," and thus illustrates his strategic use of Andalucía's Arab-Islamic past in his self-fashioning as a writer. Like many Francoist intellectuals working in the Spanish Protectorate, Gil Benumeya began his career as a regular contributor to magazines that advocated for Spain's colonial interests in Africa, such as *La Revista de la Raza* and the *Revista de tropas coloniales*. The latter publication represented the views of the Africanist military officers participating in the Rif War in the 1920s.[70] One of these officers was Francisco Franco, who cut his teeth in colonial Morocco before leading the military rebellion against the Spanish Republic in 1936. In January 1925, Franco took over as the editor of the *Revista de tropas coloniales,* and he would continue in the post until 1932. Under Franco's editorship, Gil Benumeya published articles linking *andalucismo* to Spain's colonial mission in Morocco and echoing Infante's ideas about the cultural and geographic unity between Andalucía and Morocco.

During this period, Gil Benumeya devised one of his most influential ideas: namely, the idea that Andalucía is neither of the West nor of the Orient, but rather is a propitious synthesis of the two geopolitical concepts. Gil Benumeya developed this idea in a book-length essay titled, fittingly, *Neither Orient nor Occident* (*Ni Oriente, ni Occidente,* c. 1930).[71] He dedicated the book "To the three Semitic peoples of the West [*Ponente*], who live under Spain's flag: Andalusians, the Sephardim, and Moroccans."[72] Like Infante, Gil Benumeya offers both genealogical and geographic arguments for Spain's expansion into Morocco, led by Andalucía. He calls Andalucía "a bridge between Europe and Africa, without being either Europe or Africa; a token of brotherhood between Spain and Morocco."[73] Like many other Spanish writers, Gil Benumeya claims that the Iberian Peninsula stretches "on both sides of the Strait of Gibraltar, from the Pyrenees to the Anti-Atlas."[74] This claim dates back to the mid-nineteenth century, but Gil Benumeya puts his own spin on it. Between the twin mountain ranges of the Pyrenees and the Atlas, Gil Benumeya inserts "a mountainous intermediary zone," in which are found "the old kingdom of Granada and the Spanish zone of Morocco."[75] He thus intimates an affinity between deep geological time and human history in the western Mediterranean: the Pyrenees mirror the Atlas, and the fifteenth-century kingdom of Granada mirrors the twentieth-century Spanish zone in Morocco.

Building on Infante's legacy, Gil Benumeya also worked to fuse al-Andalus, Andalucía, and Morocco in time, space, and culture. Surprisingly, Infante's influence on Gil Benumeya did not fade after the Spanish Civil War. If anything, it grew. Gil Benumeya borrows heavily from Infante in the books that he wrote about Morocco after the civil war, especially *Andalusian Morocco* (*Marruecos andaluz*, 1942) and *African Andalusianism* (*Andalucismo africano*, 1953). Infante made Morocco Andalusian; Gil Benumeya made this idea a fascist doctrine. Gil Benumeya's work also helped to codify a specific historical narrative for thinking about the transmission of Andalusi culture from fifteenth-century Granada to modern Morocco. This narrative—which I have called the "Andalus-centric" narrative of Moroccan history—would be enormously productive for both Spanish and Moroccan writers in the 1940s and 1950s.

Like Infante, Gil Benumeya was particularly enamored of the Umayyad caliphate in Cordoba. In fact, in *Andalusian Morocco*, Gil Benumeya attributes to the Umayyads the creation of Spain itself:

> The Umayyads were the creators of a concept of unity, grandness, and liberty [*unidad, grandeza y libertad*] for Spain. A more complete Peninsular patriotism than that of the Visigoths, which was based on the separation of races. Umayyadism defended the fusion of all the races, in order to make from the Visigoths, Hispano-Romans, Arabs from Arabia, Berbers of both races, etc., a single Spain. With a single type of Spaniard.[76]

The passage takes Infante's celebration of racial fusion and inserts within it a well-known Francoist motto: "Spain . . . One, grand, and free!" ("España . . . ¡Una, grande y libre!"). Gil Benumeya thus figures Umayyad Cordoba as a foreshadowing of Franco's Spain. He intensifies the comparison by signaling several parallels between the history of Umayyad al-Andalus and the history of the Spanish Protectorate in Morocco. For instance, he compares the Riffian Berbers who fought for 'Abd al-Rahman I in the eighth century to the Moroccan troops who fought for the rebel army in the Spanish Civil War.[77] While describing the military protection that 'Abd al-Rahman III gave to North African leaders in the tenth century, Gil Benumeya calls the Umayyad caliph "a sort of Cordoban high commissioner."[78] The high commissioner was the highest political office in the Spanish Protectorate in Morocco. In other words, Gil Benumeya casts the Umayyad caliphate as a precursor to Spanish colonial rule in Morocco.

Gil Benumeya shares Infante's contempt for the non-Andalusian elements of Moroccan culture, especially for the Almoravids and the Almohads, whom he depicts as the antithesis of the Umayyad ideal: "Upon the demise of the Cordoban empire, tribes and peoples from the more primitive and barbarous North African races arrived in Spain. This coarseness displeased the Andalusians."[79] According to Gil Benumeya, Morocco was unable to match the refinement of al-Andalus until it benefited from the waves of Andalusi emigrations that resulted from the Christian Reconquest of Granada in 1492 and the expulsion of the Moriscos between 1609 and 1614. He writes:

> In 1492 and in 1610, the majority of Muslims from Andalucía and Murcia went to Morocco. There, they founded neighborhoods and cities, where they faithfully preserved and reproduced all of the customs of their land of origin. Fez, Tetouan, and Rabat are the three great Andalusian capitals, the ones that are called *Hadrias* [sic] on account of their refinement and culture. They gave a Hispano-Muslim organization to the Moroccan state and government, and, to Moroccan Islam, they gave a local air that does not exist in the countries of the East because it originates on the shores of the Guadalquivir. Thanks to Fez, Tetouan, and Rabat, Morocco eventually became a living museum, where the Andalucía of the Middle Ages remains intact.[80]

Describing the migration of Andalusi culture from the Iberian Peninsula to Morocco, Gil Benumeya claims that the exiled Andalusis "conserved" and "reproduced" their lost homeland in Morocco, creating "three great Andalusian capitals": Fez, Tetouan, and Rabat. Gil Benumeya calls these cities "*Hadrias*," from the Arabic *ḥaḍariyya*, which can mean both "settled" (as opposed to nomadic) and "civilized." Thus, according to Gil Benumeya's account, the Andalusi immigrants carried the banner of civilization into a nomadic land, giving it not only "refinement and culture" but also a political structure and even a religion. Indeed, Gil Benumeya implies that Moroccan Islam, like Morocco itself, is actually Andalusian.

Religion is not the only facet of Moroccan culture that Gil Benumeya attributes to al-Andalus. He also claims that Morocco's Andalusi music is "the very same music of the Andalusian court, that which the orchestras of al-Andalus played before the Muslim sovereigns."[81] Of Moroccan architecture, he declares: "All of Morocco's old buildings, absolutely all of them, were built in the Andalusian style, and most of the time, they were made by workers of Andalusian origin."[82] For Gil Benumeya, the houses of wealthy Moroccans are "miniature Alhambras," while the houses of poor Moroccan families "are made according to traditional rules of medieval Andalusian craftsmanship" and "share the look of the houses in the towns of Andalucía."[83] Gil Benumeya's insistence that al-Andalus remains alive in Morocco appears to exemplify the anachronistic time that European colonial narratives often attribute to the "Orient" and other non-European spaces.[84] Yet, in this case, Morocco's anachronism highlights not the country's primitive alterity but rather its proximity to Spain, the colonizing power. Morocco is, for Gil Benumeya, "a living museum," where medieval Andalucía remains alive. He imagines himself and other Spanish Andalusians as the curators and docents for this museum.

Treating Morocco as part of Andalucía, Gil Benumeya includes it in the imagined territory that he calls "the Andalusian spiritual empire."[85] Like his predecessor Infante, Gil Benumeya calls on Andalusians to "reapproximate to Spanishness the descendants of Andalusians who still live throughout the Maghrib."[86] He also asserts that Spanish Andalusians are naturally suited to lead Spain's colonial projects in Morocco. On this point, he writes:

> Thus, it is understandable that the most logical works in the Protectorate zone are those that are related to *andalucismo*. Such as the renovation of arts and crafts achieved by the Granadan painter Mariano Bertuchi; the labor of renovation that the Sevillan Isidro de las Cagigas began in Tetouan and Alcázar [al-Qasr al-Kabir]; the setting in motion of the two

advanced institutes for research in Spanish and Arabic, which have been created by Tomás García Figueras, from Jerez; and the project of poetic spiritualism set into motion in Larache by the journal *Al Motamid*.[87]

Gil Benumeya places Andalusians—both past and present—at the vanguard of Spain's colonial mission. He highlights, in particular, the work of three Andalusians working in the Spanish Protectorate in the twentieth century: Mariano Bertuchi, a Granadan artist who was the director of Tetouan's School of Indigenous Arts; Tomás García Figueras, the founding director of the General Franco Institute for Hispano-Arab Studies; and Isidro de las Cagigas, the author of an early essay on *andalucismo* and, later, the Spanish consul in Tetouan.[88] The allusion to the bilingual literary magazine *Al Motamid*, founded in Larache in 1947, links Spain's cultural initiatives in Morocco to the legacy and memory of al-Muʿtamid, the eleventh-century poet-king of Seville. In later chapters, I will delve into the careers of Tomás García Figueras and Mariano Bertuchi, who played important roles in Spanish colonialism under Franco. For now, I would like to draw attention to how Gil Benumeya casts the Spanish Protectorate as both Andalusian and Andalusi: it is led by Andalusians, who revive and represent the "poetic spiritualism" of al-Andalus, embodied by al-Muʿtamid. For Gil Benumeya, Spanish colonial Morocco is where al-Andalus and Andalucía converge and become one.

While stressing the intersection of southern Spain and northern Morocco, Gil Benumeya also suggests that the Andalusi(an) heritage encompasses all of Morocco, both the Spanish zone and the French zone. In this regard, it is significant that he identifies "three great Andalusian capitals" that span the Spanish and French Protectorates in Morocco. He calls Tetouan "the stylized synthesis of all Moroccan *andalucismo*, ancient and modern," but he also emphasizes the Andalusian character of Fez and Rabat, both located in the French zone.[89] Here, again, Gil Benumeya builds on a line of argumentation that was pioneered by Blas Infante. Infante believed that the reconciliation between Andalucía and the Andalusi diaspora in Africa would give Spain a strategic advantage in its competition with France to colonize North

Africa. Reflecting on this idea in 1931, Infante wrote: "Spain is preferable to France for the natives.... Is France jealous? It does not ignore that the Andalusian families, both Muslim and Mosaic, in its African colonies nurture nostalgia for Spain through Andalucía."[90] Infante suggests that North African nostalgia for al-Andalus is Spain's trump card in the European contest for Africa.

Likewise, Gil Benumeya positions Andalucía at the center of Spain's efforts to assert itself as a world power:

> Andalucía is the indispensable instrument. Because if the Spanish bring forward to the Arabs and their Near Eastern neighbors and friends all that Spain obviously has of Europe, then it can never compete with the great world powers.... On the other hand, if it exhibits the Andalusian factor, which only Spain has, then there is no possible competition.[91]

Gil Benumeya argues for orienting Spain away from Europe and toward Andalucía. His rationale is that Spain's "Andalusian factor" (that is, its Muslim and Jewish past) is what makes Spain distinct from France and other European powers. For Gil Benumeya, a renewed focus on Andalucía responds not only to political exigencies but also to Spain's geographic destiny. Through orography (the study of mountains), Gil Benumeya fuses southern Spain with Morocco: "the South of Spain and the North of Morocco are part of a single orographic ensemble."[92] In contrast, he calls the Pyrenees "inaccesible" and muses that they convey "a command not to communicate with Europe."[93] He thus concludes that geography, human history, and political calculation all point Spain away from Europe and toward Andalucía.

This is the rhetorical point at which *andalucismo*'s cosmopolitan imperialism joins forces with its transperipheral critique. For if, as Gil Benumeya argues, Andalucía constitutes Spain's colonial trump card, then Spain's potential demise as a colonial power emanates from its most "European" region—Catalonia. In the final pages of *Andalusian Morocco*, Gil Benumeya returns to Infante's critique of Catalan nationalism, situating it within the broader program of Spanish colonialism. He defends Infante and the *andalucistas* in the following terms:

> This movement was misunderstood because its name gave the impression that it was anti-Spanish. In reality, it was a local effort to provide a counterweight to the exclusivism of some Catalans, using for that counterweight what was available [*a flor de piel*] and closest at hand—that is, Arabness [*lo árabe*]. Those Andalusian regionalists had the intention of removing from Spain everything that it had copied from encyclopedist, materialist, and skeptical Europe, bringing the entire virgin force of Morocco and Arabism to the aid of Spanish-ness.[94]

Gil Benumeya's defense of *andalucismo* and his critique of Catalan nationalism largely follow the argumentative paradigm established by Infante: Catalonia is "exclusive" and a servile copy of "materialist Europe," whereas Andalucía represents Spain's most authentic self—a self that necessarily runs through Morocco and Arabness. Here, again, a racial metaphor subtends the Andalusian claim to authenticity. Gil Benumeya says that Arab culture is, for Andalusians, "a flor de piel" (literally, "on the surface of the skin"). Finally, Gil Benumeya acknowledges his indebtedness to Infante by following the cited passage with a quotation from Infante, the one in which Infante claims that Andalusians "do not want to be, cannot be, will never be Europeans" because they are "Euro-Africans, Euro-Orientals, harmonious syntheses of men."[95] Infante's exact words were thus recycled, six years after his assassination, in defense of Franco's colonial program in Morocco and his regime's assault on Catalan nationalism.

Conclusion

Contemporary celebrations of Infante's work conveniently circumvent its influence on Francoist colonialism. On August 9, 1999, Seville's city government organized a public homage to commemorate the sixty-third anniversary of Infante's death. The event featured a keynote address by José Rodríguez de la Borbolla y Camoyán, a former president of the Junta de Andalucía. The speech was titled "In Praise of Mixing" ("Elogio del mestizaje"). In it, Rodríguez de la Borbolla y Camoyán reinvented the Infantian wheel by postulating "a new conception of identity," one based on "the truth and the goodness of mixtures."[96] Echoing Infante, he asserted that Andalucía's history of cultural and racial mixing has made the region distinct from the rest of Europe: "On our soil, diverse, unique cultures have developed and have left their footprint, making us different from other Europeans."[97] The politician concluded his speech by repeating Infante's claim that Andalusian nationalism is an "internationalist, universalist nationalism, the opposite of all those nationalisms inspired by the European principle of nationalities."[98]

Infante's ideas take on a different hue depending on the political context in which they are viewed, and the contradictory twists and turns of their afterlife are, to a certain extent, a microcosm for the malleability of al-Andalus in modern Spain. Originating as a call for regional autonomy, Infante's brand of *andalucismo* evolved into a critique of Catalan nationalism and a justification for Spanish colonialism, ideas that later fueled Francoist colonial ideology in Morocco. In the post-Franco era, Infante's ideas have resurfaced as a defense of Andalusian autonomy, grounded in the claim that Andalucía's mixed racial past makes the region exceptionally tolerant. Today, Andalusian nationalism has shed its open attack on Catalan nationalism, and it has repurposed its emphasis on racial *mestizaje* to address Andalucía's place at the frontier of African immigration to Europe.[99] But if Andalucía is to fulfill Infante's promise that it is a land where "there are no foreigners," then it cannot be foreign to its own past. The road to Andalusian tolerance might, paradoxically, run through the acknowledgment of the violence that has been committed in the name of tolerance.

In this chapter, I have highlighted the surprising transferal of Infante's ideas across the divide of the Spanish Civil War, from a Republican milieu to a fascist one. In Chapter 4, I will turn to another case of strange bedfellows: the story of the Franco regime's support for the Moroccan pilgrimage to Mecca. In both cases, my aim is to show how celebrations of Spain's Muslim past and Morocco's Andalusi heritage have bridged seemingly irreconcilable ideological divisions in Spain and Morocco.

4

FRANCO'S HAJJ

ONE EVENING IN DECEMBER 1936, the distinguished Moroccan historian and legal scholar Ahmad al-Rahuni (1878–1953) was listening to the radio while sitting at home in his garden in Tetouan, the capital of the Spanish Protectorate of Morocco.[1] At the time, al-Rahuni was at the peak of his career as a writer and public figure. Over the previous fifteen years, he had penned a diverse body of work, including a serialized newspaper account of a journey to Spain in 1930, a commentary on Arabic grammar, and a ten-volume history of his native city, *'Umdat al-rawin fi tarikh Tittawin* (*The Foundational Narrators of Tetouan's History*), today hailed as a classic of modern Moroccan historiography.[2] Meanwhile, he had assumed important leadership positions reserved for Moroccan Muslims under the Spanish Protectorate, such as chief judge in the Islamic court system from 1923 to 1934. On that evening in December 1936, al-Rahuni was listening to Radio Tetouan, when he was surprised to hear the following announcement in Arabic: "His Excellency *Generalísimo* Franco has prepared a beautiful steamship to carry the Moroccan hajj pilgrims from Ceuta to Jidda. And the aforementioned pilgrims will be under the leadership of the most erudite *Sidi* Ahmad al-Rahuni."[3] The Spanish Civil War was less than six months old, and General Francisco Franco, the leader of the military uprising against the democratically elected Spanish Republic, had taken it upon himself to organize the Moroccan hajj, the annual pilgrimage of Muslims to Mecca. After hearing the radio announcement, al-Rahuni went on to lead the Moroccan hajj sponsored by Franco, and he would write about it in his *Journey to Mecca* (*al-Rihla al-makkiyya*).

Franco is widely remembered today as a champion of Spanish Catholicism. One of the most enduring ideological legacies of Franco's fascist dictatorship (1939–1975) is what scholars now call National Catholicism (*nacionalcatolicismo*), a doctrine that espouses the political and spiritual alignment of the Spanish state with the Spanish Church.[4] Given Franco's reputation as an advocate for a militantly nationalist brand of Catholicism, it is surprising to find him sponsoring the hajj, one of the five pillars of Islam.[5] Yet Franco's hajj was part of a vast propaganda effort to represent Franco and his government as allies of Islam, not only in Morocco but also throughout the Arab world. This effort was not limited to Franco's sponsorship of the hajj, sponsorship that continued intermittently through the 1940s and 1950s.[6] Franco's outreach also included the creation of a number of institutions that were meant to bolster cultural exchange between Spain and the Arab world and to foment the academic study of al-Andalus. Among these institutions was the General Franco Institute for Hispano-Arab Research, founded in Tetouan in 1938. The General Franco Institute's publications codified the idea of "Hispano-Arab culture," which provided the cultural justification for Spanish colonialism in Morocco under Franco. Under the banner of "Hispano-Arab culture," Francoist intellectuals promoted a narrative of cultural continuity, casting modern Morocco as the legitimate heir to the culture of al-Andalus.[7]

In 1941, the General Franco Institute published al-Rahuni's *Journey to Mecca*. The text is an eloquent testament to Franco's efforts to cast himself as a friend of the Muslim world and as a defender of the legacy of al-Andalus. It is also a key text for understanding the history of Spanish colonialism in Morocco—and, in particular, the process by which Spanish colonial discourse migrated into Moroccan culture. Written by a leading Moroccan scholar and funded by the Spanish government, al-Rahuni's text has, nonetheless, been almost entirely ignored by Spanish and Moroccan scholars alike.[8] There are many reasons why al-Rahuni's

Journey to Mecca deserves critical attention in its own right. The text illuminates the surprising collaboration between Spanish fascism and the Moroccan intellectual elite. It gives insight into how an educated Moroccan viewed Spanish colonialism and, especially, the Francoist celebration of al-Andalus. It also places Hispano-Moroccan relations in a dense, transnational network that includes other colonial powers and other Muslim cultures. Any of these characteristics would justify a careful study of al-Rahuni's text. The goal of this chapter is not only, however, to recover an understudied source about a perplexing chapter in Hispano-Moroccan relations. Rather, I also hope to illuminate the scholarly practices that have made it possible to ignore or forget al-Rahuni and the journey of Moroccan pilgrims to Mecca in 1937.

Al-Rahuni's *Journey* has suffered from almost complete scholarly oblivion because it undermines the master narratives that have structured our understanding of modern Arabic literature and of European colonialism in the Arab-Islamic world. Scholars in both areas have largely taken for granted the binary distinction between Islam and the West, and between colonizer and colonized. In what follows, I will emphasize the ideological ambivalence and generic hybridity of al-Rahuni's text, which moves between pan-Islamism and colonial apology, between colonizers and colonized, and between traditional religious learning, ethnographic observation, and various modes of Arabic travel writing.

Al-Rahuni's text not only complicates our understanding of colonial relations and discourses but also exposes the conceptual assumptions that have underpinned the study of modern Arabic literature. In the conclusion, I will address al-Rahuni's vexed place within the field of modern Arabic literature, where scholars have tended to focus on Egypt, the novel, and secular epistemologies. Al-Rahuni's text speaks, instead, to the persistence of Arabic prose genres that do not fit easily under a Eurocentric notion of literature: not only hajj narratives but also biographical dictionaries, Islamic jurisprudence, and other genres that have been dismissed as "traditional."[9] In general, these genres have been ignored altogether by scholars, or they have become the exclusive province of historians and scholars of religion, who mine them for data about historical events or religious practices. Instead of treating them as vestiges of a dying literary order or as stepping-stones on the path to full-fledged modernity, I propose that we allow texts like al-Rahuni's *Journey* to point us toward other epistemic and discursive modes that coincide with and even exert force over literary forms that we have normalized as "modern."

Mecca in al-Andalus

What would Francoism sound like if it spoke Arabic and converted to Islam? Al-Rahuni's *Journey to Mecca* provides us with a tantalizing window into this hypothetical question. Yet the text eludes easy classifications of ideology, genre, and audience. Its Arabic title, *al-Rihla al-makkiyya*, signals a clear indebtedness to the Arabic *rihla* (travelogue) tradition.[10] Like al-Rahuni, the two archetypical authors of the *rihla* genre, Ibn Jubayr (d. 1217) and Ibn Battuta (d. 1368), took the pilgrimage to Mecca as the impetus for their travel narratives. Like Ibn Battuta, the medieval Arab traveler par excellence, al-Rahuni embarked on a pilgrimage to Mecca that took him far beyond Mecca. In fact, the title of al-Rahuni's text is misleading: what he writes is not merely a "journey to Mecca," but rather a journey to Spain, Libya, Egypt, Saudi Arabia, and Italy. Mecca takes center stage in al-Rahuni's narrative, but it is bookended by two separate visits to Spain, which compete with the hajj for pride of place. Al-Rahuni's text should thus be read alongside the extensive corpus of hajj narratives and also the important tradition of Arabic travel writing about Europe.[11] *Journey to Mecca* evokes both travel writing traditions but also displaces them because it subverts binary distinctions between Europe and the Muslim world, and between secular travel to Europe and religious pilgrimage to Mecca.

Beyond the thorny questions of ideology and genre, al-Rahuni's text also raises the question of audience: for what audience or audiences did al-Rahuni write? How does the text's meaning shift and adapt to the expectations of different readerships? The text espouses two key tropes of Francoist ideology vis-à-vis Morocco and the Muslim world: first, that Franco was helping to revive al-Andalus in Spain and Morocco and, second, that Franco was defending monotheistic religion against the onslaught of communism. Nevertheless, al-Rahuni parrots Francoist discourse in a language and in an epistemological framework that would have been undecipherable to a Spanish audience. He writes in Arabic at a time when few Spaniards, including those working in Morocco, could read the language.¹² Just as significantly, he peppers his text with Qur'anic language and Prophetic traditions. The text's rhetorical power thus resides in its translation of Francoist discourse into Arabic and also into an Islamic idiom. This translational movement in and out of languages and cultural codes demands what we might call a "multidirectional" hermeneutics, one that treats contradiction as productive and allows multiple meanings to run through the text without resolving them into one totalizing reading.¹³ In my translations of al-Rahuni's text, I will try to trace the Moroccan writer's movements between Francoist and Qur'anic discourses without reducing those movements to one monolithic ideological position.

It is difficult to overstate the sheer political strangeness of this moment of Hispano-Moroccan collaboration, which required both Spaniards and Moroccans to perform discursive acrobatics. Al-Rahuni's pilgrimage to Mecca coincided with the massive Spanish campaign to recruit eighty thousand Moroccan soldiers to fight in Franco's rebel army in the civil war.¹⁴ To ensure Moroccan support for the rebel cause, Franco granted unprecedented freedoms to the Moroccan nationalist movement, including the creation of an Arabic-language nationalist press and the legalization of Moroccan nationalist parties.¹⁵ The rebels also wooed the caliph, Mulay al-Hasan (r. 1925–1956), the head of the Moroccan government under the Spanish Protectorate, with vague promises of Moroccan independence in exchange for his support in the civil war.¹⁶ Despite their reliance on Muslim Moroccan soldiers, the rebels frequently referred to the Spanish Civil War as a "Crusade," a term that evokes the historical conflict between Christians and Muslims. To square this rhetorical circle, Franco audaciously transformed the meaning of the term. The Francoist crusade was an alliance of the monotheistic religions against "the godless communists," a Francoist trope for describing the Republicans that also appears in al-Rahuni's hajj narrative.¹⁷

In a similar move of symbolic inversion, al-Rahuni justified his support for Franco and his cause by casting them as part and parcel of the Muslim world. *Journey to Mecca* opens with the scene in which al-

Rahuni hears the announcement, on Radio Tetouan, of his appointment as the leader of the Moroccan delegation of pilgrims. The narrative then describes a visit that he received on the following day from Juan Beigbeder, the high commissioner of the Spanish Protectorate in Morocco and the mastermind behind the campaign to recruit Moroccan soldiers for Franco's army.[18] Al-Rahuni hails Beigbeder as "the Muslims' beloved and friend."[19] He uses similar language to describe Franco, whom he calls "the beloved of Muslims in all places."[20] Al-Rahuni's obsequiousness toward Franco is unsettling, especially when one considers that Franco launched his career in the Rif War (1921–1927), in which the Spanish army used brutal tactics, including chemical warfare, to suppress Moroccan resistance against colonialism.[21] Despite Franco's role in Spain's violent colonial occupation of Morocco and his famous Catholicism, al-Rahuni's text makes Franco appear Muslim.

The text also figures Spain as a second Mecca. Before al-Rahuni went on the hajj, Franco and Beigbeder invited him to visit Spain in order to greet wounded Moroccan soldiers from the rebel army. Al-Rahuni writes: "[Beigbeder] informed me that I was nominated first, before the trip to the hajj, to make the rounds of the Spanish hospitals and to visit the wounded Moroccans in them, to console them, and to thank them on behalf of our lord the Caliph and His Excellency the leader *Generalísimo* Franco."[22] The verbal noun that al-Rahuni uses to describe his impending visit to Spain is *al-ṭawāf,* which I have translated as "to make the rounds of," but is also the technical term to describe the ritual circumambulation of the Kaʿba during the Muslim pilgrimage to Mecca. In fact, circumambulating the Kaʿba is one of the central metaphors of al-Rahuni's narrative, where it serves to collapse the distance between Spain and Mecca. Throughout the text, al-Rahuni strategically deploys hajj terminology, such as *al-ṭawāf,* in order to cast Spain—and, in particular, the Islamic heritage sites of al-Andalus—as a metaphorical Kaʿba to which Muslims should make pilgrimage.

In al-Rahuni's description of Spain, the language of pilgrimage and the language of paradise often converge, making Spain, by turns, the Kaʿba, the heavenly paradise, and the site of bygone cultural splendor. Al-Rahuni was in Spain from January 10 to January 21, 1937. While there, his home base was Seville, a rebel stronghold during the civil war and a vibrant cultural center in eleventh- and twelfth-century al-Andalus. The Spanish authorities organized an itinerary for al-Rahuni that emphasized, in equal measures, southern Spain's Muslim past and its Francoist present. On his first full day in Seville, al-Rahuni was taken to a hospital where wounded Moroccan soldiers were receiving treatment. Of the Spanish hospital, al-Rahuni writes:

> On Monday, we began making the rounds of the hospitals. . . . We saw the excellence of their order, the fineness of their beds, the usefulness of their medicines, the kindness of their doctors, the splendor of their buildings and gardens, the delight of their restaurants (a wondrous thing!): yogurt, milk, eggs, fresh meat and also chicken, all slaughtered by a Muslim butcher. And the cook is Muslim. The nurses, *like protected eggs,* go round them *with glasses, flagons, and cups of a pure drink.*[23]

To emphasize the luxury of the Spanish hospitals, al-Rahuni quotes, without attribution, two Qur'anic descriptions of the heavenly paradise, descriptions that would be familiar to most educated Muslim readers. In my translation of the passage, I have italicized the Qur'anic citations to signal how al-Rahuni folds them into his description of the hospitals. The Moroccan traveler compares the Spanish nurses to the women of paradise, whose beauty is likened, in the Qur'an, to that of precious ostrich eggs being kept "protected" from dust and damage.[24] To intensify the comparison between the Spanish hospital and the heavenly afterlife, al-Rahuni echoes another Qur'anic image of the garden of paradise, where "everlasting youths will go round among them with glasses, flagons, and cups of a pure drink."[25] Although al-Rahuni evokes the comforts of the afterlife, his description of the hospital focuses on material matters, emphasizing its cleanliness and the Spanish attention to providing halal food for the Muslim patients. Franco's Spain, remembered today as a bastion of intransigent Catholicism, is depicted, here, as a suitable place for the earthly and spiritual needs of Muslims.

Al-Rahuni's Spanish hosts took him directly from the hospital to Seville's two most famous Andalusi monuments. First, they went to the Cathedral of Seville, whose bell tower, La Giralda, was originally the minaret of a mosque built by the Moroccan Almohad dynasty in the twelfth century. La Giralda was often deployed in Francoist culture as a sign of Hispano-Moroccan unity, and it continues to serve today as a symbol of cultural exchange between Spain and Morocco.[26] Although the building was consecrated as a church in 1248, after the Christian conquest of Seville, al-Rahuni emphasizes its Muslim identity: "Then, we went to the Mosque of Ya'qub al-Mansur the Almohad, which features a minaret that is one of three minarets in the world: the Kutubiyya in Marrakesh, the Hassan [Minaret] in Rabat, and the Mansuriyya in Seville."[27] Al-Rahuni associates La Giralda with the Almohad ruler Ya'qub al-Mansur (r. 1184–1199) and asserts its kinship with two other Almohad-era mosques in Rabat and Marrakesh. For al-Rahuni, La Giralda is not only a mosque but also, specifically, a Moroccan mosque—and one that signals Morocco's cultural proximity to al-Andalus.

Al-Rahuni's hosts led him from La Giralda to another building steeped in Andalusi lore: the nearby Alcázar, once the home of al-Mu'tamid b. 'Abbad, the eleventh-century poet-king of Seville. By the time al-Rahuni visited the Alcázar of Seville in 1937, little remained of al-Mu'tamid's original palace. The building underwent numerous transformations and restorations from the twelfth to the twentieth century—including, most famously, the construction of a Mudéjar-style palace by the Castilian rulers Alfonso XI and Pedro I in the fourteenth century. In Spanish architectural history, "Mudéjar" refers to the use of Islamicate motifs and forms in Christian settings.[28] The Mudéjar style was popular among the Christian rulers who conquered large swathes of al-Andalus from 1085 to 1492. The new Christian rulers commissioned buildings that were Islamic in style and Christian in use, and the Alcázar of Seville is one of the most famous examples. Therefore, the building that al-Rahuni visited was both a palimpsest and a house of mirrors, where origins and imitations bounced off each other in confusing combinations: it was a fourteenth-century Christian palace built in a style that was meant to evoke the Islamic structures that it supplanted and appropriated.

Whether or not al-Rahuni was familiar with the various stages in the Alcázar's historical evolution, his narration elides any reference to the building's life after the eleventh century. He writes: "Then, we made the rounds of the palace of al-Muʿtamid b. ʿAbbad, all of it from top to bottom, and we recalled those days! *Those days we deal out among people in turn!*"²⁹ For al-Rahuni, the visit to the Alcázar elicits nostalgia for al-Andalus ("We recalled those days!"), which then inspires a Qurʾanic quotation: "Those days we deal out among people in turn."³⁰ In Abdel Haleem's translation of this Qurʾanic verse, he alters the syntax of the Arabic original in order to make it more readable in English: "We deal out such days among people in turn."³¹ In my translation, I have opted to preserve the original syntax in order to highlight al-Rahuni's use of anaphora. The repetition of the phrase "those days" melds together "those days" spent in al-Andalus and "those days" cited at the beginning of the Qurʾanic verse. The Qurʾanic passage in question alludes to the Battle of Uhud (c. 625), in which the Prophet Muhammad and his followers suffered a setback at the hands of the Meccans.³² The defeat at the Battle of Uhud is often considered a test of the early Muslims' faith, and its evocation in this context suggests a parallel between the Muslims' defeat at Uhud and the loss of Muslim Seville. Al-Rahuni's allusion to the Battle of Uhud implies that the vanquished Muslims of al-Andalus will remain steadfast in their faith and will rise from the ashes of defeat, just as the Prophet Muhammad and his followers did after Uhud.

Al-Rahuni's visit to Seville thus mobilizes various layers of Spanish, Moroccan, and Islamic history, which reverberate and slip off each other. The wounded Moroccan soldiers in Franco's hospitals are reminders of the intertwined destinies of Spain and Morocco, destinies that are symbolized by the architectural hybridity of La Giralda and the Alcázar. Al-Rahuni's nostalgia for "those days" in al-Andalus evokes, in turn, the Qurʾanic representation of the struggle of the early Muslims at the Battle of Uhud. These intertextual plays obscure the lines between past and present, mosques and churches, Morocco and Spain, and Seville and Uhud. They also help to cast the wounded Moroccan soldiers as defenders of a variety of intersecting and mutually reinforcing causes: Francoism, al-Andalus, and the struggle of Muslims against nonbelievers.

After visiting Seville, al-Rahuni headed for Cordoba, the former capital of the Umayyad caliphate in al-Andalus. For modern Muslim visitors to Spain's Islamic heritage sites, the main attraction has long been the Mosque of Cordoba, which symbolizes the cultural splendor of al-Andalus.[33] Although the Mosque of Cordoba was transformed into a cathedral in the thirteenth century, al-Rahuni stresses the building's Muslim identity, as he did for La Giralda and the Alcázar in Seville:

> Then, we entered the Great Mosque of Cordoba, and with us were the *General* [*al-khanirāl*] and the entourage of notables. My companion and I prayed the midday and afternoon prayers in its prayer niche, and they looked on at us with wonder and respect for the Islamic religious rituals, and they found odd the frequency of our bending and prostrations. Then, we joined them, and we made the rounds of the whole mosque, and we entered the church that is in it and saw its precious treasures, which number in the millions. There, I had a talk with them about the possibility of reserving a section of the mosque for performing Islamic rituals. I found them to be favorably inclined to that [proposal].[34]

Al-Rahuni and his Spanish hosts "made the rounds of" the Mosque of Cordoba, as if it were the Ka'ba in Mecca. The scene of Muslims and Christians respectfully sharing the same sacred space reenacts the mythic tolerance that is often associated with al-Andalus in modern scholarship. The idea of Andalusi *convivencia* is conventionally attributed to the exiled Spanish intellectual Américo Castro (1885–1975). Nevertheless, as I have previously indicated, the myth of interfaith tolerance in al-Andalus predates Castro's work and was common to both Francoist and Republican narratives about Spain's relationship with the Muslim world.[35] Indeed, in al-Rahuni's passage about Cordoba, it is the Francoists who appear as the standard-bearers of the mythic tolerance of al-Andalus. Al-Rahuni's description of praying in the Mosque of Cordoba is particularly striking when one considers that Muslim visitors to the building today are strictly prohibited from praying, and that the Catholic Church, which administers the site, has recently come under fire for its efforts to downplay the Muslim contribution to Cordoba's history.[36] Once again, al-Rahuni's text upends our received notions about Francoism, and it also illustrates how discourses of intercultural harmony (such as *convivencia*) can be put to the service of oppressive ideologies.

Mecca at Sea

After touring hospitals and Andalusi monuments in Spain, al-Rahuni returned to Morocco, where he prepared for the pilgrimage to Mecca. In a text called *Journey to Mecca,* one would expect the hajj narrative to overshadow an account of Spain. Instead, al-Rahuni's account of Francoist Spain shapes his representation of the hajj and also his encounters with fellow Muslims on the route to Mecca. Indeed, the text culminates not with his sojourn in Islam's holiest sites but rather with his return to Seville, where Franco hosted an elaborate celebration for the Moroccan pilgrims upon their return from the hajj in April 1937. *Journey to Mecca* thus reconfigures the geography of the hajj and the parameters of the hajj narrative, inserting Spain into both. Before I analyze Franco's reception for the Moroccan pilgrims in Seville, I would like to signal two themes that connect al-Rahuni's narrative of the pilgrimage to Mecca with the two accounts of Spain that bookend it. The first is al-Rahuni's manipulation of hajj-related terms in order to blur the lines between Mecca and Franco's Spain. The second is al-Rahuni's depiction of Franco as a defender of Islam against the forces of atheism. The text thus demonstrates how the Franco-sponsored hajj helped to burnish the Spanish dictator's image in the Muslim world and to internationalize the Spanish Civil War.

When al-Rahuni returned from Spain to Morocco, a Spanish naval steamship was anchored in the port of Ceuta, waiting to transport the Moroccan pilgrims to Mecca. The ship's original name was *Dómine* ("O Lord"), but when the ship was assigned the mission of transporting the Muslim pilgrims, it was renamed *al-Maghrib al-Aqsa,* the Arabic name for Morocco.[37] After the ship arrived in Ceuta's port, throngs of Moroccans converged on the city to visit it. Al-Rahuni compares the human spectacle in Ceuta to the pilgrims' circumambulation of the Kaʿba: "The aforementioned ship arrived in Ceuta . . . and it became like the Kaʿba, to which people—men, women, and children—headed from every deep mountain pass in order to circle around it."[38] In the original

Arabic, al-Rahuni's diction bolsters the comparison between the ship and the Ka'ba. The phrase "from every deep mountain pass" (*min kull fajj 'amīq*) is used in the Qur'an to describe the massive arrival of pilgrims to the Ka'ba.[39] Al-Rahuni adopts this Qur'anic locution to describe the multitude of Moroccans who come from all over ("from every deep mountain pass") to see the Spanish ship in Ceuta's port. Moreover, the verb that he uses to describe how the Moroccans "circle around" ("*yuṭawwifūn*") the ship is the same verb that is used to describe the pilgrims' circumambulation of the Ka'ba in Mecca. Thus, al-Rahuni plays with the language of circumambulation to blur the cultural location of the hajj, pushing the site of pilgrimage toward Franco's Spain.

Al-Rahuni's comparison of the pilgrims' ship to the Ka'ba, the holiest site in Islam, bestows on the ship a sacred status. This rhetorical move sets up his description of a Republican attack on the port of Ceuta. On January 20, 1937, two Republican airplanes bombed Ceuta on a day when the caliph, Mulay al-Hasan, was scheduled to visit the pilgrims' ship. The caliph and the ship were spared in the Republican attack, but al-Rahuni interprets the bombing of the Ka'ba-like ship as an assault on Islam itself. According to al-Rahuni, the bombing not only galvanized Moroccan support for Franco's cause but also turned the entire Muslim world against the Republicans:

> This is how all of the newspapers rose against this movement . . . because it is a movement that is not only aimed at the [Spanish Protectorate] zone, in particular, but rather is aimed at Islam in general, in all places on Earth. It also happened that when this event occurred, the news flew to the entire Muslim world, and especially Egypt, Algeria, Syria, and Iraq. Muslims became furious, and they asked God Almighty to destroy every last Communist. They cried, beseeched God, and prayed the prayer of the absent [*ṣalāt al-ghā'ib*] for their brothers who had died because of this plane.[40]

Al-Rahuni both Islamizes and internationalizes the Spanish Civil War. Echoing Francoist propaganda, he casts the Republicans as "communists" who are bent on destroying Islam. He also evokes a transnational community of Muslims, who stand in solidarity with Moroccans and perform the "prayer of the absent," the prayer that is said for a dead person whose body cannot be produced. Just as Moroccans had converged on the port of Ceuta to visit the Spanish ship, the Muslim world's prayers converge on Ceuta in a communal lament. In al-Rahuni's account, the ship plays the role of the Ka'ba, around which the Muslim world revolves.

The ship transported the pilgrims along the North African coast, with stops in Melilla, Tripoli, Benghazi, and Port Said, before passing through the Suez Canal en route to the Saudi Arabian port of Jidda. Along the way, the Moroccan pilgrims spread praise for Franco and his cause. According to al-Rahuni, the ship was known, in the ports of Egypt and Saudi Arabia, as "Franco's ship," and everyone who saw it "attested that there had never been such a handsome, beautiful, and clean boat transporting hajj pilgrims."[41] In Tripoli, the Libyans praised Franco for "the excellence of his domestic and foreign policies" and said:

> This is the first time we have seen and heard of ships that transport hajj pilgrims in pure Islamic form, with all the requisite Islamic facilities, such as public mosques for prayer and for undertaking religious study, Sufi litanies [*aḥzāb*], invocations of God's name [*idhkār*], and the like. Then, they asked us about our political and economic situation, and we said that it is embodied in this ship, where the rules of our Islam are performed with complete freedom, as you can see.[42]

As the passage indicates, Franco's government outfitted the ship with a mosque in which the Moroccan pilgrims gathered to pray and study during their sea journey. In this exchange with the Libyans, al-Rahuni represents the ship as the "embodiment" of Morocco under Francoism, where Moroccans perform their religion with "complete freedom." For al-Rahuni and his Libyan interlocutors, the pilgrims' ship is not merely a mode of transport from Morocco to Saudi Arabia; it is also a symbol of the health of Moroccan Islam under Spanish colonialism.

Al-Rahuni stresses the religious unity of Moroccan Muslims living under Spanish colonialism. In particular, he asserts that Islam binds together Morocco's two main ethnic groups, Arabs and Berbers, both of which were represented on board the pilgrims' ship. On one of the first days at sea, al-Rahuni assembled the pilgrims in the ship's mosque and encouraged them to prepare for the pilgrimage by studying religious texts, especially those related to hajj rituals. He made sure that the lessons would be offered in both Arabic and Riffian Berber: "I asked the four scholars from the Rif to read from the hajj rituals [*al-manāsik*] of *al-Murshid al-Muʿin* . . . and to read Sufi litanies at midmorning and after the afternoon prayer, and for their reading to be in the two languages, Arabic and the Riffian Berber dialect, so that not a single thing escapes them."[43] Here and elsewhere in the travel narrative, al-Rahuni emphasizes that the Moroccan pilgrims are diverse in language and yet unified in their Islamic faith. Along these lines, he remarks that the other pilgrims in Mecca were amazed when they saw the unity of the Moroccan pilgrims, especially, he says:

> when they saw the blending of the Arabs and Berbers among us . . . when they saw our unity in religion and nation, and when they heard that among our Berbers there are venerable scholars, such as those present who gave lessons to their brothers, the Muslims, in Arabic first and then in Berber second, on theology, law, Prophetic traditions, Sufism, and other matters.[44]

Al-Rahuni's insistence on the religious unity of Moroccan Arabs and Berbers has a particular political resonance in 1930s Morocco. During this period, the French Protectorate came under fire for its efforts to divide Moroccans along ethnic lines and to establish separate legal systems for Arabs and Berbers.[45] Under Franco, the Spanish Protectorate worked to exploit this tension in the French zone by presenting itself as the defender of a unified Moroccan identity, under the banner of Islam. Al-Rahuni's praise of Arab-Berber unity, therefore, contains an implicit rebuke of the French Protectorate and a tacit statement of support for Spain's colonial policies.

As the leader of the Moroccan delegation of pilgrims, al-Rahuni incorporated Franco into the official discourse of the delegation when it met with Muslim leaders in Libya, Egypt, and Saudi Arabia. The most important of these meetings was the audience with King ʿAbd al-ʿAziz b. Saʿud, the founder of the modern kingdom of Saudi Arabia, who hosted the Moroccan pilgrims in Mecca on February 18, 1937. Like the Libyans, King ʿAbd al-ʿAziz wanted to hear about Moroccan life under Spanish colonialism. Al-Rahuni informed the Saudi monarch that Franco "has with our Lord the Caliph a special friendship, and he has a complete love for Muslims, in general, and for your Majesty, in particular."[46] Al-Rahuni then described the Spanish Civil War in terms that mirrored Francoist discourse. He told the Saudi king that Franco "and his supporters are turning their zeal toward combating the religionless communists. [The king] praised him greatly and hoped for his triumph over the communists, saying that communism is the ugliest trait of our time."[47] Al-Rahuni's exchange with the Saudi king demonstrates how the Moroccan pilgrims were a powerful conduit for translating and transmitting the Francoist vision of the Spanish Civil War to a far-flung Muslim and Arabic-speaking audience.

Al-Rahuni's emphasis on the "special friendship" between Franco and the caliph, Mulay al-Hasan, also points to the caliph's ambiguous position within the structure of colonial power, especially during the Francoist period. The caliph's official role was to be the sultan's representative in the Spanish zone; his authority was, in theory, tied to the sultan's authority. Despite this clear hierarchy of power, the Spanish colonial authorities, under Franco, began to surround Caliph Mulay al-Hasan with the pomp and rituals of the sultanate, such as the use of the imperial parasol in public outings and the annual celebration of the caliph's accession to the throne. Indeed, Josep Lluís Mateo Dieste has argued that the Spanish Protectorate authorities adopted these symbols as a means of representing the caliph as a second sultan, in competition with the sultan in the French zone.[48] Thus, Franco's government, while emphasizing its role as the defender of Morocco's religious and cultural unity, also sought to undermine the authority of the French Protectorate and the Moroccan sultan with the goal of casting the Spanish Protectorate zone as the legitimate center of Moroccan culture and politics.

Staging al-Andalus in Seville

On April 2, 1937, Franco hosted a lavish reception in Seville to greet the Moroccan pilgrims upon their return from Mecca. The event's elaborate staging highlighted Franco's strategic celebration of the cultural memory of al-Andalus and also his efforts to represent the civil war as a conflict between Christian-Muslim monotheism and atheist communism. Al-Rahuni's *Journey to Mecca* offers a detailed description of Franco's meeting with the pilgrims. The event in Seville was also covered by Spanish newspapers throughout the rebel-controlled territories in Spain and Morocco, with the most extensive coverage appearing in Seville's main newspaper, *ABC*.[49] In what follows, my analysis will move between al-Rahuni's narrative and the *ABC* newspaper coverage in order to give a stereophonic, multilingual account of the complex cultural encounter that took place in Seville in April 1937. I will illuminate how Franco used Morocco's Andalusi heritage as a tool of colonial propaganda, and also how al-Rahuni appropriated Francoist discourse by translating it into an Islamic idiom.

Al-Rahuni represents the Moroccans' arrival to Seville as a dizzying spectacle of sight and sound. He writes: "The ship arrived at the port of Seville. . . . And Seville came out to greet us, all without exception—men, women, children, and all of the soldiers that were there—with its music, its battalions, its *generales,* and its officers."[50] The text personifies the city of Seville, turning the crowd into a single human wave converging upon the ship. The use of the Hispanism *"khanirālāt"* (which I have translated as *"generales"*) evokes the polyphony of the scene, where Spanish and Arabic mingled with music. The *ABC* coverage also underlines the thrill and commotion of the Moroccans' arrival: "The moment when the boat docked was truly exciting. The Moors on the upper deck were saluting with their hands held high, and they were cheering Spain and General Franco with enthusiasm, while the tune of the national anthem played."[51] The Spanish newspaper paints a scene that weaves together fascist patriotism and intercultural exchange. According to this account, the Moroccans ("the Moors") greeted the Spanish crowd with their hands raised in the fascist salute. The Spanish national anthem returned the salute.

Music played an important role in the careful staging of Franco's reception for the Moroccan pilgrims. The Spanish national anthem accompanied the Moroccans' arrival at the port of Seville, but Moroccan music would soon take center stage. The Moroccans disembarked from the boat, led by the caliph's band and the grand vizier (the caliph's prime minister), and followed by the hajj pilgrims and hundreds of their relatives.[52] They then paraded through the central streets of Seville, marching to the sounds of the caliph's band, as al-Rahuni describes:

> We marched through the streets of Seville on foot. And the music was playing its heartrending sounds. They played the *qāʾim wa-naṣf* movement of *al-ʿUshshaq*, on a paved ground sprinkled with dew. The flowers were open, and their fragrance was sweet. We proceeded amongst the units of soldiers, behind whom stood the abundant crowd. . . . Each unit greeted and welcomed us, and flags fluttered from all windows and rooftops.[53]

The piece of music to which al-Rahuni alludes is the second movement from *Nubat al-ʿushshaq*, one of the eleven suites that make up the repertoire of Moroccan Andalusi music.[54] Each of the eleven suites is associated with a particular time of day and a particular state of emotion. *Nubat al-ʿushshaq* is typically performed at dawn and expresses, in the words of one Moroccan scholar, "the gushing of life, blossoming, and rejoicing."[55] The suite's lyrics describe the meeting of two lovers in a garden at dawn, surrounded by birds and blossoming flowers.[56] In al-Rahuni's description, the images of "ground sprinkled with dew" and of fragrant flowers evoke the dawn and garden imaginary found in *Nubat al-ʿushshaq*. The allusion to this particular suite also casts the event in Seville as the joyous reunion of two lovers, the Moroccans and the Spanish. Indeed, *Nubat al-ʿushshaq* is a propitious score for a scene of Hispano-Moroccan reconciliation. The suite is popularly attributed to a Christian European living in al-Andalus and thus stands as a musical testament to the cultural collaboration between Christians and Muslims in medieval Iberia.[57]

North African Andalusi music is often cast as a direct descendant of medieval al-Andalus, but it was, in fact, the object of a significant revival under Spanish and French colonial rule.⁵⁸ In the case of the Moroccan pilgrims' parade in Seville, the choice of *Nubat al-ʿushshaq* responded as much to the piece's symbolic association with dawn as it did to the material changes that Moroccan music experienced during the colonial period. Starting in the first decade of the Protectorate period, Spanish and French scholars embarked on a race to define, transcribe, and record the Moroccan Andalusi repertoire. One of the first fruits of this competition was Alexis Chottin's partial transcription and translation of *Nubat al-ʿushshaq*, published in Paris in 1931.⁵⁹ Furthermore, the *qāʾim wa-naṣf* movement, which the caliph's band performed in Seville, gained popularity in the 1930s through a European recording of the movement, in a simplified arrangement for marching bands.⁶⁰ In Chapter 6, I will return to the Andalusi music revival, which served as an arena for competition between Spain and France in Morocco. For now, I would merely like to signal that the performance of a movement from *Nubat al-ʿushshaq* in the streets of Seville in 1937 served to evoke several centuries of Spanish-Moroccan relations, from medieval al-Andalus to Spain's twentieth-century efforts to revive Moroccan Andalusi music.

In addition to music, architecture also helped to frame the Moroccans' visit to Seville as a symbolic return to al-Andalus. Franco staged the reception for the Moroccans in the Mudéjar-style Alcázar of Seville (Figure 9). The *ABC* coverage acknowledged the theatricality of the setting by calling the Alcázar "an incomparable frame for the tableau that was being prepared."⁶¹ Franco met the Moroccan pilgrims in the Alcázar's Hall of Ambassadors, decorated by Pedro I in 1366 in the style of an Islamic *qubba* (a domed square), with carved plaster, horseshoe arches, and tilework that echo the contemporaneous Hall of Ambassadors in the Alhambra.⁶²

In a gesture of strategic or unconscious anachronism, al-Rahuni associates the Alcázar with the eleventh-century figure al-Muʿtamid, despite the fourteenth-century vintage of the spaces that he and the Moroccan pilgrims visited. He writes: "We arrived, after a distance of four thousand meters, to the palace of al-Muʿtamid b. ʿAbbad, which is still a sign [*āya*] that is read after almost a thousand years, where we found His Excellency the President, the hero of Spain and her savior

Figure 9. Front page of the newspaper *ABC* (Seville edition), April 4, 1937. Reproduced with permission from DIARIO ABC, S.L., Madrid. Reproduction courtesy of the Spanish National Library, Sala de Prensa.

from communism's talons, His Excellency General Francisco Franco."⁶³ Al-Rahuni textualizes the Alcázar by calling it an *āya*, a polysemous term whose meanings include "sign," "wonder," and "miracle." *Āya* is also the technical term for a verse from the Qur'an.⁶⁴ By calling the Alcázar an *āya*, al-Rahuni associates the building with the miracle of Qur'anic language, considered inimitable in classic Islamic thought. He also makes the building legible: the Alcázar is a "sign" that allows a Moroccan visitor to read and understand al-Andalus "after almost a thousand years." Yet the tension in this passage resides in the fact that al-Rahuni's reading is also a strategic misreading: by collapsing temporal and cultural distances, al-Rahuni conflates an eleventh-century Muslim building with a fourteenth-century Christian one, and Francoist Spain with Muslim al-Andalus.

In the Alcázar, Franco delivered to the Moroccan pilgrims a speech that was reproduced in the *ABC* coverage of the event.⁶⁵ The speech emphasized two themes: first, that Franco's Spain marks the renaissance of al-Andalus and, second, that al-Andalus rivals Mecca as the center of the Muslim world. The speech relied on parallel structures to establish connections between Spain and the Muslim world across time. The first such parallel was between the pilgrimage to Mecca and the trip to Seville. Franco told the Moroccan pilgrims: "You return proudly from your Orient because you have just fulfilled the duty of every good Muslim. *There*, in contact with your Islamic brothers, you were able to see the grandeur of your people; *and here* in Seville, on Hispanic soil, you will also be able to see, in these stones and in these bricks, the work of your ancestors."⁶⁶ The syntactic parallelism between the adverbs "there" and "here" suggests a logical contiguity between the trip to Mecca and the trip to Seville. Franco thus depicts the Moroccans' contact with fellow Muslims in Mecca as the prelude to their reunion with their Muslim ancestors in Seville.

Franco's speech traces a *translatio studii* in which Andalusi culture passes from Muslims to Christians in medieval Iberia and then, in the modern era, from Spanish Christians back to the Moroccan descendants of al-Andalus. The Spanish dictator boldly asserts that "Spain and Islam have always been the peoples who understood each other best," and he argues that the special understanding between Spain and

Islam is grounded in their shared Andalusi heritage.[67] For Franco, al-Andalus embodies the Muslim world's lost grandeur: "When your ancestors passed through these places and these fields, the Muslim people had a culture, a science, a grandeur."[68] Franco evokes al-Andalus in the preterit, but he also suggests that it is poised for rebirth. Cordoba is the hinge in this narrative of rebirth; it is the place where medieval Christians learned from Muslims, and where modern-day Moroccans will, in turn, come to learn from Spaniards. Franco tells the Moroccan pilgrims: "In Cordoba, there will be a chair of Arabic studies, where we will hand over to you our books and our ancient science so that your children can study."[69] Franco thus signals Cordoba as the future capital of Andalusi culture, whose legacy is being revived by Spanish colonialism in Morocco.

Franco's performance aimed to reorient the Orient, inserting Spain in the place of Mecca. To this end, Franco juxtaposes Spain with Mecca: "*Just as today* you go to Mecca, the Orient of faith, and you purify yourselves and carry there the affirmation of your feelings and your faith; *so too tomorrow*, you, the Muslims of the world, will return to tour our places, which I hope will bloom anew and that in them you will enlighten and perfect yourselves as good Muslims."[70] The parallel structure "Just as today . . . so too tomorrow" configures the pilgrimage to Mecca as a round trip whose final destination is Spain: Muslims affirm their faith in Mecca but must "return" to Spain to find enlightenment and perfection.

Franco's attempt to conflate Mecca and al-Andalus was not lost on his Moroccan audience. In the appendix to *Journey to Mecca,* al-Rahuni furnishes a partial Arabic translation of Franco's speech. The translation does not match exactly the text reproduced in the Spanish newspaper *ABC.* In al-Rahuni's Arabic translation, Franco tells the Moroccan pilgrims that he wants "every Muslim to know that I am the Muslims' friend from the bottom of my heart, and I will prepare for them the Mosque of Cordoba and its environs so that it can be for them like a Ka'ba to which they head *from every mountain pass* for worship and learning."[71] Al-Rahuni's translation puts a Qur'anic expression related to the hajj in Franco's mouth. The Moroccan writer had previously used the same Qur'anic expression to describe the crowds of Moroccans who came "from every deep mountain pass" to circle around the pilgrims' ship in Ceuta.[72] He thus lends a Qur'anic gloss to Franco's vision of a new hajj, in which Muslims from all around the world will travel to Spain to circumambulate the Andalusi monuments, which rival the Kaʿba as sources of worship and learning. Al-Rahuni's text, therefore, registers two overlapping acts of cultural appropriation. Franco makes Moroccans Spanish and Islam Francoist. Al-Rahuni, in turn, makes Franco speak in Qur'anic idioms and locates Islam's holiest site in Cordoba.

Conclusion: Al-Rahuni in between Master Narratives

Moroccan literature has not fared well in the standard histories of modern Arabic literature. Al-Rahuni's *Journey to Mecca* exemplifies Morocco's vexed place in the dominant narrative of Arabic literary modernity. In this conclusion, I would like to explore the conceptual assumptions that underpin the study of modern Arabic literature, and to make the case for why al-Rahuni's travelogue matters—not just for the study of Spanish-Moroccan relations, but also for a deeper understanding of the intellectual and literary life of the modern Arab world.

When we attempt to define modern Arabic literature, we immediately stumble into three problematic terms: "modern," "Arabic," and "literature." Each sets off a related series of questions: What is "modernity," and are all modernities the same? What does it mean to write in "Arabic," a diglossic language with a standard register (*al-fuṣḥā*, today often called Modern Standard Arabic) and several regional dialects? What is "literature," and is it a universal category?

If one were to peruse the standard English-language reference works on Arabic literature, one could easily arrive at the conclusion that the history of modern Arabic literature is the history of how Arabs, mostly in Egypt and the Levant, learned how to write novels. That is, the history of modern Arabic literature has consolidated around a privileged geography, running from Cairo to Beirut, and a privileged literary genre, the novel. This is not the place to trace the full genealogy of this literary-historical narrative, but I will outline its broad strokes. Starting with Albert Hourani, scholars have dated the beginning of the "modern

Arab world" to the Napoleonic invasion of Egypt in 1798. This event awakened Arabs from a centuries-long decline and gave rise to an effervescent cultural movement known as the *Nahḍa* (literally, "the rising," but often translated as "the Awakening" or "the Renaissance").[73] One of the driving forces of the nineteenth-century Arab "renaissance" was a translation movement that brought European works, both technical and literary, into Arabic.[74] Through these translations, educated Arabs in Cairo and Beirut became familiar with European literary genres and began to emulate them, first by writing plays and eventually by writing novels and then free-verse poetry. Arabic literature thus becomes "modern Arabic literature" when it begins to resemble the literature produced in Europe.

In a groundbreaking recent book on Arab modernities, Tarek El-Ariss has called for scholars to challenge the teleological narrative of progress that runs from the Napoleonic invasion of Egypt to the publication of Haykal's *Zaynab* (1913), often considered the first Arabic novel.[75] El-Ariss joins a growing chorus of scholars who are debating both what "Arab (literary) modernity" is and when it begins.[76] Yet, despite these welcome interventions, I would argue that three major assumptions of the master narrative of modern Arabic literature remain operative: the centrality of Egypt, the primacy of the novel as the paradigmatic form of Arabic literary modernity, and the privileging of the secular as the ideological mode of modernity.[77] Indeed, many revisionist accounts of modern Arabic literature have unwittingly illustrated, rather than undermined, the vitality of these core assumptions.

Nowhere are the interlocking forces of Egypt, the novel, and the secular more strongly felt than in the scholarship on Moroccan literature written in Arabic. Many scholars treat Morocco as a marginal and derivative player in the story of modern Arabic literature because of the relative belatedness of the first Moroccan novel, often dated to the 1950s.[78] Recent attempts to reassess Morocco's place in the development of modern Arabic literature have focused on approximating Moroccan texts to cultural processes that were happening elsewhere—in particular, the emergence of the Arabic novel in Egypt. For that reason, scholars have sought to push back the clock on the Moroccan novel by casting earlier Moroccan texts, such as al-Tuhami al-Wazzani's

Sufi autobiography *al-Zawiya* (1942), as protonovels.[79] While I laud the renewed scholarly interest in Moroccan literature in Arabic, I worry that the incessant search for early predecessors to the Moroccan novel only serves the ambivalent goal of tying Moroccan literature to a teleological narrative whose ultimate conclusion is the Arabic-language adoption of Western literary genres.

This is where al-Rahuni's *Journey to Mecca* reenters my argument, because I believe that it furnishes us with a valuable opportunity to reassess what we study when we study modern Arabic literature. Al-Rahuni's travelogue exemplifies modern Arabic texts that challenge the current scholarly emphasis on Western literary genres and secular or rationalist epistemologies. With my reading of al-Rahuni's text, I hope to gesture toward a larger project that would entail an epistemic and methodological shift in the study of Moroccan literature—and perhaps even in the study of the literatures of the Muslim world.

First and foremost, I argue that we need to take seriously modern texts that are written from within an Islamic epistemic framework (however broadly we might construe that category) and texts that are produced by writers with a traditional religious education, such as al-Rahuni's *Journey to Mecca*. I share Talal Asad's belief that "a straightforward narrative of progress from the religious to the secular is no longer acceptable," but I do not share his optimism that scholars agree on this point—at least not within the field of Arabic studies.[80] While there has been a recent resurgence in critical attention to the representation of Islam in modern Arabic literature, this new scholarship has concerned itself almost exclusively with the representation of Islam in novels and short fiction.[81] Thus, rather than allowing religion to inform our understanding of the literary, we instead use a preconceived idea of literary form to domesticate and mediate our reading of the religious. The new scholarship on the representation of Islam in modern Arabic literature has also tended to privilege discourses that undermine institutional religious practice.[82] This emphasis is problematic in the context of modern Moroccan literature, where many of the most important figures—such as al-Rahuni and al-Wazzani—received their educations in religious institutions, such as the Qarawiyyin Mosque in Fez. To understand the poetics of this literary tradition, a familiarity with the Qur'an is at least as important as a familiarity with the evolution of the Arabic novel. Bringing the Qur'an and other Islamic sources into literary studies is not just a matter of diversifying our hermeneutic toolbox; it is also an invitation to broaden our conception of the literary, making it less provincial.

Indeed, I insert my interest in al-Rahuni's *Journey to Mecca* in the postcolonial imperative to "provincialize Europe."[83] Al-Rahuni's text not only holds the potential to revise our understanding of modern Arabic literature; it also unsettles European colonialism by making it "speak" in different languages and from different subject positions. The Moroccan writer did, indeed, spread Francoist propaganda, but he also translated European colonialism into a non-European language and into a different epistemic framework. To put this point in the boldest possible terms, we could say that *Journey to Mecca* pushes us to read the mid-century Moroccan intellectual elite as fascist and also to read Spanish fascism as Islamic. Whatever we make of these ideological paradoxes, al-Rahuni's journey charts new maps for reading the old binaries of tradition and modernity, Islam and the West.

5

THE INVENTION OF HISPANO-ARAB CULTURE

IN THIS CHAPTER, I WILL TRACE the origins and political uses of the concept of "Hispano-Arab culture," which was invented by Francoists as a discursive strategy for justifying Spanish colonialism in Morocco and for distinguishing Spanish colonialism from other European colonial enterprises, especially French colonialism in Morocco. Hispano-Arab culture was a Francoist imperialist discourse that reached backward in time and across the space of the Mediterranean. It traced the genealogical origins of Spanish colonialism back to al-Andalus. It also projected Spain's cultural influence in two geopolitical directions—southward to the Spanish Protectorate in Morocco and eastward to the eastern Mediterranean and the heartlands of the Arab and Muslim worlds.

The concept of Hispano-Arab culture was vast and multifarious, encompassing such diverse realms as interfaith relations, scholarship, literature, arts and crafts, music, and gardens. Hispano-Arab culture even became a mandatory subject in the curriculum for Spanish high schools in Morocco under Francoism.[1] In its earliest formulations, Hispano-Arab culture was a cultural ideal grounded in the myth of *convivencia*, interfaith tolerance in al-Andalus. Over the course of Francoist rule in Morocco (1936–1956), Hispano-Arabism evolved from being a cultural ideal to being a specific set of cultural and artistic practices that defined Spain and Morocco's shared Andalusi heritage. This shift, from an ideal to a set of practices, can also be thought of as the shift from Cordoba to Granada. In the historical imaginary of Hispano-Arabism, Umayyad Cordoba (755–1031) stood in for the ideal of interfaith tolerance, whereas Nasrid Granada (1237–1492)—and especially the Alhambra—stood in for the music and decorative arts that Andalusi exiles supposedly brought to Morocco after 1492. In this chapter, I will focus on the Cordoba portion of this story—that is, on the Francoist promotion of a Hispano-Arab cultural ideal that supposedly tied together interfaith life in al-Andalus and Spanish colonialism in Morocco. In Chapter 6, I will address the Granada portion of the story—that is, the people and institutions that codified and celebrated Morocco's Granadan heritage.

Hispano-Arab culture was a discourse of Spanish exceptionalism. It held that Spain's tradition of exemplary tolerance gave the Spanish colonizers an exceptional understanding for the Moroccan people. Hispano-Arab culture was implicitly, and sometimes explicitly, presented as an alternative to French colonialism. Within the domain of Spanish national politics, Hispano-Arab culture was also used to distinguish Franco's rule in Morocco from the preceding period of Republican rule, which the Francoists saw as a servile imitation of France. Through texts, institutions, and public events related to the promotion of Hispano-Arab culture, Francoist intellectuals and politicians developed a series of binary oppositions that distinguished Spanish colonialism from French colonialism. For instance, they asserted that French colonialism was driven by a desire for profit, whereas Spanish colonialism was not interested in material gain, but rather was driven by a spiritual desire to revive Hispano-Arab culture. The Francoists also argued that Spanish colonialism respected the cultural and religious unity of all Moroccans, whereas French colonialism attempted to divide Moroccans by emphasizing the ethnic distinction between Arabs and Berbers. Furthermore, they argued that the Spanish Protectorate's educational and cultural policies strengthened Islam and the Arabic language, whereas France's policies weakened them. In this same vein, they presented Spanish colonialism as a protector of Moroccan nationalism and France as a repressor of Moroccan nationalism. Finally, the

Francoists argued that Islam, Arabness, and Morocco were integral parts of Spanish history and culture, whereas they would always be alien to the French. Under Francoism, the Spanish Protectorate authorities countenanced, and even cultivated, Moroccan nationalism and pan-Arab and pan-Islamic consciousness as a strategic means of weakening France, both in Morocco and in the larger Mediterranean geopolitical sphere.

The Spanish adjective *hispano-árabe,* which will be this chapter's central concern, actually allows for two different English translations: "Hispano-Arab" (referring to *Arab* as an ethnicity) and "Hispano-Arabic" (referring to the Arabic language). The Spanish writers whose work I analyze in this chapter often conflate three distinct categories: Arab (an ethnic category), Arabic (a linguistic category), and Muslim (a religious category). The slippage between these three categories is deliberate. It allows Spanish writers and thinkers to construct malleable structures of alliance with emphases that shift between ethno-racial, linguistic, religious, and geopolitical modes of identity. Thus, "Hispano-Arab culture" might be invoked, in some contexts, to highlight the cultural affiliation between Spain and the Arab world; meanwhile, in other contexts, the same concept might be invoked to highlight the transhistorical alliance of Christianity and Islam. Therefore, a constitutive tension is built into the concept of Hispano-Arab culture: it purports to identify something that is unique and specific about Spain's relationship with Morocco, and, at the same time, that specificity is predicated on the deliberate blurring of historical, geographic, ethnic, and linguistic boundaries. Like the concept of "Orientalism," Hispano-Arab culture has no ontological stability and cannot hold up under its own weight. Nonetheless, this chapter's aim is not to expose the fallacy of Hispano-Arab culture, but rather to trace its operations within Spanish colonial culture. Hispano-Arab culture was a powerful discursive tool for asserting Spanish colonial power in Morocco and for seeking alliances between Spain and cultural elites in other Arab and Muslim contexts.

Defining Hispano-Arab Culture: Tomás García Figueras and the General Franco Institute

The adjective "Hispano-Arab(ic)" dates back to the nineteenth century, but its use was limited until the end of the Spanish Civil War.[2] The event that marked a boom in Spanish writings on Hispano-Arab culture was the foundation, in 1938, of the General Franco Institute for Hispano-Arab Research. In its prolific early years, the institute published dozens of works that emphasized the historical and cultural connections between al-Andalus, Morocco, and Francoist Spain—including Ahmad al-Rahuni's *Journey to Mecca* (1941), which I discussed in Chapter 4. The driving force behind the General Franco Institute was Tomás García Figueras (1892–1981), who collaborated on several of its early publications and became the institute's first official director in 1941.[3] In the early years of the General Franco Institute's existence, García Figueras's efforts received a boost from the enthusiastic support of Juan Beigbeder (1888–1957), the high commissioner of the Spanish Protectorate between December of 1936 and August of 1939. García Figueras, with help from Beigbeder, theorized "Hispano-Arab culture" and provided it with a historical narrative that connected al-Andalus to the Spanish Protectorate in Morocco.

Another important contributor to the General Franco Institute was Alfredo Bustani, a Lebanese Maronite who came to Tetouan in 1937 to teach Arabic at the Spanish Protectorate's Academy of Arabic and Berber. In 1938, the Academy of Arabic and Berber was transformed into the Center for Moroccan Studies, which hosted lectures on Morocco and also trained Spanish bureaucrats and military officers in Colloquial Moroccan Arabic, Classical Arabic, Riffian Berber, Moroccan geography, and other subjects tied to the advancement of Spain's colonial program in Morocco.[4] Bustani was one of the Arabic teachers at the Center for Moroccan Studies. He was also put in charge of the General Franco Institute's first project, which was to catalogue the most important Arabic manuscripts in the Spanish Protectorate zone.[5] From this project emerged the General Franco Institute's first major publication: the 1939 facsimile edition and translation of a manuscript medical treatise by the great Cordoban philosopher Ibn Rushd, known in the West as "Averroes" (d. 1198).[6] From 1939 to 1941, Bustani had a hand in several other important Arabic editions published by the General Franco Institute, such as a fifteenth-century chronicle about the conquest of Muslim Granada and two early travel narratives about Spain written by Moroccan ambassadors of Andalusi descent, al-Ghassani (seventeenth century) and al-Ghazzal (eighteenth century).[7] Bustani's Arabic editions helped to inaugurate a corpus of "Hispano-Arab" literature, stretching from medieval Cordoba to post-1492 Morocco.

Over the years of the General Franco Institute's life, from 1938 to 1956, its cast of collaborators grew to include many Spaniards and Moroccans who worked for the Spanish Protectorate, including Moroccan scholars who would later play an important role in Moroccan academic life after independence.[8] While the General Franco Institute's projects were mostly limited to the Spanish Protectorate zone, the institute's ambitions far transcended Morocco. One of the institute's earliest publications was a bilingual, Spanish-Arabic pamphlet commemorating the speeches delivered by Juan Beigbeder and the Lebanese American writer Amin al-Rihani (1876–1940) at the Center for Moroccan Studies on June 20, 1939. The event came at the tail end of al-Rihani's two-month visit to Morocco and Spain as an official guest of the Spanish Protectorate. As I will discuss later in this chapter, al-Rihani's visit to the Spanish Protectorate played an important role in the promotion of Hispano-Arab culture to an Arab and Arabic-speaking readership beyond Morocco. The visit also coincided with a boom in cultural exchange between Franco's Spain and the Arab world. During this same period, the Franco regime established the Mulay al-Hasan Institute (*Instituto "Muley el Hasan"*) in Tetouan and the Morocco House (*Bayt al-Maghrib*) in Cairo. Both institutions facilitated academic and cultural exchange between Morocco, Egypt, and Spain.[9] In the 1950s, another Francoist institution, the Hispano-Arab Institute of Culture, emerged to carry on this diplomatic outreach to the Arab world at a time when the Franco regime was isolated on the international stage.[10] Thus, the General Franco Institute, the primary organ for promoting the idea of Hispano-Arab culture, was at the forefront of a multifaceted network of Francoist cultural institutions whose mission was to solidify academic, cultural, and political ties between Spain and the Arab world.

One of the motivations for the foundation of the General Franco Institute was the need to compete with France's Institute for Advanced Moroccan Studies (*Institut des hautes études marocaines,* hereafter IHEM), founded in Rabat in 1920.[11] The flagship of French colonial research on Morocco, the IHEM helped to define the modern field of Moroccan studies through its publications and conferences. In particular, the institute's journal, *Hésperis,* shaped the field through influential scholarship on Moroccan and Andalusi history by such distinguished French Arabists as Evariste Lévi-Provençal. Edmund Burke III has argued that France's dominant position within the field of Moroccan studies bolstered France's claim that it was uniquely qualified to govern in Morocco.[12] Indeed, Burke declares that "the new field of Moroccan studies was essentially a French monopoly, with international scholars reduced to the role of observers."[13] Burke is certainly right to point out the intimate link between the production of colonial knowledge and the production of colonial power. Nevertheless, his comment about the French "monopoly" of Moroccan studies risks ignoring the important contributions that Spanish scholars made to the colonial understanding of Morocco, and also the ways in which Spanish scholars and writers, especially under Franco, tried to distance themselves from French colonial scholarship.

"Hispano-Arab culture" was one of the discursive strategies used by Francoist scholars and ideologues to distinguish themselves from French colonial scholarship on Morocco and Islam. It served as an alternative—and sometimes a tacit rebuke—to the category of the "Hispano-Moorish" (*hispano-mauresque*), which French scholars and architects used to describe Andalusi and North African architecture and decorative crafts.[14] The concept of "Hispano-Moorish" art and civilization goes back to nineteenth-century French Romantic writings about al-Andalus, but it took on new force during the French Protectorate in Morocco. The "Hispano-Moorish style" was enthusiastically adopted by Louis Hubert Lyautey, the resident-general of the French Protectorate from 1912 to 1925 and the architect of France's colonial policies in Morocco.[15] Lyautey made several trips to Spain's Islamic heritage sites, like the Mosque of Cordoba, and he encouraged French architects to adopt the "Hispano-Moorish" style as the guiding principle for major landmarks in French colonial Morocco, such as Bab Boujloud in Fez.[16] Lyautey was also a champion of the IHEM, a nursery for French colonial scholarship on "Hispano-Moorish" arts and crafts.[17]

The most important difference between the Spanish category of the "Hispano-Arab" and the French category of the "Hispano-Moorish" resided in the divergent ways in which Spanish and French colonial thinkers positioned themselves vis-à-vis these categories. The Spanish rhetorical strategy was to cast "Hispano-Arab culture" as an integral part of Spanish culture. According to this line of thought, Spain was better equipped than France to intervene in Morocco because the Spanish and the Moroccans shared a common cultural heritage. In contrast, the French never considered "Hispano-Moorish" art and design to be part of French culture; it was, instead, a sign of exotic difference. Like the Spanish, the French presented themselves as the saviors of Moroccan culture, intervening in Morocco to rescue the country from the claws of a centuries-long decline.[18] Unlike the Spanish, the French colonial preservation of Moroccan culture was predicated on policing, not blurring, the strict boundary between French and Moroccan "civilization."

In 1930s Morocco, the Spanish celebration of Morocco's "Hispano-Arab culture" would also have resonated as a critique of France's colonial policy toward Moroccan Berbers. At issue here is a long and venerable tradition of French colonial thought about the essential differences between Berbers and Arabs, beyond the obvious linguistic differences between the two groups. This tradition of thought can be traced back to nineteenth-century French ethnographic writings about Algeria, which, as Burke has noted, argued that Berber-speaking Algerians could be assimilated to French civilization by virtue of the supposedly democratic nature of their society and their superficial attachment to Islam.[19] The general premise of French colonial ethnography on the Berber-Arab divide is that Berbers are culturally, politically, and perhaps even racially closer to Europeans. Based on this premise, the French Protectorate in Morocco enacted a series of laws and policies that attempted to codify the ethnic distinction between Arabs and Berbers and to distance Berbers from Islamic and Arabic-language institutions. The most notorious episode in this story is the so-called "Berber *dahir*" (decree) of May 16, 1930, through which the French Protectorate established separate legal systems for Moroccan Berbers and Arabs. The Berber *dahir* provoked a massive backlash among Moroccans, who interpreted it as an assault on Morocco's cultural and religious unity. In the historiography on colonial Morocco, the Moroccan protests against the Berber *dahir* are often cast as a foundational event in the history of the Moroccan nationalist movement.[20] The protests against France's Berber policy soon spread from Morocco to other parts of the Muslim world, becoming a cause célèbre in the international struggle against European colonialism.

The word *Arab* in the phrase "Hispano-Arab culture" was meant to signal, to Moroccan nationalists and to pan-Arab intellectuals in other parts of the Arab world, that Spain defended the cultural and religious unity of Moroccans, under the banner of Morocco's "Arab-Islamic" identity.[21] The Franco regime pursued several other policies that bolstered its claim to be a defender of Arabic and "Arab-Islamic" culture in Morocco. Most notably, Franco, Beigbeder, and García Figueras pushed to "Arabize" (*arabizar*) Spanish schools in Morocco, making Arabic the primary language of instruction for Moroccan Muslim students and restructuring the curriculum for Spanish students in order to give more emphasis to the Arabic language (both colloquial and standard) and Moroccan geography and history.[22] The Arabization of Spanish schools in Morocco began in January of 1937, less than a year into the Spanish Civil War.[23]

At the same time, Beigbeder pursued a policy of rapprochement with the Moroccan nationalist movement, encouraging its leaders to found political parties and Arabic-language nationalist newspapers. In the first year of the Spanish Civil War, Beigbeder legalized one nationalist party, the Party of National Reform (*Hizb al-islah al-watani*), led by ʿAbd al-Khaliq al-Turris; he also financed the creation of another, the Party of Moroccan Unity (*Hizb al-wahda al-maghribiyya*), led by al-Makki al-Nasiri, a political exile from the French Protectorate zone.[24] Each party, in turn, founded its own newspaper, with Beigbeder's approval. In February of 1937, the first issue of al-Nasiri's newspaper *Moroccan Unity* (*al-Wahda al-maghribiyya*) appeared. Al-Turris and his party soon followed suit with the creation, in March of 1937, of the newspaper *Freedom* (*al-Hurriyya*).[25]

Not all of the new Moroccan newspapers created in this period were affiliated with political parties. In August of 1936, Beigbeder approached the Moroccan historian and pedagogue Muhammad Dawud with an offer of a handsome salary to be the director of a new periodical. Dawud refused Beigbeder's offer, but his close friend al-Tuhami al-Wazzani accepted it, founding the newspaper *al-Rif*, which became an important incubator for Moroccan literature and nationalist thought.[26] Notably, on November 14, 1940, *al-Rif* published, on its cover page, Muhammad Dawud's provocative article, "We Want Morocco's Independence." Its headline read: "Morocco's Lands Must Be United, and There Must Be a National Independent State in Them. All of Morocco Belongs to Us, and the Foreigners Are Guests among Us."[27] In Chapter 7, I will return to Dawud and his role in the Moroccan nationalist movement. For now, I offer this quotation as evidence of how Franco's support for the Moroccan nationalist movement might have been the victim of its own success. The Francoist patronage of the Moroccan nationalist movement, like the Francoist discourse of Hispano-Arab culture, was meant to highlight the contrast between the Spanish Protectorate and the French Protectorate. Its natural result, however, was to galvanize Moroccan calls for independence.

The best source for understanding Francoist discourse in Morocco, including the concept of Hispano-Arab culture, is the prolific oeuvre of Tomás García Figueras, the director of the General Franco Institute. In particular, García Figueras's seminal work *Morocco: Spain's Action in North Africa* (*Marruecos: La acción de España en el Norte de África*) served as a vade mecum of Francoist colonial ideology. The book was published in 1939, the last year of the Spanish Civil War. It received the Francisco Franco National Prize in 1940 and was then reissued in several editions throughout the 1940s. By the late 1940s, the book was being used as a reference work for teaching Moroccan history to Spanish high school students in Morocco.[28] In other words, García Figueras's *Morocco* both invented new ways of talking about Moroccan history and also served as a tool for transmitting those new historical narratives through the Spanish colonial education system. In this regard, it is worth noting that García Figueras was not only the director of the General Franco Institute but also in charge of the Spanish Delegation of

Education and Culture.²⁹ Thus, García Figueras contributed to the production of colonial knowledge about Morocco and also to its dissemination through the channel of the Spanish colonial education system.

García Figueras's *Morocco* is one of the first works to define "Hispano-Arab culture" and to relate it directly to Spain's colonial mission in Morocco. In the book, García Figueras traces Hispano-Arab culture back to the cultural fusion that took place in medieval Iberia:

> If nothing exists (besides the national sense) that separates the Spanish from the Arabs and Berbers of the Maghrib, there is, on the contrary, a fact of the greatest importance for humanity, which derives from the coexistence [*convivencia*] of Christian Spain and al-Andalus: *Hispano-Arab culture*. This culture is the result of the fusion, in an environment that is unique to it, of a culture elaborated by both peoples.³⁰

In this passage, García Figueras relegates the national distinction (the *sentido nacional*) between Spain and Morocco to a parenthesis, and he gives greater historical and political weight to Hispano-Arab culture. He thus suggests that Hispano-Arab culture trumps national identity. It is also important to note that García Figueras casts "Hispano-Arab culture" as a direct result of intercultural *convivencia*, a term that (as I have argued) has been associated with liberal and Republican historiographies of medieval Iberia. García Figueras not only acknowledges Spain's historical legacy of intercultural mixing but also implies that this legacy is what unites Spaniards and Moroccans in the twentieth century. In order to make this connection, he needs to perform some fancy rhetorical footwork. He agilely shifts between national categories (Spain), ethnic categories (Arab and Berber), and religious categories (Christian). These shifts allow him to connect the past and the present in two directions: he anachronistically projects the idea of Spain back onto the Middle Ages, when "Spain," as such, did not exist. He also projects the idea of al-Andalus onto the present by asserting that the cultural legacy of al-Andalus, "Hispano-Arab culture," remains alive in modern Morocco.

Throughout *Morocco*, Hispano-Arab culture serves as the lens through which García Figueras narrates Andalusi history and interprets

Spain's colonial projects in Morocco. He writes: "Spain yearns, in the future, for a free and great Moroccan people that is united to it by the bonds of the tightest brotherhood . . . a people that will collaborate with Spain in the magnificent renaissance of Hispano-Arab culture."[31] García Figueras rehearses here the familiar trope of the Hispano-Moroccan "brotherhood," but he bolsters it with a new trope—that of the "renaissance of Hispano-Arab culture." García Figueras casts the renaissance of Hispano-Arab culture as a collaboration between the Spanish and Moroccan peoples. In other words, Hispano-Arab culture, in García Figueras's view, requires the joint participation of the peoples on both sides of the Strait of Gibraltar: just as Hispano-Arab culture was the result of the *convivencia* of Christians and Muslims in al-Andalus, so too will its renaissance be the result of Spanish-Moroccan collaboration in twentieth-century Morocco.

For García Figueras, the project of Hispano-Arab culture was not limited to the Spanish Protectorate in Morocco. Instead, he inserted the Spanish colonial revival of al-Andalus within a broader program of strengthening Spain's relationship with the entire Muslim world:

> Millions of Muslims spread throughout the world, who struggle to cast off European action from their limbs, follow with enthusiastic attention the spiritual and human work that is the Spanish Protectorate in Morocco, and through it, they recognize the rebirth of that splendid cultural coexistence [*convivencia*] of both peoples in al-Andalus. . . . We Spaniards cannot forget that lesson . . . that reality of an Islamic world that returns to the spiritual empire of al-Andalus through our current action in Morocco.[32]

This passage illustrates the intersecting geographic and historical imaginaries that shape Francoist discourse in Morocco. García Figueras places the Spanish Protectorate outside the sphere of "European action"—that is, outside the sphere of European colonialism. In the same chapter, García Figueras calls Spain "a transitional country between Europe and Africa."[33] Here, Europe and Africa are understood to be both geographic and cultural locations. On account of Spain's interstitial location between them, the Spanish Protectorate embodies, in García Figueras's view, the "rebirth" of the interfaith coexistence that characterized al-Andalus. García Figueras thus performs a shift in time—placing Franco's Protectorate next to al-Andalus—and a shift in space—distancing Franco's Spain from Europe and approximating it to the Muslim world. What García Figueras dubs the "spiritual empire of al-Andalus" encompasses these intersecting temporal and spatial dimensions; it is the union of al-Andalus, Franco's Spain, and Morocco, as well as the union of the Spanish Protectorate with the greater Muslim world.

García Figueras's work helped to inaugurate the trope of "renaissance," which became one of the keywords in the Francoist lexicon in Morocco. Francoist texts, such as the publications of the General Franco Institute, often hailed the Spanish Protectorate as the "renaissance," "resurrection," or "renewal" of al-Andalus. For instance, the General Franco Institute's edition of a medical treatise by Averroes opens with an anonymous dedication that emphasizes the theme of renewal. The dedication reads: "The General Franco Institute offers Averroes's unpublished book of Generalities (*al-Kulliyyat*) to the distinguished Arab doctors and to all who admire the genius of the great philosopher and famous Andalusian doctor, as a demonstration of the affection that exists between the two races, and as proof of the renovation of the cultural bonds between the two peoples."[34] The use of the word "renovation" underlines the Francoist representation of the Spanish Protectorate as the renaissance of al-Andalus. The dedication also illustrates the trans-Mediterranean aspirations that underwrote the project of Hispano-Arab culture. It claims that the book's intended audience includes doctors from all over the Arab world. The dedication thus places the idea of *convivencia* at the heart of the Francoist project of revival. It suggests that the General Franco Institute, through the publication of works like Averroes's medical treatise, contributes to the renaissance of a historical moment in which the different "races" and "peoples" of the Mediterranean were united under the banner of Hispano-Arab culture.

The edition of Averroes's treatise features an introductory study by Alfredo Bustani, the Lebanese Maronite who taught Arabic at the Center for Moroccan Studies. Bustani dates his study December 10, 1938, and he notes that the date coincides with the anniversary of Averroes's death.[35]

Bustani thus signals a parallel between Averroes's life in twelfth-century al-Andalus and the work of the General Franco Institute in twentieth-century Tetouan. To emphasize this parallel, Bustani calls Averroes "the *caudillo* of the philosophers of Andalucía."[36] The term *caudillo* does not have a perfect equivalent in English, but it means something like "leader" or "chief," and it usually connotes a military leader. More importantly, "*el Caudillo*" was Franco's nickname. In other words, Bustani draws a comparison between Averroes, the *caudillo* of Andalusi philosophers, and Franco, the *Caudillo* of Spain. He thus situates Averroes within a cultural tradition that stretches from twelfth-century al-Andalus to Franco's Spain.

It is fitting that one of the founding gestures of Hispano-Arab culture was the publication of an edition of a medieval treatise. The Francoist revival of Hispano-Arab culture was, at its heart, a very bookish enterprise. Editions, translations, pamphlets, and academic books were among the main tools in the project of Hispano-Arab culture. In 1940, the caliph, Mulay al-Hasan, joined forces with the Spanish Protectorate to create the first "Festival of the Hispano-Arab Book" (*Fiesta del Libro Hispano-Árabe*). The following year, in 1941, the caliph issued a decree announcing that the festival would be celebrated annually on April 23. In the decree, the Caliph situates the festival within the rebirth of Hispano-Arab culture in Morocco, declaring: "The renaissance of the glorious Hispano-Arab culture is now, in our Zone, a pleasant reality, and in order to boost it adequately, new and valuable elements are coming together every day, the most distinguished elements of the Moroccan and Spanish intellectual classes."[37] The caliph's decree not only echoes the Francoist rhetoric of renaissance but also demonstrates the involvement of Moroccans in the consolidation and promotion of Hispano-Arab culture. On the same day that the caliph issued the decree, 'Abd Allah Gannun, a distinguished Moroccan scholar of Andalusi and Moroccan literature, delivered a speech in Tangier as part of the Festival of the Hispano-Arab Book.[38] In the speech, Gannun traced the historical evolution of libraries and book culture from ancient Mesopotamia to the present, placing particular emphasis on the libraries of medieval Cordoba and the medieval Maghrib. Gannun's speech did not make any specific allusions to "Hispano-Arab culture." Nonetheless, his participation in the book festival illustrates how Moroccan scholars contributed to the staging of a Spanish colonial narrative linking the Spanish Protectorate to medieval Cordoba.

The Festival of the Hispano-Arab Book was celebrated annually from 1940 until the end of the Protectorate period.[39] The centerpiece of the yearly festival was a bookfair—called the "Exhibition of the Hispano-Arab Book"—that showcased the most recent publications by the General Franco Institute and the Mulay al-Hasan Institute.[40] The festival included a symbolic exchange of books between representatives of the Spanish Protectorate and representatives of the caliph.[41] The festival was also the occasion for the awarding of two prizes for the best research on Hispano-Arab culture: the General Franco Prize, for a Spanish scholar, and the Mulay al-Hasan Prize, for a Moroccan scholar.[42] The festival focused primarily on literature and academic research, but it also included activities with a more social focus, such as the distribution of books to poor students throughout the Protectorate zone. In sum, the festival served to promote Spanish and Moroccan research on Hispano-Arab culture and to exalt the book as a material link connecting modern Morocco, Franco's Spain, and al-Andalus.

Reviving Cordoba in Tetouan: Amin al-Rihani in Morocco and Spain (1939)

The Festival of the Hispano-Arab Book was not the only public event designed to stage Hispano-Arab culture in Morocco. The Franco regime also invited prominent Arab writers and scholars to visit the Spanish Protectorate, often in conjunction with a tour of Spain's Islamic heritage sites. The most famous Arab visitor to the Spanish Protectorate was Amin al-Rihani (1876–1940), a Lebanese American poet, novelist, translator, essayist, and travel writer whose prolific oeuvre spans two languages, Arabic and English, and multiple continents. In his lifetime, al-Rihani was perhaps best known for his travel narratives about the Middle East, including several books, in Arabic and English, about the newly formed kingdom of Saudi Arabia.[43] He was also a pioneer of Arab American literature, writing the first Arab American poetry collection, *Myrtle and Myrrh* (1905), and the first Arab American novel, *The Book of Khalid*

(1911). The overarching theme that unites al-Rihani's diverse body of work is, as Waïl Hassan has argued, an attempt to bridge the East and the West.[44] Al-Rihani expressed this idea in a famous passage from his poem "A Chant of Mystics" (1921), where he wrote: "We are not of the East or the West;/ No boundaries exist in our breast:/ We are free."[45] Throughout his career, al-Rihani drew upon his bicultural and bilingual upbringing, between Lebanon and New York, in order to cast himself as a mediator and translator between Arabic and English, the Middle East and the United States—and, more broadly, between the concepts of the East and the West.

Al-Rihani was an ideal spokesman for the Francoist mission of Hispano-Arab culture, which was also predicated on the notion of bridging Europe and Africa, Christianity and Islam, Spanish and Arabic, and West and East. Al-Rihani visited Morocco and Spain in the spring of 1939 as an official guest of Juan Beigbeder, the high commissioner of the Spanish Protectorate. He went on to recount the experience in his last book *Morocco* (*al-Maghrib al-Aqsa*), written in 1939–1940 and published posthumously in Cairo in 1952.[46]

Al-Rihani arrived in the Spanish Protectorate on a small boat from Algeciras on May 9, 1939.[47] He was carrying an invitation and safe-conduct signed by Beigbeder.[48] He was accompanied by Alfredo Bustani, the Lebanese scholar and Arabic teacher, and José Aragón Cañizares, a Moroccan-born Spaniard who served as the Spanish Protectorate's adviser to the caliph. Beigbeder had dispatched Bustani and Aragón to pick up al-Rihani in Algeciras and to accompany him to the port of Ceuta and then on to Tetouan.[49] Beigbeder played host to al-Rihani in Tetouan, where the writer visited Spanish colonial institutions and met with leading Moroccan nationalists such as al-Tuhami al-Wazzani and Muhammad Dawud. After visiting Tetouan, al-Rihani embarked on a car tour of the Spanish Protectorate zone in the company of his countryman Bustani. The two made stops in Chaouen, Larache, Melilla, and many smaller towns. In June of 1939, al-Rihani and Bustani flew from Tetouan to Seville.[50] They were on their way to Burgos, Franco's capital during the Spanish Civil War. Al-Rihani interviewed Franco in Burgos, with Bustani and another Spanish translator serving as intermediaries.[51] Al-Rihani then toured Spain, including visits to Islamic heritage sites like the Great Mosque of Cordoba and the Giralda in Seville. After touring Spain, he returned to Tetouan, where he received a medal of honor from the caliph, who thanked him for "his services to Arabs, Arabism, and Morocco."[52]

Al-Rihani's visit to the Spanish Protectorate culminated with a gala event held at Tetouan's Center for Moroccan Studies on June 20, 1939. At the event, al-Rihani was named honorary director of the Center for Moroccan Studies, and he and Beigbeder delivered speeches celebrating the cultural mission of the Spanish Protectorate in Morocco. The following year, the General Franco Institute published a pamphlet—according to its cover, "as an homage to the Arab world"—that included the Spanish and Arabic texts of the two speeches, as well as photographs and a description of the event.[53] The pamphlet's anonymous prologue, perhaps written by Tomás García Figueras, hailed the event in Tetouan as "an important landmark in the rebirth of Hispano-Arab culture and friendship, guided and driven by *Generalísimo* Franco."[54] The comment echoes the familiar theme of the "rebirth of Hispano-Arab culture." This theme also animated the speeches delivered by Beigbeder and al-Rihani. The speeches and the pamphlet commemorating them illustrate how the Franco regime used the discourse of Hispano-Arab culture to legitimize Spanish colonialism and also to court the support of non-Moroccan Arabs.

The commemorative pamphlet published by the General Franco Institute is bilingual and bidirectional: the Spanish text reads from left to right, and the Arabic text reads from right to left, with the Spanish and Arabic texts meeting each other in the middle of the pamphlet (Figure 10). The pamphlet's bilingual format mirrored the bilingual staging of the event at the Center for Moroccan Studies on June 20, 1939. On that evening, Beigbeder delivered his speech dressed in a military uniform while standing below portraits of Franco and the caliph, Mulay al-Hasan.[55] Then, Alfredo Bustani read an Arabic translation of Beigbeder's speech. Next, al-Rihani, dressed in a suit and tie, stood and delivered his speech in Arabic, with Beigbeder sitting at his right elbow. Finally, another representative of the Spanish Protectorate read a Spanish translation of al-Rihani's speech. The audience, like the speeches, was mixed, featuring both Spanish and Moroccan dignitaries, including the grand vizier, Ahmad Ghanmiya.

THE INVENTION OF HISPANO-ARAB CULTURE 183

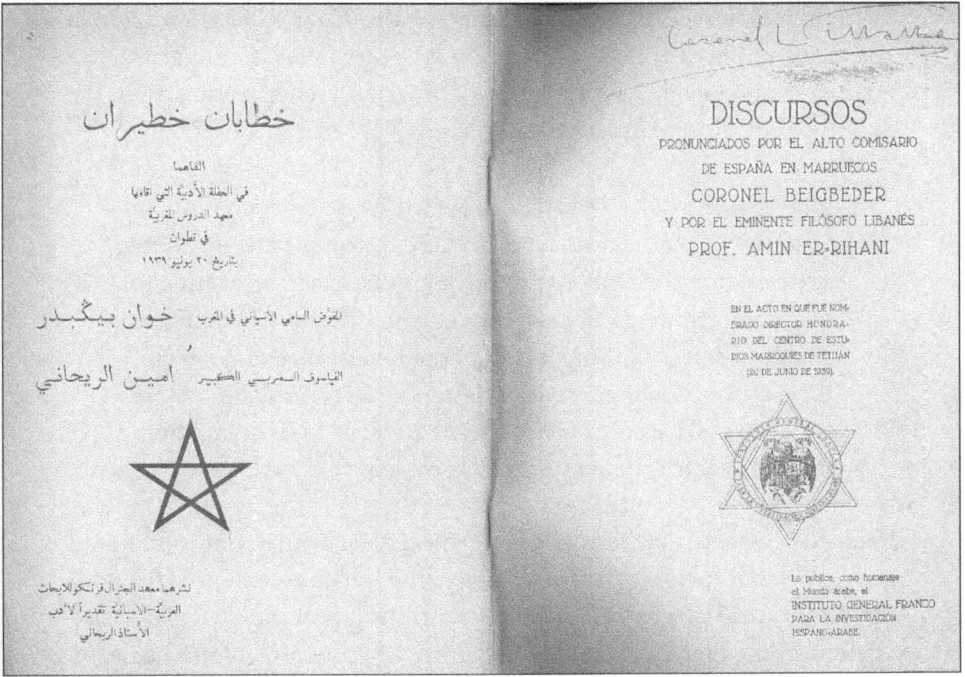

Figure 10. Spanish and Arabic covers of the pamphlet *Discursos pronunciados por el Alto Comisario de España en Marruecos Coronel Beigbeder y por el eminente filósofo libanés Prof. Amin er-Rihani,* published by the Instituto General Franco para la Investigación Hispano-Árabe (Larache: Artes Gráficas Boscá, 1940). Reproduced from the author's collection.

Beigbeder's speech cast the Spanish Protectorate as a temporal bridge between the Andalusi past and the Moroccan present and as a cultural bridge between Europe and the Muslim world. The high commissioner told the audience: "Franco's Protectorate is a sentimental, not a political, protectorate, and when it thinks about conquest, it is about the conquest of hearts. We submit to History's judgment, and now to Amin al-Rihani's testimony."[56] Beigbeder thus stresses the distinction between Spanish colonialism, which he characterizes as "sentimental," and other European colonialisms, which he calls "political." He also positions Amin al-Rihani as a witness and a guarantor to the altruistic motivations of Franco's Protectorate. That is, he uses al-Rihani's presence to lend an aura of legitimacy to his claims about Morocco.

In the next sentence, Beigbeder reiterates the distance between Spanish colonialism and other colonialisms, and he attributes the superiority of Spanish colonialism to the spirit of interfaith cooperation that the Spanish Protectorate inherited from medieval Muslim Cordoba:

> The sentimental Protectorate, which is a reflection of an imperial Spain, does not seek utilitarian conquest or primary materials or the exploitation of men or things. It aspires to something more: to the restoration of an ideal world, today in decadence. It is nothing less than the renaissance of Arab culture, of Arab feeling, of Arabic letters and of a civilization that is an integral part of Spain. We want Cordoba to rise again from its ashes, which the centuries have cooled.[57]

Beigbeder asserts that the Spanish Protectorate aspires not to material gain but rather to the revival of Cordoba, the spiritual center of Hispano-Arab culture. His use of the phrase "utilitarian conquest" is a veiled critique of the French Protectorate, which, in Francoist colonial culture, is often described as "utilitarian" or "materialist."[58] The Spanish high commissioner implies that France seeks the "exploitation" of Morocco's materials and people, while Spain seeks "the renaissance of Arab culture, of Arab feeling, of Arabic letters and of a civilization that is an integral part of Spain."[59] The statement exemplifies the conflations of time, space, ethnicity, and language that structure Francoist discourse in Morocco. In one sentence, Beigbeder oscillates between "Arab culture," grounded in ethnicity, "Arabic letters," grounded in language, and "Spain," which, in this context, is a category capacious enough to include the full run of Iberian history, from medieval Cordoba to Franco's Protectorate in Morocco. Indeed, Beigbeder's assertion "We want Cordoba to rise again from its ashes" concisely summarizes the historical imaginary of Francoist culture in Morocco. It could also serve as a motto for the Francoist project of Hispano-Arab culture, which (at least in its earliest iterations) attempted to draw a straight line between medieval Muslim Cordoba and the Spanish Protectorate in Morocco.

After calling for Cordoba "to rise from its ashes," Beigbeder jumps from the medieval period to Franco's Protectorate in Morocco. He says:

"Speaking of Arab culture, it is evident that Spain, wherever it goes, has to Arabize [*arabizar*]. It is something that we carry in our blood: culture, civilization, Arabization; for us, they are the same thing. And I am proud of having published the order radically Arabizing the education system in our happy Zone."[60] Beigbeder depicts Franco's Spain as a champion of Arab and Arabic culture in Morocco. He celebrates the Franco regime's "Arabization" of the Spanish school system in Morocco, and he ties it to deeper forces in Spanish history and culture—forces that run as deep as blood. His views on the Arabic language thus converge with the idea, frequently expressed in Spanish colonial texts, that Spaniards and Moroccans are racial "brothers." Beigbeder suggests that the Spanish drive to "Arabize" is a natural emanation of the shared racial heritage that binds Spain and Morocco.

In his speech, Beigbeder also claims that the Arabic language helped to draw Moroccan soldiers to Franco's cause in the Spanish Civil War. On this point, he says: "We must speak of our victory in this official act: We live in the enthusiasm of the Hispano-Arabic victory. We still hear the triumphal cries in two languages: it is a bilingual victory. And it is my duty to pay homage to the incomparable Moroccan soldier, the Spaniard's worthy brother."[61] Beigbeder calls the Spanish Civil War the "Hispano-Arabic victory" (*la victoria hispano-árabe*) because of the massive participation of Moroccan soldiers in Franco's army. He suggests that Moroccans and Francoists are united in a linguistic marriage, an intermingling of Spanish and Arabic, whose fruit was the "bilingual victory" in the Spanish Civil War. The bilingual staging of the event at the Center for Moroccan Studies, with speeches read back and forth in Spanish and Arabic, mirrors the bilingualism that, according to Beigbeder, fueled Franco's triumph in the civil war.

Beigbeder's attempt to draw a line between the Arabic language and the civil war sidesteps the important fact that most of the Moroccan soldiers in Franco's army came from the Berber-speaking Rif region.[62] It seems unlikely to me that Beigbeder, a longtime veteran of colonial Morocco, would be unaware of the linguistic diversity of the Spanish Protectorate zone. Instead, I interpret his comments as part of the broader effort by Spanish colonialists to distance themselves from France's colonial program of dividing Arabs and Berbers. The Spanish colonial category of the Hispano-Arab(ic) derives its force from its strategic ability to align and conflate diverse and heterogeneous elements of Mediterranean history and culture.

Indeed, Beigbeder's speech jumps from century to century, connecting Francoism and the Spanish Protectorate to earlier episodes in Spanish-Moroccan relations. He says: "What a marvelous instinct made the inhabitants of this happy Zone see that the path to well-being was in Franco's wake! Their intuition led them to fight against those people who had stolen the Arabic manuscripts of the Escorial, a national treasure."[63] The meaning of this comment might be obscure for a twenty-first-century reader, but it would have been clear for an educated Moroccan audience, especially one in the Spanish Protectorate. Beigbeder alludes to an infamous incident in Spanish-Moroccan relations: in 1612, Spanish ships sailing near the Moroccan port of Salé captured a ship that was transporting the private library of the Moroccan sultan, Mulay Zaydan, a library that consisted of three or four thousand richly illustrated volumes covering diverse topics such as Qur'anic exegesis, medicine, and philosophy. The sultan's library was confiscated and eventually taken to the Escorial, a royal palace and monastery complex outside of Madrid. The confiscated books became the nucleus of the Arabic collection at the Escorial's library, one of the largest Arabic collections in early modern Europe. About half the sultan's books were lost in a fire that ravaged the Escorial in 1671; the rest still belong to the Escorial today.[64] Not surprisingly, the confiscation of the sultan's library rankled Moroccans, especially since the library contained religious books, such as copies of the Qur'an, which could be defiled by Christians. The recovery of the Moroccan sultan's library thus became a matter of both national and religious importance. There were several unsuccessful Moroccan attempts to recover the confiscated books in the seventeenth and eighteenth centuries.[65]

The story of Mulay Zaydan's books is well known to Moroccans and to scholars interested in the history of Arabic studies in Spain. What is striking about Beigbeder's allusion to the story is that he seems to adopt the Moroccan perspective regarding it. By calling the Escorial's Arabic collection a Moroccan "national treasure," Beigbeder implicitly questions Spain's claim to it. Moreover, he associates the Republicans with the seventeenth-century confiscation of Mulay Zaydan's library. He says that the Moroccans' intuition "led them to fight against those people who had stolen the Arabic manuscripts of the Escorial." In other words, Beigbeder implies that the Republicans are the descendants of the Spaniards who stole the Moroccan sultan's books. Beigbeder thus acknowledges a contentious episode in Spanish-Moroccan relations but manages to pin it on the Spanish Republic. He argues that Franco's Protectorate in Morocco is a rejection of the Spain that plunders Morocco's cultural heritage and a return to the Spain in which Arabic culture flourishes.

Beigbeder's attempt to unite Francoists and Moroccans under the banner of the Arabic language is connected to a broader vision of pan-Mediterranean harmony. Returning to the theme of the rebirth of Muslim Cordoba, he says:

> Not only would we like the resurrection of Cordoba, and for Arabic to become again a language of world culture; we also dream of the reconciliation and compenetration of Latin and Arab cultures, and in the harmony of Islam and Christianity. The Arab people were the most tolerant of peoples, and there was tolerance and understanding when the Mediterranean was ruled in Arabic.[66]

This passage exemplifies the Francoist rhetorical strategy of conflating the Arabic language, Arabs, and Islam. According to Beigbeder, Arabic is the language not only of medieval Cordoba but also of "tolerance and understanding" in the Mediterranean. In other words, Arabic is, for Beigbeder, the language of *convivencia*. Beigbeder envisions a modern Mediterranean world fashioned in Cordoba's image, one that is guided by the reconciliation of two major religions, Islam and Christianity, and of two major cultures, Latinate and Arabic. Fueling his vision is a chronotopic imaginary that fuses, in space and time, medieval Cordoba and Franco's Protectorate in Morocco. Beigbeder's celebration of Hispano-Arab culture thus relies on strategic anachronism and also on the idea that the Andalusi heritage makes Spain and Morocco exceptional sites of intercultural and interfaith understanding.

Following Beigbeder, Amin al-Rihani delivered a speech that also emphasized the "renaissance" of Hispano-Arab culture and the importance of uniting the different cultures of the Mediterranean. Al-Rihani's speech is, to the best of my knowledge, the first Arabic text to refer to the idea of "Hispano-Arab culture." The writer opened his speech by greeting the crowd "in the name of the new Arabism and the New Spain; or rather, in the two names of the Spanish and Arab renaissances."[67] With this salutation, al-Rihani echoes the trope of renaissance, which abounds in Francoist accounts of the Spanish Protectorate. In an elegant flourish, al-Rihani's greeting uses the grammatical dual form, which the Arabic language reserves for pairs. A literal translation of al-Rihani's opening would be: "I greet you in the *two names* of the new Arabism and the New Spain; or rather, in the *two names* of the *two renaissances,* Spanish and Arab."[68] This translation, while awkward in English, gives a sense of the emphasis that al-Rihani places on the pairing of Franco's Spain and the Arab world. He suggests that the two places are united in simultaneous and interrelated processes of renaissance. He even refers to Franco's Spain as "the New Spain," a phrase that he borrows from Francoist propaganda.[69]

Al-Rihani casts Spain and Morocco as historical bridges between East and West. He outlines, for his audience, the role that Arabs played in translating Greek culture and transmitting it to Europe. He then situates al-Andalus and Morocco at the center of that process of cultural translation: "Yes, we (and I don't mean to boast) had the greatest influence in spreading that culture in the East and the West, and both the Maghrib and al-Andalus had an ample share in those glorious deeds, whose memory still blossoms in the gardens of history, and whose fragrance is diffused in scientific, philosophical, and literary works, both manuscripts and printed books."[70] Al-Rihani celebrates the Maghrib's contribution to al-Andalus and to the transmission of classical Greek culture. This comment is curious, since it stands in sharp contradiction with some of the views that al-Rihani expresses in his travel narrative *Morocco,* where he downplays the influence that North African Berbers had on the culture of al-Andalus, as I will later show. In the speech in Tetouan, however, al-Rihani treats the Maghrib as an important node in a multilingual trans-Mediterranean network that links different periods of cultural splendor.

After giving a nod to the "manuscripts and printed books" of al-Andalus, al-Rihani jumps over several centuries and lands on the General Franco Institute's efforts to publish Arabic manuscripts in twentieth-century Morocco. The writer says: "Indeed, you, in Spain and Morocco, have treasures of those manuscripts, and you've taken up the task of gathering them and publishing the most precious of them so that they might be a source of inspiration and energy in erecting the edifice of the new Hispano-Arab cultural renaissance."[71] Like the promoters of the Festival of the Hispano-Arab Book, al-Rihani sees Arabic books and manuscripts as a link between al-Andalus and the Spanish Protectorate in Morocco. He resorts to an architectural metaphor to describe the relationship between books and the revival of Hispano-Arab culture: "erecting the edifice of the new Hispano-Arab cultural renaissance [*tashyīd ṣurūḥ al-nahḍa al-thaqāfiyya al-jadīda al-'arabiyya al-isbāniyya*]." In this architectural metaphor, the building blocks of the "edifice" of Hispano-Arab culture are the Andalusi Arabic manuscripts being published in the Spanish Protectorate.

The "edifice" of Hispano-Arab culture was a metaphor on the verge of becoming a physical reality. Al-Rihani told his audience that Franco was planning to build a monumental library for Arabic manuscripts in southern Spain:

> The *Generalísimo*, on the day that I had the honor of meeting him and talking with him, said that he had made up his mind to found, in one of the capitals of al-Andalus, an Arabic library in which he would gather together all of the Arabic manuscripts so that that library would be a stopping place for scholars, historians, and all Spaniards and Arabs devoted to learning and literature.[72]

In Chapter 4, I described how Franco encouraged Moroccan hajj pilgrims to think of Cordoba as a second Mecca to which Muslims should make pilgrimage. Al-Rihani's speech offers a secular version of this pilgrimage motif. According to al-Rihani, Franco had promised to found an Arabic library that would be "a stopping place" (*mahaṭṭ*) for Arab and Spanish scholars interested in Hispano-Arab culture. Franco never made good on this promise. Instead, he helped build a virtual "library" of Hispano-Arab culture through the publications and activities of the General Franco Institute.

In his speech, al-Rihani acknowledges the imminent publication of the General Franco Institute's first book, the edition of Averroes's *Kitab al-kulliyyat,* published in the summer of 1939. Al-Rihani calls the edition the "first fruits" of Franco and Beigbeder's "glorious cultural work" in Morocco.[73] Al-Rihani was not only an admirer of the General Franco Institute; he was also a witness to its creation. His guide in Morocco was Alfredo Bustani, who wrote the prologue and the indexes for the General Franco Institute's edition of Averroes's medical treatise. While in Morocco, al-Rihani also met Tomás García Figueras, the director of the General Franco Institute, and Cristóbal Pérez Vera, who collaborated with Bustani on the edition of Averroes's medical treatise, translating the work into Spanish. Al-Rihani accompanied García Figueras and Pérez Vera on a visit to a saint's mausoleum near Larache.[74] Of García Figueras, al-Rihani wrote: "Señor Tomás García is the Spanish writer and man of letters whose research and writings are specialized in Andalusi Arabic works. He is a member of the Franco Institute, founded to publish Arabic manuscripts in Spain in order to renew Arabic culture and to pave the way for loving relations between the two nations."[75] Al-Rihani describes the General Franco Institute as a project that would inspire cultural renewal in Morocco and cultural exchange between Spain and the Arab world, which the Lebanese American writer calls "two nations." His concept of nationhood thus encompasses both nation-states, like Spain, and an expansive pan-Arab nation based on a shared ethno-cultural tradition. Al-Rihani uses the dual form "the two nations" (*al-ummatayn*) to emphasize the pairing of the Spanish nation and the Arab nation, joint partners in the renaissance of Hispano-Arab culture.

Al-Rihani's collaboration with the General Franco Institute did not end when he left Morocco. In 1940, after returning to Lebanon, al-Rihani wrote a review, in Arabic, of the General Franco Institute's edition of Averroes's medical treatise. In the review, al-Rihani celebrates the new book and says that it will soon be followed by others: "This book will be followed by other treasures of Arabic manuscripts found in Spain. General Franco referred to those manuscripts with joyful pride and enthusiasm on the day when I had the honor of visiting him in

Burgos last spring. He said to me that he was determined to publish more of them so that they would be the foundation of the new Hispano-Arab cultural renaissance."[76] Relying again on architectural language, al-Rihani describes the General Franco Institute's publications as a "foundation" for Morocco's cultural renaissance under Franco. His review depicts Franco as an enthusiastic defender of Spain's Arabic literary heritage and as an advocate for exchange between Spain and the Arab world.

The review also implies, however, that the edition of Averroes's treatise might have failed as a symbolic offering from Spain to the Arab world. Al-Rihani criticizes the editors' mistranslation of certain botanical terms.[77] He also complains that the facsimile edition of the text is difficult to read because the manuscript is written in a script that is unfamiliar to Arabs from the Mashriq, the eastern part of the Arab world.[78] Based on al-Rihani's review, it appears that the General Franco Institute's first book failed to reach its intended audience beyond Morocco and Spain. The project's failure opened up a space for al-Rihani to step into the role of cultural intermediary.

Al-Rihani believed he could succeed where the Francoists had failed; he could successfully bridge the Spanish Protectorate and the Arab East. At the end of the speech that al-Rihani delivered in Tetouan in June of 1939, he promised the audience that he would write a book bearing witness to what he had learned about the Spanish Protectorate in Morocco: "I will write about this fortunate Moroccan Arab zone a book (God willing) that will contain between its covers the truth, just as I learned it through eye-witnessing, listening, and studying."[79] In announcing his intention to write a book about Spanish colonial Morocco, al-Rihani accepted the role that Beigbeder had designated for him: that of the Arab witness whose testimony would lend legitimacy to Francoism's mission in Morocco. Like the nineteenth-century Spanish traveler Alarcón, al-Rihani emphasizes his status as an eyewitness, promising to use his own observations as the basis for his book on Morocco. Al-Rihani's claim must be tempered by the same caveat that I mentioned in my analysis of Alarcón's *Diary*: the eye only sees what it has been taught to see. In the next section, I will show how the Francoist discourse of Hispano-Arab culture served as the lens through which al-Rihani saw Morocco.

Al-Rihani's travel narrative *Morocco* translated the concept of Hispano-Arab culture into Arabic and propagated, to a broad Arab readership, the idea that Franco's aim was to resurrect al-Andalus in Morocco.

Translating Hispano-Arab Culture: Amin al-Rihani's *Morocco* (c. 1940)

Throughout *Morocco,* Amin al-Rihani stresses his role as a cultural translator—not only between the Arab world and the West but also between Morocco and the other parts of the Arab world. Indeed, the text highlights the contrast between the two large geographic units into which the Arab world is often divided: the Maghrib, the western part of the Arab world, and the Mashriq, the eastern part of the Arab world. During al-Rihani's lifetime, intellectuals from the Mashriq had very little information about life on the western edge of the Arab world. Al-Rihani acknowledges this deficit of knowledge in his book:

> The Arabs of the Mashriq are truly ignorant about what is going on in Morocco, and especially about what is going on in this zone [i.e., the Spanish Protectorate zone]. . . . Our ignorance in Syria, for example, or in Iraq and the Arabian Peninsula, concerning Morocco's affairs is greater than the Moroccans' ignorance regarding our affairs. There are no commercial or literary relations between us and them, except on the most abstract level.[80]

In the same passage, al-Rihani notes that some Moroccans have begun to study abroad in the Mashriq and to read Arabic newspapers from the Mashriq, but he claims that there is no reciprocal interest from the Mashriq toward Morocco.[81] Al-Rihani was not the first Mashriqi Arab to visit modern Morocco, but his *Morocco* is one of the only Arabic sources from the Mashriq to discuss the history, politics, culture, and geography of the Spanish Protectorate in Morocco. It thus played an important role in transmitting information about Francoism and Spanish colonialism to an Arabic readership at the eastern reaches of the Mediterranean.

Al-Rihani's account of the Spanish Protectorate shows the fingerprints of the Francoist officials who hosted him. It echoes several ideas that were integral to the Spanish colonial project—most notably, the idea that Hispano-Arab culture facilitates a special understanding between Spain and Morocco and makes Spain an ideal country to rule Morocco. Like the Francoists, al-Rihani associates Hispano-Arab culture with the legacy of al-Andalus—and, in particular, with the myth of interfaith coexistence in Muslim Cordoba. He also represents Franco and his supporters in Morocco as the champions of Hispano-Arab culture. Furthermore, he asserts that Spanish colonialism is superior to French colonialism, and he claims that Spain, unlike France, aims to protect and bolster Morocco's Arab identity. Finally, he expresses his fascination with Spanish colonial architecture, which he casts as the material embodiment of Hispano-Arab culture. In other words, al-Rihani suggests that the Spanish are, quite literally, rebuilding al-Andalus in twentieth-century Morocco.

In the prologue to *Morocco*, al-Rihani explains that he went to Morocco to understand the enigma of why so many Moroccan soldiers fought in Franco's army during the Spanish Civil War.[82] He then establishes a tacit connection between the Moroccan participation in the civil war and the memory of al-Andalus, stating that he went "to Morocco, which mobilized for Franco one hundred sixty thousand of its stouthearted sons; to Morocco, where today there is a Spanish resident-general who was born in Cartagena, in the province of Murcia, the birthplace of our Sufi poet Ibn 'Arabi."[83] This is al-Rihani's first mention of Beigbeder, whom he calls the "resident-general" (*al-muqīm al-'āmm*), following the Arabic terminology for the leader of the French zone. Al-Rihani identifies Beigbeder by the birthplace that he shares with Ibn 'Arabi (d. 1240), the most important mystic of al-Andalus.[84]

Al-Rihani thus foreshadows a rhetorical strategy that he will pursue throughout *Morocco*: He casts Beigbeder and the other Francoists not only as the descendants of al-Andalus but also as the actors who are carrying the cultural legacy of al-Andalus into the present. In Chapter 4, I showed how the Moroccan hajj pilgrim Ahmad al-Rahuni depicted Franco as a protector of Spain's Muslim heritage. In contrast, Amin al-Rihani, a Christian Arab, focuses less on the Muslim heritage of al-Andalus and more on a cultural ideal, which he describes using a phrase that he borrows from the Francoist lexicon: "Hispano-Arab culture." For al-Rihani, Hispano-Arab culture is a legacy that ties together Spain and Morocco and also connects them to the Arab heartland in the East.

Al-Rihani casts Beigbeder as the maximum representative of Hispano-Arab culture. In a chapter devoted to the high commissioner, al-Rihani reflects on what he had heard about him before traveling to Morocco:

> Back when Morocco was like a question mark in my mind, it was said to me that in Morocco there was a nationalist, cultural, civilizational, and political renaissance, which was being encouraged and supported by a foreign ruler who loved the people of the country, the Moroccan Arabs, with a sincere love and protected their interests with a fraternal, "Arab" zeal.[85]

In this passage, al-Rihani echoes the claim—often repeated by Spanish colonial texts—that Spanish colonialism inspired a "renaissance" in Morocco. By referring to the Moroccan people as "the Moroccan Arabs," al-Rihani introduces another thematic thread that runs through his text: namely, his efforts to downplay Morocco's ethnic and linguistic diversity and to attribute an Arab identity to all Moroccans, be they Arab or Berber. Elsewhere, al-Rihani argues that "Berberism" (*al-barbariyya*) is a colonial invention whose purpose is to sow division among Moroccans.[86] Perhaps it is not surprising that al-Rihani, an Arab nationalist, would try to paper over ethnic divisions within Moroccan society. It is striking, however, that he confers an Arab identity on Beigbeder, who (in al-Rihani's words) protects Moroccan interests "with a fraternal, 'Arab' zeal."[87]

Al-Rihani proposes that Beigbeder loves Arabs because he is descended from them: "I do not doubt that this love was hidden in his heart and that it descended to him from ancestors of pure Arab stock. . . . And how could it be otherwise, since Murcia was the territory where Arabs remained after the king of Castile snatched it from them in the second half of the thirteenth century?"[88] Al-Rihani traces Beigbeder's family history back to the Muslims who remained in the region of Murcia after the Christian Reconquest. To bolster this (unfounded) genealogy, he offers a spurious Arabic etymology for Beigbeder's surname: "Ibn Badr."[89] He also reiterates the observation that Beigbeder and the Andalusi mystic Ibn 'Arabi come from the same place.[90] These rhetorical moves serve to portray Beigbeder as a descendant of al-Andalus, and to imply that Beigbeder, as a descendant of al-Andalus, is particularly well positioned to contribute to Morocco's cultural renaissance.

Al-Rihani asserts that Beigbeder's mission in Morocco is nothing short of the revival of Hispano-Arab culture, embodied by Umayyad Cordoba. He writes: "It seemed to me that Coronel Beigbeder was crazy with his love and devotion for the Arabs, and with his desire to renew Hispano-Arab culture [*al-thaqāfa al-'arabiyya al-isbāniyya*] and to invigorate it in Morocco. He even wanted to resurrect Cordoba in Tetouan and to bring back the glory of the ancient Arabs for the benefit of their sons and heirs."[91] Al-Rihani asserts that Beigbeder wants "to resurrect Cordoba in Tetouan," thus echoing a claim that Beigbeder himself made several times. Al-Rihani implies that Beigbeder wants to revive the glories of medieval Cordoba and to transmit them to twentieth-century Moroccans, whom he calls the "sons and heirs" of the Arabs in al-Andalus. His statement mimics the rhetoric of revival and genealogy that underpinned the project of Hispano-Arab culture.

The Francoists who hosted al-Rihani in Morocco tried to impress upon him that their desire to revive Hispano-Arab culture trumped their pursuit of profit. In this vein, Beigbeder told al-Rihani, in one of their meetings, "Spain does not want to profit from Morocco."[92] In another passage, al-Rihani indicates that he was convinced of Beigbeder's sincerity, observing that the Spanish high commissioner "feels for Morocco and its people a sincere love that is not disfigured by benefit or tarnished by interest."[93] The "disinterested" nature of Spanish colonialism was a common theme in al-Rihani's conversations with Spanish officials in Morocco. At a ball held at a hotel in Tetouan, al-Rihani met a Spanish colonial bureaucrat, who told him:

> Spain's policy differs from the policies of all of the other European states because it is a policy of conviction, not a policy of

interest.... We are imperialists, not colonialists. We want to bring the past back to life and dress it up in new clothing, which is neither religious nor colonialist. We want to found a new Spanish state built on Hispano-Arab culture, even if we end up incurring a loss in it.[94]

The bureaucrat claims that Spanish colonialism is exceptional because it rests on a cultural ideal rather than on the pursuit of profit. He also says that Franco's Spain is creating a "new Spanish state built on Hispano-Arab culture." The bureaucrat's comments evoke García Figueras's notion of the "spiritual empire of al-Andalus," built on cultural ideals rather than on material gain. Indeed, the bureaucrat goes so far as to assert that Spain will promote the revival of Hispano-Arab culture, even if it loses money in the process.

At the same ball, al-Rihani struck up a conversation with a Spanish doctor, who asserted that Spain's Andalusi heritage makes the country uniquely well suited to collaborate with the Muslim world. The doctor had spent the majority of his life in the French Protectorate zone, where he had taken care of many Moroccan sultans.[95] The doctor explained to al-Rihani that the French and the Moroccans have trouble understanding each other, whereas the Spanish and the Moroccans share a special, fraternal understanding:

> We are brothers and relatives: brothers in a single country and relatives in Hispano-Arab culture. We need to stick together and help each other in creating a civilization[96] that brings together the Crescent and the Cross. We are the only ones in Europe who grasp the importance of Islam, and who work to strengthen it so that it can walk side by side with New Spain's grandeur.[97]

The Spanish doctor stresses the family ties between Spaniards and Moroccans, attributing them to a common "Hispano-Arab culture." Like other Spanish colonial apologists, the doctor argues that the "Hispano-Arab" cultural legacy gives Spain a unique rapport with the Muslim world. The doctor's comments slip between ethno-cultural categories and religious categories, as when he suggests that the promotion of Hispano-Arab culture goes hand in hand with the peaceful coexistence of "the Crescent and the Cross," Islam and Christianity.

Interfaith tolerance is also the cornerstone of Hispano-Arab culture for Beigbeder. The high commissioner strove to persuade al-Rihani that the coexistence of Spanish Christians and Moroccan Muslims in the Spanish Protectorate was a mirror of the mythic *convivencia* of Christians and Muslims in al-Andalus. To illustrate this point, Beigbeder took al-Rihani to visit a Spanish hospital in Tetouan. As al-Rihani tells the story, Beigbeder brought him to the hospital and said:

> It is for Muslims and Christians alike, and free for all. It has something that you won't find in all of the other hospitals of the world. Perhaps others build bigger or more beautiful hospitals for the subjects in their colonies or in the countries that are under their Protectorate.... But in this hospital—and I am proud of this fact—the church was built next to the mosque, in one building, under one roof.[98]

Beigbeder points to the hospital as evidence of what makes Spanish colonialism different from other European colonial enterprises. In this scene, the hospital symbolizes the brotherhood between Christianity and Islam, Spain and Morocco. Beigbeder stresses this point to al-Rihani, saying: "Christianity and Islam are two full brothers [*shaqīqān*] whom tolerance and love bring together in this hospital, and in this zone."[99] Beigbeder calls Christianity and Islam *shaqīqān*, two brothers who share the same mother and father. He thus adds to the diverse constellation of family metaphors used to describe Spain's relationship with Morocco and Islam. In Beigbeder's hospital, the church and the mosque live side by side, just as Spaniards and Moroccans coexist in the Protectorate, and just as Muslims and Christians coexisted in al-Andalus.

This message was reaffirmed when al-Rihani traveled to Spain to interview General Franco in June of 1939. The meeting with Franco took place in Burgos, the capital of Franco's government during the Spanish Civil War.[100] In Burgos, al-Rihani was accompanied by his hosts and guides from Morocco: Alfredo Bustani and Emilio Álvarez Sanz y

Tubau, a translator and Arabist who worked for the Spanish Protectorate.[101] Before the meeting with Franco, al-Rihani prepared a series of questions, which Álvarez Sanz y Tubau translated into Spanish and gave to Franco in advance of the interview.[102] During the meeting, al-Rihani spoke in Arabic and Franco responded in Spanish, with Álvarez Sanz y Tubau and Bustani translating between the two.

Al-Rihani posed a series of questions about Spain's objectives in Morocco and, specifically, about its plans to develop education, culture, agriculture, business, and health care in the Spanish Protectorate zone.[103] Franco did not respond to al-Rihani's questions individually. Instead, he delivered a brief speech in which he summarized his view of Spain's role in Morocco. In this speech, recorded by al-Rihani, Franco gave pride of place to the concept of Hispano-Arab culture:

> Spain desires to cooperate with the Arabs for the good of both nations, in a noble cooperation built on solid foundations. . . .
>
> Hispano-Arab culture originates in a single source. It used to occupy the first place in the world, in terms of culture. Then, it fell into neglect for quite some time. Today, we are striving to renew that old renaissance and to expand its causes.
>
> Cordoba was the base of worldwide science and the one who illuminated all of Europe with the light of science. We draw from that glorious past in order to renew activity—in particular, by creating, in one of the capitals of al-Andalus, an Arabic library in which those precious manuscripts will be collected so that it can be a pilgrimage site for cultural luminaries and men of learning from the East and the West.[104]

Franco traces the origin of Hispano-Arab culture back to medieval Cordoba. Here again, the notion of Hispano-Arab culture rests on a series of architectural metaphors: Cordoba was the "base" (*al-qāʿida*) from which science spread to Europe in the past, and the city's cultural legacy constitutes the "foundations" (*usus*) for Spanish-Arab collaboration in the present. Evoking the common theme of renaissance, Franco states that Hispano-Arab culture fell into neglect after the fall of Muslim Cordoba but that it is undergoing a "renewal" under his rule. The Spanish dictator envisions a near future when southern Spain rises again as a crossroads between East and West, a Mecca or "pilgrimage site" (*maḥajja*) for scholars from Europe and the Arab world.

It appears that al-Rihani found Franco convincing. Reflecting on his meeting with the Spanish dictator, al-Rihani writes: "I am not a partisan of dictatorship in the world. . . . Nevertheless, I was convinced of the first Spanish man's sincerity, amazed by his genius, and completely respectful of that spiritual source of far-reaching decision and scope."[105] Al-Rihani goes on to say that Franco's actions are not only "national" in scope but also "human" (a word that he writes in both Arabic and English). In a surprising allusion to American history, al-Rihani compares Franco's victory in the Spanish Civil War to Lincoln's victory in the American Civil War.[106] In short, al-Rihani implies that Franco's victory is a watershed event for world history, and that it will have positive ramifications far beyond Spain.

In particular, he argues that Franco's rise to power sparked a renaissance in Moroccan politics and education. The writer gives a detailed account of the Moroccan political parties and newspapers that emerged in the Spanish zone during the civil war, and he notes that Franco's government gave Moroccans freedoms that they had not enjoyed under previous Spanish colonial administrations:

> The press, the associations, and the parties in this zone did not enjoy freedom of thought, publication, and assembly during the two periods previous to the rebellion. It is worth mentioning and repeating that all of the manifestations of nationalist and cultural renaissance that are found in the zone today are of recent origin. They can almost be confined to the last three years [i.e., 1936–1939], in which General Franco's Moroccan policy was announced, and in which the Spanish high commissioner (Arab in spirit) has implemented it. Schools, the press, hospitals, and political parties were founded in his days and with his help.[107]

Al-Rihani mounts not a general defense of Spanish colonialism in Morocco but rather a specific defense of Francoist colonialism. He casts Franco's government as a rupture from previous Spanish rule in Morocco by claiming, for example, that Moroccan newspapers and political parties did not enjoy freedom of expression until Franco came to power. Al-Rihani also praises Franco's emphasis on Moroccan education and claims that Franco's government spends five times more on educating Moroccan students than the Spanish Republic did.[108] On this basis, he concludes that Franco's government is better for Moroccans than the Spanish Republican government was.

Al-Rihani also argues that Spanish colonialism is far superior to French colonialism. Like many Spanish writers from the same period, al-Rihani suggests that Spain represents a racial and cultural intermediary between Europe and the Arab world. In this vein, he writes that the Spanish "are the closest Europeans to the Arabs, and the most inclined toward honest and productive cooperation for the benefit of both peoples."[109] Stressing Spain's geographic and racial proximity to the Arab world, al-Rihani asserts that Spain has a natural advantage over France. He argues that Franco's government, in particular, has implemented a colonial policy that is superior to the French colonial policy. Education is at the heart of this claim. Al-Rihani harshly criticizes the French Protectorate for spending more money on the education of French and Moroccan Jewish students than on the education of Moroccan Muslim students.[110] He also observes that, under Franco, the Spanish dramatically increased their investment in schools for Moroccan students.[111]

In addition, al-Rihani contrasts the political freedom enjoyed in the Spanish Protectorate zone with the atmosphere of political repression in the French Protectorate zone. While in Tetouan, al-Rihani met with the leaders of the three Moroccan political parties that were founded during the Spanish Civil War: the Party of National Reform, the Party of Moroccan Unity, and the Liberal Party.[112] He also met with political refugees from the French Protectorate zone. One of these refugees was Ibrahim al-Wazzani, who fled the French zone in December of 1937 and settled in Tetouan, where he founded, with Beigbeder's support, the Office of National Defense.[113] Al-Wazzani gave al-Rihani a firsthand account of the nationalist demonstrations that took place throughout the French zone in the fall of 1937.[114] The French authorities responded to the wave of protests with a harsh crackdown in which they jailed and exiled many Moroccan nationalist leaders. 'Allal al-Fasi, the leader of the Moroccan nationalist movement in the French zone, was sent to a nine-year exile in Gabon. Other Moroccan nationalists took refuge in the Spanish zone.

Al-Rihani met several of these political refugees during his travels through the Spanish Protectorate, and their stories helped to solidify his conviction that Franco was an ally of the Moroccan nationalist cause. Al-Rihani even visited a village that was founded by refugees from the French zone, with land and money donated by Franco's government. The place was called the "Village of Hajj Franco."[115] The title "Hajj" is generally given to a Muslim who has performed the pilgrimage to Mecca. Al-Rihani interprets the name as an indicator of Franco's religious piety.[116] It could also be a reference to Franco's sponsorship of the Moroccan pilgrimage to Mecca. Whatever the origin of the name may be, it adds a religious connotation to Franco's protection of the Moroccan nationalists from the French zone.

For al-Rihani, the most important example of the difference between Spanish colonialism and French colonialism was the French policy toward Moroccan Berbers. In particular, he draws attention to the infamous Berber *dahir* of May 16, 1930, through which the French authorities established separate legal systems for Moroccan Berbers and Arabs. Al-Rihani compares the Berber *dahir* to the Balfour Declaration (1917), in which the British government announced its support for the establishment of a Jewish state in Palestine. He interprets both documents as examples of the colonial policy of divide and conquer.[117]

For his summary of the Berber *dahir* and the controversy it provoked, al-Rihani consulted writings by two Moroccan nationalists from the north, Muhammad Dawud, a historian and educator, and al-Makki al-Nasiri, the founder of the Party of Moroccan Unity.[118] Drawing on these Moroccan sources, al-Rihani calls the Berber *dahir* "the document of the Berbers' independence from the Arab Muslims and the strengthening of their tribal and traditional rights."[119] He accuses the French Protectorate of trying to divide Moroccan Berbers and Arabs: "[The Protectorate] declares that the tribes are not part of the conquering Arabs, but rather are European peoples; that their Islam was not, at any point in time, complete and stable; and that some of these tribes were outside of the Moroccan state and its rule."[120] With these assertions, al-Rihani summarizes the tenets of French colonial ethnography about the essential differences between Berbers and Arabs. In his view, French colonialism promotes the idea that Moroccan Berbers desire independence because they are racially and culturally distinct from the "conquering Arabs" who brought Islam to North Africa.

Al-Rihani rejects the ethnic differentiation between Arabs and Berbers, calling it a colonial invention.[121] He asks rhetorically: "Who would deny that the Berber tribes have mixed with the Arab conquerors and their descendants, and that the blood of the two peoples has become one?"[122] Al-Rihani contends that it is neither possible nor desirable to distinguish ethnically between a Berber and an Arab in Morocco. In fact, he considers the ethnic mixing of Arabs and Berbers to be a source of national strength for Moroccans: "The mixture of the two peoples through marriage is one of the causes of Moroccan nationalism."[123] In contrast, al-Rihani views France's Berber policy as a strategy to weaken Moroccan nationalism by pitting Moroccans against each other. In this vein, he writes that the purpose of the French Berber *dahir* is "to separate the Berber tribes from Moroccans with respect to language and religion, by spreading among them French education and by preaching the Catholic Christian religion."[124] Al-Rihani thus distinguishes between "Berber tribes," whom he considers a colonial invention, and "Moroccans," a category that, in his view, encompasses all of Morocco's diverse constituents. It is also worth noting that al-Rihani points to education, language, and religion as the tools through which French colonialism divides Moroccans.

Al-Rihani asserts that the Spanish Protectorate, unlike the French Protectorate, does not divide Moroccans along ethnic lines or impose Christianity on Berbers. He claims that, in the Spanish zone, "There is no evangelizing—neither in the open nor in secret. There are no missionaries in clerical or in civilian garb, and there is no propaganda that reminds one of the Protecting state."[125] Ironically, al-Rihani reproduces Spanish colonial propaganda by claiming that there is no colonial propaganda in the Spanish zone. After all, one of the central tropes of Francoist discourse in Morocco was that Spain did not want to colonize or evangelize Morocco. Beigbeder pressed this point in his conversations with al-Rihani, telling him: "Our first and highest goal in this zone is cultural, not religious. The Hispano-Arab culture that we want to revive will not be alive and strong except with an education system that is free from evangelizing."[126] Beigbeder appears to have been successful in convincing al-Rihani that the Spanish Protectorate, unlike the French Protectorate, was not driven by a missionary spirit. Al-Rihani, who was so quick to decry the French attempt to separate Moroccan Arabs and Berbers, seems to have been less skeptical about the category of "Hispano-Arab culture," a Spanish colonial invention.

Why was the idea of Hispano-Arab culture so appealing to al-Rihani, despite its colonial origins? Hispano-Arab culture was useful for the Christian Arab visitor because it allowed him to reframe Moroccan and Andalusi culture in ethnic and linguistic terms, rather than in religious ones. That is, it allowed him to think of al-Andalus and Morocco as Arab and Arabic cultures, rather than as Muslim cultures. This strategic reframing of al-Andalus as an Arab phenomenon is not unique to al-Rihani's travelogue. Since the late nineteenth century, several prominent Christian Arab artists and writers, such as the historical novelist Jurji Zaydan (1861–1914), have used this rhetorical strategy to claim a place for themselves in the history and collective memory of al-Andalus.[127] Following in the tradition of thinkers like Zaydan, al-Rihani attributes the cultural achievements of al-Andalus to Arabs. In the first edition of *Morocco*, al-Rihani concludes a summary of Andalusi history with the following remark: "The predominant rule and the greatest influence were by Arabs, not Berbers. It would be just to correct the word that is often repeated in European histories, which is *Moros* or *Moors*. It would be more correct to say *Arabs*."[128] Although this remark was removed from the second edition of the travel narrative, al-Rihani's Arab nationalist agenda remains easy to detect. In a chapter on Arabs and Berbers, he writes: "Moroccans are Arabs in their religion, Arabs in their culture, Arabs in their nationalism."[129] He goes on to say that the Spanish initiative to Arabize Moroccan schools is a boon for the Moroccan nationalist cause. Noting that Riffian Berbers in the Spanish zone are educated in Arabic, al-Rihani confidently asserts that the Riffians "have begun to understand the meaning of Arabness."[130] He thus associates Spain's Arabization policy with a respect for Morocco's cultural unity under the sign of "Arabness." Undergirding this association is the belief that Morocco's Berber identity is a product and tool of French colonialism.

Al-Rihani also suggests that the project of Hispano-Arab culture, with its attendant focus on Arabization, will respond to a serious problem in Moroccan society: a weak command of the Arabic language. He observes that few Moroccans speak standard Arabic (*al-fuṣḥā*), and he often has trouble communicating with Moroccans in Arabic.[131] He also depicts colloquial Moroccan Arabic as incomprehensible and distant from standard Arabic. For example, al-Rihani makes the following comment about a funeral procession that he witnesses in Tangier:

> Here is a Muslim's funeral procession passing in front of me. A funeral bier is carried, and in front of it, are three men who recite the Qur'an (or who try to recite the Qur'an). Behind it, the people mumble in I don't know which of the world's languages. An Islamic funeral in its external appearance and in its inner piety. As for the language and the Qur'anic recitation, they are closer to Roman, Berber, or Phoenician than they are to Arabic and Islam.[132]

In this passage, al-Rihani advances two common but pernicious stereotypes about Moroccans: first, that Moroccans do not have a solid command of standard Arabic, the language of the Qur'an; and second, that the Arabic dialect that they speak is alien and incompatible with the language spoken in other parts of the Arab world. Al-Rihani's rejection of Moroccan Arabic is striking but not extraordinary. In the hierarchy of Arabic dialects, the Maghribi dialects have often been assigned a lowly status by Western scholars and by Arabic speakers from other regions, especially Arabic speakers from the Levant.[133]

Therefore, the concept of Hispano-Arab culture was useful for al-Rihani because it allowed him to present himself, a Christian Arab born in Lebanon, as an expert on the "authentic" culture of Morocco and al-Andalus—a culture that is, for him, defined by the Arabic language and the relationship to the Arab heartlands in the East. Al-Rihani casts Hispano-Arab culture as a counterbalance to France's Berber policy, which, in his opinion, led to the erosion of the Arabic language and the Arab identity in colonial Morocco. In other words, al-Rihani adopts one colonial discourse in order to combat another. The Spanish concept of Hispano-Arab culture proves productive for al-Rihani because it allows him to articulate a critique of French colonialism. It also enables al-Rihani to stake out a place for himself in a cultural legacy that ties together Morocco, al-Andalus, and the Levant.

Conclusion: Rebuilding al-Andalus in Morocco

Al-Rihani credited the Spanish with rebuilding al-Andalus in Morocco. He casts Spanish colonial architecture as the material expression of Hispano-Arab culture. His travel narrative suggests that the Spanish revived the link between medieval al-Andalus and modern Morocco—a link that was on the verge of extinction. In particular, al-Rihani saw the Alhambra as the origin of and inspiration for Spanish colonial architecture. As the writer traveled through the Spanish Protectorate, he discovered miniature Alhambras at every turn.

Al-Rihani places particular emphasis on a Spanish architectural style known as "neo-Arab" (*neoárabe*) or "neo-Mudéjar" (*neomudéjar*), which incorporates design elements from Andalusi architecture, such as semicircular arches, crenellations, and decorative tile friezes. Many of the Spanish buildings erected in Tetouan during the first decade of the Protectorate adopted the "neo-Arab" style.[134] One of the most famous exemplars is Tetouan's train station, inaugurated in 1918. An imposing structure flanked by crenellated towers, it is a brilliant combination of whitewashed walls and sparkling green tiles.[135] Al-Rihani admired the building, calling it "an Arab-Andalusi castle in miniature."[136]

Al-Rihani associated the train station with the rebirth of al-Andalus and with the harmonious marriage of East and West. He describes the train station and two other nearby neo-Arab structures, the slaughterhouse and the military headquarters, in the following terms:

> They are the Hispano-Arab arts and spirit productively intermarried [*al-mutazāwija*]! They are the enchanting Granadan-Andalusi architecture in which the maximum desire has taken

shape, springing from the arts of the East and the West and from the longings of hearts seeking refuge in the glorious vestiges of the past and in its most captivating ruins—in the spirit and memory of the past.

Yes, they are the eternal spirit's castles, which were built, after the Alhambra and [Madinat] al-Zahra', for extended iron, coal, and fuel. And they were built for the butchers who slaughter livestock.... And they were built for the protectors of safety and order.[137]

Al-Rihani hails the three neo-Arab buildings as manifestations of "the Hispano-Arab arts and spirit" and of "the enchanting Granadan-Andalusi architecture." Spanish colonial writers often resort to family metaphors to describe the deep bond between Spaniards and North Africans. Instead, al-Rihani opts here for amorous metaphors. In his eyes, Hispano-Arab art is a fruitful "intermarriage" between the East and the West, from which springs an architectural progeny that nods to both the past and the present. Al-Rihani places the Spanish train station, slaughterhouse, and military headquarters in an architectural lineage that goes back to the Alhambra and "al-Zahra'"—that is, Madinat al-Zahra', the garden city built outside Umayyad Cordoba.[138]

The quoted passage is notable not only because of its explicit comparison between Spanish colonial architecture and Andalusi architecture but also because of its ornate style, which resembles the rhymed and rhythmic prose of the Andalusi *maqāmāt*.[139] In the original Arabic, the second paragraph features a number of internal rhymes: "the eternal spirit's castles" (*surūḥ al-rūḥ al-khālida*); "the Alhambra and [Madinat] al-Zahra'" (*al-ḥamrā' wa-l-zahrā'*); "extended iron, coal, and fuel" (*li-l-ḥadīd al-mamdūd, wa-l-faḥm wa-l-waqūd*); "livestock" (*al-anʿām*) and "order" (*al-niẓām*). In other words, the paragraph is built around a series of rhyming pairs that form harmonious combinations—much like the cultures of East and West that harmonize in Hispano-Arab architecture. The internal rhymes also facilitate the passage's quick movements across space and time. In the brief pause between rhymes, the narrator glides across several centuries—from the Alhambra and the gardens of Umayyad Cordoba to the infrastructure of twentieth-century colonial Morocco. Indeed, for al-Rihani, the Spanish Protectorate is a place that collapses both temporal and cultural distances. To be in the Spanish Protectorate is to be in al-Andalus.

Al-Rihani's description of Tetouan's "Hispano-Arab" architecture anticipates a shift that the idea of Hispano-Arab culture underwent during the period of Francoist rule in Morocco. In the earliest formulations of Hispano-Arab culture, the concept centered on the cultural ideal of *convivencia*. Over the course of Francoist rule, the concept's center of gravity shifted from the ideal of *convivencia* to a set of artistic practices that Moroccans supposedly inherited from Muslim Granada after 1492. To be sure, the idea of *convivencia* never disappeared. Increasingly, though, Francoist intellectuals tied ideas about interfaith life in al-Andalus to ideas about architecture, music, and crafts in Morocco. In Chapter 6, I will explore Spanish efforts to preserve and promote two aspects of Morocco's Andalusi heritage: crafts and music. Both art forms were central to the colonial project of Hispano-Arab culture, and they have continued to be hallmarks of Morocco's Andalusi identity in the post-independence period.

6

MOROCCAN ALHAMBRAS

ON JULY 17, 1938, Ramón Serrano Suñer (1901–2003), Franco's brother-in-law and the Spanish minister of the interior, arrived in Ceuta for a four-day tour of the Spanish Protectorate.[1] The occasion for the visit was the second anniversary of the military rebellion that took place in Spanish Morocco on July 17, 1936—the so-called Uprising (*Alzamiento*) that marked the beginning of the Spanish Civil War.[2] Franco sent Serrano Suñer to Morocco to boost the morale of the Spanish troops and to thank the Moroccan authorities and soldiers for their support in the war effort. On his first day in Ceuta, Serrano Suñer presided over the ceremonial laying of the first stone of a mosque built by Franco for the city's Muslim community. The mosque, still in use today, was named Mezquita Muley el Mehdi, after the first Moroccan caliph under the Spanish Protectorate. At the ceremony for the mosque, Serrano Suñer led a crowd of Muslims in chants of "Franco!," "Up with Spain!," and "Up with Islam!"[3] Then, Juan Beigbeder, the Spanish high commissioner, took the floor and declared: "Franco's victory is also the victory of Islam against the God-less."[4] Stressing the symbolic ties between Franco and Islam, Beigbeder informed the crowd that the new mosque's foundation would include stones taken from the Alcázar of Toledo, the site of an important early victory for the rebels in the Spanish Civil

War.[5] He explained that the mosque was not only an expression of Franco's "love for Muslims" but also the official recognition that "Islam exists within the national territory."[6] The high commissioner thus hailed the mosque in Ceuta as a symbol of the material and spiritual interpenetration of Franco's Spain and Islam.

On the same day, Beigbeder and Serrano Suñer spoke at Ceuta's stadium in front of a crowd of fifty thousand people, which included representatives from the army and the Moroccan Muslim community, as well as delegations from the French Protectorate and the Tangier international zone.[7] Addressing the vast and varied crowd, Serrano Suñer said: "Spain will never be able to forget the Muslims who were the logical echo to the heroic cry emitted by our army."[8] He then evoked al-Andalus as the explanation for the Moroccan Muslim participation in the civil war, saying: "Muslims know that they will never be able to know their history and their civilization if they do not set foot on our Spanish stones in Aragón, the Levant, and Andalucía. There, in Cordoba and Granada, in Seville and Toledo, are the highest monuments of their culture."[9] Casting Spain as an integral piece of Muslim (and Moroccan) history, Serrano Suñer called the Moroccan soldiers fighting in Franco's army "old friends who arrive at the ancestral home that they shared hundreds of years ago."[10]

On the last day of his rapid tour through the Spanish Protectorate, Serrano Suñer visited Tetouan's School of Indigenous Arts (Escuela de Artes Indígenas), founded by the Spanish in 1919.[11] A cache of photographs owned by the Spanish National Library documents the visit. In one of these photographs, a group of Moroccan carpentry apprentices raise their arms in the fascist salute as Serrano Suñer crosses the threshold of their workshop (Figure 11).[12] To the right of the doorway stands Mariano Bertuchi, the Granadan artist who served as the director of the School of Indigenous Arts from 1930 until his death in 1955. In another photograph from the same series, Serrano Suñer and Bertuchi peer over the shoulders of the young Moroccan students, who, with heads bowed, demonstrate their skill at painting intricate, multicolored designs on pieces of carved wood (Figure 12).[13] Joining Serrano Suñer and Bertuchi at the apprentices' worktable is a small group of Spanish officers, including Beigbeder, a tall, lanky figure with glasses

Figure 11. Photograph of Serrano Suñer and Moroccan students at the Escuela de Artes Indígenas in Tetouan, 1938. Photographer unknown. Spanish National Library, GC-Caja/116/18/4.

Figure 12. Photograph of Serrano Suñer, Bertuchi, Beigbeder, and Moroccan students at the Escuela de Artes Indígenas in Tetouan, 1938. Photographer unknown. Spanish National Library, GC-Caja/116/18/6.

and a severe part in his hair. The scene raises a question: Why, on an official visit to the Spanish Protectorate, during the throes of the civil war, did Serrano Suñer take time off from his meetings with Spanish officers and Moroccan dignitaries in order to visit a school where Moroccan children learned artisanal crafts such as carpentry and tilework?

This chapter responds to this question by exploring how the arts—broadly construed to include craft and performance traditions—fit into the project of Spanish colonialism in Morocco. Building on Chapter 5, I will continue to investigate the Francoist promotion of Morocco's Andalusi culture, while shifting focus away from the Hispano-Arab cultural ideal and toward a set of Andalusi cultural practices symbolized by Granada. In particular, I will examine Spanish colonial efforts to define, preserve, and administer two aspects of Moroccan culture that the Spanish associated with Muslim Granada and the Alhambra: crafts (*artesanía*) and music. My analysis will center on the careers of two Spaniards: Mariano Bertuchi (1884–1955), who trained a generation of Moroccan artisans and artists; and Patrocinio García Barriuso (1909–1997), who played an important role in the revival of Andalusi music in Morocco. Bertuchi and García Barriuso spearheaded two Spanish colonial institutions that contributed to the definition and promotion of Morocco's Andalusi heritage: the School of Indigenous Arts and the Hispano-Moroccan Music Conservatory. These institutions and the men who led them helped to codify a canon of Andalusi arts that today are upheld as essential components of Morocco's Andalusi identity. To put this claim in bolder terms, Bertuchi and García Barriuso helped to define what Moroccan culture is and where it comes from. Their work solidified a narrative of cultural transmission, linking medieval Granada to modern Morocco—and, in particular, to Tetouan. In the decades since Bertuchi and García Barriuso began their work in Morocco, their ideas about the migration of Andalusi culture to Morocco have taken on the weight of unquestioned truths, becoming anchors of modern Moroccan national identity. This chapter exposes how and why these ideas about Morocco's Andalusi arts served the needs of Spanish colonialism in Morocco.

Crafting Granada in Tetouan: Mariano Bertuchi and the School of Indigenous Arts

Spanish stewardship of Moroccan crafts dates back to the first decade of the Protectorate period. In 1916, 'Abd al-Salam Binnuna (1888–1935)—considered by some the "father of Moroccan nationalism"—advocated for the newly formed Spanish Protectorate to create a school to train young Moroccans in carpet weaving, carpentry, decorative painting, and other crafts.[14] The proposal came to fruition in 1919 with the inauguration of a school, originally named the School of Arts and Trades, installed in a symbolic location at the intersection of Tetouan's old city (the Medina), the Jewish quarter (the Mellah), and the Spanish colonial annex (the Ensanche).[15] In the ensuing years, the school grew in fits and starts, undergoing changes in its location, curriculum, and leadership. In 1921, José Gutiérrez Lescura, Tetouan's municipal architect, took over as the school's director. The school was still under Lescura's leadership when, in July of 1928, it was moved to its definitive home outside of Bab al-'Uqla, one of the gates to Tetouan's old city. That same year, one of Lescura's collaborators, Mariano Bertuchi, was named the Spanish Protectorate's Chief Inspector of Fine Arts and Indigenous Crafts.[16] In June of 1930, Bertuchi substituted Gutiérrez Lescura as the director of the School of Arts and Trades, which would be renamed the School of Indigenous Arts the following year.[17]

Bertuchi's activities at the school were so transformative that many sources credit him as the school's founder, thus ignoring the work of the two directors who preceded him in the post.[18] This characterization of Bertuchi as the sole force behind the School of Indigenous Arts is misleading, since, as I will soon explain, Bertuchi's collaboration with his predecessor Gutiérrez Lescura actually resulted in one of the school's first major projects on the international stage: the design of the Morocco Pavilion presented at the Ibero-American Exhibition of Seville in 1929. It is true, though, that Bertuchi's vision of Moroccan art (and of Moroccan artists) left an indelible mark on the culture of Spanish colonialism in Morocco—and, indeed, on debates about art in post-independence Morocco.

In recent decades, there has been a tendency, among both Spanish and Moroccan scholars, to depoliticize Bertuchi's legacy and to distance the painter from the colonial program and from Francoism. In one of the most brazen examples of this tendency, the Spanish historian Gómez Barceló has claimed that Bertuchi's projects "never had any political hue," despite the artist's prolific contributions to Francoist propaganda.[19] The attempt to distance Bertuchi from the politics of colonialism and Francoism is predicated on the belief that the artist's work was motivated by a love for Morocco, an innate understanding of Moroccans, and a desire to bridge the gap between Spain and Morocco. In this regard, Miguel Ángel Moratinos, who served as Spain's minister of foreign affairs from 2004 to 2010, has upheld Bertuchi as a model for contemporary Spanish-Moroccan relations, calling him "a precursor of cultural cooperation with Morocco."[20] The posthumous celebration of Bertuchi as a messenger of Hispano-Moroccan cooperation is reminiscent of the whitewashing that Blas Infante's work has experienced since Spain's democratic transition in the 1970s. In both cases, the politics of post-Franco Spain have obscured the legacy of Spanish colonialism in Morocco. I will argue that Bertuchi's life and work are inseparable from that colonial legacy—and, indeed, from the history of Spanish fascism.

The whitewashing of Bertuchi's legacy has gained force from the fact that the Granadan artist has also been claimed by Moroccan artists as a forefather of Moroccan art. According to the Moroccan writer and artist Abdelmajid Benjelloun, Bertuchi became, over the course of his career, a "Moroccan painter," a claim echoed by many other Moroccan luminaries, including the novelist and minister of culture Muhammad al-Ash'ari.[21] The recasting of Bertuchi as a Moroccan artist is linked to the pioneering role that Bertuchi played as an educator of Moroccan artists. In 1945, Bertuchi inaugurated Tetouan's Preparatory School of Fine Arts, the first of its kind in Morocco.[22] Through the school, Bertuchi trained a generation of Moroccan painters who became leaders in Morocco's nascent painting scene in the early independence period. Muhammad al-Sarghini (1923–1991), one of Bertuchi's first Moroccan disciples, went on to study painting and sculpture in Madrid, before returning to Tetouan in 1956 to occupy his teacher's former post as director of the School of Fine Arts.[23] Bertuchi and al-Sarghini, the colonial agent and the Moroccan disciple, are hailed today as the fathers and founders of the so-called "Tetouan School," an artistic movement that has made Tetouan one of Morocco's preeminent centers of art.[24] Bertuchi's transformation from a colonial agent to a father of Moroccan art mirrors the larger story of how Spanish colonial culture has been metabolized into Moroccan national culture. In this light, Bertuchi's career is a synecdoche for this book.

Born in Granada in 1884, Bertuchi grew up in the Realejo neighborhood, at the foot of the Alhambra. As a young boy, Bertuchi would accompany his teacher, the artist José de Larrocha, to the Generalife, the Alhambra's gardens, where he learned to paint open-air scenes.[25] Bertuchi's early works reflect his fascination with the Alhambra and with Granada's Muslim past, as evidenced by paintings like *Astrologers in the Generalife* (c. 1895) and *The Garden of the Alhambra* (1904).[26] Bertuchi was also drawn to Morocco from an early age. This interest was sparked by a close friend of his father, Aníbal Rinaldy, who was the official Arabic interpreter for the Spanish army in the War of 1859–1860 and the head of the Spanish translation service in Morocco for several decades afterward.[27] Rinaldy visited the Bertuchi family in Granada when Mariano was nine years old. The young Bertuchi, already a precocious artist, painted a portrait of the illustrious visitor. Rinaldy was apparently so impressed with Bertuchi's talents that he encouraged the young artist to come to visit him in Morocco.[28]

In the winter of 1898–1899, at the tender age of fourteen, Bertuchi made his first trip to Morocco in order to visit Rinaldy in Tangier.[29] It was the first of many trips across the Strait of Gibraltar. These trips inspired a series of works on Tangier that helped launch Bertuchi's artistic career back in Spain. In 1904, Bertuchi won an honorable mention in the National Exhibition of Fine Arts in Madrid, where he presented his *Tangier Street*, alongside paintings of the Alhambra, such as *Garden of the Generalife*.[30] In the same period, Bertuchi embarked on a long and prolific career as an illustrator for popular Spanish periodicals. He traveled to Morocco in 1903 and 1908 to draw scenes of two different armed revolts against the Moroccan sultan. Bertuchi's drawings were printed in the pages of the popular Spanish magazine *La Ilustración Española y Americana*.[31] The artist also made several trips to Tetouan, where he witnessed, in 1913, the ceremonial entrance of Caliph Mulay al-Mahdi (r. 1913–1923), an event memorialized in Bertuchi's painting *Entrada de S. A. I. el*

Jalifa Muley-el-Mehdi en Tetuán (c. 1913).[32] In 1918, Bertuchi made his definitive move to North Africa, taking up residence in Ceuta. Soon after, he became the first Spanish artist to see and paint Chaouen, when the Spanish army occupied the city in October of 1920.[33]

From 1920 until his death in 1955, Bertuchi had a hand in almost all of the visual representations of the Spanish Protectorate that circulated in Morocco, Spain, and abroad. His posters for the National Tourism Service promoted tourism to the Spanish Protectorate, promising visitors an exotic attraction "just an hour and a half away from Spain" (Figure 13). The stamps that he designed for the Spanish Protectorate's postal service adorned the envelopes that traveled from northern Morocco to the rest of the world.[34] His vast oeuvre of oil and watercolor paintings created a visual vocabulary for Spanish Morocco, emphasizing intense luminosity and chromatic contrasts. Bertuchi was also a tireless contributor to periodicals that advocated for Spain's colonial interests in Morocco. In 1924, he published several illustrations in the newly founded *Revista de tropas coloniales*, which represented the views of the Spanish army officers fighting in the Rif War. In 1925, a young Francisco Franco took over as the magazine's editor, and Bertuchi became its artistic director. The artist continued designing covers for the magazine (later renamed *África*) until May of 1955, a month before his death.[35]

Another platform for managing Morocco's image in Spain were the various exhibits and fairs of Moroccan arts and crafts that Bertuchi organized in Spain from the 1920s through the 1940s. The first of such ventures was a collaboration with the architect Gutiérrez Lescura, at the time the director of the School of Indigenous Arts. In 1924, the magazine *Revista de tropas coloniales* published an article announcing that Bertuchi and Lescura had submitted a proposal for a pavilion that would represent the Spanish Protectorate in the much anticipated Ibero-American Exhibition, scheduled to take place in Seville in 1929.[36] The article included Bertuchi's sketch of the proposed pavilion and commented that the pavilion "would symbolize, in addition to material exchange, the spiritual communion" between Spaniards and Moroccans.[37]

At first glance, it might seem odd that the Spanish Protectorate in Morocco was afforded a place in the Ibero-American Exhibition, whose main purpose was to celebrate Spain's linguistic, historic, and

Figure 13. Mariano Bertuchi, tourism poster for the Spanish Protectorate in Morocco, c. 1939. Copyright © Sucesión Mariano Bertuchi. Málaga, Spain. Reproduction courtesy of the Spanish National Library, CART. P/461.

cultural union with Hispano-America under the banner of their shared "Hispanicity" (*Hispanidad*).[38] Yet one of the implicit messages of the Morocco exhibit designed by Bertuchi and Lescura was to suggest that Moroccan culture was, in fact, a descendant of Spanish culture, much in the same way that the Spanish-speaking countries of Latin America were "children" of Spain. Bertuchi acknowledged as much when he later wrote: "Like the other countries that are sons of Spain, Morocco obtained the place that it deserved in that sentimental contest of Hispanicity."[39]

The Ibero-American Exhibition of Seville, including the Morocco Pavilion, opened to the public in May of 1929. In that month's issue of *África*, the journalist Santos Fernández published a lengthy report on the Morocco exhibit in Seville, with a photo spread illustrating the exhibit's architectural features. According to the report, the exhibit consisted of two spaces: the official Morocco Pavilion, designed by Bertuchi and Lescura, and an adjacent "Moorish Neighborhood" (Barrio Moro), featuring a minaret, a "Moorish café," and shops selling Moroccan crafts.[40] The official Morocco Pavilion gave Fernández "a strong impression of Moroccan authenticity."[41] The pavilion's façade, with its whitewashed and crenellated walls, evoked architectural motifs from northern Morocco—and, in particular, the "Hispano-Arab" style developed in the first decade of the Spanish Protectorate. Passing through an iron gateway in the shape of a horseshoe arch, the visitor to the pavilion entered the "Arab Patio," a square courtyard with a marble fountain whose water flowed into a basin made of intricate tile mosaics.[42] The courtyard's walls were divided into three horizontal bands: a lower band made of tile mosaics, a middle band of carved plaster, and an upper band of carved wood, stretching into a carved wood ceiling adorned with the honeycomb vaulting known as *muqarnas*. The space echoed decorative motifs from the Alhambra, as well as craft traditions that were being revived in Tetouan's School of Indigenous Arts. In fact, students from the school produced all of the furniture and objects on display in the Morocco Pavilion.[43] Alongside the pavilion's courtyard were exhibition halls, in which visitors could inspect crafts from the School of Indigenous Arts, as well as paintings by Bertuchi and other Spanish painters.[44] Fernández writes that visitors to the pavilion could see how, under the influence of Spanish colonialism, "Andalusian arts revive and flourish again" in Morocco.[45]

Next to the official Morocco Pavilion, there was a commercial pavilion, which was popularly known as the "Moorish Neighborhood." Its purpose was, in Fernández's words, "to condense and represent all of Morocco in miniature."[46] To that end, the pavilion's designers took inspiration from Tetouan's streets and markets in order to produce an effect of authenticity. Visitors entered the commercial exhibit through a large entranceway that was a copy of Tetouan's Tangier Gate (Bab Tanja).[47] Once inside, they walked along a commercial street that was lined with the open-faced storefronts that are common in Tetouan. The businesses were manned by Moroccan merchants and artisans, who made, displayed, and sold their crafts inside the narrow shops. Overseeing the Moroccan personnel was Antonio Got, who had served as the first director of Tetouan's School of Arts and Crafts, from 1919 until 1921.[48] If a visitor wanted to take a break from shopping, he could retire to the exhibit's "Moorish café" for a cup of mint tea. The exhibit was such a sensation that it drew two separate visits from the Spanish monarch, King Alfonso XIII.[49]

The pièce de résistance was a mosque, whose octagonal minaret, rising twenty-six meters above the "Moorish Neighborhood," was a reproduction of one of Tetouan's most famous minarets.[50] Perhaps what was most striking about the mosque was its strategic location, directly in front of the Cordoba Pavilion. Reflecting on the juxtaposition of the two structures, Fernández wrote: "It can be said that these two pavilions—the Cordoba one and the Moroccan commercial one—represent Muslim Spain and Spanish Africa in a moment of attempted approximation and understanding."[51] Fernández thus associates the Cordoba Pavilion with al-Andalus ("Muslim Spain") and the "Moorish neighborhood" with Spanish colonial Morocco. For Fernández, the two juxtaposed pavilions melded the medieval and the modern, the Islamic and the colonial, and Africa and Europe. Thus, in the journalist's eyes, the colonial exhibit not only "condensed and represented all of Morocco in miniature" but also brought into relief the intersections between Spanish colonial Morocco and medieval Muslim Iberia.

Colonial exhibitions were a common feature of European imperial culture. France also organized cultural and commercial exhibitions to showcase Moroccan art produced under the auspices of the French Protectorate. These efforts began with the Franco-Moroccan Exhibition held in Casablanca in 1915, and they continued with similar exhibitions held in Morocco and France from the first decade of the Protectorate period until the onset of World War II.[52] The key figure in the French promotion of Moroccan arts and crafts was Prosper Ricard (1874–1952), the director of the French Protectorate's Service of Indigenous Arts (Service des Arts Indigènes) from 1920 to 1935.[53] Ricard was a near contemporary of Mariano Bertuchi. A comparison of the two men is instructive because it reveals some of the commonalities between French and Spanish views of Moroccan art, but it also exposes some important differences.

Both French and Spanish colonial writers emphasized that Moroccan arts and crafts had fallen into decline by the end of the nineteenth century. According to the colonial narrative, European colonialism rescued Moroccan arts and crafts from the brink of extinction and returned them to the path of vitality and renewal. For this reason, the tropes of "rescue," "renaissance," and "restoration" run through both French and Spanish colonial writings about Moroccan art.[54] Ricard, in particular, was a major proponent of this narrative of precolonial decline followed by colonial renaissance. In a report delivered at the Imperial Economic Conference in Paris in 1935, Ricard asserted that North African crafts were, by the early twentieth century, in a state of "general decadence," in which the traditional craft centers, such as Fez and Tetouan, "witnessed the upsetting spectacle of the impoverishment and, at times, the ruin of their industries."[55] In the same report, Ricard credits the French Protectorate with rescuing Moroccan crafts from this sad state of decline, and he singles out, in particular, the work of Lyautey, the first French resident-general, "a lover of art, a born protector, and a true patron of the arts."[56] Lyautey placed Ricard at the helm of the Service of Indigenous Arts. The organization's mission was, in Ricard's words, "to protect, support, and encourage" Morocco's traditional crafts through educational programs, museums, and exhibits.[57] Ricard thus depicted French colonialism as the savior and reviver of Morocco's moribund artistic traditions.

Ricard and his colleagues at the Service of Indigenous Arts famously distinguished between Berber and Arab crafts in North Africa.

According to French colonial doctrine, Berber arts had a long history that far predated the Islamic conquest of North Africa. Essentially rural in nature, Berber arts were the manifestation of "authentic" Moroccan culture.[58] The epitome of Berber art was the Moroccan carpet, which Ricard tirelessly worked to define, classify, and promote—in Morocco and on the international market. Indeed, in 1919, the French introduced a "seal of authenticity," which they would sew on the back of Moroccan carpets that they judged to be "authentic" in quality and provenance.[59] Arab crafts, in contrast, were, in the eyes of French scholars, the product of a foreign culture forcibly imposed on the Berbers during and after the expansion of Islam into North Africa. Arab crafts were viewed as corrupting influences on the "authentically" Moroccan crafts produced in the Berber-speaking rural regions. Ricard, writing in 1930, defended the importance of studying the "specifically Moroccan objects" originating in the Sous and the Rif (both Berber-speaking regions), as opposed to the "*urban, Muslim arts,* imported by Islam" and found in Morocco's cities.[60]

Ricard and his colleagues thus established a strict separation between Berber crafts and Arab crafts, championing the former's superiority over the latter. Nevertheless, as Hamid Irbouh has argued, the French maintained that neither Berber crafts nor Arab ones had the properties of French art.[61] That is, French colonial thought divided North African craft traditions along ethnic lines, but it also held that Berber and Arab crafts were irreconcilably different from European art. The French cast themselves as experts in Moroccan culture, but not as part of Moroccan culture.

The Spanish, in contrast, saw Andalusi culture as the essential and authentic core of Moroccan culture, and they imagined themselves as direct descendants of al-Andalus, and therefore as intimately linked to Moroccan culture. Spain's School of Indigenous Arts was founded to preserve and promote the artistic traditions that Ricard dismissively called "urban, Muslim arts, imported by Islam." The Spanish Protectorate also created a School of Carpets in Chaouen and a smaller school in Tagsut, in the Rif region, but the jewel in the Protectorate's crown was the school in Tetouan, where Bertuchi and his staff forged the Spanish colonial discourse about Moroccan art. Avoiding the Arab-Berber opposition that structured the French colonial understanding of Moroccan culture, Bertuchi saw Moroccan crafts as a piece of the culture brought to North Africa by Andalusi exiles in the fifteenth century. Thus, Bertuchi viewed Moroccan crafts as not only compatible with, but *part of,* Spanish culture. When Bertuchi spoke of the "revival" of Moroccan art under Spanish colonialism, he was talking about the revival of an artistic tradition that was not only authentically Moroccan but also authentically Spanish.

This facet of Spanish colonial thought comes to light in a comment that Bertuchi made about the participation of Moroccan artisans from the School of Indigenous Arts in the Ibero-American Exhibition of 1929: "The old masters and their Muslim apprentices—some here and others in Seville—felt the rebirth of the glorious tradition of the old Hispano-Arab crafts, and it all culminated in that memorable Moroccan Pavilion at the Exhibition."[62] Bertuchi thus interprets the Morocco Pavilion of 1929—a collaboration between Spanish and Moroccan artists—as the symbol of the rebirth of al-Andalus in Spanish colonial Morocco.

The Morocco Pavilion of 1929 ushered in a new way of thinking about the origins of Moroccan crafts and a new direction for the School of Indigenous Arts in Tetouan. Bertuchi was the linchpin holding together the pavilion project and the subsequent work at the School of Indigenous Arts. He took over as the school's director in 1930 and soon became the Spanish Protectorate's primary spokesman for Moroccan art and also the main point of contact between the colonial administration and Moroccan artisans. In these roles, Bertuchi crafted a compelling narrative that charted the transmission of Andalusi culture from medieval al-Andalus to modern Morocco. He assigned the School of Indigenous Arts a leading role in this story of cultural transmission.

Writing in the newspaper *La Gaceta de África* in January of 1936, Bertuchi described Morocco's craft traditions as the vital link between al-Andalus and the Spanish Protectorate in Morocco:

> Finally, we must not forget the very important fact that these Moroccan arts are the artistic industries of old medieval Spain, conserved here miraculously. It is a duty of strict Peninsular patriotism to conserve them. And a duty of the Protectorate to promote them on account of their being the greatest link of

spiritual union that existed and that will exist between Moroccans and Spaniards. Because they are mementos of the glorious Andalusian civilization, the common mother of both brother peoples.[63]

In this passage, Bertuchi appeals to patriotism, not altruism: he argues that the Spanish Protectorate must preserve Moroccan crafts because they are miraculous "mementos" of medieval Iberian (or, here, "Spanish") culture. The preservation of Moroccan arts is, therefore, a matter of Spanish, not just Moroccan, national concern. Returning to the family metaphors that underpin many Spanish colonial texts, Bertuchi calls Andalusi civilization the "common mother" of Spaniards and Moroccans, a shared heritage that was on the verge of extinction before the Spanish Protectorate swooped in to protect it.

In the same article, Bertuchi calls on Spaniards to rekindle the craft traditions of al-Andalus, insisting that Moroccans carry those traditions on a deep instinctual, and even biological, level:

> Here, Andalusian art is a living thing that springs spontaneously from the depths of the race, just as soon as the artist is put in contact with the pure models of the past.
> The ancestors' aesthetic genius emerges instinctively and easily reproduces the decorative marvels of the Alhambra.... An innate capacity of the Moroccan to create, just as soon as he is placed on the right path, with the good models of his old forgotten culture from the Alhambra.[64]

Bertuchi implies that "Andalusian art"—understood here to be the decorative art traditions descended from al-Andalus—is an abstract good that exists independently of the artisans who practice it. He places himself in the position of a teacher who will transmit "the pure models" of that art to Moroccan artisans, who have an "innate capacity" to reproduce those models. Bertuchi thus treats Andalusi arts as a living inheritance that Moroccans understand instinctively, but he also implies that Moroccan artisans need Spanish teachers in order to reestablish contact with the appropriate models from the Andalusi past. Bertuchi's comments also signal an increasing emphasis on the Alhambra as the primary source, inspiration, and model for Moroccan craft traditions.

Just a few months after Bertuchi wrote these lines, the Spanish Civil War broke out in Morocco and soon spread to Spain. Bertuchi was not, as some have suggested, a disinterested party in the civil war. A close collaborator with Franco since the 1920s, when they both worked for the *Revista de tropas coloniales,* Bertuchi quickly put his pen and brush to the service of Franco's military uprising. A testament to these efforts is Bertuchi's painting *Crossing the Straits* (*Paso del Estrecho,* 1938), housed today in the Museum of the Spanish Legion in Ceuta (Figure 14). The painting memorializes a key episode in the civil war: the "Victory Convoy" of August 5, 1936, in which a naval convoy, protected by German and Italian bombers, transported large numbers of soldiers, artillery, and military equipment from rebel-held Morocco to Spain.[65] In Bertuchi's painting, Franco stands alone on a promontory on the North African coast, looking out on the naval convoy as it makes its way across the Strait of Gibraltar to Spain, which is visible in the painting's background. Floating above the Strait is Our Lady of Africa, the patron saint of Ceuta, who accompanies and protects the rebel convoy on its perilous journey. In her arms, she holds the limp body of Jesus, who wears a crown of thorns. Franco's resolute gaze aligns with Jesus's body, resting in the Virgin's arms. Our Lady of Africa is surrounded by rosy-colored clouds, suggesting the dawn of a new day—or, to adopt the Francoist lexicon, the dawn of a "New Spain." The horizon creates a horizontal line that divides the painting in two sections. Franco is the only figure that spans both sides of the horizon, thus bridging Morocco and Spain, Africa and Europe, as well as the convoy of ships at sea and the Virgin Mary in the heavens.

Crossing the Straits might be Bertuchi's most striking piece of Francoist propaganda, but it hardly stands alone as his only contribution to the Francoist cause. In March of 1939, the last month of the civil war, Bertuchi donated a series of several dozen paintings to Franco's government.[66] The donated works commemorated important episodes in the rebel army's march to victory in the Spanish Civil War. The following year, the paintings were presented to the public in Madrid in a special exhibition sponsored by the Spanish Ministry of Foreign Affairs, then

Figure 14. Mariano Bertuchi, "*Paso del Estretcho (Crossing the Straights)*—5 de Agosto de 1936" (1938). Original work on exhibit at the Museo Específico de La Legión, Ceuta, Spain.

under Juan Beigbeder's leadership. The exhibit, according to a journalist from the newspaper *ABC*, showcased paintings celebrating "motifs of the glorious Spanish Crusade."[67] Bertuchi's paintings of the Spanish Civil War were later turned into illustrations for the *History of the Spanish Crusade* (*Historia de la Cruzada española*, c. 1939–1943), the Franco regime's jingoistic official account of the Spanish Civil War.[68]

After the war, Bertuchi oversaw an expansion of the School of Indigenous Arts. In particular, he embarked on a mission to redesign the school in the mold of Granada's *cármenes* (from the Arabic *karm*, "vineyard"), the garden estates that dot the area around the Alhambra and the Albayzín.[69] Bertuchi's fascination with the *cármenes* dated back to his childhood. As a young student at Granada's School of Fine Arts, Bertuchi painted a study of the emblematic *Carmen de los Mártires*, which he dedicated to the translator Aníbal Rinaldy.[70] As many scholars have noted, Bertuchi's early paintings of Granada's gardens bear a striking resemblance to his later paintings of the gardens at the School of Indigenous Arts.[71] The artist often referred to his school as a "carmen," and this characterization was echoed by his contemporaries and admirers. Writing in a Madrid newspaper in 1946, Rodolfo Gil Benumeya called Bertuchi's school "the most exquisite of the Granadan *cármenes*" and limned the school's cypress trees, tile mosaics, and whitewashed walls.[72]

Gil Benumeya further observed that the school's Granada-style gardens "give access to the workshops, where three hundred students learn to continue the beautiful Hispano-Arab artisanal industries, of pure Andalusian stock."[73] As this comment implies, Bertuchi's efforts to design the School of Indigenous Arts in the mold of a Granadan *carmen* were part of a broader effort to cast the school as the torchbearer for the craft traditions that descended from al-Andalus to Morocco. In this vein, Gil Benumeya wrote that the crafts taught at the school were a source of pride for Spanish visitors because the Spanish recognized that "Moroccan artisans descend from Granadan stock, and that the detailed beauty of their technique was born in the reddish shadow of the towers of the Alhambra."[74] Under Bertuchi's leadership, the School of Indigenous Arts became a symbol and showcase for the historical link between medieval Granada and modern Tetouan, and between the Alhambra and the School of Indigenous Arts.

Bertuchi himself played an important role in this narrative of cultural transmission. A Granadan who lived and died in Morocco, Bertuchi has served—in his lifetime and to the present day—as an embodiment of the link between Granada and Tetouan. When writing about Bertuchi, scholars and journalists rarely fail to mention the artist's Granadan origins and to point to them as the explanation and justification for his work in Morocco.[75] Thus, Gil Benumeya, having traced Moroccan crafts back to Granada, posits that Bertuchi is ideally suited to spearhead the revival of Morocco's Granadan heritage:

> Perhaps that is why Bertuchi has figured out how to return to that artisanal art its hidden meaning—because he, too, is Granadan. For that reason, through his work and his person, he links together, from the School [of Indigenous Arts], space and time on the shores of the Straits, joining Andalucía with Morocco, and the centuries of Moorish Spain with those of the modern Protectorate.[76]

Gil Benumeya suggests that Bertuchi knows how to revive Moroccan crafts because he, like them, comes from Granada. Gil Benumeya asserts a natural and necessary link between Bertuchi's biography and his professional activities—"his work and his person." In other words, Bertuchi, as a Granadan, not only understands but also embodies Morocco's Andalusi heritage. Gil Benumeya concludes that Bertuchi, through the School of Indigenous Arts, bridges the spatial and temporal distances between al-Andalus and twentieth-century Morocco. For Gil Benumeya, Bertuchi stands with one foot in medieval Granada and the other in the Spanish Protectorate.

Bertuchi's Granadan credentials allowed him to adopt the role of interpreter, translator, and curator of Moroccan arts. The School of Indigenous Arts was one of Tetouan's major tourist attractions during the Protectorate period, and Bertuchi himself often served as a tour guide to the dignitaries and journalists who visited the school.[77] In 1947, a Spanish journalist writing under the pseudonym Diógenes joined Bertuchi for a tour of the school. In a report of the visit published in the Spanish magazine *Mundo ilustrado,* Diógenes introduces Bertuchi by highlighting the artist's personal connection to Muslim Granada:

> He was born in Granada, land of Christian Moors and sanctuary of glorious memories of Islam. But he has matured in Morocco, where so many of his old compatriots came to cry the nostalgia of absence. . . . Perhaps for that reason the magnificent artist does not know how to live anywhere but "there" and "here," because he is aware that any one of those points is the other, just as their spiritual atmosphere is one and the same.[78]

Diógenes signals, here, a parallel between Bertuchi and the Andalusi Muslims who emigrated to Morocco in the late fifteenth century: both were born in Granada, and both came to Morocco, where they kept alive the memory of their native land. Here, again, Bertuchi embodies a temporal and spatial collapse. Through him, Granada fuses with Tetouan until separating the two becomes impossible—"there" becomes "here," and "Moors" become "Christians."

As Bertuchi led Diógenes through the school, he underlined this fusion between past and present, Spain and Morocco. Stopping before a jug adorned with reflective tiles, Bertuchi told the visitor that the object was identical to the pottery made in Muslim Seville.[79] Pointing to a carpet made by one of the school's master artisans, Bertuchi exclaimed, "That's how they make them in the lands of the Alpujarra, and here the model has become naturalized and has received a license [albalá] of acclimatization."[80] Bertuchi ties the Tetouani carpet back to the Alpujarras, the last bastion of Muslim resistance against Christian rule in Granada. Like Granadan Muslims, the carpet has become a "naturalized" citizen in Morocco. Bertuchi uses a Spanish word of Arabic origin, albalá (from the Arabic al-barā'a), to describe the "license" of belonging that the Andalusi carpet has acquired in Morocco. The Spanish artist thus signals how the Arabic language is woven into Spanish, just like Spanish history is woven into Moroccan carpets.

While speaking for Moroccan arts in Tetouan, Bertuchi also served as the leading ambassador for Moroccan arts in Spain. In Tetouan, Bertuchi spoke with the authority of an artist born in Granada; in Spain, he spoke with the authority of an artist who had lived and worked in Morocco for decades. Both of these sources of authority were mutually reinforcing, making Bertuchi both a spokesman for and an exemplar of Hispano-Moroccan culture. During his long tenure as the director of the School of Indigenous Arts, Bertuchi organized exhibits of Moroccan crafts, produced at the school, in numerous Spanish and European cities, including Granada, Cordoba, Madrid, Valencia, Barcelona, Berlin, Leipzig, Basel, and Lisbon.[81] While these exhibits had diverse commercial and political aims, they all stressed the common theme that Spain had revived the crafts of al-Andalus through its colonial intervention in Morocco. This theme was particularly resonant in the exhibits held in the former capitals of Andalusi culture, such as Cordoba and Granada. Bertuchi was especially active in his hometown of Granada, where he organized a "Hispano-Moroccan Exhibition" in 1933, 1935, 1936, 1939, and 1940.[82]

The 1939 edition of the exhibition took place from June 7–18 in the Corral del Carbón, a caravanserai (funduq) that dates back to fourteenth-century Nasrid Granada. The event was described in loving detail by Cándido G. Ortiz de Villajos, the editor of the local newspaper, *Ideal,* and a prolific chronicler of Granadan society.[83] As Ortiz de Villajos tells the story, the exhibit was the brainchild of Granada's mayor, Antonio Gallego Burín, who conceived of the event as an "expression of gratitude" for "the noble support that the Moors have heroically given us" in the civil war, which ended two months before the exhibit's inauguration.[84] Gallego Burín was, in addition to his role as mayor, the president of the Council of the Alhambra, the government organization that oversees the Alhambra complex. In this capacity, Gallego Burín reached out to Arabists and other scholars in Granada to solicit their involvement in the exhibit. He also asked Juan Beigbeder to convene a commission of Spanish and Muslim experts from the Protectorate, including Mariano Bertuchi.[85]

The result of this network of collaborations was an event that celebrated the interconnections between Granada and Tetouan, and between Spanish crafts and Moroccan crafts. Ortiz de Villajos called the exhibit a "reminder of the shared origin and identity of the Berber artistic industries and those of Granada."[86] In this case, the term "Berber" (*bereberes*) is used in its extended sense, meaning "North African"—like the English term "Barbary." Nevertheless, Ortiz de Villajos's comment is also a reminder of the double elision at the heart of Spanish writings about Moroccan craft culture: on the one hand, the elision of Arab and Berber, and on the other, the elision of Moroccan and Spanish. Ortiz de Villajos subsumes these diverse elements into one "shared origin and identity," al-Andalus, showcased at the Granada exhibit.

The heart of the exhibit was a series of public "comparative installations," in which a Moroccan artisan worked side by side with a Granadan artisan in order to demonstrate what Ortiz de Villajos calls "the Granadan-Moroccan artistic identity."[87] Thus, for example, a Moroccan weaver worked next to a Granadan weaver, a Moroccan potter worked next to a Granadan potter, and so on. Many of the Moroccan artisans who participated in the exhibit were teachers at Tetouan's School of Indigenous Arts.[88] Alongside the comparative installations, there was also a display of artistic objects made at the school in Tetouan, including carpets, copper trays, lamps, chests, and rifles inlaid with silver and mother-of-pearl.[89]

Several other touches accentuated the exhibit's pseudo-Moroccan atmosphere. While the exhibit was up, a Moroccan cook ran a café-restaurant inside the Corral del Carbón, where patrons could enjoy mint tea and classic Moroccan dishes such as beef tagine.[90] Members of the caliph's guard were posted at the entrance to the exhibit. To cap it all off, there were daily performances of Moroccan music in the exhibit space, including a small orchestra that performed what Ortiz de Villajos called "old Andalusian airs."[91] The Spanish chronicler was referring to the North African repertoire known, today, as Andalusi music. At the Granada exhibit, selections from this repertoire were performed daily by Moroccan singers and musicians playing tambourines, drums, lutes, and the stringed instrument known as the *rabab*.[92] Such musical performances became an important feature of the Moroccan craft fairs organized by Bertuchi and the Spanish Protectorate in the 1940s and 1950s. In the years following the Spanish Civil War, Spanish scholars increasingly paired Moroccan music with crafts as dual signs of the "shared Granadan-Moroccan" artistic identity.

An example of this trend was the Exhibition of Moroccan Art held in Cordoba in May of 1946. A review of the exhibition published in the magazine *Mundo ilustrado* acknowledges that Morocco has closer ties to Granada than to Cordoba, but it nonetheless affirms Cordoba's symbolism as the setting for the event: "We cannot forget the glorious past of the Caliphate of the West . . . the seat and emporium of the most brilliant medieval civilization. And for that reason, it was chosen by our authorities."[93] Tomás García Figueras, the director of the General Franco Institute, attended the exhibition's inauguration as the official representative of the Spanish Protectorate. Muhammad Dawud, a leading Moroccan nationalist and historian, also attended the inauguration.[94] Like the exhibition in Seville in 1929, the Cordoba exhibition was set in a "Moorish Neighborhood," which featured a mosque and small stores run by craftsmen from Tetouan.[95] Inside the exhibition halls, there were displays of Moroccan crafts from the Spanish schools in Tetouan and Chaouen, as well as paintings, posters, and photographs by Bertuchi and other Spanish artists residing in Morocco.[96] The exhibition thus wove together Spanish art and Moroccan crafts into one synthetic whole, in which both elements represented a common artistic tradition. Therefore, the category of "Moroccan art," which the exhibition purportedly celebrated, was capacious enough to include watercolors by Bertuchi and woodwork from the carpenters at the School of Indigenous Arts.

Moroccan musicians from Tetouan's Hispano-Moroccan Music Conservatory, founded in 1943, performed several concerts in Cordoba as part of the Exhibition of Moroccan Art.[97] Writing about the exhibition in the magazine *África,* the art critic Cecilio Barberán mused that the concerts "worked the miracle of resuscitating the millennial echoes of Oriental music" in Cordoba.[98] The comment highlights the most common figure in Spanish colonial writings about Moroccan music—that of the "echo" that links the sounds of modern Morocco to those of medieval Iberia. In the next section, I will examine the Spanish Protectorate's efforts to define, preserve, and showcase Morocco's musical heritage, which the Spanish linked to the music of al-Andalus—and, in particular, to that of Muslim Granada.

Echoes of al-Andalus: The Revival of Andalusi Music in Spanish Colonial Morocco

The Spanish interest in the origins of Moroccan music goes back to the nineteenth century and centers on the search for a common ancestor for the modern musical traditions found in Morocco and Andalucía. In the *Diary of a Witness to the War of Africa* (1860), Alarcón compares the Muslim call to prayer to the sounds of Andalusian folk music: "We heard there, from the top of a very high minaret, the voice of a Moor who shouts or, rather, sings a slow, throbbing, melodious psalm like the sustained notes ['notas *tenidas*'] of our Andalusian songs."[99] In another passage, Alarcón compares a lullaby sung by a Tetouani woman to the *caña,* an early form of the music now known as flamenco.[100] Since Alarcón, many Andalusian writers have asserted that flamenco music is a product of southern Spain's Arab, Muslim, or African past. Blas Infante, the father of Andalusian nationalism, took this point to an extreme by inventing a spurious Arabic etymology for the word "flamenco." In several of his later writings, Infante insisted that the word "flamenco" comes from the Arabic "felah-mengu," which he translates as "expelled peasant" (*campesino expulsado*).¹⁰¹ Infante's etymology is obscure, and probably erroneous, but he appears to be referring to the Arabic phrase *fallāḥ mankūb* ("ill-fated peasant"), or perhaps *fallāḥ mujla* ("expelled peasant"). Behind Infante's dubious etymology is a desire to link modern Andalucía's most emblematic music to the culture of the Muslims who were driven out of the Iberian Peninsula between 1492 and 1614. Infante's pseudo-philological definition of flamenco as the music of the expelled Muslims of al-Andalus continues to be echoed by Andalusian writers in the twenty-first century.¹⁰²

The search for the medieval Muslim origins of flamenco has run parallel to similar efforts to trace the Spanish roots and identity of Moroccan music. At issue here is Morocco's "Andalusi music," a high-prestige music performance tradition linked to medieval Iberia and found in several North African cities, including Tetouan, Fez, Tlemcen, Algiers, and Tunis. "Andalusi music" is actually an umbrella term that was not in common use until the twentieth century, and scholars have debated whether (or to what extent) Andalusi music descends from al-Andalus.¹⁰³ In North Africa, this music is known by several alternative names, each of which is linked to a particular locale: thus, for example, it is often called *āla* ("instrument") in Morocco, whereas it is known as *gharnāṭī* ("Granadan") in western Algeria and the Algerian-Moroccan borderlands, with additional names in use further to the east in Algeria and Tunisia.¹⁰⁴ These distinct but related North African musical traditions are united by a few common formal properties: they feature *muwashshaḥ* poetry, a genre of strophic poetry that originated in al-Andalus, and they are organized into a complex suite form known as the *nūba* (in Arabic, "turn").¹⁰⁵ The modern Moroccan repertoire consists of eleven suites (*nūbāt*), but it is believed to have descended from a larger medieval repertoire of twenty-four suites. Thus, the problem of loss is, as Jonathan Glasser has argued, always already built into reflections on Andalusi music.¹⁰⁶ It is a musical tradition that claims a direct link to al-Andalus, and yet the link is fragmentary, endangered, and under threat of further loss.

In Spanish colonial culture, the Moroccan Andalusi repertoire is often represented as an echo of the music once heard in the courts of al-Andalus, especially in medieval Granada, Cordoba, and Seville. Compared to the more common trope of the palimpsest, the echo is more supple and slippery. Rather than envisioning the past as a stable subterranean layer subtending the present, the echo figures the past as a sound wave that travels across great distances, experiencing variations and distortions along the way. The figure of the echo allowed Spanish writers to represent Moroccan music as part of Spain's cultural heritage, heard from afar. To hear the "echoes" of al-Andalus, though, one must have a unique sensibility, an ear attuned to fragmentary sounds. For this reason, many Spanish colonial texts claimed that the Spanish (especially Andalusians) and Moroccans of Andalusi descent were innately qualified to study, transcribe, teach, perform, and speak for Andalusi music. The trope of the "echo" of al-Andalus thus posited a common source for Spanish and Moroccan musical culture, and it endowed Spaniards and Moroccans with a unique, hereditary claim on this shared culture. At the same time, the trope distanced Morocco from the French, who were also actively engaged in initiatives to preserve and promote Andalusi music.

As was the case with the Spanish promotion of Moroccan crafts, the Spanish intervention into Moroccan music began in the first decade of the Protectorate period and then picked up steam under the Franco regime. In 1917, Francisco Gómez Jordana, then the high commissioner of the Spanish Protectorate, sponsored a project to document Moroccan Andalusi music. The result was a full transcription of a *nūba* and the partial transcription of another.[107] The project ground to a halt in 1918 with the sudden death of its patron, Gómez Jordana, but it was resuscitated in the 1920s under the auspices of the Spanish Protectorate's Council for Historic and Artistic Monuments. In 1927, the council commissioned Antonio Bustelo, a Spanish military musician, to oversee the transcription of all eleven suites of the Moroccan Andalusi repertoire. Bustelo finished the transcription project in 1928 with the help of two renowned musicians from Tetouan: Muhammad al-Shawdri, a lute player, and Bin Salam al-Fawqi, a singer and specialist in the North African tambourine known as the *ṭār*.[108]

Bustelo's Moroccan collaborators were chosen because of their deep knowledge of the Andalusi repertoire, but also because they both claimed descent from al-Andalus. For Spanish observers, the Moroccan musicians' Andalusi ancestry served as a stamp of authenticity for their work. Patrocinio García Barriuso, a Spanish Franciscan who emerged as the leading Spanish expert on Moroccan music in the 1930s, illustrates this point in the following remark about Bustelo's Moroccan collaborators, al-Shawdri and Bin Salam:

> Both are from families of musicians that came from Spain and settled in the Spanish zone centuries ago. This detail is very important because it provides a greater guarantee of authenticity with regard to the trajectory of the classical Hispano-Morisco repertoire, and an absolute certainty for accepting that the songs that they claim are Spanish (Andalusian), are, in fact, that. We can thus discard contact with other artistic influences that could have corrupted them, or (even worse) that would have interrupted the artistic tradition of the age-old Hispano-Arab repertoire.[109]

García Barriuso traces a direct chain of transmission from al-Andalus to Morocco—and, in particular, to the "Spanish zone" in northern Morocco. A genealogical imaginary underwrites this chain of transmission. García Barriuso asserts that collaboration with Moroccans of Andalusi descent, such as al-Shawdri and Bin Salam, provides a "guarantee of authenticity" because these Moroccans carry the Andalusi music repertoire as a birthright, a cultural inheritance passed from generation to generation. He also suggests that the Spanish Protectorate zone is where Andalusi music has been preserved in its purest and most authentic state.

Unfortunately, al-Shawdri and Bin Salam did not leave any written account of their collaboration with Bustelo. Nevertheless, the collaboration foreshadowed the important role that Moroccan musicians and thinkers would play in the Spanish colonial efforts to preserve and promote Andalusi music over the ensuing three decades. The intended aim of Bustelo's project was to publish an edition of all eleven Moroccan *nūbāt*, transcribed in Western musical notation and accompanied by the lyrics found in *Kunnash al-Ha'ik* (c. 1788), an eighteenth-century Tetouani manuscript that is the earliest surviving comprehensive anthology of lyrics for the Moroccan Andalusi repertoire.[110] The projected edition was never published. However, the materials from Bustelo's collaboration with the Moroccan musicians were preserved by the

Spanish Protectorate and served as the foundation for subsequent Spanish work on Moroccan music.

Patrocinio García Barriuso arrived in Tangier in the early 1930s and soon took up the torch left behind by Bustelo. The Spanish scholar's early research appeared in the journal *Mauritania*, published by the Spanish Franciscan mission in Tangier. In 1939, the high commissioner, Beigbeder, approached García Barriuso and asked him to complete Bustelo's unpublished edition of the Moroccan *nūbāt*, which had languished in a box in a Spanish Protectorate archive for more than ten years.[111] This project bore its first fruits in 1941 when the General Franco Institute published García Barriuso's landmark study *Hispano-Muslim Music in Morocco* (*La música hispano-musulmana en Marruecos*), which features sample melodies and lyrics taken from several suites in the Moroccan Andalusi repertoire. In a prologue to the book, Tomás García Figueras announced that García Barriuso's complete edition of the Moroccan *nūbāt* was underway and would soon be published by the General Franco Institute.[112] García Barriuso's magnum opus never materialized, but the Spanish Franciscan continued to publish, through the 1940s, excerpts from the promised edition in *África* and other colonial publications.[113]

While Bustelo's transcription of the eleven Moroccan *nūbāt* sat untouched in a box in a Spanish Protectorate archive, the French were stepping up their interest and involvement in Moroccan music. An early milestone in these efforts was a three-day festival of Moroccan music organized in Rabat in April of 1928 by the Service of Indigenous Arts, under Prosper Ricard's leadership.[114] The festivities began on April 12, 1928, with a series of lectures and performances held in the Oudaias Garden in Rabat's casbah. Ricard opened the event with a speech in which he warned that Moroccan music had become "decadent" and was in danger of "losing its originality."[115] In response to this danger, Ricard affirmed the Service of Indigenous Arts's commitment to "the renovation of Moroccan musical art."[116] Following Ricard's remarks, Alexis Chottin, a teacher and music enthusiast living in Salé, delivered a lecture that surveyed the different genres of "Berber music" and "urban music" in Morocco. Moroccan musicians accompanied the lecture, illustrating the genres described by Chottin.[117] One of the performers was

Mohamed Ben Smaïl, an Algerian émigré who, in 1925, had founded an influential Andalusi music ensemble in the eastern Moroccan city of Oujda.[118] Ben Smaïl's ensemble, called Société l'Andaloussia, performed on all three days of the festival in Rabat in April of 1928, drawing on selections from the *gharnāṭī* repertoire that is associated with eastern Morocco and western Algeria. The performances were broadcast by the French Protectorate's radio station, Radio-Maroc, which soon after started a weekly radio program devoted to Moroccan music.[119]

The festival of Moroccan music in April of 1928 and the foundation of Ben Smaïl's ensemble l'Andaloussia are often cited as foundational events in the modern revival of Moroccan Andalusi music.[120] These events helped pave the way for the creation of the Conservatory of Moroccan Music, founded in Rabat in 1930, with Chottin serving as its first director. Over the next decade, Chottin produced several influential works on Moroccan Andalusi music, including the first published partial transcription and translation of a suite from the Moroccan repertoire, Chottin's *Nouba de Ochchâk* (1931). The highly visible French promotion of Moroccan music rankled Spanish scholars and politicians in the Spanish Protectorate, who felt that the French Protectorate had beaten them to the punch in publishing part of the Moroccan Andalusi repertoire. More important, the Spanish felt that the French were encroaching on a piece of Spain's national patrimony. This complaint was voiced by several Spanish scholars throughout the 1930s and 1940s, but its primary spokesman was García Barriuso.

In May of 1939, García Barriuso participated in the first Conference of Moroccan Music, organized by the French Protectorate in Fez. The conference featured lectures on Moroccan music by both European and North African scholars, as well as performances by North African music ensembles, including Ben Smaïl's orchestra l'Andaloussia.[121] The following year, García Barriuso published a trilingual account of the event, *Ecos del Magrib, Sada al-Maghrib, Échos du Maghrib*. The title both evokes the trope of the echo and performs it, as the title "echoes" across the book's cover, moving from Spanish to Arabic to French (Figure 15). The book offers, in three languages, a summary of the conference program, a narrative chronicle of the conference, and the text of the lecture that García Barriuso delivered at the conference. While acknowledging

Figure 15. Cover of Patrocinio García Barriuso, *Ecos del Magrib, Sada al-Maghrib, Échos du Maghrib* (Tangier: Editorial Tánger, 1940).

the important advances made by Andalusi music under French colonial rule, García Barriuso's book criticizes French scholars for ignoring the work of their counterparts in the Spanish Protectorate. The Franciscan also suggests that the Spanish have a deeper and more authentic claim on Andalusi music, and that Moroccan musicians in the Spanish zone are more faithful to the repertoire's Andalusi origins.

In his chronicle of the conference, García Barriuso writes: "The central theme of the Conference was the study of the traditional repertoire, known here as Andalusian music, the *nubas*; those collections of instrumental and vocal melodies that date back to the centuries of the Spanish caliphate's cultural splendor. This music has been transmitted from generation to generation up until the present day."[122] The Spanish scholar envisions the *nūba* repertoire as a continuous chain that links present-day North Africa, through several generations, back to al-Andalus. His allusion to the "Spanish caliphate" likely refers to the Umayyad caliphate in Cordoba (929–1031), but he leaves the allusion intentionally vague. The wording effaces the distinctions between the different periods of Andalusi history, from Umayyad Cordoba to Nasrid Granada. It blurs not only temporal distinctions but also spatial ones. In this description, Andalusi music unites, in time and space, modern North Africa and medieval Andalusi court culture.

While blurring toponyms and time periods, García Barriuso also draws attention to the vexed nomenclature pertaining to the *nūbāt*, which he describes as "the traditional repertoire, *known here as* Andalusian music."[123] García Barriuso does not deny the music's origins in al-Andalus; on the contrary, he exalts them. Nevertheless, he finds the terminology used to describe the repertoire inadequate because, as he observes, it ignores the related branch of Andalusian music found in Spain:

> In the present-day, we possess an Andalusian folklore, a brother to the Moorish *gharnāṭī*. . . . It therefore becomes necessary to clarify that there are two types of Andalusian music: the Hispano-Muslim one (that of the *nubas*) and the current one, which is very close to the other in its general traits and that presents itself to us in magnificent exuberance in the form of *seguidillas, granadinas, saetas, malagueñas,* etc.[124]

Listing subgenres of Spanish flamenco (*seguidillas, granadinas,* etc.), García Barriuso casts flamenco as the "brother" to the *gharnāṭī* and the other regional variants of North African Andalusi music. All of these interrelated genres are, in García Barriuso's assessment, branches of the same Andalusian tree, whose roots reach back to medieval Iberia.

García Barriuso not only draws a line between al-Andalus and Morocco but also triangulates medieval Iberia, modern North Africa, and modern Spain. He observes: "The Fez Conference has served to get to know directly the state of conservation of the traditional and classical music of the Andalusian caliphs, the NUBAS, among the different peoples who originated in Spain and now live in Tunisia, Algeria, and Morocco."[125] García Barriuso stresses the Spanishness of the *nūba* repertoire and of the people who play it—because those people, like their music, "originated in Spain." In drawing attention to Algerians and Tunisians who claim descent from al-Andalus, García Barriuso maps out an Andalusi diaspora whose borders far exceed the confines of the Spanish Protectorate in Morocco. In this imaginary cartography, all of French North Africa traces its roots back to al-Andalus. The *nūba* repertoires found in Morocco, Algeria, and Tunisia thus symbolize the deep historical bond between Spain and North Africa, a bond with both medieval roots and modern relevance. Moving freely from Umayyad Cordoba to modern North Africa and Andalucía, García Barriuso subsumes all of these disparate places and times under the malleable category of al-Andalus. This move legitimizes Spain's claim on North Africa while undermining France's influence in North Africa.

García Barriuso's belief in the essential Spanishness of the North African *nūba* repertoires serves as an undercurrent to his observations about the practice and study of Andalusi music in French colonial Morocco. The Spanish scholar acknowledges that the crowd at the Fez conference enthusiastically approved of the performances by Ben Smaïl's ensemble l'Andaloussia, but he lambasts the ensemble for its failure to adhere to "traditional music" and its efforts to resemble European orchestras.[126] He writes: "L'Andaloussia presents itself with the gloss of an Arab orchestra, but in its makeup and repertoire, it is not far from a jazz band."[127] In contrast, García Barriuso praises the orchestras in the Spanish zone for faithfully preserving the traditional Andalusi repertoire. For example, he inserts a photograph of an orchestra led by the Tetouani musician Bin Salam in between the Spanish-French text (which runs from left to right) and the Arabic text (which runs from right to left). The Tetouani orchestra is thus positioned in the center of the book, as if it were a bridge between the European and Arabic texts. Underneath the photograph, the trilingual caption reads: "Hispano-Andalusian orchestra of Tetouan, directed by the Master [m'allim] Sidi Bin Salam, one of those [orchestras] that have most faithfully been performing the traditional repertoire of the 11 *nubas*."[128] García Barriuso struck a similar note in the lecture that he delivered at the Fez conference, where he also underscored Bin Salam's Andalusi ancestry and repeated the claim that this genealogy "offers a greater guarantee of authenticity with respect to the trajectory of the classical Hispano-Morisco repertoire."[129] García Barriuso thus approaches the issue of authenticity from several mutually reinforcing perspectives. He argues that the Andalusi music performed in Tetouan is more authentic because Tetouanis come from al-Andalus, because their Andalusi ancestry inspires a more faithful adherence to the Andalusi repertoire, and because the Spanish colonizers have an innate understanding of Andalusi music, which is part of their national musical heritage.

Throughout *Echoes of the Maghrib*, García Barriuso implies that France is trying to dislodge Spain from its rightful place at the center of North African music. He states his case most forcefully when, in his summary of the conference's conclusions, he observes:

> With the goal of intensifying studies directed toward the most rapid restoration and determination of the traditional repertoire, the *nubas* of Granada, it was agreed that there would be a conference on Moroccan music every year. Where will the next one be? In Marrakesh? In Algiers? In Tunis?
> In Paris.
> The most appropriate place is Tetouan, the capital of the Spanish Protectorate in Morocco, to which is tied the glory of it being a Tetouani, al-Ha'ik, who transmitted to us the musical

treasure of Andalusian Spain. . . . No city is as deserving as Tetouan when it comes to that beloved music. . . .

Granada, Cordoba, or Seville are also signaled as appropriate places for the celebration of a conference of Hispano-Muslim music, because those cities were the fragrant cradle of this magnificent artistic flourishing. And this music is a cultural asset closely associated with Spanish Moors and Christians.[130]

García Barriuso ridicules the conference organizers' decision to hold the next edition of the meeting in Paris rather than in one of the cities associated with the Andalusi heritage. In particular, he argues that Tetouan, Granada, Cordoba, or Seville would be the most appropriate settings for the conference. These cities symbolize the trajectory of what García Barriuso calls "Hispano-Muslim music" from its initial flourishing in Umayyad Cordoba to its transmission from Nasrid Granada to Tetouan. García Barriuso sketches out not only a *translatio imperii* of Andalusi music but also a genealogy of transmission, embodied by al-Ha'ik, a Tetouani of Andalusi origin, whom he credits with transmitting al-Andalus's "musical treasure" to modern practitioners and audiences. In sum, García Barriuso's *Echoes of the Maghrib* tells a story of Andalusi music that moves between southern Spain and northern Morocco, and between Spaniards and Moroccans of Andalusi descent. Notably, this story pushes France and the French Protectorate to the margins and implicitly questions the French ability to hear the "echoes" of al-Andalus in Morocco.

In 1941, García Barriuso published his most ambitious work, *Hispano-Muslim Music in Morocco*. The book received the imprimatur of the leading Francoist intellectuals in Morocco. It was published by the General Franco Institute, the main organ for the Franco regime's colonial ideology, and it featured a prologue by the institute's director, Tomás García Figueras, and a cover illustration by Mariano Bertuchi. Bertuchi's illustration depicts a fictive historical scene from medieval court life at the Alhambra. In it, a lute player dressed in a tunic and turban sits by the pond in front of the Palacio del Partal, the oldest surviving palace in the Alhambra complex (Figure 16). The illustration epitomizes the book's main argument, which is that the music of modern

Figure 16. Cover of Patrocinio García Barriuso, *La música hispano-musulmana en Marruecos*. Published by the Instituto General Franco para la Investigación Hispano-Árabe (Larache: Artes Gráficas Boscá, 1941). With drawing by Mariano Bertuchi. Reproduction courtesy of the Spanish National Library.

Morocco (and, in particular, Tetouan) is the echo of the music performed in medieval Granada.

García Figueras's prologue to *Hispano-Muslim Music in Morocco* stresses the trope of renaissance, a common refrain in both Spanish and French writings about the development of Moroccan music under European colonialism. Evoking the concept of Hispano-Arab culture, García Figueras writes that the General Franco Institute was "created to carry out a lofty and authentic mission for Spain, which is the renaissance of a luminous period of world culture elaborated by the two peoples"—that is, the Spanish and the Arabs.[131] Warning that Moroccan music was on the verge of disappearance in the early twentieth century, García Figueras claims that Franco's Spain is ideally suited to spearhead its renaissance. "Such a task," he writes, "is a duty for Nationalist Spain [i.e., Franco's Spain], the guardian of Spain's authentic tradition, and for its action in the zone of the Moroccan protectorate, in whose capital, Tetouan, the best of that music took refuge."[132] García Figueras thus associates Moroccan music with Spain's "authentic traditions" and describes Tetouan as a "refuge" for those traditions. The comment approximates Franco's Spain to Tetouan and suggests that Spanish fascists and Moroccan Muslims are the joint standard-bearers for the traditions of al-Andalus. The Spanish Republic—often called "the anti-Spain" in Francoist writings—is understood here to be the antagonist to the "authentic tradition" embodied jointly by al-Andalus, Franco's Spain, and Morocco.[133]

García Figueras's prologue not only approximates Moroccan music to Franco's Spain and to al-Andalus but also distances the music from the rest of the Arab world and from Spain's colonial rival, France. The Spanish scholar asserts that the goal of García Barriuso's *Hispano-Muslim Music in Morocco* is "to reclaim and make known a glory shared by Spanish Christians and Moors, trying to demonstrate that the Hispano-Arabs' classical music is an art of its own, exclusive to Spanish Muslims and distinct from the music that is normally called 'Arab.'"[134] García Figueras goes on to claim that the only "Arab" component of "Hispano-Muslim music" is the Arabic text of the lyrics.[135] His goal is to assert the essential Spanishness of Moroccan music, thereby distancing Moroccan music from the Arab world and locating the origins of Moroccan culture in Spain. Although García Figueras and García Barriuso are inconsistent in their terminology, they both tend to use the term "Hispano-Muslim" to describe Moroccan Andalusi music.[136] This term allows them to assert that the *nūba* repertoire is a unique product of the cultural fusion that occurred when Islam came into contact with Spain.

By asserting the Spanishness of this musical tradition, García Figueras and García Barriuso stake a national (Spanish) claim on Moroccan music and thereby question the right of other European nations to intervene in this cultural sphere. García Figueras argues that the revival of Moroccan Andalusi music "can only be effectively achieved through the Spanish ... without it being possible for any other people to boost its renaissance, which must have a deep Spanish rootedness [*raigambre*]."[137] In the context of colonial Morocco, García Figueras's vague allusion to "other people" is clearly a jab at the French Protectorate, where Prosper Ricard and others hailed the "renovation" of Moroccan music under the auspices of French colonialism.[138]

The Spanish-French rivalry comes into greater focus in the body of García Barriuso's *Hispano-Muslim Music*. The Franciscan rails against the "Hispanophobia" of French-language scholarship that refuses to recognize the Iberian roots of the North African *nūba* tradition.[139] He, in turn, locates North African Andalusi music within an expansive (and expansionist) view of Spanish national culture, a view that encompasses the medieval and the modern, the Iberian and the North African. On this point, he writes that the Moroccan Andalusi repertoire "is a legitimate national glory. Nobody has more of a right than us to claim its excellence as another chapter in Hispanic culture. What others do for the sake of noble curiosity and love of art and culture, we must do on account of our zealous care for patriotic culture."[140] García Barriuso argues that the revival of Andalusi music is a matter of patriotic duty for the Spanish, whereas it is merely an academic exercise (a "noble curiosity") for the French.

Music was not only a proxy for the rivalry between Spain and France; it was also a resonant site for articulating a narrative of historical and cultural continuity between al-Andalus and Morocco—and, in particular, between Granada and Tetouan. García Barriuso notes that there are different versions of the *nūba* repertoire in Tetouan, Fez, Algiers, and Tunis, and he attributes each regional variant to a specific Andalusi city and to a specific wave of migration from al-Andalus to North Africa:

> The immediate origin of each one of these repertoires can be identified by relating them to their respective geographic provenance. The *nubas* of Tunis must have been brought by emigrants from Valencia; those from Algiers would come from Cordoba; those from Fez would reveal a Sevillian origin; finally, those from Tetouan would constitute the direct inheritance of the musicians from Granada. We find this Tetouani repertoire to have a more intensely defined character thanks to the subsequent migrations of the Moriscos. . . . The Tetouani al-Ha'ik was an immediate descendant of these Moriscos.[141]

García Barriuso presents a family tree of Andalusi music in which each regional branch is linked to a specific migration from al-Andalus. He attributes the Tetouani *nūba* repertoire to the post-1492 migration from Granada, whereas he attributes the other regional variants to the migrations that took place after the thirteenth-century Christian conquests of Cordoba, Valencia, and Seville. Finally, he contends that the Granadan character of Tetouan's repertoire was enriched by the subsequent waves of Muslims who came from Granada from 1492 until the Morisco expulsions in 1609–1614.

In this cultural relay between Granada and Tetouan, García Barriuso assigns a central role to al-Ha'ik, the eighteenth-century Tetouani author who compiled the earliest surviving anthology of the eleven suites that make up the Moroccan *nūba* repertoire. For García Barriuso, al-Ha'ik is a vital link between Granada and Tetouan. In his account, genealogical transmission and musical transmission mirror and reinforce each other: both al-Ha'ik and Tetouan's Andalusi music are direct descendants of Muslim Granada. García Barriuso writes that al-Ha'ik "knew how to bring together in eleven collections the majority of the classical songs that he personally knew or had the occasion to hear in

Tetouan, a still recent *echo* of the Morisco concerts on the [Iberian] Peninsula. Tetouan was, at that time, the focus from which radiated throughout the Maghrib the sonorous *echoes* of Hispano-Muslim art."[142] In this passage, García Barriuso uses acoustic language to represent Tetouan as a soundboard that takes in and amplifies the echoes of Muslim Granada. The passage both uses and mimics the trope of the echo by tracing the trajectory of sounds that carried from Muslim Granada to Tetouan and then reverberated from Tetouan to the rest of the Maghrib. Al-Ha'ik is a node in this continuous wave of echoes. The value of his anthology resides in his proximity (both temporal and genealogical) to the original source that generated the sounds of Moroccan music. García Barriuso casts the Spanish Protectorate as the next station in the cultural relay connecting medieval Muslim Granada to modern Tetouan. He thus suggests a parallel between his research on Moroccan music and al-Ha'ik's efforts to standardize the Moroccan *nūba* repertoire in the eighteenth century. Like al-Ha'ik, García Barriuso listens for the echoes of al-Andalus in order to preserve them for posterity.

García Barriuso devotes the last chapter of *Hispano-Muslim Music* to the revival of Moroccan Andalusi music under European colonialism. He titles the chapter "The Renaissance of Hispano-Moroccan Music."[143] As the title suggests, the chapter argues that European colonialism rescued Moroccan music from a long period of decline and restored it to its former splendor. In a passage that illustrates this theme, García Barriuso observes: "Currently, we are living days of intelligent Moroccan musical resurgence, in contrast with the languid life that the traditional art, born in al-Andalus, dragged along during the centuries that followed the Morisco migration."[144] Building on this theme, García Barriuso uses words like "flourishing," "renovation," and "resurrection" to describe Moroccan musical life under European colonial rule.[145] In García Barriuso's view, the major challenge facing the so-called renaissance of Moroccan music are Moroccans themselves. He accuses Moroccan musicians of corrupting the *nūba* lyrics because they do not have sufficient education to understand the Arabic texts that they sing.[146] He also contends that Moroccan musicians do not know how to read music or to teach it properly, and he blames these deficiencies for the loss of more than half of the twenty-four suites that, according to tradition, originally made up the *nūba* repertoire in al-Andalus. Finally, he calls Moroccan musicians "mechanical stiffs, rigidly attached to an insufficient practice of performance."[147] In short, he depicts Moroccans as the greatest danger to the preservation of Moroccan Andalusi music. In so doing, he appears to advocate for a Moroccan music without Moroccans.

In the face of this condescending assessment of Moroccan musicians, García Barriuso insists that European pedagogy and colonial institutions will save Moroccan Andalusi music from perdition. Noting the success of the French Protectorate's Conservatory of Moroccan Music, García Barriuso announces the imminent opening of a similar institution in the Spanish Protectorate: the Hasani Institute for Moroccan Music, named after Caliph Mulay al-Hasan. The Franciscan explains that the new conservatory will have public, scholarly, and didactic functions: it will promote Andalusi music through public concerts, foment academic research on Moroccan music, and use modern European pedagogy to teach young Moroccan musicians to read and perform music.[148] Through these activities, the conservatory will stave off, in García Barriuso's words, "the danger of the alteration and disappearance of the artistic heritage that the famous artists of al-Andalus transmitted to us."[149] Although García Barriuso presents the Hasani Institute as a European intervention to save Moroccan music, the conservatory was, in fact, the brainchild of a group of Moroccan nationalists. By way of conclusion to this chapter, I would like to discuss briefly the conservatory's history to illustrate how Moroccan nationalists became increasingly active in the definition and management of Morocco's Andalusi heritage during the 1940s and 1950s.

Conclusion

On January 31, 1940, 'Abd al-Khaliq al-Turris, the Moroccan nationalist leader, published an article in *al-Hurriyya,* the official newspaper of the Party of National Reform, calling for the creation of an institute to promote the performance and study of Moroccan music. Al-Turris envisioned an institute that would bring together Moroccan musicians, pedagogues, and scholars in order to train a new generation of musicians and to uncover the history of Moroccan music.[150] This history would reveal, in al-Turris's view, the important contributions that al-Andalus made to Morocco, and that both al-Andalus and Morocco made to the Arab world. To this point, the nationalist leader writes: "It does not escape anyone that Morocco and al-Andalus played a great role in the formation of a glorious part of the musical heritage for Arab civilization. Music and architecture might be the most important kinds of arts that our ancestors left for posterity."[151] Al-Turris goes on to call music "one of the essential elements of the renaissance" of the Moroccan people, thereby assigning music an important role in the Moroccan nationalist project.[152]

On February 15, 1940, two weeks after al-Turris published his article on music, a group of Tetouani notables addressed a letter to the Spanish high commissioner, asking him to create the Hasani Conservatory of Moroccan Music. The letter was signed by several prominent nationalist intellectuals, including M'hammad Binnuna and Muhammad Dawud.[153] Both men, as I will discuss in Chapter 7, played a leading role in consolidating al-Andalus as a central piece of Moroccan national identity. Binnuna and Dawud spearheaded the initiative to establish a Moroccan music conservatory in Tetouan, and the Spanish authorities quickly expressed their support for the project. In May of 1940, the group of Tetouani nationalists behind the project drafted bylaws for the new conservatory.[154] Drawing upon the revivalist logic that animated European interventions in Moroccan music, the bylaws stipulated that the conservatory's mission was "to revive Moroccan Andalusian music, collecting it, ordering it, and spreading it."[155]

A key piece in this project of revival was the public performance and dissemination of the Moroccan Andalusi repertoire. The bylaws indicate that the Hasani Conservatory would strive to "spread Andalusian music, and all of the songs and music produced in the Conservatory, through all possible means, attempting to write them in musical annotation, and to divulge them through the radio and phonographic records."[156] This bylaw might seem innocuous to a reader today, but in fact it signaled a tectonic shift that Moroccan Andalusi music experienced in the colonial era. Up until the 1930s, Andalusi music in Morocco was predominantly consumed in elite private settings, in soirées hosted by prominent families, or in Sufi lodges (*zawiyas*) or the royal palace.[157] The arrival of the conservatory system to colonial Morocco moved Andalusi music from the private to the public sphere. No longer would Andalusi music be a predominantly private source of entertainment limited to domestic settings; instead, it would be a public good, whose primary points of transmission would be the radio, the auditorium, and the record.[158]

The Moroccan proposal to found the Hasani Conservatory was the embryo for the eventual creation of the Hispano-Moroccan Conservatory of Music in the winter of 1943–1944. From the time of its creation until Moroccan independence, the conservatory was the primary site for the instruction and study of Andalusi music in northern Morocco, and, since independence, it has continued to function as one of Morocco's leading centers for Andalusi music.[159] Upon its foundation, the conservatory was divided into three departments: a "Spanish Section," an "Arab Section," and a "Museum-Laboratory." The first was devoted to Spanish and European music, the second to Moroccan (and especially Andalusi) music, and the third to research on Moroccan music. Patrocinio García Barriuso was in charge of the Museum-Laboratory, where he was assisted by Alfredo Bustani, who was also actively involved in the General Franco Institute.[160] The director of the "Arab Section" was ʿAbd al-Salam b. al-Amin, a former governor of Chaouen and an accomplished vocalist.[161] In the last years of the Spanish Protectorate, Ibn al-Amin joined forces with Bustani and the Spanish musicologist Arcadio de Larrea Palacín to produce a complete edition, with music and lyrics, of a suite from the Moroccan repertoire, *Nubat al-Isbahan* (1956).[162]

The Hispano-Moroccan Conservatory served as the public face of Andalusi music in the Spanish Protectorate and in Spain. In the conservatory's inaugural year, 1943–1944, its Moroccan ("Arab") orchestra gave eight public concerts in Tetouan.[163] For the rest of the Protectorate period, the Moroccan orchestra offered monthly public concerts of Andalusi music, normally held on the first Monday of each month in the auditorium of the Spanish Protectorate's Delegation of Education and Culture. The orchestra also frequently performed on Radio Tetouan, which broadcast the performances to a diverse audience of Moroccans and Spaniards.[164] In addition to its activities in Tetouan, the conservatory's orchestra represented the Spanish Protectorate in festivals and exhibitions in Spain, including performances of Andalusi music in the Exhibition of Moroccan Art, held in Cordoba in 1946, and in the International Competition of Popular Song and Dance, held in Madrid in 1949.[165] The Hispano-Moroccan Conservatory thus helped to cement Andalusi music's status as a vibrant symbol of Moroccan culture and as a public way to enact and celebrate Morocco's connection to al-Andalus.

This emphasis on public performance and commemoration has carried over into the post-independence period, and it is one of the major marks that European colonialism, both Spanish and French, made on the life of Andalusi music in Morocco. After independence, Moroccan National Radio began to broadcast a daily hour-long program on Andalusi music.[166] Moroccan public television, popularly known as "al-ūlā" ("Channel 1"), frequently broadcasts recordings of Andalusi music during the month of Ramadan and also for public celebrations of the Moroccan royal family. In recent decades, music festivals have provided another visible setting for the circulation and consumption of Andalusi music. Yearly festivals have popped up all over Morocco, and especially in cities closely associated with Morocco's Andalusi heritage, such as Tetouan, Fez, and Chaouen.[167] These festivals showcase Andalusi music as an emblem of Moroccan national tradition and mark the transformation of Andalusi music from private art to public—and national—good.

The modern trajectory of Moroccan Andalusi music, from its colonial revival in the 1930s through the contemporary festival scene, is a piece in a larger story, in which ideas about Moroccan national culture have become entangled with ideas about al-Andalus. Both Spanish and French colonial authorities played active roles in defining, administering, and disseminating Moroccan artistic culture, including music and crafts. The Spanish, though, forged a particularly cogent narrative about how Morocco's artistic culture fit into a cultural tradition that traces its roots back to al-Andalus. In particular, the Spanish emphasized the migration of the culture of medieval Muslim Granada to northern Morocco, where it supposedly took root and survived until the present. In Chapter 7, I will examine how Moroccan nationalists—particularly nationalists from Tetouan—appropriated this narrative of cultural transmission and repurposed it for their own political needs. The historical relationship between Granada and Tetouan served as a justification for Spanish colonialism, but it eventually became a centerpiece of Moroccan nationalist ideology.

7

THE DAUGHTER OF GRANADA AND FEZ

ON JUNE 18, 1930, Shakib Arslan departed his home in Lausanne, Switzerland, and embarked on his first journey to Spain.[1] A Lebanese Druze prince, Arslan (1869–1946) was one of the most famous politicians, journalists, and thinkers in the Arab and Muslim worlds from the late nineteenth century through the interwar period. His refined style in Arabic earned him the moniker "the prince of eloquence" (*amīr al-bayān*), while his tireless advocacy for pan-Islamic unity in the face of European imperialism earned him the title "warrior of the East in the West" (*mujāhid al-sharq fī al-gharb*).[2] Although Arslan had never set foot in the Iberian Peninsula before 1930, he had often traveled there in his imagination. He would later write: "I was, from the prime of my youth and my most tender age, crazy about the Arab civilization of al-Andalus and its remnants, madly in love with its history and events."[3] Arslan's early fascination with al-Andalus led him to publish, in 1897, the first Arabic translation of Chateaubriand's novella *The Adventures of the Last Abencerage*, to which he appended a condensed history of al-Andalus. Nearly thirty years later, in 1925, Arslan published a second edition of his popular translation, with an expanded appendix that included new material about the fall of Muslim Granada. The second edition was published by *al-Manar*, the Cairo-based newspaper and publishing house run by the influential Islamic reformist Muhammad Rashid Rida. Arslan's translation of Chateaubriand's novella helped rekindle popular interest in al-Andalus throughout the Arab world, and especially in Egypt and the Levant.[4]

Buoyed by the success of his early writings about al-Andalus, Arslan longed to visit Granada, Cordoba, and the other centers of the Andalusi heritage. He wrote: "All this did not quench my thirst or cure me of the desire for al-Andalus. After getting to know it with the pen, I longed to see it with my eyes and to rove about it with my legs."[5] As this passage illustrates, Arslan would often utilize amorous metaphors to talk about al-Andalus, as if it were a departed lover. His desire to move from "the pen" to "the eyes," from the page to the body, inspired him to plan, in 1930, his first trip to Spain. His initial goal seems to have been to write a travel narrative about al-Andalus, a popular destination and theme for Arab intellectuals in the late nineteenth and early twentieth centuries.[6] Instead, the trip inspired a sprawling, three-volume "Andalusi encyclopedia," titled *The Brocaded Garments about the News and Monuments of al-Andalus* (*al-Hulal al-sundusiyya fi al-akhbar wa-l-athar al-andalusiyya*, 1936–1939). The book is, at once, both more ambitious and less readable than a travel narrative. It has not fared well in posthumous assessments of Arslan's ouevre. Critics have complained that the book is boring and pedantic, and that it relies heavily on the European sources that it was meant to supplant.[7] The work's obvious flaws have, however, blinded scholars to its enormous importance. Arslan's "Andalusi encyclopedia" created a new way of talking about al-Andalus in Arabic, and the trip that gave rise to it changed the course of modern Moroccan history.

En route to Spain, Arslan stopped in Paris, where he was met, at the train station, by Muhammad al-Fasi and Ahmad Balafrij, two Moroccan students living in the French capital. Before coming to study in Paris in 1926, the two men founded, in Fez and Rabat, the first branches of a secret nationalist society (the first of its kind in Morocco) known as the Moroccan League or "The Defenders of the Truth."[8] Soon after arriving to Paris, the two men became founding members of the North African Muslim Students Association, a clearing house for a rising generation of nationalist activists from Morocco, Tunisia, and, to a lesser extent,

Algeria.⁹ At the same time, Balafrij and al-Fasi entered into contact with Arslan, who became a political mentor and surrogate father to them.¹⁰ Of his meeting with the Moroccans in Paris, Arslan would later write:

> Before noon on June 18, 1930, I departed from Lausanne, headed for Paris, and I arrived in that capital in the evening. Two young men from the elite of Moroccan letters knew about my arrival: Mr. Ahmad Balafrij, from one of the noblest Andalusi houses in Rabat, and Mr. Muhammad al-Fasi, from the great Fihri family of Andalusis, among the notables in Fez. As soon as I descended from the train, I found the two of them in front of me in the station, and we rode together to the Hotel Orleans Palace on Boulevard Brune. I spoke to them about the topic of my trip, and that was before the time of their academic break, after which they wanted to travel back to their homeland. We agreed that they would meet me in Madrid in order to accompany me for part of this trip.¹¹

It is important to note, here, how Arslan foregrounds the Andalusi roots of his Moroccan mentees. He thus implies that the Moroccan students are, by dint of genealogy, ideal companions for a research trip to Spain's Islamic heritage sites. Balafrij and al-Fasi shared their mentor's bookish enthusiasm for al-Andalus. On Arslan's second day in Paris, the Moroccans took him to Paris's most famous Orientalist bookshop, Paul Geuthner, so that he could buy books about the history of al-Andalus.¹²

Arslan's Andalusi encyclopedia, *The Brocaded Garments,* is short on autobiographical detail, but it does confirm that Balafrij and al-Fasi followed through on their promise to meet their mentor in Madrid. In July of 1930, Arslan and his two Moroccan disciples visited the Escorial, a royal monastery and palace complex outside of Madrid. While there, they perused the Escorial's Arabic collection, stolen from the Moroccan sultan in the seventeenth century.¹³ They also ran into the famous Spanish Orientalist Miguel Asín Palacios, who laid out, for Arslan, his thesis that Dante's *Divine Comedy* plagiarized an eleventh-century work by the 'Abbasid writer al-Ma'arri.¹⁴ After the visit to the Escorial, Arslan parted ways with Balafrij and al-Fasi, though the three would soon be reunited in Morocco. Arslan continued south to Cordoba, where he toured the city's famous mosque, and to Granada, where he treated himself to a two-week stay in the luxurious Hotel Alhambra Palace, a stone's throw from the eponymous fortress.[15]

Somewhere along the way, Arslan resolved to continue across the Strait of Gibraltar to Morocco, where nationalists were in an upheaval about France's controversial Berber *dahir,* which established separate legal systems for Berbers and Arabs.[16] Some historians believe that Arslan's visit to Morocco was a last-minute addition to his Spanish itinerary; others argue that his trip to Spain was merely a pretext to go to Morocco.[17] Whatever the case may be, Arslan arrived in Tangier on August 9, 1930, as a passenger on a mail steamship from the Spanish port of Algeciras.[18] Barred from entering the French Protectorate on account of his political activities, Arslan chose to arrive in Tangier, which was under joint international jurisdiction. Over the next ten days, from August 9 to August 19, Arslan met with Moroccan nationalist leaders from all over Morocco, including the Spanish zone, the French zone, and the Tangier international zone.

The story of Arslan's visit to Morocco has been told before as a milestone in the international Muslim response to France's controversial Berber policy.[19] Shortly after visiting Morocco, Arslan led the global protest campaign, stretching from Geneva to Java, against the French Protectorate's efforts to divide Moroccan Muslims along ethnic lines. As part of this campaign, he orchestrated an outpouring of letters and petitions from Muslim leaders to the League of Nations and to European governments. He also published a steady stream of polemical articles criticizing the French policy. The articles appeared in *La Nation Arabe,* the French-language journal that Arslan published in Geneva, as well as in major Egyptian periodicals like *al-Fath,* an influential Cairo newspaper aligned with the Islamic reformist movement known as Salafiyya.[20] In these articles, Arslan repeatedly accused the French of trying to convert Berbers to Christianity and to prevent them from learning the Arabic language. In an article published on the cover of *al-Fath* on October 9, 1930, Arslan decried "the removal of Berbers from Islam" and warned: "This issue is not limited to the attack on the Islam of the Berbers, but rather it implicates the entire Muslim world."[21] Arslan struck a similar note in an article published in the September issue of *La Nation Arabe*. There, he called the Berber *dahir* "the first stage in separating them [the Berbers] from Islam" and in prohibiting the use of the Arabic language.[22] In the same article, he compared Lucien Saint, the resident-general of the French Protectorate, to Ferdinand and Isabel, the Spanish Catholic Monarchs who led the Reconquest of Granada in 1492.[23]

While I acknowledge the importance of the protests against the Berber *dahir* in 1930, I also think that this episode's commemoration as a founding myth of Moroccan nationalism has obscured other important players and trends that emerged at the same time. In particular, I think that the historiography on the events of 1930 has served to center the story of Moroccan nationalism on the French zone and on French debates about Moroccan ethnic identities. In this chapter, I will use Arslan's visit to Morocco in 1930 as a starting point for telling an alternative history of Moroccan nationalism. Instead of focusing on the Berber debate, I will highlight Arslan's work on al-Andalus and the impact that this work had on the evolution of Moroccan nationalist thought, especially in northern Morocco. Arslan helped to launch the careers of several young Moroccan nationalists from Tetouan, including Muhammad Dawud and M'hammad Binnuna, who went on to leave a lasting mark on modern Moroccan representations of al-Andalus. While Arslan's relationship with Ahmad Balafrij has received ample attention, his mentorship of Moroccan nationalists from the Spanish zone, such as Dawud, has received far less attention.[24] This chapter thus reorients the history of Moroccan nationalism geographically and thematically—toward the Spanish Protectorate zone and toward the problem of Morocco's relationship with al-Andalus.

From al-Andalus to Morocco and Back: Shakib Arslan in Morocco

Upon arriving in Tangier on August 9, Arslan checked into a room at the Hotel Villa de France, one of Tangier's most exclusive addresses.[25] Soon, delegations of writers and politicians from all over Morocco converged on Tangier to greet Arslan, who was forbidden from entering the French Protectorate. Ahmad Balafrij and Muhammad al-Fasi were among the parade of men who came from Rabat and Fez to pay their respects to the visiting luminary.[26] The delegation from Tetouan, the nearby capital of the Spanish Protectorate, was led by two brothers, ʿAbd al-Salam and Mʾhammad Binnuna.

ʿAbd al-Salam Binnuna (1888–1935), sometimes called the "father of Moroccan nationalism," was a political, economic, and cultural leader in Tetouan during the first half of the Protectorate period.[27] An autodidact who taught himself Spanish and avidly followed the Egyptian press, he was the caliph's minister of finance in the 1920s, while also serving as a liaison between Morocco and Spain, and between Morocco and the Mashriq. Although advocating for cultural exchange between Morocco and Spain, Binnuna also played a major role in the early years of the Moroccan nationalist movement. In the 1920s, he bankrolled Tetouan's first nationalist school, the Madrasa Ahliyya, and its first nationalist press, the Mahdiyya Press, both of which were directed by his son-in-law Muhammad Dawud (1901–1984).[28] Dawud would later boast that the Madrasa Ahliyya was "the first free Arab Islamic school that was founded in the north of Morocco during the Protectorate period, and it was the first nucleus for the modern scientific movement and for independentist nationalism in these lands."[29] Dawud and ʿAbd al-Salam Binnuna were also both founding members of the Tetouan chapter of the secret nationalist association The Defenders of the Truth, created in August of 1926.[30]

ʿAbd al-Salam's younger brother, Mʾhammad Binnuna (1900–1967), was a founding member of both the Rabat and the Tetouan chapters of the secret society and was an early point of contact between nationalist circles in the French and Spanish zones.[31] Unlike his older brother, Mʾhammad received an extensive formal education beyond the Qurʾanic schools in Tetouan. He studied Islamic sciences at the Qarawiyyin Mosque in Fez, and then went on to study history, literature, and music in various institutions of higher education in Cairo.[32] During his first stint in the Egyptian capital, from 1922 to 1924, Mʾhammad Binnuna underwent a political awakening when he came into contact with Egyptian nationalists such as Saʿd Zaghlul. He brought these anticolonial ideas back with him when he returned to Tetouan in the fall of 1924 and took up a position as a teacher in the newly founded Madrasa Ahliyya, where the curriculum emphasized Islamic reformist thought and Moroccan patriotism.[33]

The Binnuna brothers handled the logistics of Arslan's stay in Morocco in August of 1930. M'hammad served as Arslan's tour guide in Tangier, while 'Abd al-Salam worked behind the scenes to convince Spanish officials to let the Lebanese visitor enter the Spanish Protectorate.[34] Arslan's visit happened to coincide with the feast of the Prophet Muhammad's birthday (*al-Mawlid*), a major religious holiday in Morocco, and M'hammad Binnuna shepherded Arslan through the lively streets of Tangier so that he could witness the festivities. On the night of August 13, Arslan and Binnuna attended a dinner party with the sultan's delegate, Muhammad al-Tazi. After dinner, the group went to see an Arabic play at the Teatro Cervantes, the grande dame of Tangier's theater scene.[35] M'hammad Binnuna was not only Arslan's tour guide in Morocco; he was also his chronicler. He wrote an account of Arslan's visit to Morocco, which he published in Cairo's *al-Fath* on October 16, 1930.[36] The article brought international attention to the Moroccan nationalist movement, and it also serves today as one of the best sources for reconstructing Arslan's activities in Morocco.

On August 14, 1930, M'hammad Binnuna and Ahmad Balafrij accompanied Arslan to Tetouan, where they stayed as guests in 'Abd al-Salam Binnuna's home.[37] That same night, Isidro de las Cagigas, the Spanish consul and a noted Andalusian nationalist, came to Binnuna's house to greet Arslan in the name of the Spanish Protectorate. The following day, De las Cagigas threw a tea party at his official residence in Arslan's honor. The move incensed the French Protectorate authorities, who had vociferously petitioned for Arslan's expulsion from Morocco.[38] The warm welcome that De las Cagigas extended to Arslan did not, however, come as a surprise to M'hammad Binnuna, who noted, in a letter sent to his nephew, that the Spanish consul was "one of the readers of *La Nation Arabe* and one of the lovers of Arab-Andalusi history."[39]

Among the crowd of people who came to greet Arslan on his first night in Tetouan were two of the rising stars in Tetouan's nationalist milieu, Muhammad Dawud and 'Abd al-Khaliq al-Turris.[40] Dawud was a graduate of the Qarawiyyin Mosque in Fez. He returned to his native Tetouan in 1922 and founded, with his father-in-law's financial backing, the Madrasa Ahliyya in 1924.⁴¹ One of Dawud's first students in Tetouan was the young 'Abd al-Khaliq al-Turris, who later went to Cairo in 1928 to finish his studies at the Faculty of Letters.⁴² By the time of Arslan's visit, Dawud and al-Turris were already committed nationalists and were in contact with nationalist and Islamic reformist circles in Cairo. Dawud was a frequent, though often anonymous, contributor to Cairo's major newspapers, including *al-Fath* and *al-Ahram,* and he used his publishing house, Mahdiyya Press, as a front to smuggle prohibited Egyptian periodicals into Morocco and to distribute them to his colleagues in French Morocco.⁴³ Starting in 1930, Dawud became the Moroccan distributor for Arslan's publications, including *La Nation Arabe.*⁴⁴

Upon Arslan's arrival to Tetouan, Dawud, al-Turris, M'hammad Binnuna, and a handful of other young Tetouani men formed a committee to organize an homage for the esteemed guest.⁴⁵ Binnuna was the committee's secretary; al-Tuhami al-Wazzani, the future editor of the newspaper *al-Rif,* served as the chair.⁴⁶ The committee distributed invitations for a party to be held in Arslan's honor on the afternoon of August 17 in the house of the vice-caliph, Muhammad al-Hajj.⁴⁷ On the appointed day, some two hundred guests crowded into the central courtyard of al-Hajj's house at 4:00 p.m.⁴⁸ In the packed room were Moroccan representatives from the French zone, including Balafrij and al-Fasi; representatives from the Spanish Protectorate, led by De las Cagigas; and dozens of scholars, aristocrats, and bureaucrats from Tetouan. All the Moroccans were dressed in white djellabas—"the Arabs' smoking-jacket," as Binnuna would later describe the formal attire.⁴⁹

At around 4:15 p.m., Arslan and 'Abd al-Salam Binnuna showed up to the party, and the audience erupted in cheers. Tea and pastries were served. Then, 'Abd al-Salam Binnuna stood to welcome Arslan "in the name of the Moroccan nation."⁵⁰ Following Binnuna, several young Moroccans took the floor to thank Arslan for his visit and to exalt the deep cultural ties between Morocco and the rest of the Arab-Islamic world. 'Abd al-Khaliq al-Turris, who spoke first, praised Arslan's literary accomplishments, his "reformist spirit," and "his outstanding love for Islam and Arabness."⁵¹ Al-Tuhami al-Wazzani recited a poem congratulating Morocco on Arslan's visit and enumerating the visitor's virtues.⁵²

Muhammad Dawud delivered a rousing speech on the resurgence of the Moroccan nation.[53] In Binnuna's description of the event, he notes the overtly "nationalist" tone of Dawud's speech and calls Dawud "one of the leaders of the Moroccan youth."[54] After Dawud's speech, the welcoming committee presented Arslan with a gift symbolizing the Moroccan nation: "a djellaba and a burnouse, Moroccan textiles in Morocco's name," as Binnuna described the gift.[55]

When Arslan stood to thank the committee, the room shook with thunderous applause. The text of Arslan's speech has not survived, but there are many eyewitness accounts of it, including one by Arslan himself. According to Binnuna's account, Arslan "urged Moroccan youth to learn science and to perform their duties toward their religion and their homeland."[56] Arslan's recollection of the speech emphasizes not science but rather Spain and Morocco's shared cultural heritage. He later wrote: "I responded to those speeches and explained the ancient ties between the Arab and Spanish nations and the necessity of the two being tightly interwoven [*wujūb taḍāfurihumā*]."[57] Arslan's reference to the "ancient ties" between Spain and the Arab world is a clear allusion to al-Andalus, which, in this passage, "interweaves" the destinies of Morocco and Spain. Arslan's evocation of al-Andalus is corroborated by several of the Moroccan informants who attended the event and submitted secret reports to the Spanish intelligence services. According to one of the informants, Arslan encouraged Moroccans to seek union with the Spanish because both people "come from the same place."[58] I dwell on these fleeting references to al-Andalus—fragments in the archive—because they reveal a surprising affinity between Arslan's speech and Spanish colonial thought, both of which asserted the interconnectedness of the Andalusi past and the colonial present.

After Arslan's speech, a Spanish photographer took several pictures of the group in order to commemorate the event. In the largest extant group portrait, Arslan is flanked by nationalists from the Spanish and French zones: Muhammad Dawud, Muhammad al-Fasi, M'hammad Binnuna, and Ahmad Balafrij (Figure 17). On the left side of the picture, the Spanish consul De las Cagigas sits with his legs crossed in front of 'Abd al-Salam Binnuna. The image of Arslan, the Moroccan nationalists, and the Spanish consul traveled far and wide, landing on the cover

Figure 17. Photograph of Shakib Arslan and Moroccan nationalists in Tetouan, August 17, 1930. MECD, AGA, Fondo Alta Comisaría de España en Marruecos, IDD (15)013.001, box 81/01424, file no. 896.

of Egyptian newspapers as well as in the hands of Spanish intelligence officers, who diligently worked to identify all of the people in the picture.[59] The photographs from the event were also lovingly preserved by Arslan's hosts in Tetouan, and they remain prized possessions in the Dawud and Binnuna family archives in Tetouan.

On August 18, Arslan bid farewell to Tetouan and returned to Tangier in a taxi, accompanied by Dawud and M'hammad Binnuna.[60] An unpleasant surprise awaited them. Under pressure from the French authorities, the sultan's delegate in Tangier, Muhammad al-Tazi, had issued an order to expel Arslan from the city on account of his political agitation.[61] The next day, August 19, Arslan boarded a mail steamship back to Cádiz, Spain. Or, as Binnuna described the departure, Arslan "crossed over to Cádiz in al-Andalus in order to finish his scholarly and historical research, and he left behind him throbbing hearts."[62] With this remark, Binnuna casts Arslan's stay in Morocco as an interlude in a research trip devoted to al-Andalus. In fact, al-Andalus and Morocco would become intertwined for Arslan as a result of his travels in 1930, and this interweaving of the two places left an imprint on Arslan's work with Moroccan nationalists and on his writings about al-Andalus.

After returning to Europe, Arslan granted an interview to Ahmad Balafrij, in which the two discussed the Lebanese writer's travels through Spain and Morocco. Balafrij published the interview in *al-Fath* on October 9, 1930. In the article's introduction, Balafrij highlights the historical connection between the two countries visited by Arslan:

> The greatest writer of the east visited the enchanting lands of al-Andalus, where he beheld the immortal monuments of our ancestors, but he found these monuments in an environment that was not suitable for them. He found them as foreigners in the middle of a life on whose behalf they were not created. He crossed the Strait of Gibraltar to the shores of Morocco, where he was able to behold the monuments of al-Andalus in a pure Andalusi milieu, among the descendants of those Andalusis who were the authors of these astonishing monuments.[63]

Balafrij implies that Arslan was disappointed by his trip to Spain because he found the monuments of al-Andalus to be estranged from the Spanish Christian environment in which they stand. Indeed, the adjective that Balafrij uses to describe the Islamic monuments in Spain is *gharība*, which means both "strange" and "foreign," and which is etymologically connected to the word for "homesickness" (*ghurba*). Al-Andalus thus resides in, but also against, Spain. In contrast, Balafrij depicts Morocco as a place where the "descendants" of the people who built al-Andalus have kept its civilization alive in "a pure Andalusi milieu." He thus suggests that it was in Morocco, not in Spain, where Arslan encountered the Andalusi culture that he was seeking.

Arslan reinforces this idea in the interview, telling Balafrij: "After seeing the land of al-Andalus, which I consider to be an Islamic land without Muslims . . . I was delighted when I arrived in North Africa, whose sights awakened a nostalgia in me for my land and my brothers."[64]

Arslan thus signals a contrast between Spain and Morocco: Morocco reminded him of home, while Spain's Islamic heritage sites struck him as an empty shell, devoid of the Muslims who gave them life. Arslan returns to this contrast at the end of the interview, when he tells Balafrij: "What I found to be empty and lifeless in al-Andalus, I found here to be alive with its inhabitants."[65] In other words, Arslan found in Morocco what he was missing in Spain. In his interview with Balafrij, twentieth-century Morocco emerges as a suitable substitute for al-Andalus. For both Arslan and his Moroccan mentee, Spain is a lifeless al-Andalus, whereas Morocco is a living al-Andalus.

Within a week of leaving Morocco, Arslan began a lively and prolific correspondence with ʿAbd al-Salam Binnuna and Muhammad Dawud.[66] One of the fruits of this epistolary relationship was a coordinated effort to bring Moroccan and Muslim visibility to Granada and Cordoba, the capitals of the Andalusi heritage. A month after Arslan left Tetouan, ʿAbd al-Salam Binnuna traveled to Granada to meet with the president of the University of Granada. The two men reached an agreement to appoint a Moroccan professor to teach Arabic at the University of Granada and also to establish a residence for Arab students, called Morocco House, at the university.[67] These negotiations bore fruit two years later with the creation, in 1932, of Granada's School of Arabic Studies. The school's faculty included a Moroccan instructor of Moroccan dialect, as well as many famous Spanish Orientalists, such as Emilio García Gómez, a disciple of Miguel Asín Palacios, and Leopoldo Torres Balbás, the curator of the Alhambra.[68] The school's explicit purpose was to attract Moroccan students to Granada and to serve as, in the words of one of the school's early publications, "the principal nexus of union between our fatherland and the Muslim youth."[69] To achieve this goal, the school offered scholarships to Muslim students from the Spanish Protectorate of Morocco. The Moroccan students were first housed in the school itself and were later moved to an adjacent residence named Morocco House, set inside a famous *carmen*.

Granada's School of Arabic Studies was inaugurated on May 30, 1932, in coordination with an official visit from the Moroccan caliph, Mulay al-Hasan.[70] Shakib Arslan and Ahmad Balafrij closely followed the preparations for the inauguration from their perches in Switzerland and France. On April 10, 1932, Arslan wrote a letter to Muhammad Dawud, informing him that Balafrij was planning to lead a "caravan of young Arabs" from Paris to attend the inauguration in Granada. Arslan urged Dawud to do the same, writing: "It is necessary for you all to rise up from Tetouan, Tangier, Rabat, Fez, and elsewhere, and to form a Moroccan delegation to attend the inauguration of this school so that we can teach Europe that the Arabs are still alive."[71] The school's inauguration was covered by the local newspaper *El Defensor de Granada*, which noted that, in addition to the caliph, a "numerous caravan of representatives from Tetouan and Larache" traveled to Granada to attend the event.[72] The newspaper does not specify whether Balafrij and Dawud made it to the inauguration. It is clear, however, that Arslan and the Moroccan nationalists saw Granada's School of Arabic Studies as a platform for approximating Moroccans and Muslims to Spain's Islamic heritage. The school's Spanish faculty shared this goal. At the school's inauguration, the director, García Gómez, told the caliph and the Moroccan dignitaries in the crowd: "The union of Spain with Islam—and particularly with Morocco—has a luminous projection into the future. . . . Part of our history is in your codices and in your language; part of your history is in our books and our language. We need each other."[73] García Gómez thus inserted the school's mission within a broader program of Hispano-Islamic unity, linking Granada to Morocco and to the broader Muslim world.

Arslan, Dawud, and Binnuna did not limit their efforts to Granada. In 1931 and 1932, the three men worked together to lobby the newly declared Spanish Republic to restore the Mosque-Cathedral of Cordoba to its former function as a working mosque.[74] In a letter written in May of 1931, Arslan encouraged Binnuna to bring this demand to the Spanish government and to tell the Spanish: "This is in Spain's interest because among the Spanish lands today is the Rif region, in which there are about a million Muslims. And if you want to tie their hearts to you . . . then you need to do something that shows your respect for their religious feelings."[75] Arslan continued to push this idea in the letters that he sent to Binnuna and Dawud in 1931 and 1932. In a letter from June of 1931, Arslan urged Binnuna to make the Spanish government understand the importance that the return of this mosque to Islam has in the Muslim world, and the extent of the deep impression that would be in the hearts of Muslims if Spain responded to this demand. It will be the greatest bond between Spain and all of Morocco—indeed, all of the Muslim world. . . . If the Spanish government changes the mosque back to how it was, it will prove itself to be generous to a million Muslims in Morocco under its Protectorate, and it will mollify four hundred million Muslims.[76]

Like the Spanish Arabist García Gómez, Arslan contends that Spain should use its Islamic heritage to promote cultural ties between Spain and the Muslim world. He also suggests that allowing Muslims to pray in Cordoba would advance Spain's colonial interests in Morocco by creating a "bond" between Spain and the Muslims living under its Protectorate in Morocco. Binnuna and Dawud worked behind the scenes to bring Arslan's petition to the attention of the Spanish authorities.[77] The petition was ultimately unsuccessful, but it offers another example of how Spanish colonial discourses about Morocco became entangled with Moroccan and pan-Islamic discourses about al-Andalus.

While advocating for Moroccan and Muslim visibility in Cordoba and Granada, Arslan continued to work on his Andalusi encyclopedia, *The Brocaded Garments,* the impetus behind his trip to Spain in the summer of 1930. He enlisted Moroccan nationalists, especially 'Abd al-Salam Binnuna, to help him track down books on al-Andalus and on the expansion of medieval Islam into France and Sicily.[78] Sadly, Binnuna did not live to see Arslan's Andalusi encyclopedia in print. On January 9, 1935, Binnuna died of tuberculosis while convalescing in the Andalusian city of Ronda. Announcing Binnuna's premature death in *La Nation Arabe,* Arslan called his deceased friend "one of the highest noblemen of Morocco and, we could even say, of the entire Arab world."[79] The following year, Arslan published the first two volumes of *The Brocaded Garments* in Cairo. The third volume would appear in 1939.

While Arslan was finishing his Andalusi encyclopedia, Muhammad Dawud was embarking on a major research project of his own. In a journal entry from November 1930, Dawud recorded his intention to write a history of Morocco.⁸⁰ The unassuming journal entry marked the beginning of a project that would last for the rest of Dawud's life. The projected history of Morocco eventually metamorphosed into the vast, twelve-volume *History of Tetouan (Tarikh Titwan)*.⁸¹ The work is an essential source for understanding the culture of Moroccan nationalism and the evolution of Moroccan representations of al-Andalus. Although it has often been understood as a single-author book, *The History of Tetouan* is, in fact, a collective work to which many leading Moroccan nationalists contributed. As Dawud worked on the book, from the 1930s until his death in 1984, he circulated drafts of the manuscript to his colleagues in the Moroccan nationalist movement. These colleagues made handwritten comments on the manuscript, and Dawud incorporated their comments into the final, printed version of the work, either as footnotes or as block quotes within the body of the text itself.⁸² M'hammad Binnuna and al-Tuhami al-Wazzani, Dawud's closest friends, were the most prolific contributors to the *History*. There are also sporadic contributions by 'Abd Allah Gannun and other Moroccan nationalists from both inside and outside Tetouan.

Given the work's collective authorship, *The History of Tetouan* may rightfully be considered an anthology of mid-century Moroccan nationalist thought. Since its composition and publication span the colonial and post-independence periods, the work elucidates the process by which ideas generated under colonialism took hold as national doctrine in the early independence period. In this regard, it is important to keep in mind that Dawud served as the director of the Royal Archive in Rabat from 1968–1974.⁸³ His scholarly career, like his most famous work, exemplifies the surprising migration of ideas from Spanish colonialism to Moroccan nationalism to post-independence national institutions.

The underlying thesis of Dawud's work is that the history and civilization of al-Andalus live on in Tetouan, and that Morocco's struggle against Spanish colonialism is a continuation of the struggle between Christians and Muslims for control of al-Andalus. Dawud's *History* is, therefore, one of the earliest and most important Moroccan proponents of the Andalus-centric narrative of Moroccan history. The work illustrates Arslan's influence on Moroccan ideas about al-Andalus, but it also foreshadows how Moroccans would step out from Arslan's shadow and develop their own discourse for talking about Morocco's relationship to al-Andalus. Ironically, as Morocco marched toward independence from colonial rule, Moroccan writings about al-Andalus began to sound less like Arslan and more like Spanish colonial texts.

From "Lost Paradise" to "Daughter of Granada"

Arslan's most important contribution to the modern understanding of al-Andalus was a single phrase: "the lost paradise." Arslan was not the first Arab writer to describe al-Andalus as "the lost paradise" (*al-firdaws al-mafqūd*), but he popularized the phrase through his Andalusi encyclopedia, whose full title was *The Brocaded Garments about the News and Monuments of al-Andalus: An Andalusi Encyclopedia Comprising Everything Known about That Lost Paradise*.[84] With the phrase "the lost paradise," Arslan advanced three fundamental claims about al-Andalus. First, al-Andalus is lost; it is past tense. Second, it is a pan-Muslim heritage, a past tense that the entire Muslim world shares. Third, al-Andalus is a benchmark against which the Muslim world should judge its modern decline and its weakness vis-à-vis Europe. In other words, al-Andalus is a symbol of what Islamic civilization once was, an explanatory device for a perceived decline in the Muslim world, and a model to guide the Muslim world on the path to reform. In this sense, for Arslan, al-Andalus is past tense and potential future tense, but not present tense.

These ideas about al-Andalus run through several of Arslan's writings from the 1930s, including his famous treatise *Why Did Muslims Fall Behind while Others Made Progress?*, first published in Cairo's *al-Manar* in 1930, a few months after Arslan returned from his trip to Spain.[85] As the title suggests, the treatise explores why the modern Muslim world fell behind Europe in terms of economic, political, and scientific progress. In a chapter titled "Islamic Civilization," Arslan alludes to his recent visit to Cordoba and Granada and holds up the two cities as examples of the cultural splendor that Islam is capable of producing.[86] Thus, for Arslan, the "lost paradise" of al-Andalus is not only a time and a place; it is also a metaphor for Islam's shifting relationship with Europe in the age of imperialism.

In the prologue to *The Brocaded Garments,* signed in April of 1936, Arslan draws repeatedly on the trope of the "lost paradise," using it to articulate his personal relationship to al-Andalus, and also a collective Arab relationship to al-Andalus. He writes:

> For around four hundred years, the Arab nation has been mourning this lost paradise, whose people and deeds have dwindled. Like the mourning of a bereaved father over a son whose misfortune he does not want to forget, and whose departure he continues to remember. When I was part of this nation crying for that lost paradise, from my early youth, I became enamored of reading the history of al-Andalus and delving into everything related to the Arabs in that Peninsula. So when I came across the novel of *The Last Abencerage* by the great French writer René Chateaubriand, I set out to translate it into Arabic, with an appendix about the history of al-Andalus. I published it forty years ago, and all of the copies were bought up....
>
> So, you see that forty years have passed since that first book, and that is a period that is called a lifetime. I've heard from many of the leaders of the Arab nation that they read my book when it came out, and that they followed the events of the fall of the kingdom of Granada and the last expulsion of the Muslims from al-Andalus with great interest and copious tears.[87]

This lachrymose passage combines the motif of the "lost paradise" with several synonyms for crying, thereby representing al-Andalus as an object of collective mourning. In introducing his Andalusi encyclopedia, Arslan does not give pride of place to his recent personal experience as a tourist in Spain's Islamic heritage sites. Instead, he emphasizes his literary contact with al-Andalus, suggesting that his discovery of al-Andalus came not in 1930 but rather years earlier, when he read Chateaubriand. Perhaps for this reason, Arslan calls himself and his fellow Arabs the "bereaved father" (*al-thākil*) of al-Andalus, rather than its "son." He does not portray himself as the offspring of al-Andalus; instead, al-Andalus emanates from his own imagination and is a product of reading and writing.

For the rest of this chapter, I will focus on how Moroccans adopted and eventually overcame Arslan's idea of al-Andalus as "the lost paradise." This process unfolded in two waves. In the first wave, Moroccan nationalists, especially Muhammad Dawud, adopted Arslan's idiom of "the lost paradise" and used it to insert their nationalist struggle within broader reform movements in the Arab-Islamic world, such as Arslan's brand of pan-Islamic protest against European colonialism. Even while using Arslan's lapsarian metaphor of "the lost paradise," Dawud and his contemporaries marked their distance from Arslan in a few significant ways. First, they emphatically cast themselves as the direct descendants of al-Andalus. Thus, al-Andalus was, for Dawud, an inherited and lived experience passed down through generations rather than an object of intellectual curiosity transmitted through book learning. Second, Dawud and his collaborators emphasized not the fall of al-Andalus but rather the migration of al-Andalus—its people and its culture—from Granada to northern Morocco in the fifteenth century. This narrative of migration undergirds the genealogical imaginary that animates Moroccan claims to al-Andalus. In fact, Dawud and his collaborators devised a genealogical metaphor to describe Tetouan's relationship to al-Andalus: they called Tetouan "the daughter of Granada," a nickname first coined by M'hammad Binnuna in his introduction to *Tarikh Titwan*.[88]

In a second wave of responses to Arslan's work, a younger generation of Moroccan nationalists, trained in Spanish colonial academic institutions, abandoned altogether the metaphor of "the lost paradise." They asserted that al-Andalus was not lost, but rather was alive and well in Morocco. They also pushed back against the idea that al-Andalus is a pan-Arab and pan-Muslim heritage. Instead, they insisted that it is a Moroccan national heritage. Finally, they moved away from an abstract sense of al-Andalus as a symbol of "Islamic civilization" and replaced this abstraction with a specific set of cultural attributes and practices embodied by Granada and carried into the present by Tetouan. It is not a coincidence that the intellectuals who led the charge to articulate a Morocco-centric view of al-Andalus (or an Andalus-centric view of Morocco) were scholars who came up through the ranks of Spanish colonial research institutions under Franco. A prime example is Muhammad b. Tawit (1917–1993), who joined the research faculty at the General Franco Institute in 1950 and later helped found independent Morocco's first Arabic-language scholarly journal, *Titwan* ("Tetouan").[89] In the next section, I will return to Ibn Tawit's work, tracing its relationship to Spanish colonial ideology.

It would be a mistake, though, to assume that Dawud and his generation operated independently from the colonial system. In fact, Dawud held a number of important positions in the Protectorate administration while he was working on the *History of Tetouan*. In January of 1937, the caliph appointed Dawud general inspector of Muslim education in the Spanish Protectorate.[90] In this role, Dawud helped implement the Franco regime's Arabization policy, a central pillar in the efforts to portray the Franco regime as the standard-bearer for Arab and "Hispano-Arab" culture.[91] In 1942, Dawud was named the director of Moroccan Education. In this position, he worked closely with Tomás García Figueras, the head of the Spanish Delegation of Education and Culture and the director of the General Franco Institute.[92] Franco himself bestowed the Cross of Civilian Merit on Dawud on July 18, 1944, the anniversary of the beginning of the Spanish Civil War.[93] In 1946, Dawud and García Figueras represented the Spanish Protectorate at the inauguration of the Exhibition of Moroccan Art in Cordoba, a showcase for the revival of Andalusi crafts in Spanish colonial Morocco.[94] Finally, in 1953, Dawud won the Mulay al-Hasan Prize for his *Summary of the History of Tetouan* (*Mukhtasar tarikh Titwan*), the only part of the *History of Tetouan* to be published before Moroccan independence.[95] The Mulay al-Hasan Institute and its annual prize were created by the Spanish Protectorate to promote Arabic-language research on Moroccan and Andalusi history and to solidify ties between Spain, Morocco, and the Arab world.[96]

My intention here is not to paint Muhammad Dawud as a stooge of the Francoist colonial regime. Indeed, Dawud's involvement with the Spanish Protectorate was by no means unusual. I could produce a similar list of entanglements for almost every member of the Moroccan nationalist movement in the north, including ʿAbd al-Salam Binnuna,

'Abd al-Khaliq al-Turris, al-Tuhami al-Wazzani, al-Makki al-Nasiri, and many others. To dismiss these men as colonial collaborators is to oversimplify the nature of their exchange with the Spanish colonial system. It would be more accurate to describe the exchange as an unfolding process of give-and-take. The Spanish Protectorate, especially under Franco, coopted the Moroccan nationalists in order to lend legitimacy to the idea that Spain was an ally of Islam and a defender of the Andalusi heritage. The Moroccan nationalists, in turn, coopted Spanish ideas about al-Andalus and repurposed them as building blocks of Moroccan national identity. In other words, Spanish colonialism needed the Moroccan nationalists, just as the Moroccan nationalists needed Spanish colonialism, even though the two sides were ultimately at odds with each other. Dawud's *History of Tetouan* is a fecund site for exploring this tension.

Dawud, Binnuna, al-Wazzani, and the other contributors to *The History of Tetouan* often used Arslan's phrase "the lost paradise," but they tied it to a migration story that underlined Morocco's continuous and unique relationship with Muslim Granada. In an illustrative passage, Dawud writes:

> The current city of Tetouan, with its divisions, its streets, its alleys, and its sites, is not old. Rather, it was built at the end of the ninth century *hijri* (equivalent to the fifteenth century A.D.)—that is, about five hundred years before the current date. And that was because when the great catastrophe descended upon al-Andalus—the catastrophic evanescence of the last Islamic state in *that lost Islamic paradise*—many Muslims migrated to different Islamic lands. Among them was a group of the residents of Granada and its environs. This group joined another Andalusi group, which had preceded it to this part of Morocco, and together they renewed the building of the city of Tetouan, which was, at that time, destroyed, not built or inhabited.... The reality is that the true, certain history of Tetouan starts from the date of this Andalusi building; since before that, the information about it is only disjointed fragments.[97]

For Dawud, the Andalusi migration to Morocco marks the beginning not only of Tetouan's history but also of its historical consciousness. All that comes before the Andalusi migration is limited, in Dawud's words, to "disjointed fragments." In other words, the Granadan refugees not only founded Tetouan; they also founded Tetouani history. Although Dawud acknowledges the "evanescence" (*iḍmiḥlāl*) of al-Andalus, his story is not one of total rupture but rather one of migration, from one shore to another.

The exodus from Muslim Granada furnishes Dawud with a foundation myth and also with a founding father: the Granadan leader al-Manzari. About him, Dawud writes: "The leader of the Andalusis who built modern Tetouan was the leader and *mujāhid* Abu al-Hasan 'Ali al-Manzari, the Granadan, one of the leaders of Bani al-Ahmar [i.e., the Nasrid dynasty of Granada]. . . . He was buried outside the Cemetery Gate, and his tomb is still famous and visited until today."[98] Dawud was one of the first historians to delve into al-Manzari's biography and to express interest in his tomb. *The History of Tetouan* thus contributed significantly to the mid-century revival of al-Manzari as a foundational figure. That revival would culminate with the construction of a new mausoleum for al-Manzari in the 1960s, a project that I examined in the introduction.

In 1954, Dawud drew a map that visually represented his understanding of Andalusi and Moroccan history. The map first appeared in the *Summary of the History of Tetouan* (1955), and then was used again as an illustration in the first volume of *The History of Tetouan* (1959) (Figure 18).[99] Titled "The Map of al-Andalus and Morocco," it depicts the Spanish region of Andalucía, the Strait of Gibraltar, and Morocco, along with the Mediterranean Sea and the Atlantic Ocean. Small dots mark the colonial division of Morocco into French, Spanish, and international zones. The tips of Spain and Morocco draw together and form a focus point, drawing the eye to the proximity between Granada, Cordoba, and Tetouan. The four large labels—"al-Andalus," "Mediterranean Sea," "Morocco," and "Atlantic Ocean"—form a frame around the Strait of Gibraltar, further accentuating the relationship between southern Spain and northern Morocco. Although the map is dated 1954, Dawud labels Spain as "al-Andalus," a historical toponym that, in

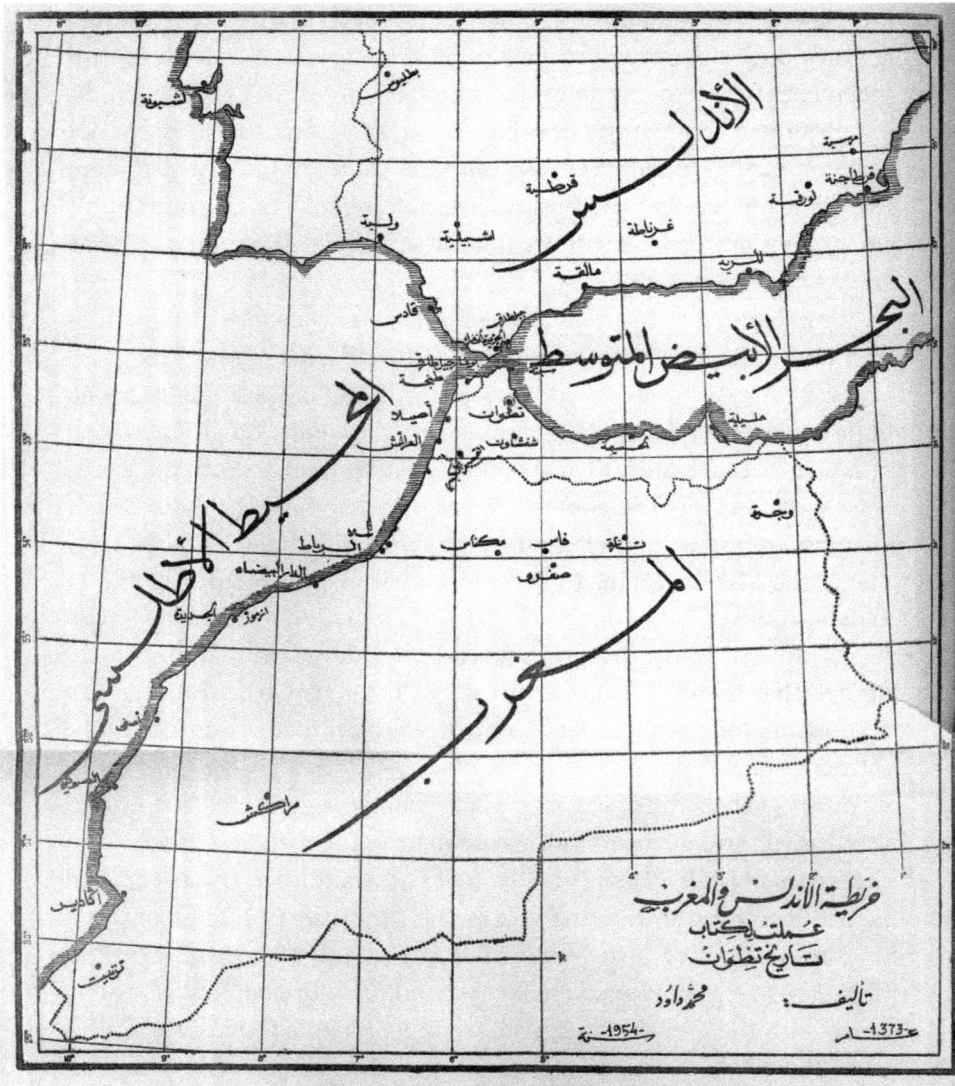

خريطة بلاد المغرب وجنوب الأندلس، وتظهر مدينة تطوان في الشمال الغربي قرب شاطئ. البحر الأبيض المتوسط. كما تظهر مدينة غرناطة الأندلسية، وهي المدينة التي هاجر منها المسلمون إلى بلاد المغرب وجددوا بها بناء. مدينة تطوان عام 888 هـ. موافق سنة 1484 م.

والنقط الصغيرة الظاهرة في الصورة. قد صارت الآن تدل على الحدود التي كان الاستعمار الفرنسي والاسباني والدولي. قد قسم بها بلاد المغرب إلى ثلاث مناطق، لكل منها حدودها وحكومتها وانظمتها كان في الجنوب سلطان المغرب تحت حماية فرنسا، وفي الشمال خليفة السلطان تحت حماية اسبانيا، وفي طنجة مجلس دولي هو المدبر لجميع شؤون منطقتها، الا ان ذلك كله قد صار في خبر كان والحمد لله، وانما يذكر الآن ليعتبر المعتبرون. ويحمد الله المؤمنون

Figure 18. Muhammad Dawud, "Map of al-Andalus and Morocco" ("Kharitat al-Andalus wa-l-Maghrib," 1954). Published in *Tarikh Titwan*, vol. 1 (Tetouan: Matba'at Maktabat "Cremades," 1959), between pages 64–65. Reproduction courtesy of the Mohamed Daoud Foundation for History and Culture, Tetouan, Morocco.

Western usage, is limited to medieval Iberia. Here, however, al-Andalus exists in an eternal present, alongside an evolving Morocco.

Indeed, Dawud's map represents multiple, overlapping temporalities: medieval Iberia, the post-1492 migration of Andalusis to Morocco, and the twentieth-century colonial division of Morocco. The map's caption underlines the relationship between Granada and Tetouan, and between the fifteenth century and the twentieth century:

> The map of the lands of Morocco and the south of al-Andalus. The city of Tetouan appears in the northwest, near to the Mediterranean coast. The Andalusi city of Granada also appears, and this is the city from which the Muslims migrated to Morocco, where they renewed the building of Tetouan in the year 888 (*hijri*), equivalent to the year 1484 AD.
>
> The small dots appearing in the image have now become historical, since they used to indicate the borders with which French, Spanish, and international colonialism divided the lands of Morocco into three zones. Each zone had its own borders, government, and laws. In the south, the sultan of Morocco was under the Protectorate of France; in the north, the sultan's caliph was under the Protectorate of Spain; in Tangier, there was an international commission, which was the director of all matters in its zone. Nevertheless, all of that now belongs to the past—and thank God! It is only mentioned now in order to teach a lesson to the lesson-takers. May the faithful praise God!

In the space between the caption's two paragraphs, Dawud vaults over several centuries, from fifteenth-century Granada to twentieth-century Moroccan independence. Although the map encapsulates nearly five centuries of Mediterranean history, the only part of it that Dawud calls "historical" are the small dots marking the division of Morocco into French, Spanish, and international zones. Dawud thus brackets the colonial period, as if it were a parenthesis in a deeper story linking Morocco to al-Andalus. The dots are superimposed on Morocco, but they are incidental: they are merely kept, as Dawud says, as a "lesson for the lesson-takers." The curious phrase revolves around a polyptoton on the

Arabic verb *i'tabara* ("to learn a lesson"), which is followed by the participle *al-mu'tabirūn* ("those who take lessons"). This wordplay points to an important facet of Dawud's work. For Dawud, history teaches. That is, his orientation toward history is fundamentally didactic.[100] It is worth remembering that some of Dawud's most important contributions to Moroccan nationalism were in the field of education, starting with his creation of the Ahliyya School. The "lesson" that Dawud's map teaches is that the people of Granada moved to Tetouan in the fifteenth century, and that European colonialism tried to divide Morocco but could not alter the country's deep attachment to its Andalusi roots.

M'hammad Binnuna also stresses the continuity between Granada and Tetouan in his contributions to *The History of Tetouan*. In a prologue to the first volume, Binnuna offers another account of the migration from al-Andalus to Morocco. In this telling, the Granadan migration marks not the beginning of Tetouani history but rather the continuation of Andalusi history. Binnuna writes:

> Yes, I would like to establish a truth that is as firm as the poles and as clear as the light of day. And that is that Tetouan did not advance gradually like other growing cities—from village to town, and from town to city. Rather, it is a city that was born whole. And from the first day in which they rebuilt the city for the last time, it was a center for Andalusi civilization, and a cradle for refined progress. Because its founders—or, to be more precise, its renewers—were the most advanced people to be found in that period. Since it is known and accepted that the district of Granada, in the east of al-Andalus, brought together, in its day, the crème de la crème of scholars and jurists, pharmacists and doctors, artisans and experts, farmers and engineers, and the heroes of thought and bravery, who cried out to it from every spot that fortune betrayed and that fell under Spanish aggression. Until it came to contain the choicest inheritors of Umayyad Cordoba and the arts of 'Abbadid Seville.... When matters became dysfunctional between the princes of the brilliant Alhambra, and betrayal appeared alongside a fierce struggle for rule amongst those who had treach-

erous schemes, and Christianity united against Islam with the marriage of the king of Aragon and the queen of Castile... then the faithful, who had their eyes on God's light, began to emigrate with their religion, honor, children, money, knowledge, and art to Morocco's shore.[101]

This passage moves backward and forward in time, offering a dizzying array of origins and offspring that is perhaps best summed up by Binnuna's paradoxical claim that Tetouan "was born whole," like Athena springing from Zeus's head.

Binnuna's narrative of Andalusi history is not one of loss but rather one of condensation and accumulation. As he surveys the full sweep of Andalusi history, from Umayyad Cordoba to Nasrid Granada, Binnuna describes a civilization that accretes, rather than dwindles, over time. Thus, for Binnuna, fifteenth-century Granada contained the best of all that came before it: "the choicest inheritors of Umayyad Cordoba and the arts of ʿAbbadid Seville." Likewise, Granada did not disappear; rather, it followed the path of the Andalusis who fled the Christian Reconquest and carried "their religion, honor, children, money, knowledge, and art to Morocco's shore." Binnuna's Andalus is a moveable collective of people and inheritances (both cultural and material) that has shifted, over the centuries, from Cordoba to Seville to Granada to Tetouan. It cannot be "lost" because it is not a fixed place or time. Like Noah's ark, everything in Binnuna's Andalus seems to come in twos. Granada synthesizes Cordoba and Seville and also brings together "scholars and jurists, pharmacists and doctors, artisans and experts, farmers and engineers." This string of dyads mirrors the pairing of Granada and Tetouan, the paragraph's overarching theme. Tetouan, therefore, was "born whole" because it always contained its other half, Granada.

As Binnuna traces the migration of Andalusis and Andalusi culture to Morocco, he introduces a new pair into the story: Granada and Fez. Most accounts of the foundation of Tetouan emphasize the collaboration between al-Manzari, the Granadan leader, and ʿAli b. Rashid, the ruler of nearby Chaouen.[102] Binnuna, in contrast, casts Tetouan as the offspring of al-Andalus and the Moroccan state, centered in Fez. According to

Binnuna's account, the Granadan exiles settled in northern Morocco, where they began to rebuild Tetouan on top of the remains of an older settlement. The Moroccan sultan, upon learning of their arrival, dispatched a delegation from Fez to help them build and populate the new city. Binnuna describes the collaboration between the Granadans and the Fasis in the following terms: "Tetouan was founded, and it was the daughter of Granada and Fez. And the two [humā] were, at the time, the two capitals ['āṣimatā] of Morocco and al-Andalus, in which were condensed all of the fortitude, subtlety, refinement, and delicacy of the civilization of the Muslim ninth century."[103] This passage is the origin of Tetouan's modern nickname, "the daughter of Granada," still in frequent use today.[104] The nickname offers an alternative to Arslan's past-tense vision of al-Andalus as "the lost paradise." In contrast with Arslan, Binnuna evokes an image of al-Andalus as a continuous family tree, stretching from medieval Iberia to modern Morocco. It is curious to note that Binnuna's phrase has been truncated in popular memory and scholarly usage. The two parents of Tetouan, "the daughter of Granada and Fez," have been reduced to one, Granada. By restoring the full context of Binnuna's phrase, a slightly different picture emerges. Binnuna suggests that Tetouan is not merely the inheritor of Granada; rather, it is the place where Morocco and al-Andalus merged and became one. Binnuna's use of the grammatical dual form underlines this point by highlighting the merging of two capitals (Granada and Fez) and two countries (Morocco and al-Andalus) into one culture, embodied in Tetouan.

Binnuna not only offers an origin story for Tetouan; he also supplements the story with a series of positive attributes that he ascribes to the Andalusi-Moroccan heritage: "fortitude, subtlety, refinement, and delicacy."[105] To this day, many Moroccans still see refinement and elegance as defining traits of Morocco's Andalusi heritage.[106] Binnuna associates these attributes with cultural and artistic practices that Moroccans inherited from al-Andalus. He goes on to enumerate these practices in his introduction to *The History of Tetouan*: "the beautiful arrangement of furniture and clothing, the great variety of food and drink, the subtle artistry in carving and engraving, good taste in presentation and subtlety in order, as well as the preservation of Andalusi music, which its first founders brought with them from Granada, Ronda, Malaga, and Fez."[107] This list indicates a shift in Moroccan thought away from the idea of al-Andalus as a "lost paradise" and toward the idea of al-Andalus as a repertoire of practices that have been preserved in Morocco since the mass exodus of Andalusi Muslims in the fifteenth century.

Among the Andalusi cultural practices cited by Binnuna are crafts and music, which, as I have argued, were revived and promoted by Spanish colonial institutions under Franco. Indeed, Binnuna and his colleague Dawud both petitioned for the creation of one of these institutions: the Hispano-Moroccan Music Conservatory.[108] In addition, Binnuna was an accomplished performer and scholar of Andalusi music, a representative of Moroccan music in the Cairo Conservatory, and a frequent organizer of Andalusi music concerts in his house in Tetouan.[109] Dawud, for his part, was an Andalusi music aficionado, an occasional lute player, and a habitué of the Andalusi music gatherings hosted on Friday nights by Tetouan's noble elite families.[110] In 1958, both Dawud and Binnuna became founding members of the Association of Lovers of Andalusi Music, perhaps the most important organization for the promotion and preservation of Andalusi music in post-independence Morocco. Binnuna was the association's deputy director; Dawud, its official archivist. In January of 1958, both men attended the association's inaugural concert, alongside Ahmad Balafrij, Muhammad al-Fasi, and Crown Prince Hassan (soon to become King Hassan II).[111] In short, both Dawud and Binnuna were instrumental in the revival of Moroccan Andalusi music at a local and national level, contributing to new national organizations and to the discourses that sustained them. In particular, they helped consolidate and disseminate a historical narrative tying twentieth-century Moroccan music to fifteenth-century Muslim Granada.

On the last page of the first volume of *The History of Tetouan*, Dawud returns to the metaphor of the "lost paradise" and combines it with the Moroccan narrative of Andalusi migration and preservation. He writes:

> It befits me to note again that the situation of this city, first upon its rebuilding and then upon the expansion of its building, then after the last Andalusi migrants settled in it, was a copy of the

> other Arab Islamic cities in the land of al-Andalus, the lost Islamic paradise. When we bear in mind that the majority of the arrivals to it from al-Andalus were from Granada, which was the last stronghold of Islam and Arabness and their civilization in Spain, we know the extent to which the inhabitants of Tetouan had civilization and progress in the styles and expressions of life, from dwelling to clothing, eating and drinking, commerce and craft. Tetouan's social life had a special stamp distinguished by fineness, pleasantness, and good taste.[112]

In this conclusion, Dawud adopts Arslan's metaphor of "the lost paradise," even while insisting that Tetouan is a "copy" of the cities of al-Andalus—and, in particular, of Granada. While paying homage to his mentor Arslan, Dawud also traces the process through which Andalusi culture was preserved and transmitted to Morocco. He reiterates the broad strokes of the narrative of cultural transmission made popular by Moroccan nationalists: Morocco's Andalusi heritage comes from Granada, is characterized by refinement, and is manifested in a repertoire of culturally specific practices. Although Andalusi music is absent from this conclusion, Dawud makes frequent allusions to it throughout his *History*. In one illustrative passage, Dawud refers to "the refined Andalusi music that the emigrants from al-Andalus brought with them from their first city, Granada the Andalusi, to their second city, Tetouan the Moroccan," and he says that the people of Tetouan preserved and transmitted the music "from generation to generation for hundreds of years until this age of ours."[113] Thus, for Dawud, the paradigm of the "lost paradise" coexists with another historical imaginary, one in which al-Andalus has been passed down by Moroccans from generation to generation until the present day.

Paradise Found

In 1953, a group of Moroccan and Spanish scholars met in Tetouan to discuss creating Morocco's first Arabic-language academic journal.[114] The group included a handful of Moroccan scholars who had played leading roles at the Mulay al-Hasan Institute, the General Franco Institute, and other colonial research institutions created under Francoism. The group's proposal for a new journal won the backing of the Spanish Delegation of Education, but the proposal was turned down by the high commissioner's office due to budgetary concerns. Three years later, in the early months of Moroccan independence, the same group of scholars revived the project and presented it to the newly created Ministry of Education, Youth, and Sports, then under the direction of Muhammad al-Fasi, a former mentee of Shakib Arslan and a scholar of al-Andalus.[115] The ministry backed the project, and thus was born Morocco's first Arabic journal, whose name was *Titwan* ("Tetouan").

The journal was described, in its masthead and on its title page, as a "journal of Andalusi Moroccan research." Its title was a reflection of its subject matter. As one of the editors, Muhammad bin Tawit, wrote in an introduction to the first issue, "We named the journal *Tetouan* . . . because this name will convey the special character of this journal (at least for the time being), and because many of the Moroccan topics that touch on al-Andalus have the closest relationship with this place."[116] Muhammad al-Fasi, the minister of education, was named the journal's editor-in-chief, but the role seems to have been largely honorary.[117] The driving forces behind the journal were three Moroccan scholars who were present at the project's conception in 1953: 'Abd Allah Gannun (b. 1908), Muhammad 'Aziman (b. 1912), and Muhammad bin Tawit (b. 1917). All three men contributed to the Spanish Protectorate's research and education programs through their work for the Mulay al-Hasan Institute, the General Franco Institute, and the Spanish Delegation of Education. Their life stories illustrate the migration of scholars and scholarship from the Spanish colonial milieu to post-independence national institutions.

'Abd Allah Gannun is considered the father of modern Moroccan literary history. His most famous work, *Moroccan Genius in Arabic Literature* (*al-Nubugh al-maghribi fi al-adab al-'arabi*), was published in Tetouan in 1938 by Dawud's Mahdiyya Press. A partial Spanish translation of the work was published by the Center for Moroccan Studies in Tetouan in 1939, the year of Franco's victory in the Spanish Civil War.[118] The same year, Gannun received an honorary doctorate from Madrid's Central University (today, the Universidad Complutense).[119] In 1941,

Gannun delivered a public lecture in Tangier to mark the Spanish Protectorate's second annual Festival of the Hispano-Arab Book.[120] In 1948, he took over as director of the Mulay al-Hasan Institute and served, in that capacity, on the jury that awarded Muhammad Dawud the Mulay al-Hasan Prize in 1953.[121] In 1956, the year of Moroccan independence, Gannun was appointed governor of Tangier, where he oversaw the dismantling of the Tangier international regime. In post-independence Morocco, Gannun occupied a number of important academic and religious posts, including his stint as the secretary-general of the League of Moroccan Scholars, a position he held from 1961 until his death in 1989.[122]

Like Gannun, 'Aziman and Ibn Tawit came up through the ranks of Francoist colonial institutions in Tetouan and then took on academic and political leadership roles in post-independence Morocco. 'Aziman studied under Muhammad Dawud at the Ahliyya School in Tetouan.[123] Like his teacher, 'Aziman delivered a speech at the tea party organized to commemorate Shakib Arslan's visit to Tetouan in August of 1930.[124] In 1942, 'Aziman became the Inspector of Moroccan Secondary Education in the Spanish Protectorate, working under his former teacher Dawud. At the same time, 'Aziman was a permanent member of the General Franco Institute's advisory council, and he also served on the jury that awarded Dawud the Mulay al-Hasan Prize in 1953.[125] After Moroccan independence, 'Aziman was appointed the deputy minister of education for northern Morocco. In this role, he helped secure the ministry's support for *Titwan* and was the journal's deputy editor.

Of the three Moroccans who led the charge to create *Titwan*, Muhammad b. Tawit was the youngest. He was one of the Moroccan students sent by the Spanish Protectorate to Cairo in 1938 to live in Morocco House, one of Beigbeder's initiatives to bolster cultural ties between Spain, Morocco, and the Arab world.[126] In 1950, Ibn Tawit joined the research faculty at the General Franco Institute.[127] In 1956, he took over as director of the Mulay al-Hasan Institute, when 'Abd Allah Gannun was appointed governor of Tangier. Ibn Tawit was the most prolific contributor to *Titwan* and was also the journal's "secretary" (roughly equivalent to managing editor, in today's parlance).

Titwan served as a bridge between the colonial period and independence, and between an old guard and a new guard of scholars and nationalists. Muhammad Dawud published an excerpt of his *History of Tetouan* in the second issue of *Titwan*. His collaborator, al-Tuhami al-Wazzani, was a member of the journal's editorial board. Another member of the board was Mariano Arribas Palau, a Spanish Arabist who served as the adjunct director of the Mulay al-Hasan Institute from 1944 to 1956, and who played an active role in the General Franco Institute and the Center for Moroccan Studies.[128] Arribas Palau's research on Hispano-Moroccan diplomatic relations was published, in Arabic translation, in the pages of *Titwan*. The journal also jump-started the careers of several young Moroccan scholars and writers, such as Muhammad al-Manuni and Muhammad al-Sabbagh. Al-Sabbagh was responsible for the bulletin of cultural events that appeared at the end of each issue of *Titwan*. He is perhaps best known today for his volume of poetry *I Am al-Andalus* (1999), a paean to Morocco's Andalusi identity. The journal *Titwan* was, likewise, a platform for asserting Morocco's Andalusi identity—and, in particular, Morocco's preservation of the cultural traditions of medieval Muslim Granada.

The cover art for *Titwan* illustrated the journal's preoccupation with Morocco's Andalusi heritage (Figure 19). The cover was designed by an artist named Fawzi who taught Islamic art at Tetouan's School of Fine Arts, founded by Mariano Bertuchi.[129] Fawzi's drawing depicts a well-known fountain that is located near Bab al-ʿUqla, one of the gates to Tetouan's old city. The fountain in the drawing has all of the design elements associated today with Andalusi arts in Morocco: an intricate tile mosaic (*zellij*), carved plaster and wood, and a green tile roof. Around the drawing runs an ornate frame with geometric and floral patterns, resembling a frieze or a carved plaster wall decoration. At the top of the frame, there is an Arabic inscription: "There is no victor but God" (*Wa-lā ghālib illā Allah*). The phrase is the motto of the Nasrid dynasty that ruled Muslim Granada until 1492. The motto is emblazoned on several walls in the Alhambra.[130] Indeed, the Arabic inscription on the cover of *Titwan* clearly evokes the look and form of the calligraphy that decorates the walls of the Alhambra. The journal's title, *Titwan*, appears in large block letters directly underneath the Nasrid motto. The juxtaposition of the two texts suggests that Tetouan is the continuation and inheritor of the culture of Nasrid Granada. In fact, since independence,

Figure 19. Cover of the first issue of the journal *Titwan* (1956). Artwork by Fawzi. Published by the Northern Delegation of the Ministry of Education, Youth, and Sports, Kingdom of Morocco. Printed by Cremades Press in Tetouan, Morocco. Reproduced from a copy at University of California Southern Regional Library Facility.

the motto of Nasrid Granada has been appropriated by Moroccans and used in some of Morocco's most famous contemporary monuments, as I will discuss in the epilogue.

Ibn Tawit's preface to the inaugural issue of *Titwan* also stresses the Moroccan claim on al-Andalus. This claim serves as the justification for the journal's existence:

> Andalusi Moroccan research is monopolized by journals that are published in languages other than Arabic, such as the French journal *Hespéris,* or the Spanish journal *Al-Andalus,* or the journal *Tamuda,* which has recently come out in Spanish. There is not in Arabic a journal of this nature, except for the journal of the Egyptian Institute in Madrid, in which (mostly) Egyptian pens pour out Andalusi research, in particular. They do not broach Moroccan subjects, except for that which is related to al-Andalus, primarily as a means of opposing them, rather than turning toward them.[131]

Ibn Tawit makes the case, here, for an Arabic and Moroccan approach to Andalusi studies. Lamenting the European "monopolization" of research on al-Andalus, he calls out three journals that were products of European colonialism in Morocco: *Hespéris,* the journal of the French Protectorate's Institute for Advanced Moroccan Studies; *Al-Andalus,* the journal of the Schools of Arabic Studies in Granada and Madrid; and *Tamuda,* the journal of the Spanish Protectorate's Delegation of Education and Culture. It is worth noting, in passing, that many of *Titwan*'s editors were also on the editorial committee for the Spanish-language journal *Tamuda*.[132] Regardless, Ibn Tawit advocates for Arabic-language scholarship on al-Andalus. At the same time, he suggests that writing in Arabic is not enough to address the current gaps in Andalusi studies. He notes that the Egyptian Institute of Islamic Studies in Madrid, founded in 1950, publishes a journal with Arabic-language scholarship on Andalusi topics, but he faults the Egyptian contributors to this journal for ignoring Moroccan subjects, or for treating Moroccan culture in opposition to Andalusi culture.[133]

Ibn Tawit suggests that the problem with Egyptian scholarship is that Egyptians do not understand Morocco—and that they might not understand al-Andalus, either. To make this point, Ibn Tawit returns to Arslan's nostalgic vision of al-Andalus as the "lost paradise":

> The excuse of our dear Egyptian brothers is acceptable, clear, and irreproachable. We admire their fidelity to science because they do not want—as they have declared more than once—to cram themselves into something over which they do not have mastery. This blessed throng stayed in al-Andalus, got to know its affairs, studied its ancient and modern culture, and prepared numerous theses, for which they worthily and appropriately earned doctoral degrees. In addition to that, they headed for "the lost paradise," and they became mad with whatever fruits were discarded under its autumnal trees, which feet trample and horseshoes tread. And they salvaged there whatever they could salvage. As for our paradise (thank God!), it is in our possession. We savor its fruits and inhale the fragrance of its flowers. It is not suitable for them to intrude into it. . . . Their slumber is what has prevented them from harvesting its fruit and taking pleasure in the perfume of its flower.[134]

In this sardonic passage, Ibn Tawit takes a few cuts at his "dear Egyptian brothers." On the one hand, he suggests that Egyptian scholars do not know enough about Morocco to write about it; on the other, he implies that Egyptian scholarship on al-Andalus is limited by the nostalgic, "autumnal" vision of al-Andalus as a lost paradise. This vision, Ibn Tawit contends, has prevented Egyptians from seeing that the Andalusi paradise is alive and well—just on the other side of the Strait of Gibraltar.

Thus, in a surprising turn, Ibn Tawit argues that Moroccans must wrest control of the historical memory of al-Andalus from both Europeans *and* non-Moroccan Arabs. He leaves behind Arslan's vision of al-Andalus as a cherished but departed past—or, to borrow the Moroccan's metaphor, as autumnal fruit discarded and trampled upon. Instead, he calls for a Moroccan al-Andalus, a living al-Andalus. There is a huge irony behind this call to arms. As Ibn Tawit encourages Moroccans to free themselves from the weight of both European and Eastern Arab scholarship, he lands upon a view of Moroccan culture that was very much created by Spanish colonialism. Spanish politicians, writers, and artists—particularly those affiliated with Spanish fascism—justified Spain's colonial projects by claiming that Moroccans were the direct descendants of medieval Muslim Granada. By the period of Moroccan independence, Moroccan scholars, like Ibn Tawit, had claimed this idea as their own and turned it into a central piece of Moroccan national identity.

EPILOGUE

The Afterlife of Colonial al-Andalus in Contemporary Morocco

WHEN I'M IN TANGIER, I like to eat lunch at Restaurant Al-Andalus on Rue du Commerce. They make a mean swordfish, grilled over charcoal and served, upon request, with fried tomatoes and herbs. From the restaurant, it is just a few steps to the nearby Petit Socco, the legendary crossroads of Tangier's old city. On the way, you pass by Buen Gusto Café Tanger, whose name is a reminder of a time when the Petit Socco was the beating heart of Tangier's vibrant Spanish community.[1] That time has now passed, but it has left its imprint on the city. Within sight of the Petit Socco, a half block down Rue Mokhtar Ahardan, is Pension Palace, a run-down hotel whose building used to be the Spanish Legation in Tangier. Inaugurated in 1786, the Spanish Legation became, in the nineteenth century, one of the most important buildings in Tangier's old city.[2] In 1918, with the building of the European *ville nouvelle,* the Spanish consul's residence was moved to a new building, outside the city walls. The old Spanish Legation was then converted into the Spanish Post and Telegraph Office, a function that the building continued to serve until 1958, when it became a hotel. According to an article published in the Spanish newspaper *ABC* in March of 1958, the closing of the Spanish post office in Tangier sent shockwaves through the city's European population, who interpreted the event as the end of an era. The article lamented that the closing of the post office meant that "a good piece of the history of international and cosmopolitan Tangier is going away."[3]

Today, few people in Tangier seem to remember Pension Palace's former life as a Spanish post office and diplomatic residence. The building, though, tells an eloquent story about how Spanish colonial culture is hiding in plain sight in contemporary Morocco. The building's courtyard (Figure 20) is an imitation of the Alhambra's Court of the Lions.[4] The four lions that flank the fountain at the center of the courtyard look more like monkeys than lions. Nevertheless, the reference to the Alhambra is clear and is borne out by other visual clues. For instance, the walls of the courtyard are decorated with mass-produced tile mosaics with green, blue, and yellow patterns that are reminiscent of the handcrafted tile mosaics in the Alhambra—or, for that matter, in Tetouan's School of Indigenous Arts. At the corners of the courtyard, there are stone columns whose capitals, like the walls of the Alhambra, carry the motto of Nasrid Granada: "There is no victor but God."

Tangier's miniature Alhambra stands today in a state of quiet abandon. During a recent visit, the water in the central courtyard was turned off, and a surfboard leaned against the wall tiles. Around the ersatz Court of the Lions, plants and trees stood in various stages of neglect. On the bannister surrounding the second-floor gallery, clothes were hung out to dry. From the courtyard, you could hear a murmur of sounds coming from the nearby Petit Socco: a quiet conversation, an exclamation of greeting, the occasional moped zooming by. Pension Palace has definitely seen better days. Inertia, not conservationism, has kept alive this colonial-era homage to the Alhambra.

From Restaurant Al-Andalus to the Pension Palace's Court of Lions, casual encounters with al-Andalus are a common occurrence in Tangier, Tetouan, and many other Moroccan cities. Allusions to al-Andalus might be more common in northern Morocco, on account of the region's colonial history and its proximity to Spain. Nevertheless, it would be wrong to think of Morocco's Andalusi identity as a regional phenomenon,

Figure 20. Courtyard of Pension Palace in Tangier, Morocco, May 2016. Photograph © Eric Calderwood.

limited to the areas formerly under Spanish colonial rule. In this book, I have argued that the way that Moroccans talk about their Andalusi identity and culture changed as a result of Spanish colonialism in Morocco. The afterlife of "colonial al-Andalus" is felt most strongly in northern Morocco, but its influence stretches across the country, including to the former centers of French colonial rule. I began this book by discussing a Tetouani mausoleum that brings together the remains of al-Manzari, Tetouan's fifteenth-century founder from Granada, and al-Turris, the leader of the Moroccan nationalist movement in northern Morocco. I will now turn to a contemporaneous mausoleum, built in the 1960s in Rabat, the capital of newly independent Morocco and the former capital of the French Protectorate. My goal will be to point, albeit briefly, to how colonial discourses about al-Andalus have made their way into the official discourse of the ruling ʿAlawi dynasty.

Building al-Andalus in Contemporary Morocco: Unfinished Projects

Rabat's most famous Andalusi monument was never finished. In 1197, the third Almohad caliph, Ya'qub al-Mansur (r. 1184–1199), ordered the construction of a colossal mosque in Rabat on a promontory overlooking the point where the Bou Regreg River meets the Atlantic Ocean.[5] The mosque was projected to be one of the largest in the world. When Ya'qub al-Mansur died in 1199, the building project ground to a halt. For the next few centuries, the site suffered from the passage of time, the occasional pillaging, a fire, and from the sea waves caused by the devastating earthquake that hit Lisbon in 1755. Today, an unfinished minaret and a forest of phantom columns mark the spot where Ya'qub al-Mansur planned his mosque.

The minaret (Figure 21), known as the Hassan Minaret ("Tour Hassan," or Ṣawmaʻat Ḥassān), soars forty-four meters into the sky and is visible from many points in Rabat. It echoes many of the design elements of the two other famous minarets built during Ya'qub al-Mansur's reign, the Kutubiyya Mosque in Marrakesh and the Giralda in Seville. The three minarets, sometimes called "the three sisters," have often been upheld as symbols of the cultural and political unity of al-Andalus and the Maghrib during the period of Almohad rule, and of the Andalusi cultural legacy that unites contemporary Spain and Morocco.[6] The Hassan Minaret, like its "sisters" in Seville and Marrakesh, sits on a square foundation and is built with earth-colored stone and bricks that serve both structural and decorative purposes. The four sides of the minaret's façade are decorated with stones cut in geometric and floral patterns and with decorative columns connected by arches.[7]

In the decades since Moroccan independence, the twelfth-century Hassan Minaret has been incorporated into a complex of monuments celebrating the ruling 'Alawi dynasty, which came to power in the seventeenth century. On October 9, 2015, King Muhammad VI inaugurated the archive of the 'Alawi dynasty (known as the Khizanat al-Dawla al-'Alawiyya) in a space built directly underneath the foundation of the Hassan Minaret.[8] The archive's façade is adorned with the 'Alawi dynasty's family tree, tracing the family's lineage back to the Prophet

Figure 21. Hassan Minaret in Rabat, Morocco, September 2016. Photograph © Eric Calderwood.

Muhammad. The archive contains the official documents of the 'Alawi dynasty, including diplomatic correspondence and sultans' decrees from the period of 'Alawi rule. Thus, the official archive of the ruling Moroccan dynasty literally undergirds the foundation of the Hassan Minaret, which is, in turn, an architectural symbol of the cultural unity between Morocco and al-Andalus.

The recently inaugurated 'Alawi archive joins a group of related monuments that were built near the Hassan Minaret in the 1960s. King Muhammad V, who helped lead Morocco to independence, died unexpectedly in 1961 from complications related to a minor surgery. After his death, his son Hassan II (r. 1961–1999) decided to erect a mausoleum complex in his honor. It was Hassan II's first major public commission as king. For the project, he hired the Vietnamese-born architect Vo Toan, who was trained at the School of Fine Arts in Paris.[9] Hassan II instructed Vo to incorporate the mausoleum complex into the site of the ruined Hassan Mosque. The location had both historic and contemporary symbolic resonances. As one of the most famous architectural monuments from the Almohad dynasty, the Hassan Mosque evoked a time when Moroccan political and cultural influence spread across North Africa and the Iberian Peninsula. The monument was also a symbol of the Moroccan nationalist struggle for independence from European colonial rule. It was the place where Muhammad V led a crowd in prayer when he returned to Morocco from exile in 1955, on the eve of independence.[10] When Muhammad V died in 1961, his body lay in state on the spot of the former prayer niche of the Hassan Mosque, and throngs of Moroccans visited the site in order to pay their respects to the deceased king.[11] Therefore, when Hassan II chose the area surrounding the Hassan Minaret as the site for his father's mausoleum, he was choosing a space that symbolized Morocco's past glory, its cultural connections with the Iberian Peninsula, and its recent fight for independence.

The mausoleum complex, built from 1962 to 1971, consists of three buildings: a mausoleum, a mosque, and a museum. The complex contains numerous intertextual references to the Hassan Minaret, which stands in front of it. Indeed, several features serve to cast the mausoleum complex as the continuation and completion of the Almohad mosque that was left unfinished at the end of the twelfth century. The Hassan

Minaret is connected to the twentieth-century mausoleum complex by a long esplanade populated by columns from the abandoned twelfth-century mosque. The Moroccan historian Kamal Lakhdar has described the esplanade as a temporal bridge linking eight centuries of Moroccan history: "With the Hassan Minaret and the Muhammad V Mausoleum, eight centuries meet on this esplanade."[12] The esplanade is a place of blinding light. Though surrounded by palm trees, it has no trees or vegetation, thereby giving the visitor the impression of a vast, open-air courtyard connecting the minaret to the buildings in front of it.

The mausoleum complex for Muhammad V was built along the former Hassan Mosque's *qibla* wall, signaling the direction of Mecca.[13] The mosque, which is in the middle of the complex, is directly aligned with the Hassan Minaret. This spatial composition ties together the twelfth-century minaret and the twentieth-century mosque. In fact, Vo designed the new mosque without a minaret because, as the architect explained, "this function is served by that of the old Tower of Hassan itself."[14] As you walk from the Hassan Minaret toward the mosque, you walk in the direction of the *qibla* wall—that is, in the direction of prayer. The abandoned medieval columns, which once supported a roof, now play the role of a courtyard leading you to the modern mosque. The mosque itself mirrors the design of the Almohad monument that is in front of it. It is built with earth-colored stones that are very similar to the ones that were used to build the Hassan Minaret. The stones are cut in geometric and floral patterns that mimic the patterns on the Hassan Minaret's façade. The same patterns adorn the exterior walls of Muhammad V's mausoleum, connected to the mosque by a lateral courtyard. Thus, the spatial composition, materials, and decorative patterns of the mausoleum complex reflect the Almohad monument to which it was appended.

The Muhammad V mausoleum complex does not merely mirror the Hassan Minaret; it also embodies the modern revival of Morocco's Andalusi identity. King Hassan II, the mastermind behind Muhammad V's mausoleum, was a major patron of Morocco's Andalusi cultural heritage. Hassan II frequently incorporated references to Morocco's Andalusi roots in his speeches and interviews.[15] Under his rule, the Moroccan Ministry of Culture oversaw the first recording of the complete repertoire of Moroccan Andalusi music.[16] Hassan II also encouraged the publication of modern Moroccan editions of Andalusi texts and supported academic conferences about Morocco's relationship with al-Andalus.[17] Finally, he championed Morocco's "Andalusi" craft traditions, such as tile mosaics (*zellij*), through major building projects, like the Hassan II Mosque in Casablanca.[18] In 1992, Muhammad Binsharifa, the director of the Moroccan National Library, declared:

> These traditional arts and crafts descended from the Moroccan-Andalusi heritage are experiencing today an important blossoming, thanks to the brilliant royal guidance. . . . His Majesty the King's order to restore the historic royal palaces in Fez, Marrakesh, and elsewhere, caused a revival of these Andalusi-Moroccan arts, and rescued them from ruin when they were on the verge of dying out.[19]

Binsharifa's description of the revival of Morocco's Andalusi arts under Hassan II recalls earlier Spanish claims about the renaissance of Morocco's Andalusi arts under colonial rule. Binsharifa, however, presents an alternative narrative of decline and rebirth. In contrast with Spanish and French writers, who claimed that colonialism rescued Morocco's crafts from a centuries-long decline, Binsharifa insists that Moroccan crafts were "on the verge of dying out" by the end of European colonial rule.

The Muhammad V mausoleum project was, as Roberson has argued, a major landmark in Hassan II's efforts to promote Moroccan craft traditions. Four hundred craftsmen worked on the mausoleum complex under the direction of Mohamed Ben Abdelkrim, a master craftsman (*mu'allim* or, in Moroccan dialect, *m'allim*) from Fez.[20] In a 1976 illustrated guide to the mausoleum, Abdelwahab Benmansour, the mausoleum's curator and the official historian of Morocco under Hassan II, called the complex a "living testimony of the rebirth of Moroccan art and handicrafts."[21] Benmansour went on to say, "Future generations will speak of the Muhammad V mausoleum built in the reign of His Majesty King Hassan II as the symbol of the Moroccan Renaissance."[22] In the same guide, the architect Vo Toan deployed a similar rhetoric of rebirth, calling the mausoleum complex a "living testimony of a renaissance in traditional Moroccan art" and "the symbol of Morocco's independence."[23] Here, it is important to note that Vo aligns the rebirth of Moroccan art with the rebirth of Morocco as an independent nation.

The trope of "independence as national rebirth" runs throughout the guide, but it is particularly emphatic in a preface written by Muhammad al-Fasi, the former minister of education, editor of the journal *Titwan*, and mentee of Shakib Arslan. Al-Fasi calls Muhammad V "the Hero of Independence who freed his people from the foreign yoke" and "the Savior who snatched them out of the grip of foreign domination."[24] Al-Fasi casts Moroccan independence as a clean break from European colonialism. He treats Muhammad V's mausoleum as a symbol of Moroccan independence and, thus, as a symbol of Morocco's rupture with the colonial period. In a similar vein, al-Fasi praises the architect, Vo Toan, for achieving "the renovation of architectural art *in the purest Moroccan tradition.*"[25] Such invocations of "pure traditions" should raise a red flag for scholars of nationalism. They often serve as a cover for invented traditions. Indeed, upon closer inspection, Muhammad V's mausoleum seems less like a rupture from colonialism and more like a prolongation of discourses and cultural practices carried over from the colonial period.

The mausoleum complex was Vo's first commission in Morocco and in the Muslim world. To familiarize himself with Moroccan architecture, Vo traveled throughout the country and visited famous mosques and religious monuments.[26] Notably, he also traveled to Spain, where, he writes, "centuries of Islamic history and civilization left in Cordoba, Seville, Granada, or in Toledo prestigious palaces and mosques which constitute immense and invaluable jewels of the art of an inventive and refined people most of whom came from Morocco, either under the Almoravids, the Almohads, or the Nasrids."[27] In Spanish colonial writings, the best parts of Moroccan culture come from al-Andalus, not the other way around. In contrast, Vo makes Andalusi art Moroccan. That is, he casts the Islamic monuments of Cordoba, Seville, Granada, and Toledo as exemplars of the art that North Africans brought to the Iberian Peninsula. He thus suggests that Andalusi art has always been Moroccan at its core.

Vo writes that the Muhammad V mausoleum complex was built as a "prolongation" of the Hassan Minaret.[28] Nevertheless, the Almohad structure was not the only monument from which he drew inspiration. He writes: "Like the Alhambra of Granada, the mosque of Cordoba, or the palaces and medersas of Morocco in their time, the mausoleum, mosque, and museum complex is destined to become a symbol of the renaissance of Moroccan art under King Hassan II."[29] Vo places the mausoleum complex within an architectural lineage that goes back to the eighth-century Mosque of Cordoba and moves forward through the Alhambra and then shifts to the other side of the Strait of Gibraltar. Like many of the writers I have analyzed in this book, Vo imagines a direct chain of transmission that links medieval Muslim Granada to modern Morocco. The "renaissance of Moroccan art under King Hassan II" is, thus, also the return of al-Andalus.

Vo's allusions to the Alhambra and the Mosque of Cordoba are not haphazard. In fact, he visited these and other Islamic monuments in Spain and consciously incorporated references to them in the design for the mausoleum complex. Vo details these references to Andalusi architecture in his guide to the mausoleum. He notes, for example, that the columned porch surrounding the mausoleum features tapered columns, rather than the cylindrical columns that are more common in Moroccan buildings. The architect explains that tapered columns are found in Greco-Roman monuments but also in the Mosque of Cordoba.[30] The allusions to al-Andalus proliferate in the mausoleum's interior. Visitors enter the mausoleum at a gallery level that is one floor above the chamber where Muhammad V's sarcophagus sits on a sea of onyx and dark blue granite. The inner side of the gallery's balcony is covered with multicolored tile mosaics. The outside of the balcony, facing into the tomb chamber, is covered with bronze plating carved in a polygonal design. Above the polygonal design is a frieze that repeats the motto of Nasrid Granada, written in Andalusi script: "There is no victor but God."[31]

This use of the Nasrid motto is not the only homage to the Alhambra in Vo's design for the mausoleum complex. Vo also planned to build "Granada gardens," based on the Generalife gardens at the Alhambra, around the mausoleum and the Hassan Minaret.[32] The architect envisioned gardens with paths paved with pebbles and with flowerbeds bordered by hedges trimmed in geometric designs.[33] Vo seems to have been unaware of the fact that the Generalife's design, which he was emulating, was a recent invention, based on late nineteenth-century work in the Alhambra's gardens.[34] The plan to build the "Granada gardens" was never fully realized, but it serves as further evidence of the influence that the Alhambra exercised on Vo's design for the mausoleum complex.

Vo also drew upon an Andalusi model to design the large cupola that crowns the tomb chamber. The cupola rises from a square base to form a twelve-sided dome of carved mahogany covered in gold leaf. The dome's mahogany is carved in the intricate stalactite forms known as *muqarnas,* which are found in the Alhambra and many other Andalusi buildings. Indeed, Vo points to the Alcázar of Seville as the inspiration for the mausoleum's cupola. He writes: "A similarly vivid example of the virtuosity of Moroccan cabinet-making still exists in the Alcázar in Seville, in the Ambassadors Hall, where one can admire the cupola of wooden open-work starting on a square base and rising to a half sphere."[35] Vo alludes to the Hall of the Ambassadors in Seville's Alcázar, one of the most famous examples of the Mudéjar style that was popular among Christian rulers who conquered Muslim territories in medieval Iberia. As I have previously indicated, the hall was commissioned by the Castilian ruler Pedro I in 1366. Visitors to the Hall of the Ambassadors in Seville are often struck by its resemblance to the eponymous Hall of the Ambassadors in the Alhambra. The resemblance is not a coincidence. The Nasrid ruler of Granada, Muhammad V, sent Muslim artisans from his court to work on Pedro I's Alcázar, perhaps because the Christian ruler had helped Muhammad V to regain his throne in 1362.[36]

It is worth pausing for a moment to draw attention to the intricate web of influences on display in the mausoleum: the French-trained architect Vo modeled part of his mausoleum for a twentieth-century Moroccan king on a fourteenth-century Spanish Christian palace that emulated, in turn, the Islamic architecture of Nasrid Granada. Vo's design attempted to synthesize these diverse influences into a single, coherent style that encompassed buildings as diverse as the Mosque of Cordoba, the Hassan Minaret in Rabat, the Alcázar of Seville, the Alhambra, and Muhammad V's mausoleum complex. This style—an amalgam of medieval and modern, Andalusi and Maghribi—became, under Hassan II, something akin to a national architectural style, one that gave independent Morocco a visual identity rooted in craft traditions from al-Andalus. This national style cannibalized historical narratives and artistic practices developed under colonialism, while at the same time eliminating any explicit reference to colonialism.

Hassan II and his collaborators cast the mausoleum project as a symbol of Morocco's independence and of its break from colonial rule. Yet, the project illustrates the significant imprint that Spanish colonialism left on Moroccan culture and politics. I am not suggesting that Hassan II or the architect Vo read any of the Spanish colonial authors whose work I have analyzed in this book. Rather, I mean to argue that, by the 1960s, the key precepts of Spanish colonialism had successfully been transformed into unquestioned truths about Moroccan culture. The Muhammad V mausoleum complex, like al-Manzari's mausoleum in Tetouan, embodies this transfer of ideas from the Spanish colonial imaginary to the Moroccan national imaginary. Both mausoleums compress time, bracket the colonial period, and represent Moroccan independence as the restoration of the Andalusi-Moroccan heritage. They both link post-independence Moroccan identity to medieval Granada and to the migration of Andalusi culture from the Iberian Peninsula to Morocco in the fifteenth century. The Muhammad V mausoleum complex not only embodies this narrative of cultural transmission but also serves as a showcase for the repertoire of Andalusi arts that were revived under the auspices of European colonialism. Thus, the mausoleum is both a tribute to the father of Moroccan independence and a sign of the long shadow that colonialism casts over independence.

While Muhammad V's mausoleum is one of Rabat's principal tourist attractions, al-Manzari's mausoleum in Tetouan receives almost no visitors. In this sense, the two mausoleums also represent the very different paths that Rabat and Tetouan, the respective capitals of the French and Spanish Protectorates, have taken in the post-independence period. Tetouan was notoriously underserved and shunned during Hassan II's reign. The city has experienced something of a rebirth under Muhammad VI, who summers nearby, but it still lags far behind Rabat in terms of economic development and social services. Today, the main drivers of Tetouan's economy are the drug trade and the business of smuggling goods from the nearby Spanish enclave of Ceuta. There is an intimate relationship between Tetouan's current struggles, the oblivion that surrounds al-Manzari's mausoleum, and the story that this book has sought to tell. During the colonial period, Spanish and Moroccan writers, politicians, and artists worked in surprising collaboration to create and disseminate a new set of ideas about the relationship between medieval al-Andalus and modern Morocco. The diverse actors who participated in this unlikely project are largely forgotten today, and the city where most of them lived and worked exists at the margins of Moroccan political and economic life. Nevertheless, their ideas animated nearly a century of Spanish policy toward Morocco and have persisted into the twenty-first century as defining characteristics of Moroccan identity. In this sense, the mausoleum that al-Manzari shares with 'Abd al-Khaliq al-Turris in Tetouan is both a symbol of what Morocco has become and also a reminder of the people who have been forgotten along the way.

NOTES

BIBLIOGRAPHY

ACKNOWLEDGMENTS

INDEX

NOTES

INTRODUCTION

1. For Tetouan's Medina, see Benaboud, "Medina de Tetuán"; Benaboud and Torres López, "Murallas y mazmorras." For Tetouan's Ensanche, see Malo de Molina and Domínguez, *Tetuán, el Ensanche*; Bravo Nieto, *Arquitectura*, 71–86. For an introduction to the Spanish Protectorate in Morocco, see Madariaga, *Marruecos*.

2. For Tetouan's cemetery, see Calderwood, "Letter from Morocco"; Ibn al-Hajj al-Sulami, "La mémoire silencieuse." For al-Manzari, see Gozalbes Busto, *Al-Mandari*; Dawud, *Tarikh Titwan*, 1:85–110. For al-Turris, whose name is often rendered "Abdelkhaleq Torres," see Wolf, *Secrets*; Benjelloun, *Mouvement*; Madariaga, *Marruecos*, 223–237, 292–402.

3. Dawud, *Tarikh Titwan*, 1:95–96; Gozalbes Busto, *Al-Mandari*, 43–49.

4. Several historians have noted the military nature of al-Manzari's original settlement in Tetouan, including Benaboud, "Medina de Tetuán," 44; al-Sharif, *Titwan*, 15; Miège, Benaboud, and Erzini, *Tétouan*, 15.

5. Harvey, *Islamic Spain*, 314–322.

6. The campaign to force Spanish Muslims to convert to Christianity began in Granada in 1500. By the mid-1520s, it had spread to all Spanish territories, as discussed by Harvey, *Muslims in Spain*, 1–101.

7. The population figures are based on Gozalbes Busto's estimates in *Al-Mandari*, 110. See also García-Arenal, "Los moriscos en Marruecos," 276–281.

8. Benaboud and Torres López, "Murallas y mazmorras," 72; Gozalbes Busto, *Al-Mandari*, 107–110.

9. Ibn al-Hajj al-Sulami, "La mémoire silencieuse," 138–141. For the *qubba* in Andalusi cemeteries, see Pavón, *Ciudades hispanomusulmanas*, 79–84.

10. In order to reconstruct the history of al-Manzari's shared mausoleum with al-Turris, I have relied on interviews with Kenza Torres, the daughter of ʿAbd al-Khaliq al-Turris, and Boubkir Bennouna (Binnuna), the brother of Saʿd Binnuna and the son of ʿAbd al-Salam Binnuna. My interviews with

Kenza Torres took place by phone and email on May 10–12, 2016. I met with Boubkir Bennouna in person in his house in Tetouan on May 11 and 12, 2016.

11. For ʿAbd al-Salam Binnuna, see Ibn ʿAzzuz Hakim, *Ab*; Benjelloun, *Approches*, 95–108.

12. Wolf, *Secrets*, 33–51.

13. Al-Turris delivered this speech in Spanish on Radio Sevilla on October 14, 1936. The text of the speech, written in al-Turris's hand on the stationery of Seville's Alfonso XIII Hotel, is currently held in Boubkir Bennouna's private archive in Tetouan.

14. Benaboud, "Medina de Tetuán," 40. All English translations are mine, unless otherwise noted.

15. Binsharifa, "al-ʿInaya"; El-Khatib Boujibar and Mezzine, "Le Maroc andalou"; al-Sharif, *Titwan*, 5–50; Benaboud, "Medina de Tetuán"; González Alcantud, "Los andalusíes hoy"; González Alcantud and Rojo Flores, "Al-Ándalus"; Shannon, *Performing al-Andalus*, 84–118; Saaf, "Elementos"; Bouali, *Poemas marroquíes y al-Andalus*; Benmansour, "Khitab al-iftitah."

16. See Bouali, *Poemas marroquíes y al-Andalus*; Fernández Parrilla, *La literatura marroquí contemporánea*, 140–150; Allen, "Rewriting Literary History," 316–317.

17. For Andalusi music in North Africa, see Glasser, *Lost Paradise*; Glasser, "Andalusi"; Davila, *Andalusian Music*; Shannon, *Performing al-Andalus*, 84–118; Chaachoo, *Música andalusí*.

18. Calderwood, "Proyectando al-Ándalus," 219–232.

19. Tourism accounts for roughly 11.4 percent of Moroccan GDP and is Morocco's second largest source of GDP and employment, according to the Moroccan Ministry of Tourism. "Chiffres Clés," Secrétariat d'État chargé du Tourisme, accessed June 27, 2017, www.tourisme.gov.ma/fr/tourisme-en-chiffres/chiffres-cles.

20. One of these tourism initiatives is described in Calderwood, "Invention of al-Andalus," 36–45.

21. Binnuna coined Tetouan's nickname in his introduction to *Tarikh Titwan*, 15. It also appears in al-Sharif, *Titwan*, 5–50; Benaboud, "Tétouan, le patio," 164.

22. "Medina of Tétouan (formerly known as Titawin)," UNESCO World Heritage Centre, accessed June 28, 2017, http://whc.unesco.org/en/list/837.

In current academic practice, Anglophone scholars use the adjective "Andalusi" to refer to al-Andalus (medieval Muslim Iberia) and the adjective "Andalusian" to refer to Andalucía (the region in contemporary Spain). In this book, I will try to maintain a strict distinction between what is "Andalusi" and what is "Andalusian." The only exception is when I am citing a source, such as the UNESCO report, that uses the adjective "Andalusian" to refer to medieval al-Andalus.

23. Al-Sharif, *Titwan*, 5–50; Dawud, *Tarikh Titwan*, 1:431; Razzuq, *al-Andalusiyyun*, 293–299; Benaboud, "Medina de Tetuán," 42.

24. *La Constitution*, Secrétariat Général du Gouvernement, July 29, 2011, www.sgg.gov.ma/Portals/o/constitution/constitution_2011_Fr.pdf.

25. The scholarship on the concept of *convivencia* is quite extensive. Helpful introductions are found in Akasoy, "*Convivencia* and Its Discontents"; Martin-Márquez, *Disorientations*, 300–307; Nirenberg, *Communities of Violence*, 8–10.

26. See Calderwood, "Reconquista"; Shannon, *Performing al-Andalus*, 158–179; Goytisolo, "Américo Castro," 30–31; Manzano Moreno, "Qurtuba," 233–234.

27. For example, in 2011, the Moroccan Ministry of Foreign Affairs presented a "National Action Plan" to the United Nations Alliance of Civilizations program. The report says: "The history of Morocco has been that of an uninterrupted cultural, religious, and ethnic mixing between Muslims, Christians and Jews, Arabs and Berbers, peoples of European origin and others of African descent. Its location at the junction of two continents and at the heart of the Mediterranean Basin—this cosmopolitan space where both East and West meet—has made it especially possible for Morocco to be a country of intercultural exchange." See "National Action Plan for the Alliance of Civilizations," United Nations Alliance of Civilizations, March 18, 2011, www.unaoc.org/wp-content/uploads/National-Plan-of-Morocco.pdf. The Spanish-language version of Morocco's "National Action Plan," available at the same website, uses the word *convivencia* to describe the successful integration of Jews and Moriscos in Morocco.

28. González Alcantud and Rojo Flores, "Al-Ándalus"; González Alcantud, "Los andalusíes hoy"; Saaf, "Elementos," 308–310; Wolf, *Secrets*, 37–55; Binsharifa, "al-'Inaya," 33.

29. I discuss the Spanish-Moroccan War of 1859–1860 in Chapters 1 and 2. For al-Andalus in Spanish colonial discourse, see also Martin-Márquez, *Disorientations*; González Alcantud, *Mito*, 86–103; Mateo Dieste, *La "hermandad" hispano-marroquí*, 223–227.

30. For the participation of Moroccan soldiers in the Spanish Civil War, see Madariaga, *Marruecos*, 325–335; Balfour, *Deadly Embrace*, 268–317. The Francoists referred to themselves as the "Nationalists" (*Nacionales*), but throughout this book, I will refer to them as "the rebels." I thus follow the practice of many contemporary scholars who have used the term "rebels" (*sublevados*) to emphasize the Francoists' rebellion against the democratically

elected Republic. See, for example, Martin-Márquez, *Disorientations;* Álvarez Junco, prologue to *Las historias de España.*

31. The Andalusi migration to Morocco is documented in García-Arenal, "Los moriscos en Marruecos"; Razzuq, *al-Andalusiyyun;* Gozalbes Busto, *Los Moriscos en Marruecos.*

Following the current convention in Moroccan studies, I use the term "Andalusi" to refer to two groups that are often kept separate in modern European and American scholarship: "Andalusis" and "Moriscos." In European and American scholarly writings, the term "Andalusi" is generally reserved to describe the people who lived under Muslim rule in the Iberian Peninsula from 711 to 1492, whereas the term "Morisco" generally refers to the Muslims and crypto-Muslims who remained on the Iberian Peninsula from 1492 until the expulsion decrees of 1609-1614. In Moroccan scholarship, both groups of people are called "Andalusis." See García-Arenal, "Los moriscos en Marruecos," 275. For the problems associated with the term "Morisco," see Harvey, *Muslims in Spain,* 1–6.

32. Elinson, *Looking Back,* 134–150; Gómez-Rivas, "Exile."

33. See Saaf, "Elementos"; González Alcantud, "Los andalusíes hoy"; González Alcantud and Rojo Flores, "Al-Ándalus," 8–9.

34. Gil Benumeya, *Marruecos andaluz,* 139–140.

35. Ibid., 122–176.

36. Binsharifa, "al-ʿInaya," 27.

37. Al-Sharif, *Titwan,* 5.

38. García Figueras, *Marruecos,* 341.

39. For example, Álvarez Junco and Fuente Monge assert that the first years of Francoism "constituted a radical rupture with the recent past and an open offensive against everything that the liberal tradition stood for." "Evolución," 405–406. For the conflict between two competing views of Spain in the Spanish Civil War, see Juliá, *Historias;* Álvarez Junco and Fuente Monge, "Evolución," 353–457.

40. In particular, the idea of *convivencia* is often attributed to the exiled Republican intellectual Américo Castro (1885–1975). See Álvarez Junco and Fuente Monge, "Evolución," 385–396; Martin-Márquez, *Disorientations,* 303–304; Subirats, ed., *Américo Castro.*

41. Similar critiques of early Moroccan nationalist historiography may be found in Miller, *History,* 2–3; Guerin, "'Not a Drop,'" 227–230; Wyrtzen, *Making Morocco,* 7.

42. Burke III, *Ethnographic State.* In recent years, a number of excellent studies have explored the impact of European colonialism on postcolonial Moroccan life. For example, Wyrtzen's *Making Morocco* argues that Euro-

pean colonial intervention politicized Moroccan ethnic, religious, and gender identities in ways that continue to resonate in Morocco today. Other prominent examples of this line of scholarship include Amster, *Medicine and the Saints*; González Alcantud, *Invención*; Irbouh, *Art*.

43. See, for example, McDougall's work on Algerian nationalism.

44. On the anachronistic nature of the nationalist imaginary, Anderson observes: "If nation-states are widely conceded to be 'new' and 'historical,' the nations to which they give political expression always loom out of an immemorial past, and, still more important, glide into a limitless future." *Imagined Communities*, 11–12. For an introduction to the vast scholarly literature on nationalism, see also Hobsbawm and Ranger, *Invention of Tradition*; Chatterjee, *Nation*.

45. For an overview of the Protectorate period (1912–1956), with an emphasis on the French Protectorate, see Miller, *History*, 88–153.

46. Madariaga, *Marruecos*; Villanova, *Protectorado*.

47. The history of Spanish colonialism in the Sahara remains the most understudied facet of Moroccan colonial history, and, unfortunately, it falls outside the purview of this book. The most detailed studies of Spain's colonial presence in the Sahara were written by Spaniards who worked for the Spanish Protectorate in Morocco. See, in particular, García Figueras, *Santa Cruz*; Hernández-Pacheco and Cordero Torres, *El Sahara español*, 119–175. More recently, Zunes and Mundy's *Western Sahara* covers not only the colonial period but also the ongoing conflict over sovereignty in Western Sahara (formerly "Spanish Sahara").

48. See Soto Bermant, "Consuming Europe"; al-'Attar, *Sabta wa-Maliliya*.

49. On the importance of Muhammad V University and other Rabat-based institutions in the development of post-independence Moroccan culture, see Kably et al., *Histoire du Maroc*, 719–721.

50. For the emphasis that Moroccan nationalists put on Arabic-language education and culture, see Wyrtzen, *Making Morocco*, 138–160. In a speech delivered on the first Throne Day of the independence period, King Muhammad V announced his plan to Arabize the entire Moroccan educational system. *Le Maroc*, 34. The plan was only partially implemented, and language policy remains a contentious issue in Morocco. For language debates in contemporary Morocco, see Boukous, *Société*; Elinson, "*Dārija*"; Allen, "Rewriting Literary History."

51. For North Africa's vexed place within Middle East and Arabic studies, see Burke III, "Theorizing"; Clancy-Smith, introduction to "Maghribi Histories." For an example of the Egypt-centric narrative of the modern Arab world, see Badawi, "Background."

52. See, for example, Nogué and Villanova, *España en Marruecos;* Martín Corrales, *Marruecos;* Rodríguez Mediano and Felipe, *Protectorado;* Mateo Dieste, *La "hermandad" hispano-marroquí;* Martin-Márquez, *Disorientations;* Madariaga, *Marruecos.*

53. Many American historians take the "colonial period" to be coterminous with the Protectorate period (1912–1956). I, instead, follow the lead of Spanish historians and of Moroccan historians from the former Spanish zone, for whom the colonial period starts in 1859, with the Spanish-Moroccan War.

54. Scholars have adopted the term "transcolonial" to refer to such frameworks. See Lionnet and Shih, "Thinking through the Minor"; Harrison, *Transcolonial Maghreb.*

55. Harrison, *Transcolonial Maghreb*, 7.

56. Said, *Orientalism*, 2.

57. Ibid.

58. Ibid., 3.

59. Foucault explores the notion of "productive power" in several of his works, including *Discipline and Punish*, 26–28, 194.

60. Said, *Orientalism*, 20.

61. Behdad, *Belated Travelers*, 11; Ahmad, *In Theory*, 166–168; Martin-Márquez, *Disorientations*, 8–9.

62. In fact, Said asserts that there is no corresponding equivalent to Orientalism in the non-Western world. *Orientalism*, 204. In response to Said's dubious claim, a number of scholars have documented and analyzed the historical evolution and ideological contours of Arabic writings about Europe. See, in particular, the work of Matar; Paradela.

63. Said explicitly acknowledges his decision to focus on France and Britain: "Historically and culturally there is a quantitative as well as a qualitative difference between the Franco-British involvement in the Orient and . . . the involvement of every other European and Atlantic power. To speak of Orientalism therefore is to speak mainly, although not exclusively, of a British and French cultural enterprise." *Orientalism*, 3–4. Said takes almost all of his examples from British and French writings about Egypt and the Levant. With the exception of a few passing references to Algeria, he does not address European colonialism in the Maghrib.

64. Renan, *Peuples sémitiques*, 27. For Renan's role within the project of European Orientalism, see Said, *Orientalism*, 130–148.

65. Mallette, *European Modernity.*

66. The phrase is discussed in Calderwood, "Invention of al-Andalus"; Martin-Márquez, *Disorientations.*

67. Martin-Márquez, *Disorientations*, 9.

68. Martin-Márquez, *Disorientations*; Mateo Dieste, *La "hermandad" hispano-marroquí*.

69. See Conklin, *Mission to Civilize*.

70. Chatterjee calls this idea "the rule of colonial difference." *Nation*, 10–34.

71. Fernand Braudel's *La Méditerranée et le monde méditerranéen à l'époque de Philippe II* (1949) inaugurated the study of the Mediterranean as a unified region with a distinctive ecology or culture. In 2000, Horden and Purcell's *The Corrupting Sea* revived the Mediterranean paradigm in literary and historical studies. For recent reflections on the state of Mediterranean studies, see Horden, introduction to *Companion to Mediterranean History*; Herzfeld, "Practical Mediterraneanism."

72. For the trope of the Mediterranean as a "bridge" between cultures, see Shannon, *Performing al-Andalus*, 168–169. "Connectivity" is one of the key terms that Horden and Purcell use to describe the underlying unity of the Mediterranean in *Corrupting Sea*, 123–172.

73. "History," Union for the Mediterranean, accessed June 28, 2017, http://ufmsecretariat.org/history/.

74. Even if Moroccans had wanted to identify themselves as "Mediterraneans" during the colonial period, it was not an identity that was available to them. As Clancy-Smith has noted, "By the late nineteenth century, deeply entrenched racial bias against Arabs and Muslims excluded them from constructions of a Mediterranean identity, indeed from Mediterranean history *tout court.*" *Mediterraneans*, 10.

75. For the geographic imaginary of Spanish colonialism, see Martin-Márquez, *Disorientations* 58–59, 223–224; Calderwood, "Invention of al-Andalus," 40.

76. For rhetorical uses of the Mediterranean in contemporary Spanish culture, see Calderwood, "Invention of al-Andalus," 36–45; Shannon, *Performing al-Andalus*, 158–179. Morocco's claim to a Mediterranean identity is a more recent phenomenon, but today, the Mediterranean is frequently invoked in Moroccan political discourse and foreign policy initiatives. In fact, the current secretary-general of the Union for the Mediterranean, Fathallah Sijilmassi, is a Moroccan diplomat. For contemporary Moroccan uses of the Mediterranean, see Shannon, *Performing al-Andalus*, 158–179; Benaboud and Sijelmassi, "Terre." See also the allusions to the Mediterranean in the preface to the Moroccan Constitution, www.sgg.gov.ma/Portals/0/constitution/ccnstitution_2011_Fr.pdf.

77. The Mediterranean identity was initially projected onto southern European countries (such as Greece and Italy) by travelers and writers from

the more powerful countries in northern Europe. Herzfeld, "Practical Mediterraneanism," 54, 62–63; Horden and Purcell, *Corrupting Sea*, 28–29.

78. I am alluding, here, to Aristotle's idea that history speaks of particulars and poetry of the universal. *Poetics*, 95.

1. TETOUAN IS GRANADA

1. For Martínez Sánchez, see Yeves Andrés, *Imagen*, 185–186. Many scholars have reproduced Alarcón's Moroccan portraits without identifying their date or the context of their production. See, for example, Romano, *Pedro Antonio de Alarcón*, 112; Lara Ramos, *Pedro Antonio de Alarcón*, 76. I would like to thank Isabel Ortega García and Juan Antonio Yeves Andrés for helping me to locate the original photographs and to identify their date and author.

2. This portrait is part of an album housed in the Sala Goya at the Spanish National Library, call number 17 / LF / 51, page 41r.

3. For the *Diary*'s publication history, see Palomo, *Diario*, XLVI–LI; Alarcón, "Historia de mis libros," 14–15.

4. I have based my description of the Duchess of Medinaceli's costume ball on accounts that were published between April 2 and April 6, 1861, in three Spanish newspapers: *La Época, El Contemporáneo,* and *La Iberia*. These newspapers are digitized in the Spanish National Library's *Hemeroteca Digital*, http://hemerotecadigital.bne.es/.

5. "El baile de trajes de la Excma. señora duquesa de Medinaceli," *El Contemporáneo*, April 3, 1861, 3–4, http://hemerotecadigital.bne.es/issn/2174-7083. For Mulay al-'Abbas, see al-Nasiri, *Kitab al-istiqsa*, 8:101–118; Alarcón, *Diario*, 526–538.

6. "Artículo de traje, o sea carta de Muley-Abbas al poeta Chorby, en Tetuán," *La Época*, April 3, 1861, 3–4, http://hemerotecadigital.bne.es/issue.vm?id=0000156305&search=&lang=en.

7. A number of factors substantiate the hypothesis that Alarcón is the author of the article narrated from the fictional perspective of Mulay al-'Abbas. First of all, Alarcón attended the duchess's ball dressed as the Moroccan general. Second, the article is addressed to Chorby, who plays an important role in Alarcón's representation of Morocco, as I will discuss at the end of this chapter. Third, Alarcón was a regular contributor to *La Época*, according to Romano, *Pedro Antonio de Alarcón*, 110. Fourth, an article printed in *La Época* on April 2, 1861, promised that the newspaper would publish, on the following day, a detailed account of the costume ball written by "one of our most distinguished literary figures, who attended the party." Lasandro, "Baile," 3.

8. "Artículo de traje," 3.

9. Ibid.

10. Ibid.

11. The duchess publicized her plan to make a photo album in an announcement that was published in several Madrid newspapers on April 6, 1861. The announcement appears in *El Contemporáneo* and *La Iberia*, both of which are digitized in the Hemeroteca Digital.

12. For the Alpujarras Rebellion, see Harvey, *Muslims in Spain*, 204–237. Alarcón returns to this historical event in his travel narrative *La Alpujarra* (1874).

13. The anecdote and the quote come from Pardo Bazán's *Alarcón*, 56–58. This anecdote also appears in Palomo, *Diario*, LXIV; González Alcantud, "Poética," 25.

14. For Burton's alter ego, see Grant, *Postcolonialism*, 56–88; Said, *Orientalism*, 194–196.

15. Jacobson, *Odalisques*, 62–67.

16. Martin-Márquez, *Disorientations*, 8–9.

17. Ibid., 106.

18. The description of Spain (and, in particular, Granada) as "neither Orient, nor occident" comes from the writer Gil Benumeya, whose work I discuss in Chapter 3.

19. For detailed accounts of the war, from different perspectives, see al-Nasiri, *Kitab al-istiqsa*, 8:101–118; Miège, *Maroc*, 2:349–393; Calderwood, "Writing."

20. Ferhat, "Sabta"; Villada Paredes et al., *Historia de Ceuta*; Ibn Tawit, *Tarikh Sabta*.

21. Al-Nasiri, *Kitab al-istiqsa*, 8:101.

22. For the newspaper coverage of the war, see Lécuyer and Serrano, *Guerre*, 35–92; Palomo, *Diario*, xxxvii–lvii.

23. Ibo Alfaro, *Españoles*, 3.

24. The quote comes from an untitled article published on the cover of the October 12, 1859, issue of *La Discusión*, http://hemerotecadigital.bne.es/issue.vm?id=0002222247.

25. Tejado, "El Pensamiento Español," 2.

26. Alarcón, *Diario*, 8–9, 18–22.

27. Fernández Cuesta, "Muley-Abd-el-Rahman," 173.

28. Martin-Márquez, *Disorientations*, 58–59; Calderwood, "Invention of al-Andalus," 40.

29. Fernández y González's Orientalist historical fiction included the novel *Los monfíes de la Alpujarra*, published in 1859 by the same editors who

serially published Alarcón's *Diary* in 1859–1860. Both Fernández y González and Alarcón were members of a Granadan literary circle known as the "Cuerda granadina." See Gallego Roca, *"La Cuerda Granadina."*

30. Fernández y González, "A España," 178.

31. Ibid.

32. Lécuyer and Serrano, *Guerre*, 17, 40; Serrallonga Urquidi, "La guerra de África," 144.

33. Ros de Olano, *Leyendas de África*, 13.

34. Alarcón, *Diario*, 476–478; Ros de Olano, *Leyendas de África*, 12–13.

35. A different version of the story appears in Martínez Kleiser, *Obras completas*, 165–170. Martin-Márquez analyzes the version of the text edited by Martínez Kleiser, and her analysis focuses on the North African protagonist's conversion to Christianity. *Disorientations*, 101–104.

36. Alarcón, "Una conversación," 158. For Boabdil, see Álvarez de Morales, "Boabdil"; Arié, "Boabdil."

37. Alarcón, "Una conversación," 158.

38. Ibid.

39. Ibid., 159.

40. Other scholars have also noted the influence of Romantic literature on Alarcón's perception of Morocco. See Martin-Márquez, *Disorientations*, 102–113; Lécuyer and Serrano, *Guerre*, 188–196.

41. Alarcón, "Una conversación," 159.

42. For Pérez de Hita, see Carrasco Urgoiti, *Moro*; Carrasco Urgoiti, *Moriscos*.

43. For the Abencerraje myth in Romantic literature, see Carrasco Urgoiti, *Moro*.

44. Chateaubriand wrote the novella in 1810–1811 and circulated the manuscript among friends, but he did not publish it until 1826, according to Berchet, *Atala*, 60, 283–284.

45. Alarcón, "Una conversación," 159.

46. Ibid.

47. Ibid.

48. Martin-Márquez calls this process of historical revision "second-wave" Spanish nationalism. *Disorientations*, 18–38.

49. Alarcón, "Una conversación," 159.

50. For the fandango, see Meira Goldberg and Pizà, "Introduction."

51. Alarcón, "Una conversación," 159.

52. Ibid.

53. Alarcón, *Diario*, 4. I have opted to provide my own translations of Alarcón's *Diary*, rather than relying on Keating's translation, which is

plagued by errors and inaccuracies. Also, Keating inexplicably omits Alarcón's prologue to the *Diary*, which is arguably the most important part of the text.

54. Alarcón, *Diario*, 4.
55. Said, *Orientalism*, 230–231.
56. Martin-Márquez, *Disorientations*, 105.
57. Alarcón, *Diario*, 4.
58. Said, *Orientalism*, 2.
59. Smith, *National Identity*, 78–79; McClintock, *Imperial Leather*, 44–45.
60. Alarcón, *Diario*, 4.
61. Ibid.
62. Ibid.
63. Susan Martin-Márquez calls this narrative of Spanish nationhood "first-wave nation building in Spain." *Disorientations*, 12–18. See also Álvarez Junco and De la Fuente Monge, "Evolución," 69–73.
64. Alarcón, *Diario*, 4–5.
65. *OED Online*, s.v. "Talisman, n. 2," accessed July 1, 2017, www.oed.com.
66. Quoted in Flores Morales, *África*, 28.
67. Alarcón, *Diario*, 7.
68. Ibid., 20.
69. Alarcón, *Diario*, 7–8.
70. Ibid., 55.
71. I am building, here, on Scott's essay "The Evidence of Experience," in which Scott interrogates the epistemic status of "experience" as an explanatory framework for historical analysis.
72. For this building's history, see Erzini, "El Serrallo."
73. Alarcón, *Diario*, 38.
74. All three buildings have received significant scholarly attention. For helpful introductions, see Ruggles, "Stratigraphy of Forgetting"; Ruggles, "Alcazar"; González Alcantud and Malpica Cuello, *Pensar la Alhambra*.
75. For two versions of this standard, Cordoba-centered account of Andalusi history, see Menocal, *Ornament*; Lévi-Provençal et al., "Al-Andalus."
76. Alarcón, *Diario*, 38–39.
77. This conflation of al-Andalus with Medina and Mecca emerges as a motif in several twentieth-century Moroccan and Spanish texts, as I discuss in Chapters 3 and 4.
78. Alarcón, *Diario*, 155.
79. Carrasco Urgoiti, *Moro*, 55–71; Correa Rodríguez, *Historia*.
80. Alarcón, *Diario*, 159.
81. Correa Rodríguez, *Historia*, cxix–cxx; Arié, "Boabdil," 94–98.
82. Chateaubriand, *Dernier Abencérage*, 204.

83. Alarcón, *Diario*, 224–225.

84. In fact, Alarcón cites a full Spanish translation of that passage from Chateaubriand as the epigraph to chapter 31 (*Diario*, 213). Alarcón's passage about the similarities between Granada and Tetouan appears in the same chapter. Martin-Márquez also examines this passage as an example of how Alarcón envisions the journey to Morocco as a journey to al-Andalus. *Disorientations*, 106.

Chateaubriand's novella was translated into Spanish in 1826 and was published in several Spanish editions throughout the nineteenth century, as discussed in Palomo, *Diario*, 213.

85. Alarcón, *Diario*, 363.
86. Ibid., 534.
87. For Muza, often known as "el moro Muza," see Correa Rodríguez, *Historia*, cxxxv–cxliv; Carrasco Urgoiti, *Moro*, 67–68.
88. Carrasco Urgoiti, *Moro*, 67–68.
89. Alarcón, *Diario*, 525.
90. Ibid., 395.
91. Ibid., 396.
92. Ibid., 397.
93. Ibid.
94. Ibid.
95. Ibid., 412–413.
96. Ibid., 416–417.
97. Ibid., 417.
98. Ibid.
99. Derrida, "Différance," 1–9.
100. Alarcón, *Diario*, 416–417.
101. This tendency starts with Pardo Bazán's biography, but it has continued into the twenty-first century. For example, González Alcantud speaks of Alarcón's "radical desire to get to know the Other." "Poética," 18.
102. Alarcón, *Diario*, 434.
103. Ibid., 554.
104. Ibid., 556.
105. Ibid.
106. Ibid.
107. Ibid.
108. Ibid.
109. I would like to thank Jaʿfar b. al-Hajj al-Sulami, the modern editor of ʿ*Umdat al-rawin*, for helping me to confirm that al-Shurbi ("Chorby") does not appear in al-Rahuni's massive work.

110. Hasna' Dawud has recently completed an edition of Muhammad Dawud's 'A'ilat Titwan. I would like to thank her for sending me the entry on the Shurbi family, which appears in the third volume. She has helped me to confirm that Muhammad Dawud (her father) does not mention a poet named Shurbi in any of his works.

111. Alarcón, Diario, 458. I thank the historian Nadia Erzini for providing me with information about Muhammad b. Ahmad al-Shurbi.

112. "Artículo de traje."

113. The poem appears in Alarcón's volume *Poesías serias y humorísticas* (1870) with the epigraph "Tetouan—1860" (152). Martínez Kleiser, in his edition of Alarcón's complete works, adds the following note to the poem: "The author wrote this sonnet when he served as a volunteer soldier in the War of Africa." *Obras completas*, 292.

114. My translation is based on Martínez Kleiser's edition of the poem.

115. The peace treaty is reproduced in De las Cagigas, *Tratados*, 39–44.

116. For the Spanish press's reaction to the peace treaty, see Lécuyer and Serrano, *Guerre*, 45–92; Serrallonga Urquidi, "La guerra de África," 156–159.

117. Miège, *Maroc*, 2:369–371. Miège offers a detailed account of the Moroccan government's struggles to pay for the war indemnity in *Maroc*, 2:371–382. I summarize Miège's work in this paragraph.

118. Miège, *Maroc*, 2:381–393; Miller, *History*, 25–27; Rodríguez Esteller, "Intervención."

119. Al-Nasiri, *Kitab al-istiqsa*, 8:116. For al-Nasiri, see Calderwood, "Beginning."

120. See Lécuyer and Serrano, *Guerre*, 44, 52–53, 59–60, 69, 76–77.

121. Alarcón, *Diario*, 484–486.

122. Ibid., 488.

123. Ibid., 383.

124. Ibid., 577.

125. Ibid., 578.

126. For scholarly assessments of Alarcón's sudden loss of faith in the war, see Martin-Márquez, *Disorientations*, 112–113.

127. Alarcón, *Diario*, 578–582.

128. The devastating role of cholera in the war is documented in Serrallonga Urquidi, "La guerra de África."

129. Alarcón, *Diario*, 381.

130. See Martin-Márquez, *Disorientations*; Mateo Dieste, *La "hermandad" hispano-marroquí*.

131. Costa et al., *Intereses*, 14.

132. See Chapter 7.

2. AL-ANDALUS AND MOROCCAN LITERARY HISTORY

1. "Father, I dreamed of eleven stars and the sun and the moon: I saw them all bow down before me." *Surat Yusuf,* 4; Abdel Haleem, *Qur'an,* 236. All Qur'anic citations in English come from Abdel Haleem's translation, unless otherwise noted.

2. Sacks, *Iterations of Loss,* 31–44; García Moreno, "Al-Andalus."

3. Darwish, *Ahad 'ashar kawkaban,* 21.

4. For a prominent use of oxymoron in Darwish's work, see the title of his memoir *In the Presence of Absence* (*Fi hadrat al-ghiyab,* 2006).

5. See Martínez Montávez, *Al-Andalus;* Snir, "Al-Andalus"; al-'Adwani, *Zaman al-wasl.*

6. Granara, "Nostalgia"; Martínez Montávez, *Al-Andalus.*

7. I am drawing on the dual meaning of topos, which is discussed in Boym, *Future of Nostalgia,* 77; Elinson, *Looking Back,* 15.

8. Darwish, *Ahad 'ashar kawkaban,* 10. Ellipsis in the original.

9. Aristotle, *Poetics,* 95. For the Arabic transmission of Aristotle's *Poetics* to Christian Europe, see Mallette, "Beyond Mimesis."

10. For the Andalusi emigration to Chefchaouen, see García-Arenal, "Los moriscos en Marruecos," 276–282.

11. For 'Abd al-Salam b. Mashish, see Le Tourneau, "'Abd al-Salām b. Mashīsh."

12. The best introduction to the Andalusi city elegy is Elinson, *Looking Back.* See also al-Zayyat, *Ritha' al-mudun.*

13. See Said, "Return to Philology"; de Man, "Literary"; Mallette, *European Modernity,* 5–6.

14. Said, "Return to Philology," 64.

15. Ibid., 61.

16. Geertz, *Interpretation of Cultures,* 3–30. Geertz's ideas have had significant influence on literary studies, as discussed in Gallagher and Greenblatt, *Practicing New Historicism,* 20–31.

17. For an introduction to nineteenth-century Moroccan literary culture, see Abdulrazak, "Kingdom of the Book"; al-Manuni, *Mazahir yaqzat al-Maghrib al-hadith,* 1:22–40, 364–377. These sources are helpful, but, in my opinion, they suffer from the epistemic limitations that I outline in the following paragraphs.

18. Abdulrazak, "Kingdom of the Book"; Abdulrazak, *Al-Matbu'at al-hajariyya fi al-Maghrib.*

19. The manuscript is number 158 in the Dawud Library's manuscript collection. The historian Muhammad Dawud mentions that he has heard of a

second manuscript containing Afaylal's writings from the last third of his life. *Tarikh Titwan,* 7:179. Dawud never saw the second manuscript, and I have not been able to locate it.

20. Afaylal's elegy for Tetouan first appeared in print in al-Nasiri's *Kitab al-istiqsa,* 8:108–110. In the twentieth century, Muhammad Dawud quoted extensively from Afaylal's manuscripts in his multivolume *Tarikh Titwan,* particularly in volumes 4, 5, and 7. In 2008, the Moroccan historian M'hammad Benaboud edited Afaylal's chronicle of the Spanish-Moroccan War. Benaboud, "Harb Titwan." Hasna' Dawud, the director of the Dawud Library, has produced an unpublished critical edition of the *Kunnash,* which she generously shared with me. In this chapter, I will rely primarily on the excerpts from the *Kunnash* that have been edited by al-Nasiri, Muhammad Dawud, and Benaboud, but I will also make occasional reference to the original manuscript of the *Kunnash* and to Hasna' Dawud's introduction to it.

21. The scholarship on Afaylal is limited to al-Nasir, "al-Haraka al-thaqafiyya fi Titwan"; Akmir, "Aproximación," 286–292; M. Dawud, *Tarikh Titwan,* 7:177–216. To the best of my knowledge, there is no published scholarship on Afaylal produced by non-Moroccan scholars. Afaylal does, however, appear as a character in Pérez Galdós's novel *Aita Tettauen* (1905).

22. For a recent summary and critique of this literary-historical narrative, see Allen, "Post-Classical Period."

23. Jayyusi, "Arabic Poetry," 27–37.

24. For this narrative of the *Nahḍa,* see Hourani, *Arabic Thought;* Badawi, "Background." I will return to the scholarly debates about the *Nahḍa* in Chapter 4.

25. Badawi, for example, totally excludes Morocco from his influential introduction to *Modern Arabic Literature* ("Background"). In recent years, there have been attempts to reassess Morocco's place in Arabic literary history. See, for example, Allen, "Rewriting Literary History"; Fernández Parrilla, *La literatura marroquí contemporánea.*

26. Sahar Bazzaz strikes a similar note when she observes that scholars of nineteenth-century Morocco have tended to ignore "Islamic historical texts reflecting non-positive and/or non-rationalist epistemologies or lacking linear narrative structure." "Reading Reform," 2.

27. In 2010, the Moroccan Ministry of Islamic Affairs organized an exhibit of Afaylal's calligraphy in Rabat. See Maghrawi et al., *Al-Faqih al-Mufaddal Afaylal.*

28. Sacks, *Iterations of Loss,* 20.

29. Afaylal, *Kunnash,* 5.

30. For al-Harraq, see M. Dawud, *Tarikh Titwan*, 6:289–391. For al-Saffar, see Miller, *Disorienting Encounters*, 33–48; M. Dawud, *Tarikh Titwan*, 7:78–97.

31. Afaylal, *Kunnash*, 5. Afaylal gives dates in the Islamic (*Hijri*) calendar. I have converted the dates to the Common Era.

32. M. Dawud, *Tarikh Titwan*, 7:78.

33. Miller, *Disorienting Encounters*, 33.

34. Ibid., 36–38.

35. Ibid., 28–29, 118.

36. See Susan Miller's masterful translation and study of al-Saffar's travel narrative, *Disorienting Encounters*.

37. Miller, *Disorienting Encounters*, 42–44.

38. For Ibn Malik, see Fleisch, "Ibn Mālik."

39. Afaylal, *Kunnash*, 5; M. Dawud, *Tarikh Titwan*, 7:180–183; Ben Cheneb, "Khalīl b. Isḥāk."

40. Afaylal, *Kunnash*, 25.

41. Afaylal describes the journey to Meknes in his *Kunnash*, 47–51.

42. For Europe's intervention in nineteenth-century Morocco, see Miège, *Maroc*; Miller, *History*, 7–55; Kably et al., *Histoire du Maroc*, 473–550.

43. For example, Burke III writes: "Prior to 1860 Morocco was but little affected by European influences." *Prelude*, 19. In a similar vein, Lewis calls seventeenth- and eighteenth-century Morocco "a remote and isolated outpost." *Muslim Discovery*, 118.

44. See Miller, *Disorienting Encounters*, 87, 90, and 178. For Hispanisms in Moroccan travel writing about Europe, see Paradela, *El otro laberinto español*, 50.

45. Afaylal, "Harb Titwan," 188, 191, and 192.

46. The account appears in Afaylal, *Kunnash*, 45–46; quoted in M. Dawud, *Tarikh Titwan*, 7:138–139.

47. For the mausoleum of Sidi al-Mubarak ("Sidi Embarek"), see Gómez Barceló, "Santuarios," 330–336.

48. In Modern Standard Arabic, the town's name would be written *al-Funaydiq* (the diminutive of *al-Funduq*), but it is often written *Fnideq* in order to reflect the Moroccan pronunciation of the town's name.

49. Afaylal, *Kunnash*, 45; quoted in M. Dawud, *Tarikh Titwan*, 7:138.

50. Ibid. For the Moroccan siege of Ceuta in 1790–1791, see Carmona Portillo, *Relaciones*.

51. Quoted in M. Dawud, *Tarikh Titwan*, 7:138.

52. The complex, known as "El Serallo" in Spanish, is analyzed in Erzini, "El Serrallo."

53. Afaylal, *Kunnash*, 45–46; quoted in M. Dawud, *Tarikh Titwan*, 7:138–139.
54. Ibid.
55. H. Dawud, *Kunnash Afaylal*, 6–7; Benaboud, "Harb Titwan," 182; Akmir, "Aproximación," 286.
56. For Ibn al-Murahhal, see Gómez García, "Ibn al-Muraḥḥal"; Jubran, *Malik b. al-Murahhal*, 39–125.
57. Jubran, *Malik b. al-Murahhal*, 1.
58. See Knysh, "Ibn al-Khatib," the source for the biographical information in this paragraph.
59. See al-'Abbadi, *Mushahadat*; Elinson, *Looking Back*, 142–150; Gómez-Rivas, "Exile."
60. Elinson, *Looking Back*, 142; Knysh, "Ibn al-Khatib," 363; Lévi-Provençal and Pellat, "al-Maḳḳari."
61. Ferhat, "Sabta."
62. Talbi, "'Iyāḍ b. Mūsā."
63. The poems are found in al-Maqqari, *Azhar al-riyad*, 1:29. Afaylal does not explicitly mention *Azhar al-riyad* in his *Kunnash*. Nevertheless, there are three factors that lead me to believe that Afaylal encountered these two poems in al-Maqqari's work. The first is that *Azhar al-riyad* is, to the best of my knowledge, the only work in which Ibn al-Murahhal and Ibn al-Khatib's poems about Ceuta appear together. The second factor is that several manuscripts of al-Maqqari's work circulated in Morocco, including a manuscript that ended up in 'Abd Allah Gannun's library in Tangier. The third factor is that Afaylal quotes from al-Maqqari's *Nafh al-tib* in another text, reproduced in M. Dawud, *Tarikh Titwan*, 7:214. For the Moroccan manuscripts of *Azhar al-riyad*, see Qara, *Diwan*, 100; Lévi-Provençal and Pellat, "al-Maḳḳari."
64. These descriptions appear in Afaylal's *Kunnash*, 57–58. They come from Ibn al-Khatib's travel narrative, *Mi'yar al-ikhtiyar* (c. 1359), 103–105. Afaylal attributes the descriptions to Ibn al-Khatib, but he does not identify their source. Afaylal also refers to another travel narrative by Ibn al-Khatib, *Khatrat al-tayf fi rihlat al-shita' wa-l-sayf*, an account of a journey through the kingdom of Granada in 1347. *Kunnash*, 3.
65. Afaylal, *Kunnash*, 3. The title of al-Rundi's work translates, roughly, to *Treatise on Composing Rhymes*.
66. Qara, *Diwan*, 92–94; Muhsin, *Kitab al-wafi*, 26–27; Gannun, "Abu al-Baqa'," 216–220. Muhsin has edited the first of the four volumes of the text, and I refer to his edition below.
67. For al-Rundi's citations of these poets, see *Kitab al-wafi*, 43–44, 60, 68–69, 87–88.

68. The episode appears in Afaylal's *Kunnash*, 42. The poem that Afaylal recites is from al-Rundi's *Kitab al-wafi*, 71.

69. Al-Rundi's elegy appears in al-Maqqari, *Nafh al-tib*, 4:486–488; al-Maqqari, *Azhar al-riyad*, 1:46–50. An eloquent example of the elegy's popularity may be found in the work of the Moroccan poet Yasin ʿAdnan (b. 1970), who wrote in 2012: "We cry for Granada, and we long for / pomegranates. / We elegize Ronda, / and we ask God to have mercy on Abu al-Baqaʾ [al-Rundi], as if we never left. / As if we / are still there." *Daftar al-ʿabir*, 37–38. For al-Rundi's elegy in Morocco, see also Gannun, "Abu al-Baqaʾ."

70. Afaylal notes that he finished the poem in Chefchaouen on 20 Rajab 1277 (1 February 1877). *Kunnash*, 62.

71. Elinson, *Looking Back*. I summarize Elinson's work in this paragraph.

72. Ibid., 16.

73. Although Elinson highlights this theme in several Andalusi texts, it is particularly prominent in his analysis of Ibn Shuhayd's elegy for Cordoba. *Looking Back*, 38–49.

74. Zarqa al-Yamama is the heroine of an Arab folk narrative that dates back to the pre-Islamic period. In Arabic letters, she often personifies vision and foresight. See Khoury, "Zarqāʾ."

75. *Maqāmāt* (sing. *maqāma*) are brief episodic texts written in rhymed and rhythmic prose. See Stewart, "*Maqāma*." Ibn al-Khatib was known for his *maqāmāt*. See Elinson, *Looking Back*, 148–150. Afaylal also wrote a *maqāma* about a journey to Marrakesh. It appears in his *Kunnash*, 67–71.

76. "Qasr Kutama" is an old name for the city al-Qasr al-Kabir ("Alcazarquivir" in Spanish sources), which lies to the southwest of Tetouan. Ibn al-Khatib also refers to the city as "Qasr Kutama" in *Miʿyar al-ikhtiyar*, 103–104. In 1861, during Afaylal's two-year exile from occupied Tetouan, he taught classes in grammar and logic in al-Qasr al-Kabir, as discussed in M. Dawud, *Tarikh Titwan*, 7:207–208.

77. "The everlasting Home" is one of the names for Heaven used in the Qurʾan. See, for example, *Surat al-Fatir*, 35; Abdel Haleem, *Qurʾan*, 439.

I have based my translation of Afaylal's elegy on the text that appears in al-Nasiri's *Kitab al-istiqsa* (8:108–110), which is widely available. The elegy also appears in Afaylal's *Kunnash* (62), with a few variants that do not affect the poem's overall meaning. I thank Jaafar Ben Elhaj Soulami and Mohammed Sawaie for their helpful suggestions for my translation.

78. Kennedy, *Wine Song*, 86–148; Granara, "Remaking Muslim Sicily," 177; Kadhim, *Poetics*, 78. Afaylal wrote a short commentary on his elegy. In it, he says that he opened the elegy "with the address to Fate, in the manner and custom of the poets." Quoted in M. Dawud, *Tarikh Titwan*, 7:212.

79. For these images in the city elegy tradition, see Elinson, *Looking Back*, 32–41; Stetkevych, *Zephyrs of Najd*, 106–107, 189–201; Kadhim, *Poetics*, 66–69.

80. Elinson discusses these rhetorical figures in *Looking Back*, 17–47. See also Kadhim, *Poetics*, 60, 77, 80; Sacks, *Iterations of Loss*, 43–45.

81. I have transliterated the rhyme words as they would be pronounced, in order to clarify the rhyme scheme. The third word is actually *lijāmahu* ("his bridle"). Nevertheless, according to the rules of Arabic prosody, you do not pronounce the final short vowel of the word at the end of a line of poetry. Thus, the words *al-karāma* ("miracle") and *lijāmahu* ("his bridle") rhyme when the two words appear at the end of a line.

82. For the English text of al-Rundi's elegy, I rely on Monroe's translation in *Hispano-Arabic Poetry*, 332–337. Monroe's translation is based on the Arabic text found in al-Maqqari, *Nafh al-tib*, 4:486–488.

83. Elinson, *Looking Back*, 25–29.

84. See al-Rundi's elegy (vv. 40–41); Kadhim, *Poetics*, 68–69.

85. *Surat al-Baqara*, 25; Abdel Haleem, *Qur'an*, 6.

86. For water imagery in the city elegy, see Elinson, *Looking Back*, 35–38. For the topos of weeping over an abandoned campsite, see Stetkevych, *Zephyrs of Najd*, 50–102; Elinson, *Looking Back*, 40–41; Granara, "Remaking Muslim Sicily," 174.

87. Heinrichs, "Rhetorical Figures," 660; Elinson, *Looking Back*, 28, 38–49.

88. See al-Zayyat, *Ritha' al-mudun*, 426–441; Kadhim, *Poetics*, 75–81.

89. Jubran, *Malik b. al-Murahhal*, 336–338; Continente, "Dos poemas"; Elinson, *Looking Back*, 33.

90. Kadhim, *Poetics*, 35–84.

91. For the dove as the modern symbol of Tetouan, see Benaboud, "Medina de Tetuán," 41.

92. Kadhim, *Poetics*, 30–31, 47–56.

93. The terms "Christians" and "Muslims" are used in almost every paragraph of Afaylal's chronicle, so I have not bothered to cite individual examples. The terms "the enemy" and "the infidels" are also common, though they are used less frequently. For examples of each term, see pages 189 and 194 respectively. All page numbers refer to Benaboud's edition ("Harb Titwan"), which I have used because it is more readily accessible to readers outside of Morocco.

94. Bazzaz, "Reading," 2.

95. Afaylal, "Harb Titwan," 188.

96. Ibid., 191–192.

97. These words appear in Afaylal, "Harb Titwan," 189 and 196. Benaboud glosses the dialectal term *al-ghawth* in a footnote on page 189.

98. Afaylal, "Harb Titwan," 188–189.

99. Ibid., 189.

100. Afaylal often uses the verb *shāhadnā* ("we witnessed") to describe the things that he sees in his journey to Marrakesh. Afaylal, *Kunnash*, 66–71; quoted in M. Dawud, *Tarikh Titwan*, 7:201–206.

101. For the autoptic, see Pagden, *European Encounters*, 51–87.

102. This Prophetic tradition (hadith) is narrated in ʿAbd al-Razzaq, *al-Musannaf*, 5:284. Nevertheless, ʿAbd al-Razzaq's hadith collection was not known in nineteenth-century Morocco, so it is likely that Afaylal learned the hadith orally. I thank Michael Dann, Jaafar Ben Elhaj Soulami, and Issam Eido for helping me to locate the source for this hadith.

103. According to the conversion from the website Islamic Finder, this date corresponds to a Friday, not a Monday. The calendar converter on Islamic Philosophy Online gives the date as Saturday, November 12. In any case, it is clear that Afaylal is narrating events that took place in early November 1859.

104. Afaylal, "Harb Titwan," 189. My italics.

105. In Islamic theology, the Christian doctrine of the Holy Trinity is considered a form of polytheism because it accords divine status to both Jesus and the Holy Spirit.

106. Afaylal, "Harb Titwan," 189.

107. Ibid., 192. Literally, "with a *fatḥa* on the *hamza*." Afaylal is recording the speech of illiterate Moroccans who, in a misguided attempt to speak in classical Arabic, say *aymān* ("right hands") instead of *īmān* ("faith").

108. Afaylal, "Harb Titwan," 192–193.

109. Ibid., 193.

110. The meaning of the term "caliph" (*khalīfa*, lit. "successor") has varied over time and in different geographical contexts. In Morocco, the term generally refers to the second in command, often the sultan's brother. During the Protectorate period, the caliph was the highest Moroccan authority in the Spanish zone, as discussed in Chapters 4 and 5.

111. Afaylal, "Harb Titwan," 196.

112. Benaboud's edition signals an ellipsis in the text here. In Afaylal's *Kunnash*, a line of text is crossed out after the word "caliph" (32). The crossed-out text is not legible.

113. *Ḥizb* is a technical term, referring to the sixtieth part of the Qur'an.

114. Afaylal, "Harb Titwan," 196.

115. For the Islamic conception of impurity, see Maghen, "Ablution."

116. Afaylal, "Harb Titwan," 198.

117. Alarcón, *Diario*, 345–365; Afaylal, "Harb Titwan," 200–203.

118. Afaylal, "Harb Titwan," 201.
119. Ibid., 201–202. My italics.
120. For this motif, see Kadhim, *Poetics,* 26; Elinson, *Looking Back,* 40–43.
121. Freud develops the concept of "working through" in his essay "Remembering, Repeating and Working-Through" (1914). In the essay, Freud speculates that the "compulsion to repeat" is a way of remembering and working through something that has been repressed. Building on Freud's insights, LaCapra has argued that the compulsion to repeat is one of the symptoms of writing trauma. *Writing History, Writing Trauma,* 186.
122. LaCapra, *Writing History, Writing Trauma,* 186.
123. Afaylal, "Harb Titwan," 202.
124. Ibid.
125. Scott, "Evidence of Experience."
126. M. Dawud, *Tarikh Titwan,* 7:110.
127. Afaylal, *Kunnash,* 75.
128. The Moroccan Andalusi repertoire is described in Chaachoo, *Música andalusí;* Davila, *Andalusian Music;* Valderrama Martínez, *Cancionero de al-Ḥāʾik.*
129. Davila, *Andalusian Music,* 323.
130. Glasser, "Andalusi Musical Origins," 720–724; Davila, *Andalusian Music,* 7–8.

3. AL-ANDALUS, ANDALUCÍA, AND MOROCCO

1. I have based my narration of Blas Infante's travels in Morocco on Iniesta Coullaut-Valera, *Blas Infante,* 205–240, which quotes extensively from Infante's manuscripts. Infante was declared "Padre de la Patria Andaluza" by a decree from the Parliament of Andalucía in 1983. "Blas Infante, Padre de la Patria Andaluza," Parlamento de Andalucía, accessed June 30, 2017, www.parlamentodeandalucia.es/opencms/export/portal-web-parlamento/elparlamento/historia/blasinfantepadredeandalucia.htm.
2. For the Rif War, see Balfour, *Deadly Embrace;* Madariaga, *Marruecos,* 115–170; Wyrtzen, *Making Morocco,* 116–135.
3. For al-Muʿtamid in modern Arabic literature, see Shawqi, *Amirat al-Andalus;* Bouali, *Poemas marroquíes y al-Andalus,* 30–31. Al-Muʿtamid is also a protagonist in the recent Syrian soap opera *Muluk al-tawaʾif* (2005), discussed in Calderwood, "Proyectando al-Ándalus."
4. Quoted in Iniesta Coullaut-Valera, *Blas Infante,* 216.
5. For the pilgrimage of Andalusi writers to al-Muʿtamid's tomb in Aghmat, see García Gómez, "Supuesto sepulcro."

6. Infante, *Motamid*, 163. Infante appears to confuse the Arabic word *qaṣba* (citadel or casbah) with the *kaʿba* (Kaʿba), the main shrine in Mecca.

7. Ibid.

8. Quoted in Iniesta Coullaut-Valera, *Blas Infante*, 224.

9. "Blas Infante, Padre de la Patria Andaluza."

10. "Nuevo texto del Estatuto andaluz," Junta de Andalucía, March 2007, www.juntadeandalucia.es/html/especiales/estatuto/aj-nuevoestatuto-estatutodc67.html?idSeccion=1&idApartado=1. For debates about the loaded term *mestizaje*, see Lund, *Impure Imagination*.

11. Calderwood, "Invention of al-Andalus"; Rogozen-Soltar, "Al-Andalus in Andalusia"; Rosón Lorente, *¿El retorno de Tariq?*.

12. Martin-Márquez, *Disorientations*; Mateo Dieste, *La "hermandad" hispano-marroquí*.

13. For the history of *andalucismo*, see Lacomba, *Regionalismo*; Fernández-Montesinos, *García Lorca*.

14. For Catalonia as Europe, see Epps, "Between Europe and Africa"; Martin-Márquez, *Disorientations*, 43–44, 147.

15. I discuss this phrase in the Introduction.

16. *Andalucismo* is generally left out of critical conversations about Iberian peripheral nationalisms, but there are some notable exceptions, including Stallaert, *Etnogénesis*, 70–126; Martin-Márquez, *Disorientations*, 39–50.

I will insist on referring to *andalucismo* as a nationalism, although scholars have oscillated between calling it a "regionalism" (Lacomba, *Regionalismo*) and a "nationalism" (Fernández-Montesinos, *García Lorca*). It is not surprising that scholars have had trouble categorizing *andalucismo*, since the historical *andalucistas*, going back to Blas Infante, referred to their movement as both a "regionalism" and a "nationalism." I address the evolving terminology of Andalusian nationalism later in this chapter.

17. Lacomba, *Regionalismo*, 23–31.

18. "Proyecto de la Constitución," 9.

19. Acosta Sánchez, *Andalucía*, 9.

20. Resina, "Iberian Modalities," 16.

21. Ibid., 2.

22. Ibid., 2–3.

23. Deleuze and Guattari, *Kafka*.

24. I am building here on Lionnet and Shih's insight: "Critiquing the center, when it stands as an end in itself, seems only to enhance it; the center remains the focus and the main object of study. The deconstructive dyad center / margin thus appears to privilege marginality only to end up containing it." "Thinking through the Minor," 3.

25. Calderwood, "'In Andalucía.'" The term "transperipheral" is my play on Lionnet and Shih's term "transcolonial," which refers to transversal movements of culture that laterally connect postcolonial subjects and spaces while circumventing the metropole. Through this term, Lionnet and Shih offer a critique of the excessive emphasis, in postcolonial studies, on the vertical power relationship between a dominant colonizer and a marginal colonized. "Thinking through the Minor."

26. Prat de la Riba, *Nacionalitat catalana*, 26. For the concept of *Volksgeist* in modern Spanish thought, see Serrano, "Conciencia," 353–363.

27. Prat de la Riba, *Nacionalitat catalana*, 18.

28. The *Renaixença* is conventionally dated back to Aribau's poem "La pàtria" (1833), which Resina has read as "a summons to mine the modern potential of the [Catalan] language." "Catalan *Renaixença*," 472.

29. Epps, "Between Europe and Africa," 114–119.

30. Martin-Márquez, *Disorientations*, 43–44.

31. Prat de la Riba, *Nacionalitat catalana*, 12.

32. Ibid., 57.

33. Ibid., 12–13.

34. De las Cagigas, "Apuntaciones," 84.

35. Ibid., 88.

36. Infante, *Ideal andaluz*, 102.

37. Stepan, "Racial Degeneration."

38. Infante, *Ideal andaluz*, 84.

39. Ibid., 96.

40. Ibid., 99.

41. Ibid., 72.

42. Ibid., 102.

43. Ibid., 77–78.

44. Ibid., 57.

45. Infante et al., "Manifiesto," 83.

46. Infante, *Verdad*, 23.

47. Ibid., 66.

48. Ibid., 63.

49. Junta Liberalista de Andalucía, prologue to *La verdad sobre el complot de Tablada*, by Blas Infante, 14.

50. Infante, *Verdad*, 69.

51. Prat de la Riba and Muntañola, "Compendi," 97.

52. Infante, *Verdad*, 68.

53. Ibid., 69. Italics in the original.

54. Goode, *Impurity of Blood*, 1–4.

55. For the history of this idea, see Gonzàlez i Vilalta, *La nació imaginada*.
56. Infante, *Verdad*, 82.
57. Ibid.
58. Quoted in Iniesta Coullaut-Valera, *Blas Infante*, 217.
59. I discuss the metaphorical relationship between al-Andalus and Palestine in Chapter 2.
60. Quoted in Iniesta Coullaut-Valera, *Blas Infante*, 228.
61. Infante, *Verdad*, 84.
62. Ibid., 82–83.
63. Ibid., 81.
64. Martin-Márquez, *Disorientations*, 52–60. See also my discussion of family metaphors in Chapter 1.
65. Infante, *Verdad*, 81.
66. Infante, *Ideal andaluz*, 96.
67. Infante, *Motamid*, 129.
68. Ibid., 75, 98.
69. González Alcantud surveys Gil Benumeya's life and work in the introduction to *Ni Oriente, ni Occidente*; and in *Mito*, 82–85.
70. Balfour, *Deadly Embrace*, 99–100, 171–174.
71. The year of the book's publication is unknown, but it is likely in the late 1920s or in the early 1930s, according to González Alcantud, *Ni Oriente, ni Occidente*, lxvii.
72. Gil Benumeya, *Ni Oriente, ni Occidente*, 5.
73. Ibid., 219.
74. Ibid., 216.
75. Ibid.
76. Gil Benumeya, *Marruecos andaluz*, 97–98.
77. Ibid., 88.
78. Ibid., 93–94.
79. Ibid., 101.
80. Ibid., 139–140.
81. Ibid., 161.
82. Ibid., 167.
83. Ibid., 172–174.
84. Martin-Márquez, *Disorientations*, 22; McClintock, *Imperial Leather*, 40–42.
85. Gil Benumeya, *Andalucismo africano*, 119.
86. Ibid., 112.
87. Ibid., 123.
88. For García Figueras, see Chapter 5. For Bertuchi, see Chapter 6. For De las Cagigas in his role as Spanish consul, see Chapter 7.

89. Gil Benumeya, *Marruecos andaluz*, 149.
90. Infante, *Verdad*, 91.
91. Gil Benumeya, *Andalucismo africano*, 126.
92. Gil Benumeya, *Marruecos andaluz*, 11.
93. Ibid., 13.
94. Ibid., 201.
95. Gil Benumeya, *Marruecos andaluz*, 201–202; quoting Infante, *Verdad*, 63.
96. Rodríguez de la Borbolla y Camoyán, *Elogio del mestizaje*, 33.
97. Ibid., 34.
98. Ibid., 39.
99. For representations of immigration to contemporary Spain, see Flesler, *Return*; Rogozen-Soltar, "Al-Andalus in Andalusia"; Calderwood, "Invention of al-Andalus."

4. FRANCO'S HAJJ

1. This anecdote comes from al-Rahuni, *al-Rihla al-makkiyya*, 5.
2. Ibn al-Hajj al-Sulami recently completed a critical edition of al-Rahuni's *'Umdat al-rawin*. In the introduction, he gives an overview of al-Rahuni's life and situates al-Rahuni's work within the Moroccan historiographic tradition. *'Umdat al-rawin*, 1:7–50.
3. Al-Rahuni, *al-Rihla al-makkiyya*, 5.
4. Botti, *Cielo y dinero*; Casanova, *La Iglesia de Franco*.
5. For the history and significance of the hajj, see Peters, *Hajj*; Porter and Saif, *Hajj*. For efforts to control the hajj under European colonialism, see Brower, "Colonial Hajj"; Low, "Empire and the Hajj."
6. Franco's support of the hajj is also discussed in Solà Gussinyer, "L'organització"; Mateo Dieste, "Franco North African Pilgrims."
7. I discuss the General Franco Institute and the concept of "Hispano-Arab culture" in Chapter 5.
8. In the only published scholarship on al-Rahuni's travelogue, al-Sharif discusses al-Rahuni's impressions of Saudi Arabia. *Titwan*, 195–214.
9. For innovative scholarship on these neglected genres, see Terem, *Old Texts, New Practices*; Bazzaz, "Reading Reform."
10. Introductions to the Arabic *rihla* tradition may be found in Netton, "Rihla"; Euben, *Journeys*.
11. For hajj narratives, see Peters, *Hajj*. For Arabic travel narratives about Europe, see Matar, *In the Lands*; Matar, *Europe through Arab Eyes*; Paradela, *El otro laberinto español*; Miller, *Disorienting Encounters*.
12. Zarrouk, *Traductores*, 15–16, 234–236; Villanova, *Los interventores*, 230–231.

13. I am playing here with Rothberg's *Multidirectional Memory*.

14. See Madariaga, *Marruecos*, 325–335; Balfour, *Deadly Embrace*, 268–317.

15. Madariaga, *Marruecos*, 283–299; Benjelloun, *Mouvement*, 113–178.

16. Balfour, *Deadly Embrace*, 273–274.

17. In a 1937 interview with a French newspaper, Franco asserted: "Our war is not a civil war . . . but rather a Crusade of men who believe in God . . . [and] who fight against men without faith." Franco, *Palabras del Caudillo*, 453.

18. For Beigbeder, see Madariaga, *Marruecos*, 257–335; as well as Chapter 5.

19. Al-Rahuni, *al-Rihla al-makkiyya*, 5–6.

20. Ibid., 21.

21. Balfour, *Deadly Embrace*.

22. Al-Rahuni, *al-Rihla al-makkiyya*, 6.

23. Ibid., 30. My italics.

24. The image comes from *Surat al-Saffat*, verses 48–49: "With them will be spouses—modest in gaze and beautiful of eye—like protected eggs." Abdel Haleem, *Qur'an*, 448. In a footnote on the same page, Abdel Haleem explicates the phrase "like protected eggs."

25. *Surat al-Waqiʿa*, 17–18; Abdel Haleem, *Qur'an*, 536.

26. Asín Palacios, "Por qué lucharon," 20–21; Martin-Márquez, *Disorientations*, 226–227; Calderwood, "Invention of al-Andalus," 42–44.

27. Al-Rahuni, *al-Rihla al-makkiyya*, 30. I discuss Rabat's Hassan Minaret (or "Tour Hassan") in the epilogue.

28. Ruggles, "Alcazar."

29. Al-Rahuni, *al-Rihla al-makkiyya*, 31. My italics.

30. *Surat Al ʿImran*, 140.

31. Abdel Haleem, *Qur'an*, 68.

32. Abdel Haleem, *Qur'an*, 68; Robinson, "Uḥud."

33. See Paradela, *El otro laberinto español*.

34. Al-Rahuni, *al-Rihla al-makkiyya*, 32.

35. The *convivencia* theme appears in several Francoist texts about Morocco, including García Figueras, *Marruecos*, 46; Asín Palacios, "Por qué lucharon," 20.

36. Calderwood, "Reconquista."

37. For the ship's name change, see Box 81 / 02428, Archivo General de la Administración, Alcalá de Henares (Spain).

38. Al-Rahuni, *al-Rihla al-makkiyya*, 38.

39. In *Surat al-Hajj*, verse 27, God tells the prophet Abraham: "Proclaim the Pilgrimage to all people. They will come to you on foot and on every kind

of lean camel, emerging from every deep mountain pass." Abdel Haleem, *Qur'an*, 336.

40. Al-Rahuni, *al-Rihla al-makkiyya*, 39.
41. Ibid., 38.
42. Ibid., 59.
43. Ibid., 55–56.
44. Ibid., 216–217.
45. I will return to this controversy in Chapters 5 and 7.
46. Al-Rahuni, *al-Rihla al-makkiyya*, 112.
47. Ibid., 113.
48. Mateo Dieste, "Muley Hassan."
49. In Spanish archives, I have found newspaper accounts of the event in Seville that were published in Cordoba, Palencia, Zamora, Santa Cruz de Tenerife, and Ceuta. While this list is not meant to be exhaustive, it gives a sense of the rebels' concerted effort to publicize the event to a broad Spanish audience.
50. Al-Rahuni, *al-Rihla al-makkiyya*, 219.
51. "Los musulmanes peregrinos," 13.
52. Al-Rahuni, *al-Rihla al-makkiyya*, 220.
53. Ibid.
54. For the eleven suites, see Davila, *Andalusian Music*; Chaachoo, *Música andalusí*.
55. Al-Fasi, "Musique," 94. For the suite's association with dawn, see Chottin, *Nouba de Ochchâk*; García Barriuso, *Música*, 175–180.
56. In fact, the literal translation of the suite's name is "The Lovers" (*al-ʿushshāq*), although such literal translations are rarely given, since, according to Jonathan Glasser, the suites' names are generally understood to be abstract and somewhat independent from their referential meaning. Email message to author, July 24, 2017.
  Some of the lyrics for *Nubat al-ʿushshaq* appear in Chottin, *Nouba de Ochchâk*; Valderrama Martínez, *Cancionero de al-Ḥāʾik*, 149–154.
57. García Barriuso, *Música*, 178; Valderrama Martínez, *Cancionero de al-Ḥāʾik*, 150.
58. Glasser, *Lost Paradise*; Chaachoo, *Música andalusí*, 93–100; Davila, *Andalusian Music*, 154–168.
59. Chottin, *Nouba de Ochchâk*.
60. García Barriuso, *Música*, 186.
61. "Los musulmanes peregrinos," 13.
62. For the Alcázar's Hall of Ambassadors, see Ruggles, "Alcazar," 91–92.
63. Al-Rahuni, *al-Rihla al-makkiyya*, 220.

64. Rippin, "Āya."

65. "Los musulmanes peregrinos," 14.

66. Ibid. My italics.

67. Ibid.

68. Ibid.

69. Ibid.

70. Ibid. My italics.

71. Al-Rahuni, *al-Rihla al-makkiyya*, 228. My italics.

72. Ibid., 38.

73. For versions of this narrative of the *Nahḍa*, see Hourani, *Arabic Thought*; Abu-Lughod, *Arab Rediscovery of Europe*; Badawi, "Background"; Kassab, *Contemporary Arab Thought*, 17–47. See also my discussion in Chapter 2.

74. Cachia, "Translations."

75. El-Ariss, *Trials of Arab Modernity*, 8–9.

76. See, for example, Allen, "Post-Classical Period"; El-Rouayheb, *Islamic Intellectual History*; Terem, *Old Texts, New Practices*.

77. For the power of the secular in formulations of modernity, see Asad, *Formations of the Secular*, 1–17; Scott and Hirschkind, "Anthropological Skepticism."

78. For example, Badawi asserts: "the states of North Africa . . . began to make their distinct literary contribution only some time after the Second World War." "Background," 23.

79. Allen, "Rewriting Literary History"; Fernández Parrilla, *La literatura marroquí contemporánea*, 103–114.

80. Asad, *Formations of the Secular*, 1.

81. Elmarsafy, *Sufism*; al-Musawi, *Islam on the Street*.

82. See, for example, Elmarsafy's observation on Sufism in the contemporary Arabic novel: "The turn to Sufism in the literature of the post-war period . . . marks an attempt at reappropriating and redefining individuality along lines that evade the dogmas of institutional religious and political restriction." *Sufism*, 5.

83. Chakrabarty, *Provincializing Europe*.

5. THE INVENTION OF HISPANO-ARAB CULTURE

1. See *Bachillerato Hispano-Marroquí*, 7, 25–26.

2. There is much evidence that allows me to date the emergence of the category of "Hispano-Arab culture" to the Francoist period. For example, in the Real Academia Española's historical database, CORDE (Corpus Di-

acrónico del Español), there are only three cases of the word *hispano-árabe* between 1700 and 1939. Likewise, in the catalogue of the Spanish National Library, there are very few instances of the term before 1939, but there is an explosion of publications on "Hispano-Arab culture" after the Spanish Civil War. One of the exceptions to this chronology is the nomenclature of the Spanish education system in Morocco. From 1907 on, the Spanish used the term "Hispano-Arab schools" (*escuelas hispano-árabes* or *centros hispano-árabes*) to describe Spanish schools for Moroccan Muslims. In this specific context, the adjective "Hispano-Arab" was not attached to the broader project of "Hispano-Arab culture," which took shape under Francoism. For the "Hispano-Arab schools," see González González, *Escuela*, 111–147.

3. For a brief history of the General Franco Institute, see Valderrama Martínez, *Historia*, 814–832.

4. For Bustani, see Valderrama Martínez, *Historia*, 511. For the Academy of Arabic and Berber of Tetouan and the Center for Moroccan Studies, see Valderrama Martínez, *Historia*, 499–527.

5. Valderrama Martínez, *Historia*, 814–816.

6. Averroes, *Quitab el Culiat*. The edition's prologue and indexes were written by Bustani. Cristóbal Pérez Vera did the Spanish translation. Although this edition of Averroes's treatise was hailed as the General Franco Institute's first publication, it was actually preceded by a few short works published by the institute in 1938.

7. Bustani, *Fragmento*; Bustani, *Rihlat al-wazir*; Bustani, *Kitab natijat al-ijtihad*.

8. A good example is Muhammad b. Tawit, who joined the General Franco Institute in 1950, according to Valderrama Martínez, *Historia*, 819. In 1956, Ibn Tawit helped found the academic journal *Titwan*, which I discuss in Chapter 7.

9. Valderrama Martínez, *Historia*, 795–814; González González, *Escuela*, 271–273; Khatib, *Culture*, 32–45; Stenner, "Centering the Periphery," 445–446.

10. Larramendi, González González, and López García, *Instituto Hispano-Árabe*.

11. For the IHEM, see Burke, *Ethnographic State*, 124–126; Miller, *History*, 101–102.

12. Burke, *Ethnographic State*, 124–125.

13. Ibid., 126.

14. For the "Hispano-Moorish" style in French colonial thought, see González Alcantud, "Fábrica."

15. For Lyautey, see Miller, *History*, 89–119.

16. González Alcantud, "Fábrica"; Holden, "When It Pays," 303–304.

17. A prominent example of this scholarly tradition is Henri Terrasse's *L'art hispano-mauresque des origins au XIIIe siècle*, published by the IHEM in 1932.

18. For this narrative of decline in French colonial writing about Morocco, see Irbouh, *Art*, 31–33, 228; González Alcantud, "Fábrica."

19. Burke, *Ethnographic State*, 33. The treatment of the Arab-Berber distinction in French colonial discourse has generated a vast corpus of scholarship. For helpful introductions, see Burke III, "Image"; Wyrtzen, *Making Morocco*, 136–178.

20. For the Berber *dahir* episode and its impact on the Moroccan nationalist movement, see Wyrtzen, *Making Morocco*, 1–4, 136–178; Miller, *History*, 125–136.

21. For Morocco's "Arab-Islamic" identity, see Wyrtzen, *Making Morocco*.

22. See García Figueras, *Marruecos*, 293–294; García Figueras, *Líneas*; González González, *Escuela*, 240–241.

23. Beigbeder, "Ordenanza."

24. Madariaga, *Marruecos*, 292–294; Benjelloun, *Mouvement*, 130–133.

25. Madariaga, *Marruecos*, 294; Benjelloun, *Mouvement*, 131, 158.

26. For the foundation of the newspaper *al-Rif*, see Benjelloun, *Approches*, 115–124; H. Dawud, *'Ala ra's*, 191–193. Al-Wazzani serially published his autobiographical text *al-Zawiya*, sometimes called the first Moroccan novel, in the pages of the newspaper *al-Rif*. See Fernández Parrilla, *La literatura marroquí contemporánea*, 104–108.

27. Dawud, "Nurid istiqlal al-Maghrib," 1.

28. *Bachillerato Hispano-Marroquí*, 24.

29. Valderrama Martínez, *Historia*, 110–111; González González, *Escuela*, 229–230.

30. García Figueras, *Marruecos*, 46. Italics in the original.

31. Ibid., 290.

32. Ibid., 341.

33. Ibid., 339.

34. Dedication to *Quitab el Culiat*, by Averroes, 5.

35. Bustani, introduction to *Quitab el Culiat*, 33.

36. Ibid., 9.

37. "Dahir creando," 310.

38. The Spanish National Library owns a typed Spanish text of the speech delivered by Gannun, "Fiesta del Libro Hispano-Árabe." It is dated in Tangier on April 23, 1941.

39. For the history of the Festival of the Hispano-Arab Book from 1940–1948, see García Figueras, "Fiesta."

40. The caliph's 1941 decree mentions the annual celebration of the Exhibition of the Hispano-Arab Book. "Dahir creando," 310–311. The General Franco Institute produced catalogs of its publications for the Festival of the Hispano-Arab Book in 1941 and 1942. Both catalogs are titled *Fiesta del Libro Hispano-Árabe*, and they are owned by the Spanish National Library.

41. García Figueras, "Fiesta," 75.

42. "Dahir creando," 311; García Figueras, "Fiesta"; Valderrama Martínez, *Historia*, 820–822.

43. For an introduction to al-Rihani's Arabic oeuvre, see Ruiz Bravo-Villasante, *Testigo*; Hassan, *Immigrant Narratives*, 38–40.

44. Hassan, *Immigrant Narratives*, 38–39.

45. Quoted in Hassan, *Immigrant Narratives*, 45.

46. Al-Rihani dates the book's prologue August 11, 1939. Nevertheless, there are details in the travel narrative that make it clear that al-Rihani was still working on it in 1940. For instance, he refers to the Spanish occupation of Tangier in June of 1940. *Al-Maghrib al-Aqsa*, 98.

Al-Rihani died on September 13, 1940. The travelogue was first published in 1952, with a second edition in 1975. All of my references are to the second edition, unless otherwise noted.

47. I have reconstructed al-Rihani's itinerary based on information found in *al-Maghrib al-Aqsa*. The travel narrative is thin on dates, but it does provide the date for al-Rihani's arrival to Morocco. *Al-Maghrib al-Aqsa*, 111.

48. The Ameen Rihani Museum in Freike, Lebanon, owns a few documents related to al-Rihani's visit to the Spanish Protectorate, including the *salvoconducto* signed by Beigbeder on May 8, 1939. The museum also has a telegram that Beigbeder sent to al-Rihani, inviting him to visit the Spanish Protectorate. I thank the Ameen Rihani Organization for sharing these documents with me.

49. Al-Rihani, *al-Maghrib al-Aqsa*, 110–111. The information about Aragón comes from al-Rihani, *al-Maghrib al-Aqsa*, 294–295.

50. This information appears in the first edition of the travel narrative (p. 485), but not in the second edition, in which some of the chapters are omitted.

51. Al-Rihani, *al-Maghrib al-Aqsa*, 498–514.

52. Ibid., 534.

53. Beigbeder and al-Rihani, *Discursos*.

54. Ibid. The quote appears on an unnumbered page that comes after the title page.

55. I am basing my description of the event on the photographs and texts included in Beigbeder and al-Rihani, *Discursos*.

56. Beigbeder and al-Rihani, *Discursos*, 7. The pamphlet has two sets of pagination: one for the Spanish text (running left-to-right) and another for the Arabic text (running right-to-left). For the quotes from Beigbeder's speech, I will refer to the pagination of the Spanish text; for the quotes from al-Rihani's speech, I will refer to the pagination of the Arabic text.

57. Ibid., 7–8.

58. García Figueras also stresses the contrast between Spain's "spiritual" mission and France's material or utilitarian ambitions in *Marruecos*, 289–290.

59. Beigbeder and al-Rihani, *Discursos*, 7–8.

60. Ibid., 8.

61. Ibid., 9.

62. See Madariaga, *Marruecos*, 325–335.

63. Beigbeder and al-Rihani, *Discursos*, 10.

64. Hershenzon, "Traveling Libraries"; Justel Calabozo, *Real Biblioteca*, 171–191.

65. Hershenzon, "Traveling Libraries," 551–557; Paradela, *El otro laberinto español*, 38–45; Justel Calabozo, *Real Biblioteca*, 191–197.

66. Beigbeder and al-Rihani, *Discursos*, 10.

67. Ibid., 13.

68. Ibid.

69. The phrase "the New Spain" also appears in García Figueras, *Marruecos*, 289.

70. Beigbeder and al-Rihani, *Discursos*, 14.

71. Ibid.

72. Ibid., 15.

73. Ibid.

74. Al-Rihani, *al-Maghrib al-Aqsa*, 339–340.

75. Ibid., 340.

76. Ibid., 551. The review was published in the appendix of both editions of *al-Maghrib al-Aqsa*. My citations refer to the text reproduced in the second edition, 548–553.

77. Ibid., 549–550.

78. Ibid., 551.

79. Beigbeder and al-Rihani, *Discursos*, 16.

80. Al-Rihani, *al-Maghrib al-Aqsa*, 183.

81. Ibid.

82. Ibid., 15–16.

83. Ibid., 16. Al-Rihani inflates the number of Moroccans who fought in Franco's army. There were roughly 80,000, not 160,000, according to Madariaga, *Marruecos*, 335.

84. For Ibn ʿArabi, see Knysh, "Ibn ʿArabi."
85. Al-Rihani, *al-Maghrib al-Aqsa*, 270.
86. Ibid., 453.
87. Ibid., 270.
88. Ibid., 288.
89. Ibid.
90. Ibid., 267.
91. Ibid., 271.
92. Ibid., 272.
93. Ibid., 184.
94. Ibid., 298.
95. Ibid., 297.
96. The Arabic text reads *madīna* ("city"), which appears to be an erratum. From the context, I believe that al-Rihani meant *madaniyya* ("civilization").
97. Al-Rihani, *al-Maghrib al-Aqsa*, 297.
98. Ibid., 284.
99. Ibid., 282.
100. Al-Rihani describes his meeting with Franco in *al-Maghrib al-Aqsa*, 498–514.
101. For Álvarez Sanz y Tubau, see Zarrouk, *Traductores*, 123–133, 244; al-Rihani, *al-Maghrib al-Aqsa*, 125–126, 293–294.
102. Al-Rihani, *al-Maghrib al-Aqsa*, 499–500.
103. Ibid., 500–501.
104. Ibid., 501–502.
105. Ibid., 507–508.
106. Ibid., 508.
107. Ibid., 210–211.
108. Ibid., 185–186.
109. Ibid., 122.
110. Ibid., 160–161.
111. Ibid., 185–186.
112. For these political parties, see al-Rihani, *al-Maghrib al-Aqsa*, 210–224; Madariaga, *Marruecos*, 292–299.
113. For Ibrahim al-Wazzani, see al-Rihani, *al-Maghrib al-Aqsa*, 215–216; Madariaga, *Marruecos*, 295–296.
114. For the nationalist uprisings in the fall of 1937, see al-Rihani, *al-Maghrib al-Aqsa*, 215–216; Guerin, "'Not a Drop'"; Wyrtzen, *Making Morocco*, 166–170.
115. Al-Rihani, *al-Maghrib al-Aqsa*, 423–424.

116. Ibid.

117. Ibid., 225, 236. Al-Rihani was a fierce advocate of the Palestinian cause. For this facet of his career, see his prologue to *al-Maghrib al-Aqsa*, 7–20.

118. For al-Rihani's Moroccan sources, see al-Rihani, *al-Maghrib al-Aqsa*, 224–226. For Muhammad Dawud, see Chapter 7. For al-Makki al-Nasiri, see al-Rihani, *al-Maghrib al-Aqsa*, 213; Madariaga, *Marruecos*, 294–299.

119. Al-Rihani, *al-Maghrib al-Aqsa*, 226.

120. Ibid.

121. Al-Rihani writes that European colonizers and missionaries "invented Pharaohism in Egypt, and Phoenicianism in Lebanon, and Berberism in Morocco." *Al-Maghrib al-Aqsa*, 453.

122. Ibid., 227.

123. Ibid., 246.

124. Ibid., 228.

125. Ibid., 191.

126. Ibid., 192.

127. For example, in Zaydan's novel *Sharl wa-'Abd al-Rahman* (1904), the Arab-Berber rivalry is at the root of the Muslim army's defeat at the Battle of Poitiers (732), which put an end to Islam's expansion in western Europe. In Zaydan's fictional retelling of the event, the army's Arab leaders are exemplary Muslims who are tolerant of their Christian and Jewish subjects. In contrast, the Berber soldiers are insincere Muslims, who only converted to Islam out of greed for war booty.

128. Amin al-Rihani, *al-Maghrib al-Aqsa*, 1st ed. (Cairo: Dar al-Ma'arif, 1952), 637.

129. Amin al-Rihani, *al-Maghrib al-Aqsa*, 2nd ed. (Beirut: Dar al-Thaqafa, 1975), 467.

130. Ibid., 469.

131. Ibid., 129, 340.

132. Ibid., 86.

133. Hachimi, "Maghreb-Mashriq"; Calderwood, "Proyectando al-Ándalus," 228–232.

134. Bravo Nieto, *Arquitectura*, 157–170; Malo de Molina and Domínguez, *Tetuán, el Ensanche*, 45. French colonial architecture also made abundant use of elements from Moroccan design arts, such as tile mosaics, whitewashed walls, and stalactite *muqarnas*. The result was an architectural style now known as *Arabisances*. See Wright, *Politics*, 108–114.

135. Bravo Nieto, *Arquitectura*, 55, 159. The station was recently restored by the Junta de Andalucía and is now Tetouan's Center for Modern Art.

136. Al-Rihani, *al-Maghrib al-Aqsa*, 125.

137. Ibid., 300–301.
138. For Madinat al-Zahra' see Ruggles, *Gardens*, 53–109.
139. For the *maqāmāt*, see Stewart, "*Maqāma*"; Elinson, *Looking Back*.

6. MOROCCAN ALHAMBRAS

1. Serrano Suñer's visit to Morocco is described in Serrano Suñer and Beigbeder, *Discursos*. This source is a pamphlet containing the speeches delivered by Serrano Suñer and Beigbeder from July 17–20, 1936, as well as a brief chronicle of Serrano Suñer's travels through Morocco.
2. For the events of the military uprising in July of 1936, see Madariaga, *Marruecos*, 257–262; Balfour, *Deadly Embrace*, 268–270.
3. Serrano Suñer and Beigbeder, *Discursos*, 5.
4. Ibid.
5. Ibid., 6.
6. Ibid., 5.
7. Ibid., 6.
8. Ibid., 9.
9. Ibid.
10. Ibid.
11. At its foundation, the school was named the School of Arts and Trades (Escuela de Artes y Oficios). In 1931, its name was changed to the School of Indigenous Arts. Finally, in 1947, the name was changed to School of Moroccan Arts (Escuela de Artes Marroquíes). Valderrama Martínez, *Historia*, 374. In this chapter, I will use the name "School of Indigenous Arts" for the sake of consistency, and also because I will focus on the period in which this name was in use.
12. The photograph, belonging to the Fondo Fotográfico de la Guerra Civil, carries the following call number: GC-Caja / 116 / 18 / 4.
13. GC-Caja / 116 / 18 / 6.
14. Valderrama Martínez describes the origins of the School of Indigenous Arts in *Historia*, 367–372. For 'Abd al-Salam Binnuna, see Chapter 7.
15. For the school's original location, see Valderrama Martínez, *Historia*, 370.
16. Santos Moreno, "Mariano Bertuchi Nieto," 62.
17. Valderrama Martínez, *Historia*, 372–374.
18. For example, writing in 1946, Gil Benumeya calls Bertuchi the "creator of the School of Indigenous Arts." "Veinte," 3.
19. Gómez Barceló, "Mariano Bertuchi," 87–88.
20. Moratinos, foreword to *Mariano Bertuchi*.

21. Benjelloun, "L'École picturale de Tétouan," 11; Achaâri, foreword to *Mariano Bertuchi*.

22. Valderrama Martínez, *Historia*, 383–385; Dizy Caso, "Bertuchi," 111–112.

23. Benaboud and Bouzaid, *Rassamun Titwan*, 2:18–21; Valderrama Martínez, *Historia*, 384.

24. Benaboud and Bouzaid, *Rassamun Titwan*; Achaâri, foreword to *Mariano Bertuchi*.

25. For Bertuchi's art education, see Santos Moreno, "Mariano Bertuchi Nieto," 55–61.

26. Santos Moreno, "Mariano Bertuchi Nieto," 57–61.

27. For Rinaldy, see Zarrouk, *Traductores*, 11–93; Calderwood, "Beginning," 414–416.

28. This anecdote appears in Martín de la Escalera, "Mariano Bertuchi," 42; Santos Moreno, "Mariano Bertuchi Nieto," 59.

29. Santos Moreno, "Mariano Bertuchi Nieto," 59–60; García Figueras, "A la Escuela," 16.

30. *Catálogo oficial*, 13; Santos Moreno, "Mariano Bertuchi Nieto," 61.

31. Utande Ramiro and Utande Igualada, "Mariano Bertuchi."

32. This painting is currently held at the Spanish Embassy in Moscow. I thank Ana Pernia and Domingo Guerrero Borrull, of the Spanish Ministry of Foreign Affairs, for sending me images of the painting and information about it.

33. Santos Moreno, "Mariano Bertuchi Nieto," 62; Serna et al., *Mariano Bertuchi*, 118–123.

34. Hernández Ramos, *Emisión*; Gil Benumeya, "Veinte."

35. The Spanish National Library's *Hemeroteca Digital* has digitized the issues of the *Revista de tropas coloniales* published between 1924 and 1936. I used this digital resource to document Bertuchi and Franco's early involvement in the magazine. The magazine resumed publication in 1942, after a break on account of the Spanish Civil War. I would like to thank Ethan Madarieta and the Interlibrary Loan Office at the University of Illinois for helping to me to track down the issues published in the 1940s and 1950s, which include dozens of illustrations by Bertuchi.

36. For the Ibero-American Exhibit, see Darias Príncipe, "Marruecos en España"; Graciani García, *Participación*.

37. Arbizu, "Hispanismo," 40.

38. The concept of *Hispanidad* is discussed in Martin-Márquez, *Disorientations*, 49–50; Krauel, *Imperial Emotions*, 175–179.

39. Bertuchi, "Escuela," 68.

40. Fernández, "Marruecos," 112–113.

41. Ibid., 112.
42. Ibid.
43. Ibid.
44. Ibid.; Martín de la Escalera, "Mariano Bertuchi," 42.
45. Fernández, "Marruecos," 112.
46. Ibid., 113.
47. Ibid.
48. Ibid. For Got, see Valderrama Martínez, *Historia*, 369–370.
49. Fernández, "Marruecos," 113.
50. The structure reproduced the minaret of the Basha's Mosque, built in the eighteenth century. Graciani García, *Participación*, 421; Fernández, "Marruecos," 113.
51. Fernández, "Marruecos," 113.
52. Irbouh, *Art*, 59–60, 187–188; Ricard, "Arts marocains," 17–19.
53. For an introduction to Ricard's career, see Mokhiber, "'Le protectorat dans la peau.'"
54. Examples of these tropes are found in Ricard, *Artisanat*; Ricard, "Arts marocains," 20–21; Mokhiber, "'Le protectorat dans la peau,'" 265–271; Bertuchi, "Artesanía," 213–214; Gil Benumeya, "Actualidad."
55. Ricard, *Artisanat*, 3.
56. Ibid., 9.
57. Ibid., 15.
58. For the distinction between "Berber" and "Arab" crafts, see Ricard, "Arts ruraux"; Ricard, "Arts marocains," 13–14; Irbouh, *Art*, 29–31.
59. See Ricard "Arts marocains," 20; Ricard, *Artisanat*, 12; Mokhiber, "'Le protectorat dans la peau,'" 266–269; Irbouh, *Art*, 182–187.
60. Ricard, "Arts marocains," 13–14. Italics in the original.
61. Irbouh, *Art*, 30–31.
62. Bertuchi, "Escuela," 68.
63. Bertuchi, "Industrias artísticas tetuaníes," 45.
64. Ibid.
65. For the "Victory Convoy," see Balfour, *Deadly Embrace*, 287–288.
66. This episode is narrated in the anonymous article "Arte y artistas: Exposición Bertuchi," *ABC*, April 16, 1940, http://hemeroteca.abc.es/nav/Navigate.exe/hemeroteca/madrid/abc/1940/04/16/014.html.
67. Ibid.
68. Gómez Barceló, "Mariano Bertuchi," 88.
69. For the school's remodeling, see Bertuchi, "Escuela," 70. For the *cármenes*, see Tito Rojo and Casares Porcel, *Carmen*, 17–45.
70. Santos Moreno, "Mariano Bertuchi Nieto," 57; Vallina, "Pintura," 77.

71. See Vallina, "Pintura," 76; Serna et al., *Mariano Bertuchi*, 174–176.
72. Gil Benumeya, "Veinte," 3.
73. Ibid.
74. Ibid.
75. See, for example, Santos Moreno, "Mariano Bertuchi Nieto," 55; Serna, "Arte," 16.
76. Gil Benumeya, "Veinte," 3.
77. In 1954, the school received 10,718 visitors from more than 40 nationalities. Valderrama Martínez, *Historia*, 373–374.
78. Diógenes, "Mariano," 57.
79. Ibid.
80. Ibid.
81. Bellido Gant, "Difundir una identidad," 75–80.
82. The exhibit's name varied slightly over time. In 1933, it was called the Exposición Hispano-Africana, whereas the 1939 edition was called the Exposición de Industrias Artísticas Hispano-Marroquíes.
83. The description appears in Ortiz de Villajos, *Crónica*, 89–93. I have also relied on information found in the online catalog of Granada's Escuela de Estudios Árabes, which has a collection of documents and photographs related to the event.
84. Ortiz de Villajos, *Crónica*, 89–90.
85. Ibid., 90.
86. Ibid., 91.
87. Ibid.
88. Ibid., 91–92.
89. Ibid., 92.
90. Ibid., 91.
91. Ibid., 90.
92. Ibid., 90–91.
93. "Arte marroquí," 112.
94. Ibid., 113. I discuss Dawud's work at length in Chapter 7.
95. Barberán, "Exposición," 29; "Arte marroquí," 112.
96. Barberán, "Exposición," 29–30; "Arte marroquí," 113.
97. Barberán, "Exposición," 30; "Arte marroquí," 113. For the Hispano-Moroccan Music Conservatory, see Valderrama Martínez, *Historia*, 404–428.
98. Barberán, "Exposición," 30.
99. Alarcón, *Diario*, 472.
100. Ibid., 429.
101. See Infante, *Verdad*, 76–77; Infante, *Orígenes*.

102. See, for example, Iniesta Coullaut-Valera, *Blas Infante*, 231–246; Manuel, *Huella morisca*, 141–145.

103. Glasser, "Andalusi"; Glasser, *Lost Paradise*; Davila, *Andalusian Music*; Shannon, *Performing al-Andalus*, 94–95.

104. Glasser, "Andalusi," 722–723; Glasser, *Lost Paradise*, 32–34; Davila, *Andalusian Music*, 7–8; Chaachoo, *Música andalusí*, 115.

105. For the *nūba*, see Davila, *Andalusian Music*, 8–12, 28–33; Glasser, *Lost Paradise*, 14–16; García Barriuso, *Música*, 173–222. For the *muwashshaḥ*, see Glasser, *Lost Paradise*, 84–91; Davila, *Andalusian Music*, 15–18, 267.

106. Glasser, *Lost Paradise*.

107. García Barriuso, *Ecos*, 70; García Barriuso, *Música*, 13.

108. García Barriuso, *Ecos*, 72; García Barriuso, *Música*, 14–15. García Barriuso transcribes the names of the Moroccan musicians as "Mohamed Ech-Chaudri" and "Es-Salam el Foki."

109. García Barriuso, *Música*, 14.

110. For the *Kunnash*, see Valderrama Martínez, *Cancionero de al-Ḥā'ik*; Davila, *Andalusian Music*, 149–160.

111. Writing in the spring of 1939, García Barriuso said that he received the commission from Beigbeder "a few months ago." *Ecos*, 82. For García Barriuso's work on Bustelo's unfinished project, see García Barriuso, *Ecos*, 80–102.

112. García Figueras, prologue to *Música*, vii–viii.

113. For example, García Barriuso published an excerpt from his edition of *Nubat Ramal al-Maya* in *África* in April of 1944. García Barriuso, "Plan."

114. A detailed account of this event appears in Ricard, *Essai*, 4–10.

115. Ricard, *Essai*, 6.

116. Ibid., 7.

117. Ibid., 8.

118. For Ben Smaïl, see Glasser, *Lost Paradise*, 1–3, 113–115.

119. Ricard, *Essai*, 13.

120. Shannon, *Performing al-Andalus*, 94–95; Davila, *Andalusian Music*, 163; Glasser, *Lost Paradise*, 210, 272.

121. The Fez conference is also discussed in Glasser, *Lost Paradise*, 208–213.

122. García Barriuso, *Ecos*, 32.

123. Ibid. My italics.

124. Ibid., 38.

125. Ibid., 28.

126. Ibid., 44.

127. Ibid., 44–46.

128. The photograph and caption appear on an unnumbered page in between the Spanish-French and the Arabic sections.

129. García Barriuso, *Ecos*, 72.
130. Ibid., 60–62.
131. García Figueras, prologue to *Música*, vii.
132. Ibid., viii.
133. For the Republic as the "anti-Spain," see García Figueras, *Marruecos*, 243, 289–290, 341.
134. García Figueras, prologue to *Música*, viii.
135. Ibid.
136. García Barriuso expresses an explicit preference for the term "Hispano-Muslim" over the term "Hispano-Arab" (*Música*, 4), but he uses both terms interchangeably in his book.
137. García Figueras, prologue to *Música*, ix.
138. See, for example, Ricard, *Essai*, 7.
139. García Barriuso, *Música*, 172.
140. Ibid., 18.
141. Ibid., 85.
142. Ibid. My italics.
143. Ibid., 253.
144. Ibid., 255.
145. Ibid., 260–261, 263.
146. Ibid., 261–262.
147. Ibid., 262.
148. Ibid., 262–263.
149. Ibid., 263.
150. Al-Turris, "Al-'Inaya," 72–73.
151. Ibid., 72.
152. Ibid., 74.
153. Valderrama Martínez, *Historia*, 404.
154. The bylaws are reproduced in Valderrama Martínez, *Historia*, 404–407.
155. Quoted in Valderrama Martínez, *Historia*, 405.
156. Ibid.
157. Chaachoo, *Música andalusí*, 91–103; Davila, *Andalusian Music*, 141–148, 162.
158. Glasser traces a similar movement from the private to the public sphere in his discussion of Andalusi music in Algeria. *Lost Paradise*.
159. See Valderrama Martínez, *Historia*, 408–428; Chaachoo, *Música andalusí*, 106–111.
160. Valderrama Martínez, *Historia*, 421–422.
161. Valderrama Martínez, *Historia*, 421; García Barriuso, *Música*, 260.

162. For this collaboration, see Larrea Palacín and Bustani, *Nawba Iṣbahān*; Chaachoo, *Música andalusí*, 96.

163. Valderrama Martínez, *Historia*, 411.

164. Garrido, "Conservatorio"; Valderrama Martínez, *Historia*, 427.

165. "Arte marroquí," 113; Alta Comisaría de España en Marruecos, *Conservatorio*.

166. Chaachoo, *Música andalusí*, 109.

167. See Shannon, *Performing al-Andalus*, 84–118; Davila, *Andalusian Music*, 167–175; Glasser, *Lost Paradise*, 23–27.

7. THE DAUGHTER OF GRANADA AND FEZ

1. Arslan, *Tarikh ghazawat al-'arab*, 24. I have reconstructed Arslan's travels in 1930 by piecing together information found in the following sources: Arslan, *Tarikh ghazawat al-'arab*; Arslan, *al-Hulal*; Balafrij, "al-Amir"; Binnuna, "'Utufat al-amir"; Ibn 'Azzuz Hakim, *Watha'iq*; Paradela, *El otro laberinto español*, 201–212; Cleveland, *Islam against the West*, 93–99. I have also relied on documents from the Archivo General de la Administración (hereafter cited as AGA).

2. Arslan also used the hereditary title *amīr* (roughly equivalent to "prince"). Cleveland, *Islam against the West*, 4, 13, 53.

3. Arslan, *Tarikh ghazawat al-'arab*, 21–22.

4. For the translation and its impact in the Arab world, see Arslan, *Tarikh ghazawat al-'arab*, 22–23; Arslan, *al-Hulal*, 1:10–11; Cleveland, *Islam against the West*, 13.

5. Arslan, *Tarikh ghazawat al-'arab*, 23.

6. Paradela's *El otro laberinto español* provides an excellent introduction to Arabic travel literature about Spain.

7. Cleveland, *Islam against the West*, 184; Lévi-Provençal, "L'Émir Shakib Arslan," 11; Paradela, *El otro laberinto español*, 206–207.

8. Benjelloun, *Approches*, 102–103; Halstead, *Rebirth of a Nation*, 165–169.

9. Ageron, "L'Association"; Halstead, *Rebirth of a Nation*, 170–172; Miller, *History*, 122–123.

10. Cleveland, *Islam against the West*, 90–134; Ryad, "New Episodes"; Halstead, *Rebirth of a Nation*, 129–130.

11. Arslan, *Tarikh ghazawat al-'arab*, 24.

12. Ibid., 24–25.

13. I discuss the origin of the Escorial's Arabic collection in Chapter 5.

14. Arslan, *al-Hulal*, 1:249. For the theory about al-Ma'arri's influence on Dante, see Asín Palacios, *Escatología*.

15. Arslan's stay in Cordoba is memorialized by a portrait taken in front of a studio picture of the Mosque of Cordoba. The image is reproduced in several sources, including Paradela, *El otro laberinto español*, 208. For Arslan's two-week stay at the Hotel Alhambra Palace, see "Viaje a Tetuán del Emir Xekib Arslan," AGA, Box 81-1424.

16. For this controversy, see Chapter 5.

17. In an interview with Balafrij, Arslan suggests that the choice to go to Morocco was not premeditated, but Ibn ʿAzzuz Hakim is one of several historians who argue that Arslan always intended to go to Morocco during his trip to Andalucía. Balafrij, "al-Amir," 4; Ibn ʿAzzuz Hakim, *Wathaʾiq*, 19-20.

18. "Emir Chekib Arslam," AGA, Box 81-1424; Balafrij, "al-Amir," 4.

19. Wyrtzen, *Making Morocco*, 148-150; Cleveland, *Islam against the West*, 96-100; Ibn ʿAzzuz Hakim, *Wathaʾiq*, 12-16; Miller, *History*, 127; Stenner, "Centering the Periphery," 437-438.

20. Cleveland, *Islam against the West*, 61, 68-69, 97-99.

21. Arslan, "Masʾalat ikhraj al-barbar," 1.

22. Arslan, "Tribunaux Berbères," 28.

23. Ibid., 27.

24. For Arslan and the Moroccan nationalists in the north, see also Ryad, "New Episodes"; Ibn ʿAzzuz Hakim, *Ab*; Ibn ʿAzzuz Hakim, *Wathaʾiq*; Stenner, "Centering the Periphery."

25. "Emir Chekib Arslam," AGA, Box 81-1424.

26. Binnuna, "ʿUtufat al-amir," 4.

27. See Ibn ʿAzzuz Hakim, *Ab*; Benjelloun, *Approches*, 95-108; Rézette, *Les partis politiques marocains*, 72, 83-84.

28. For the Madrasa Ahliyya, see H. Dawud, *ʿAla raʾs al-thamanin*, 22-77; Benjelloun, *Approches*, 100-102. For the Mahdiyya Press, see H. Dawud, *ʿAla raʾs al-thamanin*, 95-103; Benjelloun, *Approches*, 105-106.

29. The quote comes from Dawud's autobiographical appendix to the first volume of *Tarikh Titwan*, b.

30. Benjelloun, *Approches*, 102-103.

31. Ibid., 102-105.

32. M. Dawud, *ʿAla raʾs al-arbaʿin*, 194-197; Benjelloun, *Approches*, 96-97.

33. H. Dawud, *ʿAla raʾs al-thamanin*, 22-77.

34. Ibn ʿAzzuz Hakim, *Wathaʾiq*, 22-23.

35. For Arslan's stay in Tangier, see "Emir Chekib Arslam," AGA, Box 81-1424; as well as several untitled documents in the same box. See also Ibn ʿAzzuz Hakim, *Wathaʾiq*, 22-30; Binnuna, "ʿUtufat al-amir."

36. Binnuna, "'Utufat al-amir." In the same issue, *al-Fath* published a handful of articles on the international Muslim response to the French Berber *dahir*.

37. Binnuna, "'Utufat al-amir," 4; Ibn 'Azzuz Hakim, *Watha'iq*, 30–31.

38. Ibn 'Azzuz Hakim, *Watha'iq*, 23–37; Tomás García Figueras to the Director General de Marruecos y Colonias, 11 October 1930, AGA, Box 81–1424.

39. Quoted in Ibn 'Azzuz Hakim, *Watha'iq*, 35.

40. Ibn 'Azzuz Hakim, *Watha'iq*, 30–33; "Viaje a Tetuán del Xekib Arslan," Box 81–1424, AGA.

41. For Dawud, see H. Dawud, *'Ala ra's al-thamanin*; Benjelloun, *Approches*, 94–106; M. Dawud, *Tarikh Titwan*, 1:a–h.

42. H. Dawud, *'Ala ra's al-thamanin*, 9–47; Benjelloun, *Approches*, 94–107.

43. Benjelloun, *Approches*, 94–95; "Nota de información," Oficina Mixta de Información, 18 February 1931, AGA, Box 81–1424.

44. Ryad, "New Episodes." Dawud's efforts to distribute Arslan's works in Morocco were closely monitored by the Spanish intelligence services. See, for example, the untitled report numbered 1224 in AGA, Box 81–5642.

45. Binnuna, "'Utufat al-amir," 4; Ibn 'Azzuz Hakim, *Watha'iq*, 37; H. Dawud, *'Ala ra's al-thamanin*, 122–123.

46. For al-Wazzani, see al-Sa'ud et al., *al-Tuhami al-Wazzani*; Benjelloun, *Approches*, 111–118.

47. Binnuna, "'Utufat al-amir," 4; Ibn 'Azzuz Hakim, *Watha'iq*, 38.

48. My description of the event relies principally on Binnuna's account in "'Utufat al-amir." Supplemental information comes from Ibn 'Azzuz Hakim, *Watha'iq*; Arslan, *'Urwat al-ittihad*, 144–145; H. Dawud, *'Ala ra's al-thamanin*, 123; as well as from documents found in AGA, Box 81–1424.

49. Binnuna, "'Utufat al-amir," 4.

50. Ibid.

51. Ibn 'Azzuz Hakim reproduces al-Turris's speech in full, based on a manuscript from al-Turris's private library. *Watha'iq*, 115–118.

52. Binnuna, "'Utufat al-amir," 4.

53. According to a Spanish intelligence report, Dawud told the crowd that Moroccans were leaving behind the yoke of oppression and moving into a "century of light and liberty." See "Emir Chekib Arslam," AGA, Box 81–1424.

54. Binnuna, "'Utufat al-amir," 5.

55. Ibid.

56. Ibid.

57. Arslan, *'Urwat al-ittihad*, 144.

58. "Emir Chekib Arslan," Negociado Central de Vigilancia y Seguridad, AGA, Box 81-1424.

59. A copy of the picture, with an accompanying list of sixty-eight people in it, is preserved in AGA, Box 81-1424. In the same box, there are numerous references to the coverage that Arslan's visit received in Egyptian newspapers. The Cairo newspaper *al-Lata'if al-musawwara* printed two pictures from Arslan's visit to Tetouan in the issue published on September 22, 1930. Clippings of these pictures are in Boubkir Bennouna's archive in Tetouan.

60. Binnuna, "'Utufat al-amir," 5; H. Dawud, *'Ala ra's al-thamanin*, 123.

61. Comunicado a Marruecos y Colonias, "Emir Chekib Arslam," AGA, Box 81-1424; H. Dawud, *'Ala ra's al-thamanin*, 124.

62. Binnuna, "'Utufat al-amir," 5.

63. Balafrij, "al-Amir," 4.

64. Ibid.

65. Ibid., 5.

66. This correspondence is collected in Arslan and Binnuna, *Nidaluna*; Arslan and Dawud, *Murasalat al-amir*.

67. For this episode, see Ibn 'Azzuz Hakim, *Ab*, 2:60–62. Fittingly, Binnuna proposed a Moroccan named Ahmad al-Andalusi ("Ahmad the Andalusi") to fill the post of Arabic instructor in Granada.

68. Ministerio de Instrucción Pública y Bellas Artes, *Escuela*.

69. Ibid., 4.

70. Gracia Mechbal, Font Ubalde, and Torre, "Noticias."

71. Arslan and Dawud, *Murasalat al-amir*, 122.

72. The quote comes from the cover page of the May 28, 1932, issue of *El Defensor de Granada*. I thank Mariam Gracia Mechbal for bringing this document to my attention.

73. Quoted in Gracia Mechbal, Font Ubalde, and Torre, "Noticias," 117.

74. Ibn 'Azzuz Hakim, *Ab*, 2:440–445; Ryad, "New Episodes," 127–128.

75. Arslan and Binnuna, *Nidaluna*, 235.

76. Ibid., 240–241.

77. Ibn 'Azzuz Hakim, *Ab*, 2:441–442.

78. See Arslan and Binnuna, *Nidaluna*, 100–101; Arslan, *Tarikh ghazawat al-'arab*, 210–214.

79. Arslan, "Une perte très douloureuse," 209.

80. H. Dawud, *'Ala ra's al-thamanin*, 127.

81. For the shift in the project's focus, see H. Dawud, *'Ala ra's al-thamanin*, 127–128.

82. I would like to acknowledge the extensive help I received from Muhammad Dawud's daughter, Hasna' Dawud, who explained to me her

father's writing process and showed me his manuscripts, which contain extensive comments from Binnuna, al-Wazzani, and others.

83. H. Dawud, 'Ala ra's al-thamanin, 285–288.

84. For al-Andalus as "the lost paradise," see Glasser, Lost Paradise, 3–7; Paradela, El otro laberinto español, 132–145.

85. I will refer to the first edition (1930), but the book was reprinted in several editions and translations during Arslan's lifetime. See Cleveland, Islam against the West, 115–134.

86. Arslan, Li-madha?, 77–80.

87. Arslan, al-Hulal, 1:10–11.

88. Binnuna, introduction to Tarikh Titwan, 15.

89. Valderrama Martínez, Historia, 819; Kably et al., Histoire du Maroc, 718.

90. H. Dawud, 'Ala ra's al-thamanin, 199.

91. For the Arabization policy and "Hispano-Arab culture," see Chapter 5.

92. Valderrama Martínez, Historia, 110–111.

93. The certificate, with Franco's signature, is hanging today in the Dawud Library in Tetouan.

94. "Arte marroquí."

95. The prize is mentioned on the book's cover and in Valderrama Martínez, Historia, 810.

96. Valderrama Martínez, Historia, 795–814; González González, Escuela, 270–272.

97. M. Dawud, Tarikh Titwan, 1:61. My italics.

98. Ibid., 1:90.

99. In the Summary, the map appears inside the book's front cover. In the History, it is inserted in between pages 64 and 65.

100. Dawud develops this didactic theory of history in his introduction to Tarikh Titwan, 1:23–35.

101. Binnuna, introduction to Tarikh Titwan, 14–15.

102. See, for example, Gozalbes Busto, Al-Mandari; Gozalbes Busto, Los Moriscos en Marruecos; Yebbur, Los Ber-Rached.

103. Binnuna, introduction to Tarikh Titwan, 15.

104. Tetouan's nickname appears in al-Sharif, Titwan, 5–50; Benaboud, "Tétouan, le patio," 164; Rojo Flores, "Lo andalusí," 235–240.

105. Binnuna, introduction to Tarikh Titwan, 15.

106. Rojo Flores, "Lo andalusí"; González Alcantud, "Los andalusíes hoy," 44–45.

107. Binnuna, introduction to Tarikh Titwan, 16.

108. Valderrama Martínez, *Historia*, 404.

109. Chaachoo, *Música andalusí*, 102–110; Benjelloun, *Approches*, 97; H. Dawud, *'Ala ra's al-thamanin*, 315.

110. H. Dawud, *'Ala ra's al-thamanin*, 313–315.

111. Ibid., 315–318. Davila discusses the history of the Association of Lovers of Andalusi Music in *Andalusian Music*, 171–173.

112. M. Dawud, *Tarikh Titwan*, 1:431.

113. Ibid., 7:110.

114. For this meeting, see Ibn Tawit's introduction to the first issue of *Titwan*, 9.

115. Al-Fasi's interest in al-Andalus went back at least as far as his student days in Paris, when he translated, in collaboration with Ahmad Balafrij, a French work on Andalusi history. After Moroccan independence, al-Fasi published an influential essay on Moroccan Andalusi music. See al-Fasi and Balafrij, *Azhar al-basatin*; al-Fasi, "Musique."

116. Ibn Tawit, introduction to *Titwan*, 9.

117. To the best of my knowledge, al-Fasi never published an article in *Titwan*. After the first issue, his name was moved from the top of the masthead to the list of the members of the editorial committee.

118. For a brief introduction to the work and its Spanish translation, see Carrillo Ordóñez and Tayeddin Buzid, *Genio*, 3–10. The Spanish translation only covers the first volume of Gannun's two-volume work.

119. Al-Idrisi, *'Abd Allah Gannun*, 15.

120. Gannun, "Fiesta."

121. Valderrama Martínez, *Historia*, 803–810.

122. Al-Idrisi, *'Abd Allah Gannun*, 16.

123. Valderrama Martínez offers a brief biography of 'Aziman in *Historia*, 111–112.

124. Binnuna, "'Utufat al-amir."

125. Valderrama Martínez, *Historia*, 808, 819.

126. Khatib, *Culture*, 41; González González, *Escuela*, 272–273.

127. Valderrama Martínez, *Historia*, 819.

128. Ibid., 803–834.

129. I would like to thank the artist Bouabid Bouzaid for helping me to identify Fawzi, about whom little is known today.

130. Castilla Brazales, "Inscripciones," 10; Villafranca Jiménez and Yusty, *Corpus epigráfico*.

131. Ibn Tawit, introduction to *Titwan*, 9–10.

132. Such was the case of Gannun, Arribas Palau, and 'Aziman. See Valderrama Martínez, *Historia*, 837.

133. For the Egyptian Institute and its journal, see Instituto de Estudios Islámicos, *Instituto*.

134. Ibn Tawit, introduction to *Titwan*, 11.

EPILOGUE

1. For Spanish Tangier, see España, *Pequeña historia*.
2. For the building's history, see Bravo Nieto, "Dos palacios."
3. Colón, "Adiós," 18.
4. My description of the building is based on site visits that I made in May and September of 2016.
5. For Yaʿqub al-Mansur's unfinished mosque in Rabat, known as the Hassan Mosque, see Lévi-Provençal and Troin, "Ribāṭ al-Fatḥ"; Lakhdar, "Flux," 227–228.
6. Lakhdar, "Flux"; Olmedo, *Itinerario;* Vo, *Le Mausolée Mohammed V,* 32. Many of the authors studied in this book have also emphasized the connection between the Hassan Minaret, the Giralda, and the Kutubiyya. See, for example, al-Rahuni, *Al-Rihla al-makkiyya,* 30.
7. My description of the Hassan Minaret and of the surrounding monuments is based on visits I made to the site in September of 2016. I would also like to thank Caitlin Scholl, who returned to the site on my behalf in October of 2016 in order to confirm a few details in my description.
8. The inauguration was described in an article published the same day on the Moroccan Ministry of Culture and Communication's official website, Maroc.ma (accessed June 30, 2017).
9. For the history of the Muhammad V mausoleum complex, see Vo, *Le Mausolée Mohammed V;* Roberson, "Changing Face."
10. Benmansour, introduction to *Le Mausolée Mohammed V,* 18–20; Vo, *Le Mausolée Mohammed V,* 34. For Muhammad V's exile in Madagascar (1953–1955), see Miller, *History,* 150–153.
11. Benmansour, introduction to *Le Mausolée Mohammed V,* 18–20; Vo, *Le Mausolée Mohammed V,* 34.
12. Lakhdar, "Flux," 229.
13. Vo, *Le Mausolée Mohammed V,* 30; Roberson, "Changing," 67.
14. Vo, *Le Mausolée Mohammed V,* 48. The guide *Le Mausolée Mohammed V* is written in four languages: French, English, German, and Arabic. Unfortunately, the English text has several grammatical and typographical errors. When quoting from the guide, I have occasionally used the French original to correct the errors in the English translation.

15. Saaf, "Elementos," 306–307.

16. The project was inaugurated in 1989 with the release of the recording of *Nubat Gharibat al-Husayn*, performed by Fez's Orchestre al-Brihi. Over the next ten years, the Moroccan Ministry of Culture, in conjunction with the Maison des Cultures du Monde in Paris, released recordings of all eleven suites in the Moroccan Andalusi repertoire.

17. Binsharifa, "Al-'Inaya"; Benmansour, "Khitab al-iftitah."

18. Roberson, "Changing."

19. Binsharifa, "Al-'Inaya," 24.

20. Roberson, "Changing," 68–70; Vo, *Le Mausolée Mohammed V*, 48, 58–60.

21. Benmansour, introduction to *Le Mausolée Mohammed V*, 20.

22. Ibid.

23. Vo, *Le Mausolée Mohammed V*, 48, 50.

24. Al-Fasi, preface to *Le Mausolée Mohammed V*, 10, 12.

25. Ibid., 12. My italics.

26. Vo, *Le Mausolée Mohammed V*, 36.

27. Ibid.

28. Ibid., 51.

29. Ibid., 42.

30. Ibid., 68.

31. Ibid., 76.

32. Ibid., 56.

33. Ibid.

34. For the historical evolution of the Generalife, see Casares Porcel, "El Generalife."

35. Vo, *Le Mausolée Mohammed V*, 46.

36. Ruggles, "Alcazar," 91–95.

BIBLIOGRAPHY

'Abbadi, Ahmad Mukhtar al-, ed. *Mushahadat Lisan al-Din Ibn al-Khatib fi bilad al-Maghrib wa-l-Andalus*. Alexandria: Mu'assasat Shabab al-Jami'a, 1983.

'Abd al-Razzaq. *Al-Musannaf*. Edited by Habib al-Rahman al-A'zami. 2nd ed. 11 vols. Beirut: al-Maktab al-Islami, 1983.

Abdel Haleem, M. A. S., trans. *The Qur'an: English Translation and Parallel Arabic Text*. Oxford: Oxford University Press, 2010.

Abdulrazak, Fawzi (*see also* 'Abd al-Razzaq, Fawzi). "The Kingdom of the Book: The History of Printing as an Agency of Change in Morocco between 1865 and 1912." PhD diss., Boston University, 1990.

———. *Al-Matbu'at al-hajariyya fi al-Maghrib: Fihris wa-muqaddima tarikhiyya*. Rabat: Dar Nashr al-Ma'rifa, [1989].

Abu-Lughod, Ibrahim. *Arab Rediscovery of Europe*. Princeton, NJ: Princeton University Press, 1963.

Achaâri, Mohamed. Foreword to *Mariano Bertuchi: Pintor de Marruecos*, by Alfonso de la Serna et al., 9.

Acosta Sánchez, José. *Andalucía: Reconstrucción de una identidad y la lucha contra el centralismo*. Barcelona: Anagrama, 1978.

'Adnan, Yasin. *Daftar al-'abir*. Casablanca: Dar Tubqal li-l-Nashr, 2012.

'Adwani, Ahmad al-. *Zaman al-wasl: al-Andalus fi al-qasida al-'arabiyya al-mu'asira*. Beirut: al-Intishar al-'Arabi, 2014.

Afaylal, Mufaddal. "Harb Titwan min khilal masdar jadid." Edited by M'hammad Benaboud. In *Al-Maghrib wa-l-Andalus 2*, edited by M'hammad Benaboud and Muhammad al-Sharif, 179–203. Tetouan: Jami'at 'Abd al-Malik al-Sa'di, 2008.

———. *Kunnash*. MS 158. Dawud Library. Tetouan, Morocco.

———. "Ya dahr . . ." (Elegy for Tetouan, 1861). In *Kitab al-istiqsa li-akhbar duwal al-Maghrib al-Aqsa*, by Ahmad b. Khalid al-Nasiri, edited by Ahmad al-Nasiri, Muhammad Hajji, Ibrahim Bu Talib, and Ahmad al-Tawfiq, 8:108–110. Casablanca: Wizarat al-Thaqafa wa-l-Ittisal, 2001.

Ageron, Charles-Robert. "L'Association des étudiants musulmans nord-africains en France durant l'entre-deux-guerres. Contribution à l'étude des nationalismes maghrébins." *Revue française d'histoire d'outre-mer* 70 (1983): 25–56.

Ahmad, Aijaz. *In Theory: Classes, Nations, Literatures.* London: Verso, 1992.

Akasoy, Anna. "*Convivencia* and Its Discontents: Interfaith Life in al-Andalus." *International Journal of Middle East Studies* 42, no. 3 (2010): 489–499. doi:10.1017/S0020743810000516.

Akmir, Youssef. "Una aproximación historiográfica a la cultura en el Marruecos de finales del siglo XIX: Los aires de cambio y el caso de Sidi Mfedal Afailal." In *Regenerar España y Marruecos,* edited by Francisco Javier Martínez Antonio and Irene González González, 277–292. Madrid: Consejo Superior de Investigaciones Científicas, 2011.

Alarcón, Pedro Antonio de. "A Chorby, poeta marroquí." In *Obras completas de D. Pedro A. de Alarcón,* edited by Luis Martínez Kleiser, 292. Madrid: FAX, 1943.

———. *La Alpujarra.* Madrid, 1874.

———. "Una conversación en la Alhambra." *El Museo Universal,* October 15, 1859, 158–160. http://hemerotecadigital.bne.es/issn/1889-8440.

———. *Diario de un testigo de la guerra de África.* Edited by María del Pilar Palomo. Seville: Fundación José Manuel Lara, 2005.

———. "Historia de mis libros." In *Obras completas de D. Pedro A. de Alarcón,* edited by Luis Martínez Kleiser, 3–28. Madrid: FAX, 1943.

Allen, Roger. "The Post-Classical Period: Parameters and Preliminaries." In *Arabic Literature in the Post-Classical Period,* edited by Roger Allen and D. S. Richards, 1–21. Cambridge: Cambridge University Press, 2006.

———. "Rewriting Literary History: The Case of Moroccan Fiction in Arabic." *Journal of North African Studies* 16, no. 3 (2011): 311–324. doi:10.1080/13629387.2010.550725.

Alta Comisaría de España en Marruecos, Delegación de Educación y Cultura. *Conservatorio Hispano-Marroquí de Música: Concurso internacional de canciones y danzas populares que se celebrará en Madrid el 1 de junio de 1949.* Tetouan: Imp. del Majzen, [1949].

Álvarez de Morales, Camilo. "Boabdil." In *Encyclopedia of Islam.* 3rd ed. Accessed June 29, 2017. http://dx.doi.org/10.1163/1573-3912_ei3_COM_24349.

Álvarez Junco, José. Prologue to *Las historias de España: Visiones del pasado y construcción de identidad,* xv–xxvii. Vol. 12 of *Historia de España,* edited by Josep Fontana and Ramón Villares. Barcelona: Crítica/Marcial Pons, 2013.

Álvarez Junco, José, and Gregorio de la Fuente Monge. "La evolución del relato histórico." In *Las historias de España: Visiones del pasado y construcción de identidad,* 1–437. Vol. 12 of *Historia de España,* edited by Josep Fontana and Ramón Villares. Barcelona: Crítica / Marcial Pons, 2013.

Amster, Ellen. *Medicine and the Saints: Science, Islam, and the Colonial Encounter in Morocco, 1877–1956.* Austin: University of Texas Press, 2013.

Anderson, Benedict. *Imagined Communities.* Rev. ed. London: Verso, 1991.

Arbizu, Julio. "Hispanismo (africano-americano)." *Revista de tropas coloniales,* March 1924, 40–41.

Arié, Rachel. "Boabdil, sultan nasride de Grenade: Le personnage historique et la figure littéraire." In *Aspects de l'Espagne musulmane: Histoire et culture,* 83–106. Paris: De Boccard, 1997.

Aristotle. *Poetics.* Translated by Richard Janko. In *The Norton Anthology of Theory and Criticism,* edited by Vincent B. Leitch, William E. Cain, Laurie A. Finke, Barbara E. Johnson, John McGowan, T. Denean Sharpley-Whiting, and Jeffrey J. Williams, 88–115. 2nd ed. New York: Norton, 2010.

Arslan, Shakib. *Al-Hulal al-sundusiyya fi al-akhbar wa-l-athar al-andalusiyya.* 3 vols. Beirut: Dar al-Kutub al-ʿIlmiyya, 1997.

———. *Li-madha taʾakhkhara al-muslimun wa-li-madha taqaddama ghayruhum?* Cairo: Matbaʿat al-Manar, 1930.

———. "Masʾalat ikhraj al-barbar min al-Islam." *Al-Fath,* October 9, 1930 (17 Jumada al-Ula 1349), 1–3.

———. "Une perte très douloureuse: La mort de Hadje Abdessalam Bennuna." *La Nation Arabe,* January / February 1935, 209–210.

———. *Tarikh ghazawat al-ʿarab fi Faransa wa-Siwisira wa-Italiya wa-jazaʾir al-bahr al-mutawassit.* Beirut: Maktabat al-Hayat, 1966.

———. "Tribunaux Berbères." *La Nation Arabe,* September 1930, 22–28.

———. *ʿUrwat al-ittihad bayna ahl al-jihad.* Buenos Aires: al-ʿAlam al-ʿArabi, 1941.

Arslan, Shakib, and ʿAbd al-Salam Binnuna. *Nidaluna al-qawmi fi al-rasaʾil al-mutabadala bayna al-amir Shakib Arslan wa-l-hajj ʿAbd al-Salam Binnuna.* Edited by al-Tayyib Binnuna. Tangier: Dar Amal, 1980.

Arslan, Shakib, and Muhammad Dawud. *Murasalat al-amir Shakib Arslan maʿa muʾarrikh Titwan Muhammad Dawud.* Edited by ʿUmar Riyad. Cairo: Dar al-Kutub wa-l-Wathaʾiq al-Qawmiyya, 2015.

"Arte marroquí en la sede del Califato." *Mundo ilustrado,* May 1947, 112–113.

"Artículo de traje, o sea carta de Muley-Abbas al poeta Chorby, en Tetuán." *La Época,* April 3, 1861, 3–4. http://hemerotecadigital.bne.es/issue.vm?id=0000156305&search=&lang=en.

Asad, Talal. *Formations of the Secular: Christianity, Islam, Modernity.* Stanford, CA: Stanford University Press, 2003.

Asín Palacios, Miguel. *La escatalogía musulmana en la* Divina Comedia. Madrid: Estanislao Maestre, 1919.

———. "Por qué lucharon a nuestro lado los musulmanes marroquíes." *Boletín de la Universidad Central*, 1940, 1–25.

'Attar, Bu Ghalib al-. *Sabta wa-Maliliya: Maghariba tahta al-ihtilal*. [Casablanca]: Dar al-Nashr al-Maghribiyya, 1996.

Averroes. *Quitab el Culiat (Libro de las generalidades)*. Instituto General Franco para la Investigación Hispano-Árabe. Larache: Artes Gráficas Boscá, 1939.

Bachillerato Hispano-Marroquí. Tetouan: Cremades, 1949.

Badawi, M. M. "The Background." In *Modern Arabic Literature,* edited by M. M. Badawi, 1–23. Cambridge: Cambridge University Press, 1992.

Balafrij, Ahmad. "Al-Amir Shakib Arslan fi al-Maghrib al-Aqsa." *Al-Fath,* October 9, 1930 (17 Jumada al-Ula 1349), 4–5.

Balfour, Sebastian. *Deadly Embrace: Morocco and the Road to the Spanish Civil War.* Oxford: Oxford University Press, 2002.

Barberán, Cecilio. "La Exposición de Arte Marroquí en Córdoba." *África,* July 1946, 29–30.

Bazzaz, Sahar. "Reading Reform beyond the State: *Salwat al-Anfas,* Islamic Revival, and Moroccan National History." *Journal of North African Studies* 13, no. 1 (2008): 1–13. doi:10.1080/13629380701528853.

Behdad, Ali. *Belated Travelers: Orientalism in the Age of Colonial Dissolution.* Durham: Duke University Press, 1994.

Beigbeder, Juan. "Ordenanza del Excmo. Sr. Alto Comisario Reorganizando la Enseñanza en la Zona de Protectorado." *Boletín oficial de la zona de Protectorado español en Marruecos,* February 10, 1937, 99–100.

Beigbeder, Juan, and Amin al-Rihani. *Discursos pronunciados por el Alto Comisario de España en Marruecos Coronel Beigbeder y por el eminente filósofo libanés Prof. Amin er-Rihani.* Instituto General Franco para la Investigación Hispano-Árabe. Larache: Artes Gráficas Boscá, 1940.

Bellido Gant, María Luisa. "Difundir una identidad: La promoción exterior de Marruecos." In *Al-Andalus: Una identidad compartida,* edited by Federico Castro Morales, 75–90. Madrid: Universidad Carlos III, 1999.

Benaboud, M'hammad (*see also* Ibn 'Abbud, Mahammad). "Harb Titwan min khilal masdar jadid." In *Al-Maghrib wa-l-Andalus 2,* edited by M'hammad Benaboud and Muhammad al-Sharif, 179–203. Tetouan: Jami'at 'Abd al-Malik al-Sa'di, 2008.

———. "La Medina de Tetuán: Pasado y presente." In *La Medina de Tetuán: Guía de arquitectura,* edited by Ramón de Torres López, 37–48. 2nd ed. Sevilla: Consejería de Obras Públicas y Transportes, 2002.

———. "Tétouan, le patio d'une civilisation." In *Le Maroc andalou: À la découverte d'un art de vivre*, 163–179. Casablanca: EDDIF; Aix-en-Provence: Édisud, 2000.

Benaboud, M'hammad, and Bouabid Bouzaid, eds. *Rassamun Titwan / Peintres de Tétouan*. 2 vols. Tetouan: Association Tétouan-Asmir, 2009.

Benaboud, M'hammad, and Mohamed Sijelmassi. "Terre de dialogue et de cultures." In *Maroc Méditerranée*, edited by Mohamed Sijelmassi, 190–192. Casablanca: Oum Éditions, 2007.

Benaboud, M'hammad, and Ramón de Torres López. "Murallas y mazmorras." In *La Medina de Tetuán: Guía de arquitectura*, edited by Ramón de Torres López, 63–72. 2nd ed. Sevilla: Consejería de Obras Públicas y Transportes, 2002.

Ben Cheneb, M. "Khalīl b. Isḥāk." *Encyclopedia of Islam*. 2nd ed. Accessed June 29, 2017. http://dx.doi.org/10.1163/1573-3912_islam_SIM_4162.

Benjelloun, Abdelmajid. *Approches du colonialisme espagnol et du mouvement nationaliste marocain dans l'ex-Maroc Khalifien*. Rabat: OKAD, 1988.

———. "L'École picturale de Tétouan." In *Rassamun Titwan / Peintres de Tétouan*, edited by M'hammad Benaboud and Bouabid Bouzaid, 1:11–12. Tetouan: Association Tétouan-Asmir, 2009.

———. *Le mouvement nationaliste marocain dans l'ex-Maroc khalifien (1930–56)*. Rabat: El Maarif Al Jadida, 2011.

Benmansour, Abdelwahab (*see also* Ibn Mansur, ʿAbd al-Wahhab). "Khitab al-iftitah." In *al-Turath al-hadari al-mushtarak bayna Isbaniya wa-l-Maghrib*, 15–19. Rabat: Akadimiyyat al-Mamlika al-Maghribiyya, 1993.

———. Introduction to *Le Mausolée Mohammed V*, by Vo Toan, 18–23. Casablanca: Sochepress, 1976.

Berchet, Jean-Claude, ed. *Atala, René: Les aventures du dernier Abencérage*. By Chateaubriand. Paris: Flammarion, 1996.

Bertuchi, Mariano. "La artesanía marroquí a través de la Escuela de Artes Indígenas de Tetuán." In "Congreso de Estudios Sociales." Special issue, *Revista de trabajo*, 1945: 213–219.

———. "La Escuela de Artes Indígenas desde su fundación hasta el año 1947." *África*, August–October 1947, 68–70.

———. "Las industrias artísticas tetuaníes." *Gaceta de África*, núm. extraordinario, 1936, 43–45.

Binnuna, M'hammad. Introduction to *Tarikh Titwan*, by Muhammad Dawud, 1:7–18. Tetouan: Maktabat "Cremades," 1959.

———. "ʿUtufat al-amir Shakib Arslan fi al-Maghrib al-Aqsa." *Al-Fath*, October 16, 1930 (24 Jumada al-Ula 1349), 4–5.

Binsharifa, Muhammad. "Al-'Inaya bi-turath al-Andalus fi al-Maghrib wa-Isbaniya." In *al-Turath al-hadari al-mushtarak bayna Isbaniya wa-l-Maghrib,* 23–36. Rabat: Akadimiyyat al-Mamlika al-Maghribiyya, 1993.

Botti, Alfonso. *Cielo y dinero: El nacionalcatolicismo en España (1881–1975).* Madrid: Alianza, 1992.

Bouali, Abderrahmane. *Poemas marroquíes y al-Andalus.* Granada: Universidad de Granada, 2009.

Boukous, Ahmed. *Société, langues et cultures au Maroc: Enjeux symboliques.* Rabat: Faculté des Lettres et des Sciences Humaines, 1995.

Boym, Svetlana. *The Future of Nostalgia.* New York: Basic Books, 2001.

Braudel, Fernand. *La Méditerranée et le monde méditerranéen à l'époque de Philippe II.* 2nd rev. ed. 2 vols. Paris: Librairie Armand Colin, 1966.

Bravo Nieto, Antonio. *Arquitectura y urbanismo español en el norte de Marruecos.* Seville: Consejería de Obras Públicas y Transportes, 2000.

———. "Dos palacios del Barroco tardío en Marruecos: Las legaciones diplomáticas de España en Larache y Tánger." *Boletín de Arte* 34 (2013): 33–54.

Brower, Benjamin Claude. "The Colonial Hajj: France and Algeria, 1830–1962." In *The Hajj: Collected Essays,* edited by Venetia Porter and Liana Saif, 108–114. London: British Museum, 2013.

Burke III, Edmund. *The Ethnographic State: France and the Invention of Moroccan Islam.* Berkeley: University of California Press, 2014.

———. "The Image of the Moroccan State in French Ethnological Literature: A New Look at the Origin of Lyautey's Berber Policy." In *Arabs and Berbers: From Tribe to Nation in North Africa,* edited by Ernest Gellner and Charles Micaud, 175–199. Lexington: D. C. Heath, 1972.

———. *Prelude to Protectorate in Morocco: Precolonial Protest and Resistance, 1860–1912.* Chicago, IL: University of Chicago Press, 1976.

———. "Theorizing the Histories of Colonialism and Nationalism in the Arab Maghrib." In *Beyond Colonialism and Nationalism in the Maghrib: History, Culture, and Politics,* edited by Ali Abdullatif Ahmida, 17–34. New York: Palgrave, 2000.

Bustani, Alfredo, ed. *Fragmento de la época sobre noticias de los Reyes Nazaritas.* Instituto General Franco para la Investigación Hispano-Árabe. Larache: Artes Gráficas Boscá, 1940.

———, ed. *Kitab natijat al-ijtihad fi al-muhadana wa-l-jihad (Consecuencia del esfuerzo en la paz y en la guerra).* Instituto General Franco para la Investigación Hispano-Árabe. Larache: Artes Gráficas Boscá, 1941.

———. Introduction to *Quitab el Culiat (Libro de las generalidades)*, by Averroes, 7–35. Instituto General Franco para la Investigación Hispano-Árabe. Larache: Artes Gráficas Boscá, 1939.

———, ed. *Rihlat al-wazir fi iftikak al-asir (El viaje del visir para la liberación de los cautivos)*. By al-Ghassani. Tangier: Instituto General Franco para la Investigación Hispano-Árabe, 1940.

Cachia, Pierre. "Translations and Adaptations, 1834–1914." In *Modern Arabic Literature*, edited by M. M. Badawi, 23–35. Cambridge: Cambridge University Press, 1992.

Calderwood, Eric. "The Beginning (or End) of Moroccan History: Historiography, Translation, and Modernity in Ahmad b. Khalid al-Nasiri and Clemente Cerdeira." *International Journal of Middle East Studies* 44, no. 3 (2012): 399–420. doi:10.1017/S0020743812000396.

———. "'In Andalucía, There Are No Foreigners': *Andalucismo* from Transperipheral Critique to Colonial Apology." *Journal of Spanish Cultural Studies* 15, no. 4 (2014): 399–417. doi:10.1080/14636204.2014.991488.

———. "The Invention of al-Andalus: Discovering the Past and Creating the Present in Granada's Islamic Tourism Sites." *Journal of North African Studies* 19, no. 1 (2014): 27–55.

———. "Letter from Morocco: The Living and the Dead." *The American Scholar* (Fall 2009): 7–11.

———. "Proyectando al-Ándalus: Alegorías andalusíes en el cine árabe moderno." In *Andalusíes: Antropología e historia cultural de una elite magrebí*, edited by José Antonio González Alcantud and Sandra Rojo Flores, 213–240. Madrid: Abada, 2015.

———. "The Reconquista of the Mosque of Córdoba." *Foreign Policy*, April 10, 2015. http://foreignpolicy.com/2015/04/10/the-reconquista-of-the-mosque-of-cordoba-spain-catholic-church-islam/.

———. "Writing the Hispano-Moroccan War of 1859–1860: Spanish and Moroccan Reflections on Spanish Colonialism in Morocco." PhD diss., Harvard University, 2011.

Carmona Portillo, Antonio. *Las relaciones hispano-marroquíes a finales del siglo XVIII y el cerco de Ceuta de 1790–1791: Historia militar y diplomática*. Málaga: Sarriá, [2004].

Carrasco Urgoiti, María Soledad. *Los moriscos y Ginés Pérez de Hita*. Barcelona: Bellaterra, 2006.

———. *El moro de Granada en la literatura (Del siglo XV al XX)*. Madrid: Revista de Occidente, 1956.

Carrillo Ordóñez, Jerónimo, and Mohammad Tayeddin Buzid, trans. *El genio marroquí en la literatura árabe*. By ʿAbd Allah Gannun. Larache: Artes Gráficas Boscá, 1939.

Casanova, Julián. *La Iglesia de Franco*. Madrid: Temas de Hoy, 2001.

Casares Porcel, Manuel. "El Generalife: Historia de un jardín entre la conservación y la innovación." In *El jardín hispanomusulmán: Los jardines de al-Andalus y su herencia*, edited by José Tito Rojo y Manuel Casares Porcel, 223–260. Granada: Universidad de Granada, 2011.

Castilla Brazales, Juan. "Las inscripciones árabes de la Alhambra." In *Corpus epigráfico de la Alhambra: Palacio de Comares*, edited by María del Mar Villafranca Jiménez and Carmen Yusty. Granada: Patronato de la Alhambra y el Generalife, [2007?]. CD-ROM.

Catálogo oficial ilustrado de la Exposición General de Bellas Artes. Madrid: Casa Editorial "Mateu," 1904.

Chaachoo, Amin. *La música andalusí al-Ála: Historia, conceptos y teoría musical*. Cordoba: Almuzara, 2011.

Chakrabarty, Dipesh. *Provincializing Europe: Postcolonial Thought and Historical Difference*. Princeton, NJ: Princeton University Press, 2000.

Chateaubriand. *Les aventures du dernier Abencérage*. In *Atala, René: Les aventures du dernier Abencérage*, edited by Jean-Claude Berchet, 199–244. Paris: Flammarion, 1996.

Chatterjee, Partha. *The Nation and Its Fragments: Colonial and Postcolonial Histories*. Princeton, NJ: Princeton University Press, 1993.

Chottin, Alexis, trans. and ed. *Nouba de Ochchâk*. Vol. 1 of *Corpus de musique marocaine*. Paris: Heugel, 1931.

Clancy-Smith, Julia. Introduction to "Maghribi Histories in the Modern Era." Special issue, *International Journal of Middle East Studies* 44, no. 4 (2012): 625–630. doi:10.1017/S0020743812000785.

———. *Mediterraneans: North Africa and Europe in an Age of Migration, c. 1800–1900*. Berkeley: University of California Press, 2011.

Cleveland, William L. *Islam against the West: Shakib Arslan and the Campaign for Islamic Nationalism*. Austin: University of Texas Press, 1985.

Colón, Antonio. "Adiós al Correo español de Tánger." *ABC*, March 7, 1958, 18. http://hemeroteca.abc.es/nav/Navigate.exe/hemeroteca/sevilla/abc .sevilla/1958/03/07/018.html.

Conklin, Alice L. *A Mission to Civilize: The Republican Idea of Empire in France and West Africa, 1895–1930*. Stanford, CA: Stanford University Press, 1997.

Continente, José Manuel. "Dos poemas de Malik b. al-Murahhal: Poeta malagueño al servicio de los benimerines." *Awraq* 2 (1979): 44–54.

Correa Rodríguez, Pedro. Introduction to *Historia de los bandos de Zegríes y Abencerrajes*, by Ginés Pérez de Hita, ix–clxxxi. Granada: Universidad de Granada, 1999.

Costa, Joaquín, Francisco Coello, Gabriel Rodríguez, Gumersindo de Azcárate, Eduardo Saavedra, and José de Carvajal. *Intereses de España en Marruecos*. Madrid: Fortanet, 1884.

"Dahir creando la Fiesta del 'Día del Libro Árabe.'" *Boletín oficial de la zona de Protectorado español en Marruecos*, April 30, 1941, 310–311.

Darias Príncipe, Alberto. "Marruecos en España: La Exposición Ibero-Americana de Sevilla." In *Al-Andalus: Una identidad compartida*, edited by Federico Castro Morales, 91–98. Madrid: Universidad Carlos III, 1999.

Darwish, Mahmud. *Ahad 'ashar kawkaban*. Beirut: Dar al-Jadid, 1992.

———. *Fi hadrat al-ghiyab*. 2nd ed. Beirut: Riad El-Rayyes Books, 2009.

Davila, Carl. *The Andalusian Music of Morocco: Al-Āla*. Wiesbaden: Reichert, 2013.

Dawud, Hasna'. *'Ala ra's al-thamanin*. Tetouan: Jam'iyyat Titwan-Asmir, 2011.

———. Introduction to *Kunnash Afaylal*. MS 158. Dawud Library. Tetouan, Morocco.

Dawud, Muhammad. *'A'ilat Titwan*. Edited by Hasna' Dawud. 3 vols. Tetouan: Jam'iyyat Titwan-Asmir, 2016–2017.

———. *'Ala ra's al-arba'in*. Edited by Hasna' Dawud. Tetouan: Jam'iyyat Titwan-Asmir, 2001.

———. *Mukhtasar tarikh Titwan*. Tetouan: al-Matba'a al-Mahdiyya, 1955.

———. "Nurid istiqlal al-Maghrib." *Al-Rif*, June 14, 1940, 1.

———. *Tarikh Titwan*. Vol. 1. Tetouan: Krimadis [Cremades], 1959.

———. *Tarikh Titwan*. Vol. 4. Tetouan: al-Matba'a al-Mahdiyya, 1964.

———. *Tarikh Titwan*. Vol. 5. Tetouan: al-Matba'a al-Mahdiyya, 1965.

———. *Tarikh Titwan*. Vol. 6. Tetouan: al-Matba'a al-Mahdiyya, 1966.

———. *Tarikh Titwan*. Vol. 7. Tetouan: al-Matba'a al-Mahdiyya, 1975.

De las Cagigas, Isidro. "Apuntaciones para un estudio del regionalismo andaluz." In *Ensayistas del Mediodía*, edited by Manuel Ruiz Lagos, 73–102. Seville: Editoriales Andaluzas Unidas, 1985.

———. *Tratados y convenios referentes a Marruecos*. Madrid: Instituto de Estudios Africanos, 1952.

Deleuze, Gilles, and Félix Guattari. *Kafka: Toward a Minor Literature*. Translated by Dana Polan. Minneapolis: University of Minnesota Press, 1986.

de Man, Paul. "Literary History and Literary Modernity." *Daedalus* 99, no. 2 (1970): 384–404. www.jstor.org/stable/20023950.

Derrida, Jacques. "Différance." In *Margins of Philosophy*, translated by Alan Bass, 1–27. Chicago, IL: University of Chicago Press, 1982.

Diógenes [pseud.]. "Mariano Bertuchi y su obra." *Mundo ilustrado,* May 1947, 56–57.
Dizy Caso, Eduardo. "Bertuchi, maestro de artesanos y artistas: Fidelidad a un patrimonio histórico." In Serna et al., *Mariano Bertuchi,* 103–115.
El-Ariss, Tarek. *Trials of Arab Modernity: Literary Affects and the New Political.* New York: Fordham University Press, 2013.
Elinson, Alexander E. "*Dārija* and Changing Writing Practices in Morocco." *International Journal of Middle East Studies* 45, no. 4 (2013): 715–730. doi:10.1017/S0020743813000871.
———. *Looking Back at al-Andalus: The Poetics of Loss and Nostalgia in Medieval Arabic and Hebrew Literature.* Leiden: Brill, 2009.
El-Khatib Boujibar, Naïma, and Mohamed Mezzine. "Le Maroc andalou." In *Le Maroc andalou: À la découverte d'un art de vivre,* 50–63. Casablanca: EDDIF; Aix-en-Provence: Édisud, 2000.
Elmarsafy, Ziad. *Sufism in the Contemporary Arabic Novel.* Edinburgh: Edinburgh University Press, 2012.
El-Rouayheb, Khaled. *Islamic Intellectual History in the Seventeenth Century: Scholarly Currents in the Ottoman Empire and the Maghreb.* Cambridge: Cambridge University Press, 2015.
Epps, Brad. "Between Europe and Africa: Modernity, Race, and Nationality in the Correspondence of Miguel de Unamuno and Joan Maragall." *Anales de la literatura española contemporánea* 30 (2005): 97–132. www.jstor.org/stable/27742338.
Erzini, Nadia. "El Serrallo: A Palace and Mosque Built by the Basha Ahmad b. ʿAli ar-Rifi outside Ceuta." *Hespéris-Tamuda* 32 (1994): 63–79.
España, Alberto. *La pequeña historia de Tánger.* Tangier: Distribuciones Ibérica, 1954.
Euben, Roxanne L. *Journeys to the Other Shore: Muslim and Western Travelers in Search of Knowledge.* Princeton, NJ: Princeton University Press, 2006.
Fasi, Muhammad al- (*see also* El Fasi, Mohammed). Preface to *Le Mausolée Mohammed V,* by Vo Toan, 10–17. Casablanca: Sochepress, 1976.
———. "La musique marocaine dite 'musique andalouse.'" *Hespéris-Tamuda* 3 (1962): 79–106.
Fasi, Muhammad al-, and Ahmad Balafrij, trans. *Azhar al-basatin fi akhbar al-Andalus wa-l-Maghrib ʿala ʿahd al-murabitin wa-l-muwahhidin.* Rabat: al-Matbaʿa al-Wataniyya, 1930.
Ferhat, Halima. "Sabta." *Encyclopedia of Islam.* 2nd ed. Accessed June 29, 2017. http://dx.doi.org/10.1163/1573-3912_islam_SIM_6384.

Fernández, Santos. "Marruecos en la Exposición Ibero-Americana de Sevilla." *África*, May 1929, 109–115. http://hemerotecadigital.bne.es/issn/0001-9763.

Fernández Cuesta, Nemesio. "Muley-Abd-el-Rahman." *El Museo Universal*, November 11, 1859, 171–173. http://hemerotecadigital.bne.es/issn/1889-8440.

Fernández-Montesinos, Alberto Egea. *García Lorca, Blas Infante y Antonio Gala: Un nacionalismo alternativo en la literatura andaluza*. Seville: Fundación Blas Infante, 2001.

Fernández Parrilla, Gonzalo. *La literatura marroquí contemporánea: La novela y la crítica literaria*. Cuenca: Ediciones de la Universidad de Castilla-La Mancha, 2006.

Fernández y González, Manuel. "A España: Recuerdos y esperanzas." *El Museo Universal*, December 1, 1859, 177–178. http://hemerotecadigital.bne.es/issn/1889-8440.

Fleisch, H. "Ibn Mālik." *Encyclopedia of Islam*. 2nd ed. http://dx.doi.org/10.1163/1573-3912_islam_COM_0336.

Flesler, Daniela. *The Return of the Moor: Spanish Responses to Contemporary Moroccan Immigration*. West Lafayette, IN: Purdue University Press, 2008.

Flores Morales, Ángel. *África a través del pensamiento español: De Isabel la Católica a Franco*. Madrid: Instituto de Estudios Africanos, 1949.

Foucault, Michel. *Discipline and Punish: The Birth of the Prison*. Translated by Alan Sheridan. New York: Pantheon Books, 1977.

Franco, Francisco. *Palabras del Caudillo: 19 abril 1937—19 abril 1938*. Edited by La Delegación Nacional de Falange Española Tradicionalista y de las JONS. N.p.: Fe, 1938.

Freud, Sigmund. "Remembering, Repeating and Working-Through." In *The Standard Edition*, edited by James Strachey, Anna Freud, Alix Strachey, and Alan Tyson, 12:145–156. Logan: Hogarth Press, 1958.

Gallagher, Catherine, and Stephen Greenblatt. *Practicing New Historicism*. Chicago, IL: University of Chicago Press, 2000.

Gallego Roca, Miguel. *"La Cuerda Granadina": Una sociedad literaria del postromanticismo*. Granada: Comares, 1991.

Gannun, ʿAbd Allah (*see also* Guennún, Abdal-lah). "Abu al-Baqaʾ al-Rundi wa-kitabuhu *al-Wafi fi nazm al-qawafi*." *Revista del Instituto de Estudios Islámicos en Madrid* 6 (1958): 205–220.

———. "La Fiesta del Libro Hispano-Árabe." 1941. AFRGFB / 195 / 17. Spanish National Library.

———. *Al-Nubugh al-maghribi fi al-adab al-ʿarabi*. 2 vols. Tetouan: al-Matbaʿa al-Mahdiyya, [1938].

García-Arenal, Mercedes. "Los moriscos en Marruecos: De la emigración de los granadinos a los hornacheros de Salé." In *Los moriscos: Expulsión y diáspora,* edited by Mercedes García-Arenal and Gerard Wiegers, 275–311. Valencia: Universitat de València, 2013.

García Barriuso, Patrocinio. *Ecos del Magrib, Sada al-Maghrib, Échos du Maghrib.* Tangier: Editorial Tánger, 1940.

———. *La música hispano-musulmana en Marruecos.* Instituto General Franco para la Investigación Hispano-Árabe. Larache: Artes Gráficas Boscá, 1941.

———. "Plan de composición de la nuba." *África,* April 1944, 93–96.

García Figueras, Tomás. "A la Escuela de Artes y Museo Marroquí de Tetuán los titula el pueblo 'Escuela y Museo de Bertuchi.'" *Ideal,* June 17, 1956, 15–16.

———. "La fiesta del Libro Hispano-Árabe en nuestra Zona de Protectorado." *África* 77–78 (1948): 74–75.

———. *Líneas generales de la obra de educación y cultura que se desarrolla en nuestra Zona de Protectorado en Marruecos.* Tetouan: Alta Comisaría de España en Marruecos, [1944].

———. *Marruecos: La acción de España en el Norte de África.* Barcelona: Fe, 1939.

———. Prologue to *La música hispano-musulmana en Marruecos,* by Patrocinio García Barriuso, vii–ix. Larache: Artes Gráficas Boscá, 1941.

———. *Santa Cruz de Mar Pequeña, Ifni, Sahara.* Madrid: Fe, 1941.

García Gómez, Emilio. "El supuesto sepulcro de Muʿtamid de Sevilla en Āgmāt." *Al-Andalus* 18 (1953): 402–411.

García Moreno, Beatriz. "Al-Andalus en el poeta palestino Maḥmūd Darwīš." In *El saber en al-Andalus: Textos y estudios,* 4:135–146. Seville: Universidad de Sevilla, 2006.

Garrido, José María. "El Conservatorio Hispano-Marroquí de Música, de Tetuán." *Mundo ilustrado,* May 1947, 114.

Geertz, Clifford. *The Interpretation of Cultures: Selected Essays.* New York: Basic Books, 1973.

Gil Benumeya, Rodolfo. "Actualidad de la artesanía hispano-marroquí." *Levante,* May 19, 1945, 4.

———. *Andalucismo africano.* Madrid: Instituto de Estudios Africanos; Consejo Superior de Investigaciones Científicas, 1953.

———. *Marruecos andaluz.* Madrid: Ediciones de la Vicesecretaría de Educación Popular, 1942.

———. *Ni Oriente, ni Occidente: El universo visto desde el Albayzín.* Facsimile of the first edition, with an introduction by José Antonio González Alcantud. Granada: Universidad de Granada, 1996.

———. "Veinte años de arte hispanomarroquí." *Madrid,* May 28, 1946, 3.

Glasser, Jonathan. "Andalusi Musical Origins at the Moroccan-Algerian Frontier: Beyond the Charter Myth." *American Ethnologist* 42, no. 4 (2015): 720–733. doi:10.1111/amet.12166.

———. *The Lost Paradise: Andalusi Music in Urban North Africa*. Chicago, IL: University of Chicago Press, 2016.

Gómez Barceló, José Luis. "Mariano Bertuchi: Cuando el pintor vence al cronista." In Serna et al., *Mariano Bertuchi*, 83–91.

———. "Los santuarios islámicos de Sidi Bel Abbas, Sidi Embarek y Sidi Brahim." *Cuadernos del Archivo Central de Ceuta* 17 (2008): 325–342.

Gómez García, Luz. "Ibn al-Muraḥḥal, Mālik." In *Biblioteca de al-Andalus*, edited by Jorge Lirola Delgado, 4:278–286. Almería: Fundación Ibn Tufayl de Estudios Árabes, 2006.

Gómez-Rivas, Camilo. "Exile, Encounter, and the Articulation of Andalusi Identity in the Maghrib." *Medieval Encounters* 20 (2014): 340–351. doi:10.1163/15700674-12342178.

González Alcantud, José Antonio. "Los andalusíes hoy: Una elite viva frente al pasado futuro de al-Ándalus." In *Andalusíes: Antropología e historia cultural de una elite magrebí*, edited by José Antonio González Alcantud and Sandra Rojo Flores, 15–57. Madrid: Abada, 2015.

———. "La fábrica francesa del estilo *hispano-mauresque*, en la galería mediterránea de los espejos deformantes." In *La invención del estilo hispano-magrebí: Presente y futuros del pasado*, edited by José A. González Alcantud, 15–76. Barcelona: Anthropos, 2010.

———, ed. *La invención del estilo hispano-magrebí: Presente y futuros del pasado*. Barcelona: Anthropos, 2010.

———. *El mito de al Ándalus: Orígenes y actualidad de un ideal cultural*. Córdoba: Almuzara, 2014.

———. Introduction to *Ni Oriente, ni Occidente: El universo visto desde el Albayzín*, by Rodolfo Gil Benumeya, xlvii–xcvi. Granada: Universidad de Granada, 1996.

———. "Poética de la conquista en la obra orientalista de Pedro Antonio de Alarcón." In *Pedro Antonio de Alarcón y la Guerra de África: Del entusiasmo romántico a la compulsión colonial*, edited by José A. González Alcantud, 11–30. Barcelona: Anthropos, 2004.

González Alcantud, J. A., and A. Malpica Cuello, eds. *Pensar la Alhambra*. Barcelona: Anthropos, 2001.

González Alcantud, José Antonio, and Sandra Rojo Flores. "Al-Ándalus y los andalusíes: Tras el mito habitan seres vivos." In *Andalusíes: Antropología e historia cultural de una elite magrebí*, edited by José Antonio González Alcantud and Sandra Rojo Flores, 7–12. Madrid: Abada, 2015.

González González, Irene. *Escuela e ideología en el Protectorado español en el norte de Marruecos, 1912–1956.* Barcelona: Bellaterra, 2014.

Gonzàlez i Vilalta, Arnau. *La nació imaginada: Els fonaments dels Països Catalans (1931–1939).* Catarroja: Afers, 2006.

Goode, Joshua. *Impurity of Blood: Defining Race in Spain, 1870–1930.* Baton Rouge: Louisiana State University Press, 2009.

Goytisolo, Juan. "Américo Castro en la España actual." In *Américo Castro y la revision de la memoria,* edited by Eduardo Subirats, 23–37. Madrid: Libertarias, 2003.

Gozalbes Busto, Guillermo. *Al-Mandari, el granadino fundador de Tetuán.* 2nd ed. Granada: T. G. Arte, 1993.

——. *Los Moriscos en Marruecos.* Granada: T. G. Arte, 1992.

Gracia Mechbal, Mariam, Miriam Font Ubalde, and Concha de la Torre. "Noticias sobre la visita del Jalifa Muley el Hasan Ben el Mehdi en el Archivo de la Escuela de Estudios Árabes de Granada." In *El príncipe Muley El Hasan Ben El Mehdi: Jalifa del Sultán en el Norte de Marruecos y en el Sahara,* edited by Jaafar Ben Elhaj Soulami, 105–124. Tetouan: Fundación Mhammad Ahmed Benaboud, 2016.

Graciani García, Amparo. *La participación internacional y colonial en la Exposición Iberoamericana de Sevilla de 1929.* Sevilla: Universidad de Sevilla, 2010.

Granara, William. "Nostalgia, Arab Nationalism, and the Andalusian *Chronotope* in the Evolution of the Modern Arabic Novel." *Journal of Arabic Literature* 36, no. 1 (2005): 57–73.

——. "Remaking Muslim Sicily: Ibn Ḥamdīs and the Poetics of Exile." *Edebiyat* 9 (1998): 167–198.

Grant, Ben. *Postcolonialism, Psychoanalysis and Burton: Power Play of Empire.* New York: Routledge, 2009.

Guerin, Adam. "'Not a Drop for the Settlers': Reimagining Popular Protest and Anti-Colonial Nationalism in the Moroccan Protectorate." *Journal of North African Studies* 20, no. 2 (2015): 225–246. doi:10.1080/13629387.2014.917586.

Hachimi, Atiqa. "The Maghreb-Mashriq Language Ideology and the Politics of Identity in a Globalized Arab World." *Journal of Sociolinguistics* 17, no. 3 (2013): 269–296.

Halstead, John P. *Rebirth of a Nation: The Origins and Rise of Moroccan Nationalism, 1912–1944.* Harvard: Harvard University Press, 1967.

Harrison, Olivia C. *Transcolonial Maghreb: Imagining Palestine in the Era of Decolonization.* Stanford, CA: Stanford University Press, 2016.

Harvey, L. P. *Islamic Spain: 1250 to 1500.* Chicago, IL: University of Chicago Press, 1990.
———. *Muslims in Spain: 1500 to 1614.* Chicago, IL: University of Chicago Press, 2005.
Hassan, Waïl S. *Immigrant Narratives: Orientalism and Cultural Translation in Arab American and Arab British Literature.* New York: Oxford University Press, 2011.
Heinrichs, Wolfhart P. "Rhetorical Figures." In *Encyclopedia of Arabic Literature*, edited by Julie Scott Meisami and Paul Starkey, 2:656–662. London: Routledge, 1998.
Hernández-Pacheco, Francisco, and José María Cordero Torres. *El Sahara español.* Madrid: Instituto de Estudios Políticos, 1962.
Hernández Ramos, José María. *La emisión de Marruecos de 1928 y Mariano Bertuchi: Correo y filatelia en el Protectorado Español.* San Sebastián: AFINET, 2013.
Hershenzon, Daniel. "Traveling Libraries: The Arabic Manuscripts of Muley Zidan and the Escorial Library." *Journal of Early Modern History* 18 (2014): 535–558.
Herzfeld, Michael. "Practical Mediterraneanism: Excuses for Everything, from Epistemology to Eating." In *Rethinking the Mediterranean*, edited by W. V. Harris, 45–63. Oxford: Oxford University Press, 2005.
Hobsbawm, Eric. "Introduction: Inventing Traditions." In *The Invention of Tradition*, edited by Eric Hobsbawm and Terence Ranger, 1–14. Cambridge: Cambridge University Press, 1992.
Hobsbawm, Eric, and Terence Ranger, eds. *The Invention of Tradition.* Cambridge: Cambridge University Press, 1992.
Holden, Stacy E. "When It Pays to Be Medieval: Historic Preservation as a Colonial Policy in the Medina of Fez, 1912–1932." *The Journal of the Historical Society* 6, no. 2 (2006): 297–316.
Horden, Peregrine. Introduction to *Companion to Mediterranean History*, edited by Peregrine Horden and Sharon Kinoshita, 1–7. Chichester, UK: Wiley Blackwell, 2014.
Horden, Peregrine, and Nicholas Purcell. *The Corrupting Sea: A Study of Mediterranean History.* Malden, MA: Blackwell, 2000.
Hourani, Albert. *Arabic Thought in the Liberal Age: 1798–1939.* Oxford: Oxford University Press, 1962.
Ibn 'Azzuz Hakim, Muhammad. *Ab al-haraka al-wataniyya al-maghribiyya: al-Hajj 'Abd al-Salam Binnuna.* 3 vols. Rabat: al-Hilal al-'Arabiyya li-l-Tiba'a wa-l-Nashr, 1987–1988.

———. *Watha'iq sirriyya hawla ziyarat al-amir Shakib Arslan li-l-Maghrib.* Tetouan: Mu'assasat 'Abd al-Khaliq al-Turris, 1980.
Ibn al-Hajj al-Sulami, Ja'far (*see also* Ben Elhaj Soulami, Jaafar). "La mémoire silencieuse." In *Tétouan: Reflets souterrains de l'histoire d'une cité,* 138–170. Mohammedia: Senso Unico, 2009.
———, ed. *'Umdat al-rawin fi tarikh Tittawin.* By Ahmad al-Rahuni. 11 vols. Tetouan: Jam'iyyat Titwan-Asmir, 1998–2015.
Ibn al-Khatib. *Mi'yar al-ikhtiyar fi dhikr al-ma'ahid wa-l-diyar.* In *Mushahadat Lisan al-Din Ibn al-Khatib fi bilad al-Maghrib wa-l-Andalus,* edited by Ahmad Mukhtar al-'Abbadi, 67–115. Alexandria: Mu'assasat Shabab al-Jami'a, 1983.
Ibn Tawit, Muhammad. *Tarikh Sabta.* Casablanca: Dar al-Thaqafa, 1982.
———. Introduction to *Titwan* 1 (1956): 9–11.
Ibo Alfaro, Manuel. *Españoles . . . a Marruecos.* Madrid: Manuel de Ancos, 1859.
Idrisi, 'Abd al-Qadir al-. *'Abd Allah Gannun wa-mawqi'uhu fi al-fikr al-islami al-siyasi al-hadith.* Cairo: al-Zahra' li-l-I'lam al-'Arabi, 1992.
Infante, Blas. *El ideal andaluz.* Edited by Enrique Tierno Galván and Juan Antonio Lacomba. Madrid: Tucar, [1976].
———. *Motamid: Último rey de Sevilla.* Edited by Manuel Ruiz Lagos. Seville: Fundación Blas Infante, 1983.
———. *Los orígenes de lo flamenco y secreto del cante jondo (1929–1933).* Seville: Junta de Andalucía, 1980.
———. *La verdad sobre el complot de Tablada y el Estado libre de Andalucía.* 2nd ed. Granada: Aljibe, 1979.
Infante, Blas, Inocencio Fe, Emilio Álvarez, Juan García Jiménez, Manuel Rosi, Dionisio Pastor, Eloy Vaquero, Francisco Azorín, and Francisco Córdoba. "Manifiesto de los regionalistas: La autonomía de la región andaluza." In *Cuatro textos políticos andaluces (1883–1933),* edited by Juan Antonio Lacomba, 75–95. Granada: Universidad de Granada, 1979.
Iniesta Coullaut-Valera, Enrique. *Blas Infante. Toda su verdad.* Vol. 2, *1919–1933.* Granada: Atrio, 2003.
Instituto de Estudios Islámicos. *Instituto de Estudios Islámicos en Madrid.* Madrid, 1966.
Irbouh, Hamid. *Art in the Service of Colonialism: French Art Education in Morocco, 1912–1956.* London: Tauris Academic Studies, 2005.
Jacobson, Ken. *Odalisques & Arabesques: Orientalist Photography, 1839–1925.* London: Quaritch, 2007.
Jayyusi, Salma Khadra. "Arabic Poetry in the Post-Classical Age." In *Arabic Literature in the Post-Classical Period,* edited by Roger Allen and D. S. Richards, 25–59. Cambridge: Cambridge University Press, 2006.

Jubran, Muhammad Masʿud, ed. *Malik b. al-Murahhal: Adib al-ʿudwatayn.* Abu Dhabi: al-Majmaʿ al-Thaqafi, 2005.
Juliá, Santos. *Historias de las dos Españas.* Madrid: Taurus, 2004.
Justel Calabozo, Braulio. *La Real Biblioteca de El Escorial y sus manuscritos árabes.* 2nd ed. Madrid: Patrimonio Nacional, 1987.
Kably, Mohamed, et al. *Histoire du Maroc: Réactualisation et synthèse.* Rabat: Institut Royal pour la Recherche sur l'Histoire du Maroc, 2011.
Kadhim, Hussein N. *The Poetics of Anti-Colonialism in the Arabic Qaṣīdah.* Leiden: Brill, 2004.
Kassab, Elizabeth Suzanne. *Contemporary Arab Thought: Cultural Critique in Comparative Perspective.* New York: Columbia University Press, 2010.
Keating, Bern, trans. *Diary of a Witness.* By Pedro Antonio de Alarcón. Memphis: White Rose Press, 1988.
Kennedy, Philip F. *The Wine Song in Classical Arabic Poetry: Abū Nuwās and the Literary Tradition.* Oxford: Clarendon, 1997.
Khatib, Toumader. *Culture et politique dans le mouvement nationaliste marocain au Machreq.* Tetoun: Association Tétouan-Asmir, 2016.
Khoury, Jeries. "Zarqāʾ al-Yamāma in Modern Arabic Poetry: A Comparative Reading." *Journal of Semitic Studies* 53, no. 2 (2008): 311–328. doi:10.1093/jss/fgn006.
Knysh, Alexander. "Ibn al-Khatib." In *The Literature of al-Andalus,* edited by María Rosa Menocal, Raymond P. Scheindlin, and Michael Sells, 358–371. Cambridge: Cambridge University Press, 2000.
———. "Ibn ʿArabi." In *The Literature of al-Andalus,* edited by María Rosa Menocal, Raymond P. Scheindlin, and Michael Sells, 331–344. Cambridge: Cambridge University Press, 2000.
Krauel, Javier. *Imperial Emotions: Cultural Responses to Myths of Empire in Fin-de-Siècle Spain.* Liverpool: Liverpool University Press, 2013.
LaCapra, Dominick. *Writing History, Writing Trauma.* Baltimore, MD: The Johns Hopkins University Press, 2001.
Lacomba, Juan Antonio. *Regionalismo y autonomía en la Andalucía contemporánea (1835–1936).* Granada: Caja General de Ahorros y Monte de Piedad de Granada, 1988.
Lakhdar, Kamal. "Flux et reflux, rayonnement et éclipse." In *Le Maroc andalou: À la découverte d'un art de vivre,* 215–246. Casablanca: EDDIF; Aix-en-Provence: Édisud, 2000.
Lara Ramos, Antonio. *Pedro Antonio de Alarcón.* Granada: Comares, 2001.
Larramendi, Miguel H. de, Irene González González, and Bernabé López García, eds. *El Instituto Hispano-Árabe de Cultura: Orígenes y evolución de la diplomacia pública española hacia el mundo árabe.* Madrid: AECID, 2015.

Larrea Palacín, Arcadio de, and Alfredo Bustani. *Nawba Iṣbahān*. Instituto General Franco de Estudios e Investigación Hispano-Árabe. Tetouan: Editora Marroquí, 1956.

Lasandro [pseud.]. "Baile de trajes en el palacio Medinaceli." *La Época*, April 2, 1861, 3–4. http://hemerotecadigital.bne.es/issue.vm?id =0000156257&search=&lang=es.

Lécuyer, M. C., and C. Serrano. *La Guerre d'Afrique et ses repercussions en Espagne: Idéologies et colonialism en Espagne, 1859–1904*. Paris: Presses Universitaires de France, 1976.

Le Tourneau, R. "'Abd al-Salām b. Mashīsh." *Encyclopedia of Islam*. 2nd ed. Accessed June 30, 2017. http://dx.doi.org/10.1163/1573-3912_islam_SIM _0127.

Lévi-Provençal, E. "L'Émir Shakib Arslan (1869–1946)." *Cahiers de l'Orient contemporain* 9–10 (1947): 5–19.

Lévi-Provençal, E., J. D. Latham, L. Torres Balbás, and G. S. Colin. "Al-Andalus." *Encyclopedia of Islam*. 2nd ed. Accessed June 30, 2017. http://dx.doi.org/10.1163/1573-3912_islam_COM_0054.

Lévi-Provençal, E., and Ch. Pellat. "al-Maḳḳari." *Encyclopedia of Islam*. 2nd ed. Accessed June 30, 2017. http://dx.doi.org/10.1163/1573-3912_islam_SIM_4832.

Lévi-Provençal, [Évariste], and J.-F. Troin. "Ribāṭ al-Fatḥ." *Encyclopedia of Islam*. 2nd ed. Accessed June 30, 2017. http://dx.doi.org/10.1163/1573-3912 _islam_SIM_6283.

Lewis, Bernard. *The Muslim Discovery of Europe*. New York: Norton, 1982.

Lionnet, François, and Shu-mei Shih. "Introduction: Thinking through the Minor, Transnationally." In *Minor Transnationalism*, 1–23. Durham: Duke University Press, 2005.

Low, Michael Christopher. "Empire and the Hajj: Pilgrims, Plagues, and Pan-Islam under British Surveillance, 1865–1908." *International Journal of Middle East Studies* 40, no. 2 (2008): 269–290. doi:10.1017/ S0020743808080549.

Lund, Joshua. *The Impure Imagination: Toward a Critical Hybridity in Latin American Writing*. Minneapolis: University of Minnesota Press, 2006.

Madariaga, María Rosa de. *Marruecos, ese gran desconocido: Breve historia del Protectorado español*. Madrid: Alianza, 2013.

Maghen, Ze'ev. "Ablution." *Encyclopedia of Islam*. 3rd ed. Accessed June 30, 2017. http://dx.doi.org/10.1163/1573-3912_ei3_COM_0150.

Maghrawi, Muhammad, et al. *Al-Faqih al-Mufaddal Afaylal: Masarat fanniyya*. Rabat: Wizarat al-Awqaf wa-l-Shu'un al-Islamiyya, 2010.

Mallette, Karla. "Beyond Mimesis: Aristotle's *Poetics* in the Medieval Mediterranean." *PMLA* 124, no. 2 (2009): 583–591. www.jstor.org/stable/25614301.

———. *European Modernity and the Arab Mediterranean: Toward a New Philology and a Counter-Orientalism*. Philadelphia: University of Pennsylvania Press, 2010.
Malo de Molina, Julio, and Fernando Domínguez. *Tetuán, el Ensanche: Guía de arquitectura, 1913–1956*. 2nd ed. Sevilla: Consejería de Obras Públicas y Transportes, 1996.
Manuel, Antonio. *La huella morisca*. Cordoba: Almuzara, 2010.
Manuni, Muhammad al-. *Mazahir yaqzat al-Maghrib al-hadith*. 2 vols. Beirut: Dar al-Gharb al-Islami, 1985.
Manzano Moreno, Eduardo. "Qurtuba: Algunas reflexiones críticas sobre el califato de Córdoba y el mito de la convivencia." *Awraq* 7 (2013): 225–246. www.awraq.es/index.aspx?r=43.
Maqqari, Ahmad b. Muhammad al-. *Azhar al-riyad fi akhbar 'Iyad*. 5 vols. [Rabat]: Sunduq Ihya' al-Turath al-Islami, 1978.
———. *Nafh al-tib min ghusn al-Andalus al-ratib*. Edited by Ihsan 'Abbas. 8 vols. Beirut: Dar Sadir, 2004.
Martín Corrales, Eloy, ed. *Marruecos y el colonialismo español (1859–1912): De la guerra de África a la "penetración pacífica."* Barcelona: Bellaterra, 2002.
Martín de la Escalera, A. M. "Mariano Bertuchi y su labor en Marruecos." *África: Revista de Tropas Coloniales,* February 1926, 41–43. http://hemerotecadigital.bne.es/issn/0001-9763.
Martin-Márquez, Susan. *Disorientations: Spanish Colonialism in Africa and the Performance of Identity*. New Haven, CT: Yale University Press, 2008.
Martínez Kleiser, Luis, ed. *Obras completas de D. Pedro A. de Alarcón*. Madrid: FAX, 1943.
Martínez Montávez, Pedro. *Al-Andalus, España, en la literature árabe contemporánea: La casa del pasado*. Madrid: MAPFRE, 1992.
Matar, Nabil. *Europe through Arab Eyes, 1578–1727*. New York: Columbia University Press, 2009.
———, ed. and trans. *In the Lands of the Christians*. New York: Routledge, 2003.
Mateo Dieste, Josep Lluís. "The Franco North African Pilgrims after WWII: The Hajj through the Eyes of a Spanish Colonial Officer (1949)." In *The Hajj and Europe in the Age of Empire*, edited by Umar Ryad, 240–264. Leiden: Brill, 2017.
———. *La "hermandad" hispano-marroquí: Política y religión bajo el Protectorado español en Marruecos (1912–1956)*. Barcelona: Bellaterra, 2003.
———. "Muley Hassan b. el Mehdi y el aparato colonial español: Escenificaciones rituales entre el jalifato y el sultanato." In *El príncipe Muley El*

Hasan Ben El Mehdi: Jalifa del Sultán en el Norte de Marruecos y en el Sahara, edited by Jaafar Ben Elhaj Soulami, 157–173. Tetouan: Fundación Mhammad Ahmed Benaboud, 2016.

McClintock, Anne. *Imperial Leather: Race, Gender, and Sexuality in the Colonial Contest.* New York: Routledge, 1995.

McDougall, James. *History and Culture of Nationalism in Algeria.* Cambridge: Cambridge University Press, 2006.

Meira Goldberg, K., and Antoni Pizà. Introduction to "Españoles, indios, africanos y gitanos: El alcance global del fandango en música, canto y danza." Special issue, *Música oral del Sur* 12 (2015): 25–32. www.centrode documentacionmusicaldeandalucia.es/opencms/documentacion /revistas/revistas-mos/musica-oral-del-sur-n12.html.

Menocal, María Rosa. *The Ornament of the World.* New York: Little, Brown, 2002.

Miège, Jean-Louis. *Le Maroc et l'Europe (1830–1894).* 4 vols. Paris: Presses Universitaires de France, 1961.

Miège, Jean-Louis, M'hammad Benaboud, and Nadia Erzini. *Tétouan: Ville andalouse marocaine.* Paris: CNRS Éditions; Rabat: Kalila wa dimna, 1996.

Miller, Susan Gilson, trans. *Disorienting Encounters: Travels of a Moroccan Scholar in France in 1845–1846. The Voyage of Muḥammad aṣ-Ṣaffār.* Berkeley: University of California Press, 1992.

———. *A History of Modern Morocco.* Cambridge: Cambridge University Press, 2013.

Ministerio de Instrucción Pública y Bellas Artes. *Escuela de Estudios Árabes de Granada (Casa del Chapiz): Curso 1934–1935.* Madrid: Estanislao Maestre, [1934].

Mokhiber, James. "'Le protectorat dans la peau': Prosper Ricard and the 'native arts' in French colonial Morocco, 1899–1952." In *Revisiting the Colonial Past in Morocco,* edited by Driss Maghraoui, 257–284. London: Routledge, 2013.

Monroe, James T. *Hispano-Arabic Poetry.* Piscataway, NJ: Gorgias Press, 2004.

Moratinos, Miguel Ángel. Foreword to *Mariano Bertuchi: Pintor de Marruecos,* by Alfonso de la Serna et al., 5.

Muhammad V (*see also* Mohammed V). *Le Maroc à l'heure de l'indépendance.* Vol. 1, *1955–1957.* Rabat: Ministère de l'Information et du Tourisme, [1957].

Muhsin, Inqadh 'Ata Allah, ed. *Kitab al-wafi fi nazm al-qawafi.* By al-Rundi. *Majallat Jami'at Anbar li-l-lughat wa-l-adab* 1 (2009): 21–160. www.iasj .net/iasj?func=fulltext&aId=63727.

Musawi, Muhsin al-. *Islam on the Street: Religion in Modern Arabic Literature.* Lanham, MD: Rowman & Littlefield, 2009.

"Los musulmanes peregrinos de la Meca." *ABC,* April 3, 1937, 13–14. http://hemeroteca.sevilla.abc.es/nav/Navigate.exe/hemeroteca/sevilla/abc.sevilla/1937/04/03.html.

Nasir, Sa'ad al-. "Al-Haraka al-thaqafiyya fi Titwan: Sidi al-Mufaddal Afaylal namudhijan." In *Titwan qabla al-himaya (1860–1912),* 197–203. Tetouan: n.p., 1994.

Nasiri, Ahmad b. Khalid al-. *Kitab al-istiqsa li-akhbar duwal al-Maghrib al-Aqsa.* 9 vols. Edited by Ahmad al-Nasiri, Muhammad Hajji, Ibrahim Bu Talib, and Ahmad al-Tawfiq. Casablanca: Wizarat al-Thaqafa wa-l-Ittisal, 2001.

Netton, I. R. "Riḥla." *Encyclopedia of Islam.* 2nd ed. Accessed June 30, 2017. http://dx.doi.org/10.1163/1573-3912_islam_SIM_6298.

Nirenberg, David. *Communities of Violence: Persecution of Minorities in the Middle Ages.* Princeton, NJ: Princeton University Press, 1996.

Nogué, Joan, and José Luis Villanova, eds. *España en Marruecos (1912–1956): Discursos geográficos e intervención territorial.* Lleida: Milenio, 1999.

Olmedo, Fernando, ed. *Itinerario cultural de Almorávides y Almohades: Magreb y Península Ibérica.* 2nd ed. [Seville]: Junta de Andalucía, 2003.

Ortiz de Villajos, Cándido G. *Crónica de Granada en 1939: Año de la Victoria.* Granada: Urania, 1940.

Pagden, Anthony. *European Encounters with the New World.* New Haven, CT: Yale University Press, 1993.

Palomo, María del Pilar, ed. *Diario de un testigo de la guerra de África.* By Pedro A. de Alarcón. Seville: Fundación José Manuel Lara, 2005.

Paradela, Nieves. *El otro laberinto español: Viajeros árabes a España entre el siglo XVII y 1936.* Madrid: Siglo XXI, 2005.

Pardo Bazán, Emilia. *Alarcón: Estudio biográfico.* Madrid: Imp. de la Comp. de Impresores y Libreros, [c. 1891].

Pavón, Basilio. *Ciudades hispanomusulmanas.* Madrid: MAPFRE, 1992.

Pérez Galdós, Benito. *Aita Tettauen.* Edited by Francisco Márquez Villanueva. Madrid: Akal, 2004.

Pérez de Hita, Ginés. *Historia de los bandos de Zegríes y Abencerrajes.* 1595. Facsimile. Granada: Universidad de Granada, 1999.

Peters, F. E. *The Hajj: The Muslim Pilgrimage to Mecca and the Holy Places.* Princeton, NJ: Princeton University Press, 1994.

Porter, Venetia, and Liana Saif, eds. *The Hajj: Collected Essays.* London: British Museum, 2013.

Prat de la Riba, Enric. *La nacionalitat catalana. Compendi de la doctrina catalanista.* Edited by Jordi Casassas. Barcelona: Edicions de la Magrana, 1993.
Prat de la Riba, Enric, and Pere Muntañola. "Compendi de la doctrina catalanista." In *La nacionalitat catalana. Compendi de la doctrina catalanista,* edited by Jordi Casassas, 83–100. Barcelona: Edicions de la Magrana, 1993.
"Proyecto de la Constitución Federal Regional para Andalucía." In *Cuatro textos políticos andaluces (1883–1933),* edited by Juan Antonio Lacomba, 7–32. Granada: Universidad de Granada, 1979.
Qara, Hayat, ed. *Diwan Abi al-Tayyib Salih b. Sharif al-Rundi.* [Kuwait]: Markaz al-Babtayn li-Tahqiq al-Makhtutat al-Shiʿriyya, 2010.
Rahuni, Ahmad al-. *Al-Rihla al-makkiyya.* Tetouan: Maʿhad Khaniral Franku li-l-Abhath al-ʿArabiyya al-Isbaniyya (Instituto General Franco para la Investigación Hispano-Árabe), 1941.
———. *ʿUmdat al-rawin fi tarikh Tittawin.* Edited by Jaʿfar b. al-Hajj al-Sulami. 11 vols. Tetouan: Jamʿiyyat Titwan-Asmir, 1998–2015.
Razzuq, Muhammad. *Al-Andalusiyyun wa-hijratuhum ila al-Maghrib.* 3rd ed. Casablanca: Afriqiya al-Sharq, 1998.
Renan, Ernest. *De la part des peuples sémitiques dans l'histoire de la civilisation.* Paris: Michel Lévy Frères, 1862.
Resina, Joan Ramon. "The Catalan *Renaixença*." In *The Cambridge History of Spanish Literature,* edited by David T. Gies, 470–478. Cambridge: Cambridge University Press, 2013.
———. "Iberian Modalities: The Logic of an Intercultural Field." In *Iberian Modalities: A Relational Approach to the Study of Culture in the Iberian Peninsula,* edited by Joan Ramon Resina, 1–19. Liverpool, UK: Liverpool University Press, 2013.
Rézette, Robert. *Les partis politiques marocains.* Paris: Librairie Armand Colin, 1955.
Ricard, Prosper. *L'Artisanat indigène en Afrique du Nord.* Rabat: École du Livre, 1935.
———. "Les Arts marocains et leur rénovation." *Revue d'Afrique* 6 (1930): 10–22.
———. "Arts ruraux et arts citadins dans l'Afrique du Nord." *France-Maroc* 5 (1917): 20–27.
———. *Essai d'Action sur la Musique et le Théâtre Populaire Marocains.* Rabat: Imprimerie Nouvelle, 1928.
Rihani, Amin al-. *Al-Maghrib al-Aqsa.* 1st ed. Cairo: Dar al-Maʿarif, 1952.
———. *Al-Maghrib al-Aqsa.* 2nd ed. Beirut: Dar al-Thaqafa, 1975.

Rippin, Andrew. "ʿĀya." *Encyclopedia of Islam*. 3rd ed. Accessed June 30, 2017. http://dx.doi.org/10.1163/1573-3912_ei3_SIM_0335.

Roberson, Jennifer. "The Changing Face of Morocco under King Hassan II." *Mediterranean Studies* 22, no. 1 (2014): 57–83. https://muse.jhu.edu/article/547158.

Robinson, C. F. "Uḥud." *Encyclopedia of Islam*. 2nd ed. Accessed June 30, 2017. http://dx.doi.org/10.1163/1573-3912_islam_SIM_7685.

Rodríguez de la Borbolla y Camoyán, José. *Elogio del mestizaje*. Seville: Ayuntamiento de Sevilla, 1999.

Rodríguez Esteller, Omar. "La intervención española de las aduanas marroquíes (1862–1835)." In *Marruecos y el colonialismo español (1859–1912)*, edited by Eloy Martín Corrales, 79–131. Barcelona: Bellaterra, 2002.

Rodríguez Mediano, Fernando, and Helena de Felipe, eds. *El Protectorado español en Marruecos. Gestión colonial e identidades*. Madrid: Consejo Superior de Investigaciones Científicas, 2002.

Rogozen-Soltar, Mikaela. "Al-Andalus in Andalusia: Negotiating Moorish History and Regional Identity in Southern Spain." *Anthropological Quarterly* 80, no. 3 (2007): 863–886. www.jstor.org/stable/30052728.

Rojo Flores, Sandra. "Lo andalusí: Melancolía, nostalgia y ecos contemporáneos de un mito." PhD diss., Universidad de Granada, 2015.

Romano, Julio. *Pedro Antonio de Alarcón: El novelista romántico*. Madrid: Espasa-Calpe, 1933.

Ros de Olano, Antonio. *Leyendas de África*. Madrid: Gaspar y Roig, 1860.

Rosón Lorente, Francisco Javier. *¿El retorno de Tariq?: Comunidades etnorreligiosas en el Albayzín granadino*. Granada: Editorial de la Universidad de Granada, 2008.

Rothberg, Michael. *Multidirectional Memory: Remembering the Holocaust in the Age of Decolonization*. Stanford, CA: Stanford University Press, 2009.

Ruggles, D. Fairchild. "The Alcazar of Seville and Mudejar Architecture." *Gesta* 43, no. 2 (2004): 87–98. www.jstor.org/stable/25067097.

———. *Gardens, Landscapes, and Vision in the Palaces of Islamic Spain*. University Park: Pennsylvania State University Press, 2000.

———. "The Stratigraphy of Forgetting: The Great Mosque of Cordoba and Its Contested Legacy." In *Contested Cultural Heritage: Religion, Nationalism, Erasure, and Exclusion in a Global World*, edited by H. Silverman, 51–67. New York: Springer, 2011.

Ruiz Bravo-Villasante, Carmen, ed. and trans. *Un testigo árabe del siglo XX: Amin al-Rihani en Marruecos y en España (1939)*. 2 vols. Madrid: Cantarabia, 1993.

Rundi, Abu al-Baqa' Salih b. al-Sharif al-. *Kitab al-wafi fi nazm al-qawafi.* Edited by Inqadh 'Ata Allah Muhsin. *Majallat Jami'at Anbar li-l-lughat wa-l-adab* 1 (2009): 21–160. www.iasj.net/iasj?func=fulltext&aId=63727.

Ryad, Umar. "New Episodes in Moroccan Nationalism under Colonial Rule: Reconsideration of Shakib Arslan's Centrality in Light of Unpublished Materials." *Journal of North African Studies* 16, no. 1 (2011): 117–142. doi:1 0.1080/13629387.2010.511013.

Saaf, Abdallah. "Elementos para la indagación en el mito andaluz en el discurso político marroquí actual." In *Andalusíes: Antropología e historia cultural de una elite magrebí*, edited by José Antonio González Alcantud and Sandra Rojo Flores, 303–313. Madrid: Abada, 2015.

Sabbagh, Muhammad al-. *Ana al-Andalus.* Tangier: Silsilat Shira', 1999.

Sacks, Jeffrey. *Iterations of Loss: Mutilation and Aesthetic Form, al-Shidyaq to Darwish.* New York: Fordham University Press, 2015.

Said, Edward. *Orientalism.* 25th Anniversary ed. New York: Vintage, 2003.

———. "The Return to Philology." In *Humanism and Democratic Criticism*, 57–84. New York: Columbia University Press, 2004.

Santos Moreno, María Dolores. "Mariano Bertuchi Nieto, de Granada a Tetuán." In Serna et al., *Mariano Bertuchi,* 55–71.

Sa'ud, 'Abd al-'Aziz al-, et al. *A'mal nadwat shakhsiyyat al-Tuhami al-Wazzani wa-musahamatihi al-fikriyya.* Tetouan: Jam'iyyat Titwan-Asmir, 2002.

Scott, David, and Charles Hirschkind. "Introduction: The Anthropological Skepticism of Talal Asad." In *Powers of the Secular Modern: Talal Asad and His Interlocutors,* 1–11. Stanford, CA: Stanford University Press, 2006.

Scott, Joan W. "The Evidence of Experience." *Critical Inquiry* 17, no. 4 (1991): 773–797. www.jstor.org/stable/1343743.

Serna, Alfonso de la. "El arte de un reencuentro." In *Mariano Bertuchi: Pintor de Marruecos,* by Alfonso de la Serna et al., 13–16. Barcelona: Lunwerg, 2000.

Serna, Alfonso de la, et al. *Mariano Bertuchi: Pintor de Marruecos.* Barcelona: Lunwerg, 2000.

Serrallonga Urquidi, Joan. "La guerra de África: Una revisión." In *La política en el reinado de Isabel II,* edited by Isabel Burdiel, 139–159. Madrid: Marcial Pons, 1998.

Serrano, Carlos. "Conciencia de la crisis, conciencias en crisis." In *Más se perdió en Cuba: España, 1898 y la crisis de fin de siglo,* edited by Juan Pan-Montojo, 335–403. Madrid: Alianza, 1998.

Serrano Suñer, Ramón, and Juan Beigbeder. *Discursos pronunciados por los excelentísimos señores don Ramón Serrano Suñer, Ministro del Interior,* y don Juan Beigbeder, Alto Comisario de España en Marruecos, en los actos conmemorativos del 17 de julio, fecha histórica del glorioso Alzamiento del Ejército de África. Ceuta: Imprenta África, [1938].

Shannon, Jonathan Holt. *Performing al-Andalus: Music and Nostalgia across the Mediterranean*. Bloomington: Indiana University Press, 2015.

Sharif, Muhammad al-. *Titwan: Hadinat al-hadara al-maghribiyya al-andalusiyya*. Tetouan: Manshurat Jamʿiyyat Titwan-Asmir, 2013.

Shawqi, Ahmad. *Amirat al-Andalus*. [Cairo]: al-Hayʾa al-Misriyya al-ʿAmma li-l-Kitab, 1982.

Smith, Anthony D. *National Identity*. Reno: University of Nevada Press, 1991.

Snir, Reuven. "'Al-Andalus Arising from Damascus': Al-Andalus in Modern Arabic Poetry." In *Charting Memory: Recalling Medieval Spain*, edited by Stacy N. Beckwith, 263–293. New York: Garland, 2000.

Solà Gussinyer, Mercè. "L'organització del pelegrinatge a la Meca per Franco durant la Guerra Civil." *L'Avenç* 256 (2001): 56–61.

Soto Bermant, Laia. "Consuming Europe: The Moral Significance of Mobility and Exchange at the Spanish-Moroccan Border of Melilla." *Journal of North African Studies* 19, no. 1 (2014): 110–129.

Stallaert, Christiane. *Etnogénesis y etnicidad en España: Una aproximación histórico-antropológica al casticismo*. Barcelona: Proyecto A, 1998.

Stenner, David. "Centering the Periphery: Northern Morocco as a Hub of Transnational Anti-Colonial Activism, 1930–43." *Journal of Global History* 11 (2016): 430–450. doi:10.1017/S174002281600022X.

Stepan, Nancy. "Racial Degeneration: Races and Proper Places." In *Degeneration: The Dark Side of Progress*, edited by J. Edward Chamberlin and Sander L. Gilman, 97–120. New York: Columbia University Press, 1985.

Stetkevych, Jaroslav. *The Zephyrs of Najd: The Poetics of Nostalgia in the Classical Arabic Nasīb*. Chicago, IL: University of Chicago Press, 1993.

Stewart, Devin. "The *maqāma*." In *Arabic Literature in the Post-Classical Period*, edited by Roger Allen and D. S. Richards, 145–158. Cambridge: Cambridge University Press, 2006.

Subirats, Eduardo, ed. *Américo Castro y la revisión de la memoria: El Islam en España*. Madrid: Libertarias, 2003.

Talbi, M. "ʿIyāḍ b. Mūsā." *Encyclopedia of Islam*. 2nd ed. Accessed July 4, 2017. http://dx doi.org/10.1163/1573-3912_islam_SIM_3715.

Tejado, Gabino. "El Pensamiento Español." *El Pensamiento Español*, February 18, 1860, 2–3. http://hemerotecadigital.bne.es/issn/2173-254X.

Terem, Etty. *Old Texts, New Practices: Islamic Reform in Modern Morocco*. Stanford, CA: Stanford University Press, 2014.

Terrasse, Henri. *L'Art hispano-mauresque des origines au XIIIe siècle*. L'Institut des Hautes Études Marocaines. Paris: G. Van Oest, 1932.

Tito Rojo, José, and Manuel Casares Porcel. *El Carmen de la Victoria: Un jardín regionalista en el contexto de la historia de los cármenes de Granada*. Granada: Universidad de Granada, 1999.

Turris, ʿAbd al-Khaliq al-. "Al-ʿInaya bi-l-musiqa al-maghribiyya." In *Min turath al-Turris*, 72–74. Rabat: Matbaʿat al-Risala, [1980?].

Utande Ramiro, María del Carmen, and Manuel Utande Igualada. "Mariano Bertuchi y sus dibujos de la guerra civil marroquí (1903 y 1908) en el Museo de la Academia." *Academia* 75, no. 2 (1992): 321–361.

Valderrama Martínez, Fernando. *El Cancionero de al-Ḥāʾik*. Tetouan: Editora Marroquí, 1954.

———. *Historia de la acción cultural de España en Marruecos (1912–1956)*. Tetouan: Editora Marroquí, 1956.

Vallina, Sonsoles. "La pintura de Bertuchi: Un diario personal de luz y color." In Serna et al., *Mariano Bertuchi*, 73–81.

Villada Paredes, Fernando, et al. *Historia de Ceuta*. 2 vols. Ceuta: Instituto de Estudios Ceutíes, 2009.

Villafranca Jiménez, María del Mar, and Carmen Yusty, eds. *Corpus epigráfico de la Alhambra: Palacio de Comares*. Granada: Patronato de la Alhambra y el Generalife, [2007?]. CD-ROM.

Villanova, José Luis. *Los interventores: La piedra angular del Proctectorado español en Marruecos*. Barcelona: Bellaterra, 2006.

———. *El Protectorado de España en Marruecos: Organización política y territorial*. Barcelona: Bellaterra, 2004.

Vo, Toan. *Le Mausolée Mohammed V*. Casablanca: Sochepress, 1976.

Wazzani, al-Tuhami al-. *Al-Zawiya*. Edited by ʿAbd al-ʿAziz al-Saʿud. Tetouan: Manshurat Jamʿiyyat Titwan-Asmir, 2008.

Wolf, Jean. *Les secrets du Maroc espagnol: L'épopée d'Abd-el-Khaleq Torres*. Paris: Balland; Casablanca: Eddif, 1994.

Wright, Gwendolyn. *The Politics of Design in French Colonial Urbanism*. Chicago, IL: University of Chicago Press, 1991.

Wyrtzen, Jonathan. *Making Morocco: Colonial Intervention and the Politics of Identity*. Ithaca, NY: Cornell University Press, 2015.

Yebbur, Abderrahim. *Los Ber-Rached de Chefchauen y su significación en la historia de Marruecos septentrional*. Tetouan: Cremades, 1953.

Yeves Andrés, José Antonio. *Una imagen para la memoria: La carte de visite—Colección de Pedro Antonio de Alarcón*. Madrid: Fundación Lázaro Galdiano, 2011.

Zarrouk, Mourad. *Los traductores de España en Marruecos (1859–1939)*. Barcelona: Bellaterra, 2009.

Zaydan, Jurji. *Shar! wa-'Abd al-Rahman*. Cairo: al-Hilal, 1904.
Zayyat, 'Abd Allah Muhammad al-. *Ritha' al-mudun fi al-shi'r al-andalusi*. Benghazi: Jami'at Qaryunis, 1990.
Zunes, Stephen, and Jacob Mundy. *Western Sahara: War, Nationalism, and Conflict Irresolution*. Syracuse, NY: Syracuse University Press, 2010.

ACKNOWLEDGMENTS

In 2007, I went to Morocco intending to work on a project about religious and ethnic identities in medieval Iberia and North Africa. Ten years later, I have emerged with a book about modern Spanish-Moroccan relations—and, in particular, about the political uses of medieval al-Andalus in Spanish colonial Morocco. Along the journey, from one project to another, from the medieval period to the modern, I have had the great fortune to meet and learn from numerous teachers, colleagues, and friends, who have contributed to this book with their ideas and encouragement.

I would like to acknowledge the extensive support I have received from colleagues in Tetouan, Morocco, the heart of this book and the main site of my research. This book simply would not have been possible without the generosity of Jaafar Ben Elhaj Soulami and M'hammad Benaboud, both of whom are distinguished scholars of al-Andalus as well as experts in the history and culture of northern Morocco. Despite the fact that I arrived to Tetouan as an unknown (and green) graduate student, Dr. Ben Elhaj Soulami and Dr. Benaboud did not hesitate to take me under their wings and guide me toward new sources and new ideas. Thanks to their fortuitous intervention, I was introduced to many of the Moroccan authors who appear here. Dr. Ben Elhaj Soulami and Dr. Benaboud also spent countless hours responding to my questions about Tetouani and Moroccan history. Their assistance has proven invaluable, and I'm deeply indebted to them. I am also profoundly grateful to Hasna Daoud, the director of the Muhammad Dawud Foundation for History and Culture, one of the main archives for my research in Tetouan. She not only helped me navigate the foundation's impressive collections, but also responded to numerous inquiries about the work of her father, Muhammad Dawud, one of the main figures in my study.

In Morocco, I have also received significant support from the historian Nadia Erzini, the historian Mohamed Reda Boudchar, and the artist and art historian Bouabid Bouzaid, as well as from several American scholars based in North Africa and Spain, including Jessie Stoolman, Caitlin Scholl, Serena Van Buskirk, and James A. Miller. I would also like to thank the staff of the Tangier American Legation Institute for Moroccan Studies—especially John Davison, Yhtimad Bouziane, and Jerry Loftus—for helping me to create a community of interlocutors and a second home in Tangier.

My research has often taken me to Spain, where I have benefited greatly from the support of Mariano Bertuchi Alcaide, Gonzalo Fernández Parrilla, Mercedes García-Arenal, José Luis Gómez Barceló, José Antonio González Alcantud, Domingo Guerrero Borrull, Eloy Martín Corrales, Fernando Rodríguez Mediano, Sandra Rojo Flores, and Amalia Zomeño Rodríguez. I spent significant time at the Spanish National Library in Madrid. Among the very knowledgeable staff there, I would like to single out Isabel Ortega García, the head of the Department of Drawings and Engravings, who helped me locate several uncataloged and unstudied visual sources, including the portraits of Alarcón that I discuss in Chapter 1. Finally, I thank Patricia Estevan and David Sucunza for years of friendship and hospitality in Madrid.

The embryo for this book, including source materials that led to Chapters 1 and 2, was my doctoral research on the Spanish-Moroccan War of 1859–1860, conducted at Harvard University and completed in 2011 under the very capable direction of Brad Epps (now of the University of Cambridge), Luis Girón Negrón, and William Granara. At the time I proposed my topic, there were very few scholars in the United States working on modern Spanish–North African relations. I am therefore lucky to have found three advisers who believed in my unorthodox research interests and fostered them from the very beginning. Over the years, they have continued to mentor me and advocate for me tirelessly. They taught me to think, read, and write across the two shores of the Mediterranean, as well as across centuries, and I am grateful for the scholarly skills and ethical values I learned from them. At Harvard, I also benefited greatly from the mentorship of Mary Gaylord, my first graduate adviser, who continues to inspire me with her perceptive eye for literary texts. In addition, I was also fortunate to study under Susan Miller, at the time the head of Harvard's Moroccan Studies Program and now a professor at UC Davis. She introduced me to Tetouan and to scholarly contacts there. Without her, I never would have embarked on this long (and happy) journey.

My argument took shape during a productive three-year stint at the University of Michigan. While at the Michigan Society of Fellows, I was surrounded by inspiring colleagues from diverse disciplinary backgrounds who, through their feedback on my work and through the examples of their own work, helped me frame my project for a broad audience. For this wonderful intellectual community, I thank the Chair of the Society of Fellows, Donald S.

ACKNOWLEDGMENTS 379

Lopez, and all the postdoctoral scholars, especially Lydia Barnett, Claudia Brittenham, Lily Cox-Richard, Clare Croft, Roger Grant, Elizabeth Hinton, S. E. Kile, Erik Linstrum, Sara McClelland, Laura Miles, Adedamola Osinulu, and Elizabeth Pringle. I would also like to thank my colleagues in the Departments of Romance Languages and Literatures, Near Eastern Studies, and Comparative Literature for making Michigan a congenial and productive home. In particular, I thank Wijdan Alsayegh, Barbara Alvarez, Carol Bardenstein, Michael Bonner, Hussein Fancy, Enrique García Santo-Tomás, Mayte Green-Mercado, Michele Hannoosh, Alexander Knysh, Karla Mallette, Peggy McCracken, Cristina Moreiras-Menor, Ellen Muehlberger, Dan Nemser, Yopie Prins, Anton Shammas, Andrew Shryock, and Ryan Szpiech.

I wrote the bulk of *Colonial al-Andalus* at the University of Illinois, where I have been an Assistant Professor of Comparative Literature since 2014. This book has been immensely enriched by wonderful dialogue with my colleagues in the Program of Comparative and World Literature, as well as in the other programs with which I am affiliated: the Department of Spanish and Portuguese, the Center for South Asian and Middle Eastern Studies, the Program in Medieval Studies, the Unit for Criticism and Interpretive Theory, and the Program in Jewish Culture and Society. I would like to thank those at Illinois who have read and commented on parts of the manuscript or otherwise contributed with suggestions and encouragement: Ericka Beckman, Nancy Blake, Clara Bosak-Schroeder, Antoinette Burton, Paula Mae Carns, Michael Dann, Catharine Fairbairn, Maria Gillombardo, Dara Goldman, Glen Goodman, Waïl S. Hassan, Laila Hussein Moustafa, Gordon Hutner, Javier Irigoyen-García, Lilya Kaganovsky, Brett Kaplan, Craig Koslofsky, Eduardo Ledesma, Avital Livny, Jean-Philippe Mathy, Rini Bhattacharya Mehta, John Meyers, Ben Miller, Harriet Murav, Mimi Thi Nguyen, Bruce Rosenstock, Michael Rothberg, D. Fairchild Ruggles, Rob Rushing, Carol Symes, Robert Tierney, Joyce Tolliver, Oscar Vázquez, and Yasemin Yildiz. I have also been lucky enough to work with two talented graduate research assistants, Ethan Madarieta and Mandy Rector, who helped me with the final stages of research. Finally, I would like to thank the entire staff at the Interlibrary Borrowing Office, especially Kathy Danner, for their unflagging efforts to track down rare sources from Europe and North Africa and to bring them to Illinois.

This project bears the unique mark of each of the institutional environments in which it gestated, but it has also benefited from a decade's worth of exchanges with colleagues spread out across the world. I am particularly grateful for the feedback and suggestions I received from Samer Ali, Michael Allan, Roger Allen, Colette Apelian, Elena Arigita, Sahar Bazzaz, Naor H. Ben-Yehoyada, Julia Clancy-Smith, Jeffrey Culang, Tarek El-Ariss, Alexander

Elinson, Daniela Flesler, Itzea Goikolea, Adam Guerin, Greg Halaby, Daniel Hershenzon, William Hoisington, Stacy Holden, Ahmed Idrissi Alami, Catherine Infante, Seth Kimmel, Jo Labanyi, Luke Leafgren, Jessica Marglin, Susan Martin-Márquez, Josep Lluís Mateo Dieste, Phillip Naylor, Robert P. Parks, Camila Pastor, Daniel Pollack-Pelzner, Jennifer Rappaport, Janell Rothenberg, Umar Ryad, Mohamed Sawaie, Susan Slyomovics, Jonathan Smolin, Diana Sorensen, Justin Stearns, David Stenner, Etty Terem, Nick Valvo, and Jonathan Wyrtzen. I would especially like to acknowledge Jonathan Glasser, who read the manuscript and made several insightful suggestions for improvement. Thanks also to Arnold Weinstein, who has been a model mentor and friend since my days as an undergraduate at Brown University.

This book was made possible by the generous financial support of a number of organizations and institutions, including a fellowship from the National Endowment for the Humanities; a fellowship from the Illinois Program for Research in the Humanities; a postdoctoral fellowship from the Michigan Society of Fellows; the Theodore H. Ashford Dissertation Fellowship from the Graduate School of Arts and Sciences at Harvard University; two grants from the American Institute for Maghrib Studies; the John L. Loeb Fellowship from the Harvard Divinity School; a fellowship from the Fulbright-Hays DDRA program; and research funding from the Campus Research Board at the University of Illinois and from the College of Literature, Science, and the Arts at the University of Michigan.

It has been a true privilege to work with the entire staff at Harvard University Press. I simply could not imagine a better editor than Sharmila Sen, who has given me constant support, while still pushing me to hone my arguments and polish my language. I am grateful for her insight and expert guidance throughout the publishing process, especially when she provided perceptive feedback on the first draft of my manuscript. I also want to thank her assistant, Heather Hughes, who has fielded countless questions with intelligence, patience, and good cheer. Stephanie Vyce, the press's Director of Intellectual Property, has been a font of knowledge, helping me to secure permissions for the images in this book. Thanks to Kimberly Giambattisto for shepherding my book through the production process. I am also extremely grateful to the two anonymous reviewers who read my manuscript with care and offered cogent feedback on its argumentation, clarity, and style.

Chapter 3 expands on " 'In Andalucía, There Are No Foreigners': *Andalucismo* from Transperipheral Critique to Colonial Apology," *Journal of Spanish Cultural Studies* 15, no. 4 (2014): 399–417. I thank the journal for permission to reprint portions of the text of the article. Chapter 4 reprints and expands on "Franco's Hajj: Moroccan Pilgrims, Spanish Fascism, and the Unexpected

Journeys of Modern Arabic Literature," *PMLA*, October 2017. The text is reprinted by permission of the copyright owner, the Modern Language Association of America.

I would like to thank my family and friends for standing by me and providing moral and material support throughout the long life of this project. In particular, I thank my mother and father, Nancy and Stephen Calderwood, for instilling in me a deep curiosity about the world and a love of travel and reading. I also thank Michael, Audrey, Sam, and Katie Calderwood; the entire Beaven clan; Becky and Skip Curtiss; Karen and Charlie Frazier; Karen and Connell Jones; Peter Kitlas and Susan Abraham; Cindy and Tim McGinn; Jacob Okada; Rachel and Greg Pollock; and Sandy Steiner and Aaron Rackoff.

Finally, I thank my wife and partner, Jamie Jones, to whom I dedicate this book. You have been here from inception to completion. Along the way, you have read every page, offering crucial advice and encouragement, while also helping me to maintain a large and vibrant life outside of this project. Thank you for everything that you have done, which has made this book possible and paved the way for the work and adventures that are still to come.

INDEX

Abbasid caliphate, 92, 93
ABC (Spanish newspaper), 157, 159, *160*, 162, 224, 287
'Abd al-'Aziz b. Sa'ud, King, 156
'Abd al-Rahman, Sultan, 84
'Abd al-Rahman III, 135
Abdel Haleem, M.A.S., 150
Abdou in the Time of the Almohads (film, dir. Naciri, 2006), 7
Abencerraje (Abencerage, Abencerrage), 41, 53
"A Chorby, poeta marroquí" ["To Chorby, Moroccan Poet"] (Alarcón), 64–67
Afaylal, Mufaddal, 26, 49, 72, 76, 77, 78–79, 113–115; calligraphy of, 81, *82*, 315n27; chronicle of Spanish-Moroccan War, 73, 79, 81, 84, 101, 102–113; elegy for Tetouan, 92–101, 112–113; as nineteenth-century Moroccan scholar, 83–92; pilgrimage to Ceuta, 85–88.
See also *Kunnash Afaylal*
Afaylal, Muhammad b. al-Hashimi, 83
Africa, 17, 21, 37, 46, 66, 86
África (journal), 217, 230, 234.
See also *Revista de tropas coloniales* (journal)
Aghmat, 116, 117

Ahliyya School [Madrasa Ahliyya] (Tetouan), 256–257, 258, 274, 280
'A'ilat Titwan [*Families of Tetouan*] (Dawud), 63, 313n10
Alarcón, Pedro Antonio de, 25, 33, 118, 230; "Chorby" alter ego, 32, 62–67; as eyewitness, 48, 55, 58, 62, 72, 191; identification with Mulay al-'Abbas, 54–55; Moroccan portraits of, 30, *31*, 32, 33, *34*, 62; as opponent of colonialism, 69, 71; Orientalism and, 44–45, 58, 60, 73; self-citation of, 61–62; self-fashioning as "Moor," 33, 35, 70; as war correspondent for *El Museo Universal*, 38
'Alawi dynasty, 17, 29, 288, 289, 291
Alcázar (Seville), 50, 149–150, 159–161, 296
Alfonso XI, 149
Alfonso XIII, 218
Algeria, 51, 76, 173, 231, 235, 238, 253
Alhambra (Granada), 28, 40, 50, 59, 125, 228, 262, 287; Andalusi music and arts associated with, 168, 240, *241*; crafts and music associated with, 211; Gate of Justice, 4; Generalife gardens, 295–296; Hall of the Ambassadors, 41–42, 159; miniature Alhambra of Tangier, 287, *288*; Nasrid dynasty

384 INDEX

Alhambra *(continued)*
motto in, 125, 281, 287, 295; "neo-Arab" architecture and, 206; Patio of the Lions, 40, 287; School of Indigenous Arts and, 225
Almohad dynasty, 120, 133, 136, 149, 289, 291, 294
Almoravid dynasty, 116, 120, 133, 136, 294
Alpujarras Rebellion (1568–1570), 33, 45, 227
Álvarez Sanz y Tubau, Emilio, 197–198
Ana al-Andalus [I Am al-Andalus] (al-Sabbagh), 8, 281
Andalucía, 26, 54, 56, 124, 225, 302–303n22; "African blood" of, 127; classical Greek culture and, 132; conflated with al-Andalus, 117, 120; Constitution of Antequera (1883), 121–122; cultural and racial mixing in, 141; "Euro-African" character of, 129, 134; as frontier of African immigration into Europe, 141; historical claims over Morocco, 131; Junta de Andújar (1835), 121; as "nationality," 128; as "region," 127; Statute of Autonomy, 119
Andalucismo africano [African Andalusianism] (Gil Benumeya, 1953), 135
Al-Andalus (journal), 283
Al-Andalus (medieval Muslim Iberia), 3, 12, 72, 188, 298, 302–303n22; Alarcón's vision of, 58; "Andaluscentric" narrative of Moroccan history, 6, 28, 115, 135, 265, 268–269; Christian reconquest of, 3, 74, 100–101, 129; conflated with Andalucía, 117, 120; cultural legacy of, 41; cultural memory of, 5, 25, 157, 203;

East–West distinction and memory of, 21; fragmentary link with Andalusi music, 231; Francoist celebration of, 27; Hispano-Arab culture concept and, 176, 193; interfaith tolerance in, 127; Islamic heritage sites in, 147; as "lost paradise," 28, 52, 266–270, 276, 277, 278, 284; in Mediterranean perspective, 19–25; in Moroccan literary history, 74–81, 83; in Moroccan nationalist thought, 259; nostalgia for, 139, 150; "renaissance" of, 178
Andalusian nationalism *(andalucismo)*, 18, 26, 129, 230; as anti-nationalist nationalism, 130; as cosmopolitan imperialism, 130–140; Francoist colonial discourse and, 119–120, 121; racial and cultural mixing defended by, 125–126; relation to Castilian culture and language, 122–123; relation to Catalan nationalism, 26, 122, 123, 126, 127–130, 139–140, 141
Andalusi identity, 11, 18, 25; arts as essential components of, 28; as modern invention, 8; Moroccan national culture and, 9; uninterrupted transmission of, 12
Ángel Moratinos, Miguel, 213
Al-Anis al-mutrib (Ibn al-Tayyib), 81
Anjara clan, 37
Arab (Arab-Islamic) world, 27, 28, 58, 144, 258, 268
Arabic language, 17, 47, 51, 142, 155, 199; in Afaylal's city elegy, 96, 99; *convivencia* and, 187; Francoist discourse in, 146; French colonial policy and, 204–205; Hispanisms and European loanwords in, 84–85, 103–104, 105, 157; standard Arabic,

105, 163, 204; Spanish "Arabization" policy and, 174, 185, 203–204; Spanish-French colonial rivalry and, 168; *Titwan* as Morocco's first academic journal in, 278–279; woven into Spanish in carpet metaphor, 227
Arabic studies, 18
Arabs, 33, 92, 155; Arab nationalism, 194; French colonial doctrine and, 168, 173–174, 201–202, 203, 219–220
Architecture, 11, 12, 50, 295; architectural metaphors for Hispano-Arab culture, 198–199; Gothic, 124–125; "Hispano-Arab," 217; Mudéjar style, 149, 159, 296; "neo-Arab" or "neo-Mudéjar," 205–207
Aristotle, 75
Arribas Palau, Mariano, 281
Arslan, Shakib, 28, 52, 251–254, 279, 294; on al-Andalus as "lost paradise," 266–270, 276, 284; Berber *dahir* opposed by, 254–255; Islamic heritage of Spain promoted by, 262–266; in Morocco, 28, 255–266, 260, 280, 341n1; in Paris, 252–253; on relationship of Spain and Morocco, 261–262; in Spain, 251–252, 253–254
Asad, Talal, 165
Ash'ari, Muhammad al-, 213
Ash'ash, 'Abd al-Qadir, 83
Asín Palacios, Miguel, 253, 262
Association of Lovers of Andalusi Music, 277
Astrologers in the Generalife (Bertuchi painting, c. 1895), 214
Atlas Mountains, 53
Aventures du dernier Abencérage, Les [The Adventures of the Last Abencerage] (Chateaubriand, c. 1826), 41, 51, 72, 267, 310n44, 312n84; Arabic translation of, 251–252; "Moor's Last Sigh" story retold in, 52
Averroes. *See* Ibn Rushd
Azhar al-riyad fi akhbar 'Iyad (al-Maqqari), 90, 317n63
'Aziman, Muhammad, 279

Baghdad, 92, 93
Balafrij, Ahmad, 252–253, 255–256, 258, 277; Arslan interviewed by, 261–262; School of Arabic Studies in Granada and, 262–263
Barberán, Cecilio, 230
Barcelona, 123, 227
Basque Country, 121, 124
Basque language, 123
Bazzaz, Sahar, 103
Beigbeder, Juan, 147, 171, 174, 181, 191; in Ceuta during Spanish Civil War, 208–209; cultural legacy of al-Andalus and, 193; family history in Murcia, 194–195; Hispano-Arab culture concept and, 194; "Hispano-Moroccan Exhibition" and, 228; on interfaith coexistence, 197; Morocco House and, 280; refugees from French zone and, 200; on Spanish versus French policy in Morocco, 202–203; speech on Spanish Protectorate policy, 182–187; visit to School of Indigenous Arts, 209, *210*, 211
Ben Abdelkrim, Mohamed, 293
Benaboud, M'hammad, 6–7
Benjelloun, Abdelmajid, 213
Benmansour, Abdelwahab, 293
Ben Smaïl, Mohamed, 235, 238
Berber *dahir* (1930), 174–175, 201, 202, 254–255
"Berberism" (*al-barbariyya*), 194

Berbers, 10–11, 33, 86, 92, 132–133; "Berber" in extended sense of "North African," 228; French colonial doctrine and, 168, 173–174, 201–205, 219–220; on hajj (pilgrimage to Mecca), 155; Riffian Berber dialect, 155

Bertuchi, Mariano, 28, 137, 138, 240, 281; as close collaborator of Franco, 223; early life of, 214–215; effort to depoliticize legacy of, 212–213; Granadan roots of, 225–226, 227; "Hispano-Moroccan Exhibition" organized by, 227–229; paintings by, 214–215, 223–224, *224*, 230; Ricard compared with, 219–223; School of Indigenous Arts and, 209, *210*, 212–215, 217–230; tourism posters by, 215, *216*

Bética magazine, 125

Binnuna, 'Abd al-Salam, 5, 212, 256–257; Arslan's trip to Morocco and, 258, 259, *260*; death of, 264; Francoist colonial regime and, 269

Binnuna, M'hammad, 28, 247, 255; on Andalusi migration from Granada, 274–276; Arslan's trip to Morocco and, 257–260; Moroccan League ("Defenders of the Truth") and, 256; on Tetouan as "daughter of Granada," 7, 268, 276

Bin Salam al-Fawqi, 232–233, 238

Binsharifa, Muhammad, 12, 293

"Boabdil" (Abu 'Abd Allah Muhammad b. 'Ali), 40, 52, 54, 55

Book of Khalid, The (al-Rihani, 1911), 180–181

Britain, 21, 68, 70

Brocaded Garments about the News and Monuments of al-Andalus, The (Arslan, 1936–1939), 252, 253, 264, 266, 267

Brotherhood discourse, 22, 71, 132, 177

Burgos, as Franco's capital during Spanish Civil War, 181, 190–191, 197

Burke, Edmund, III, 14, 172

Burton, Sir Richard, 35

Bustani, Alfredo, 170, 171, 178–179, 181, 197–198, 248

Bustelo, Antonio, 232–234

Cairo, 163, 164, 256, 258, 264, 277; Morocco House (Bayt al-Magrib), 171, 280; newspapers, 251, 254, 257, 258, 266, 344n59. *See also* Egypt

Caliph (office in Spanish Protectorate), 17, 146, 156, 320n110. *See also* Mulay al-Hasan

Capitulations of Granada, 4

Casablanca, 116, 219, 293

Castile, 3, 122, 123–124

Castro, Américo, 151, 304n40

Catalan language, 18, 123, 124

Catalan nationalism, 26, 122, 125–126; Infante's repudiation of, 127–130, 139–140; *Països Catalans* homeland idea, 131; rejection of African influences, 124–125

Catalonia, 121, 123, 124, 129, 139

Catholicism, 143, 147, 148, 202

Catholic Monarchs, 3, 4, 39, 46, 255

Center for Moroccan Studies, 171, 178, 182, 279, 281

Ceuta, 17, 38, 47, 108–109, 298; Afaylal's pilgrimage to, 85–88; as contested border, 85, 90; hajj sea voyage from, 142, 152, 163; history of al-Andalus and, 85; Mezquita Muley el Mehdi mosque, 208–209; Our Lady of

INDEX 387

Africa as patron saint of, 223; sieges of, 86; Serrallo, 50; Spanish-Moroccan War and, 36–37
Chaouen. *See* Chefchaouen
Chateaubriand, 41, 51, 52, 53, 72, 267
Chefchaouen (Chaouen), 76, 106, 181, 220, 229, 249, 275
"Chorby" (alter ego of Alarcón), 32, 62–67
Chottin, Alexis, 159, 234, 235
Christianity, 40, 55, 69; Berber *dahir* and, 254; conflict with Islam in literary representation, 95–96, 98; Hispano-Arab culture concept and, 169; peaceful coexistence with Islam, 197; representation of conflict with Islam, 76; Spain as vanguard of, 47; Spanish Muslims forcibly converted to, 4
Christians, 25, 32, 87; in Afaylal's chronicle of Spanish-Moroccan War, 102–103, 105, 108; Arab, 203, 204; as "barbarians," 92, 95–98, 100, 103; conflict with Muslims in al-Andalus, 92–93; *convivencia* ("coexistence") and, 8, 119
City elegy, as literary genre, 26, 76; Afaylal's elegy for occupation of Tetouan, 92–101; antithesis in, 95, 96–97, 98; apostrophe in, 95; paronomasia in, 95, 98–99; pre-Islamic poetry and, 112; repetition (anaphora) in, 95, 96–97; rhetorical conventions of, 77; al-Rundi's elegy for Seville, 92, 95–98; *taḥrīḍ* (incitement) motif in, 100–101, 107; water imagery in, 95, 96–97, 98
"Clash of civilizations," 8
Colonialism, European, 2, 76, 114, 166, 283; Andalusi music and, 249; anticolonial nationalism and, 10, 19; Moroccan discourses shaped by, 14; pan-Islamic protest against, 268; postcolonial national identity shaped by, 20, 294; revival of Andalusi arts under, 297; self-destruction of, 13; shaped by Islamic history, 20
Colonialism, French, 9, 27, 168, 193; Andalusi music and, 232, 234–235; "civilizing mission" trope of, 22; Moroccan colonial history dominated by, 17. *See also* French Protectorate
Colonialism, Spanish, 9, 11, 26, 62, 101, 193, 285; *andalucismo* and, 141; Andalusi cultural practices promoted by, 211; "brotherhood" trope of, 22; colonial period (1859–1956), 8, 13–14, 18, 23, 24, 25, 306n53; exceptional nature claimed for, 195–196; marginalized in Moroccan colonial history, 17, 18; Moroccan responses to, 36; Orientalism and, 22; origins of, 88; policy toward Berbers, 201–202; "renaissance" in Morocco attributed to, 194; renaissance of al-Andalus attributed to, 12; "sentimental" nature of, 183. *See also* Spanish Protectorate
Communism, 145, 156, 157
Compendi de la doctrina catalanista [*Compendium of the Catalanist Doctrine*] (Prat de la Riba and Muntañola, 1894), 129
Conference of Moroccan Music (Fez, 1939), 235, 237–240
Constitution, Moroccan, 8
"Conversación en la Alhambra, Una" ["A Conversation in the Alhambra"] (Alarcón), 39–43

Convivencia ("coexistence"), 8, 12, 127; al-Andalus as symbol of cultural tolerance, 10; Andalusian nationalism and, 119; Arabic language and, 187; in Francoist and Republican narratives, 151, 326n35; Hispano-Arab culture concept and, 27, 167, 177, 178, 207; Infante's work and, 26; Mediterranean discourses and, 23; Spanish Protectorate as mirror of, 197

Cordoba, 27, 60, 79, 162; in Andalucía region, 120; Andalusi music and, 230, 231; Christian conquest of, 244; Exhibition of Moroccan Art (1946), 229, 249; "Hispano-Arab" literature and, 171; Islamic heritage sites in, 294; Mosque (later, Cathedral) of, 50, 151, 161, 172, 182, 295; myth of interfaith coexistence in, 193; al-Rahuni in, 150–151; "renaissance" of Hispano-Arab culture in, 198–199; revived in Tetouan, 180–192. *See also* Umayyad caliphate

Cordoba Manifesto (1919), 128

Cosmopolitan imperialism, 130–140

Costa, Joaquín, 71

Covadonga, 39

Crafts, 11, 28, 115, 172; centrality to Hispano-Arab culture, 207, 221–223; French distinction between Berber and Arab crafts, 219–220; mosaics (*zellij*), 293; paired with music in exhibitions, 229–230

Damascus, 101, 131

Darwish, Mahmud, 74, 75

Dawud, Muhammad, 5, 28, 63, 175, 181, 229; Ahliyya School and, 256, 257–258, 274; Andalusi migration and, 268, 271; on Andalusi music, 114, 115, 278; Arslan and, 255, 264; as director of Royal Archive in Rabat, 265; Francoist colonial regime and, 269; French policy toward Berbers and, 201; Hasani Conservatory of Moroccan Music and, 247; history of Morocco by, 264–265; "lost paradise" idea and, 270, 277–278; Mahdiyya Press and, 279; map of al-Andalus and Morocco, 271, 272, 273; at Moroccan nationalist meeting in Tetouan, 259, *260;* as Protectorate general inspector of Muslim education, 269; at welcome party for Arslan, 259. *See also Tarikh Titwan* [*History of Tetouan*]

Decorative arts, 27, 168, 172

Delacroix, Eugène, 44

De las Cagigas, Isidro, 125–126, 127, 137; Arslan welcomed by, 257; at Moroccan nationalist meeting in Tetouan, 258, 259, *260;* as Spanish consul in Tetouan, 138

Deleuze, Gilles, 123

De Man, Paul, 78

Derrida, Jacques, 60–61

Dersa, Mount, 1, 56

Diario de un testigo de la guerra de África [*Diary of a Witness of the War of Africa*] (Alarcón, 1860), 25, 30, 32, 35, 59, 191; on Andalusian folk music, 230; brotherhood discourse in, 71; colonialist discourses influenced by, 71; colonial ventriloquism in, 62–64, 67; contradictory impulses in, 70; motifs of, 36; Orientalist tropes in, 40, 44–45, 60; prologue, 43–48, 56, 60; Ros de Olano and, 39, 43–44; on the Spanish taking of Tetouan, 69; as visual text, 48–49

Différance, Derridean concept of, 60–61

Ecos del Magrib / Sada al-Maghrib / Échos du Maghrib (García Barriuso), 235, 236, 237–240
Egypt, 18, 19, 145; hajj pilgrims and, 155; modern Arabic literature and, 80, 163; Napoleonic invasion (1798), 164; as part of "the Orient," 21; popularity of al-Andalus in, 76. *See also* Cairo
El-Ariss, Tarek, 164
Eleven Stars [*Ahad 'ashar kawkaban*] (Darwish, 1992), 74, 75
Elinson, Alexander, 10, 92
Entrada de S.A.I. el Jalifa Muley-el-Mehdi en Tetuán (Bertuchi painting, c. 1913), 214–215
Epps, Brad, 124
Erzini (al-Razini) family, 63
Escorial, Arabic collection of, 186–187, 253
Europe: al-Andalus as civilizing influence on, 127; Catalonia associated with, 121, 124–125, 127, 128–129, 139, 140; migration crisis in European Union, 17; north-south cultural divide, 24; Pyrenees as southern border of, 21, 121, 139; symbolic separation of Spain from, 128
Exhibition of Moroccan Art (Cordoba, 1946), 229–230, 243, 269
Eyewitness testimony, 48, 49, 55, 72; of Afaylal, 88, 102, 106, 108, 110; of Alarcón, 88; history and, 77

Fanatics of Tangier, The (Delacroix painting, 1837–1838), 44
Fascists, Spanish, 9, 10, 23, 72, 242; Moroccan intellectual elite and, 27, 144, 166; point of convergence with Republican liberalism, 120
Fasi, 'Allal al-, 201
Fasi, Muhammad al-, 252–255, 258, 277, 279, 294, 346n115
Al-Fath (Cairo newspaper), 254, 258, 261
Fawzi, 281
Fernández, Santos, 217–218
Fernández y González, Manuel, 38
Festival of the Hispano-Arab Book (*Fiesta del Libro Hispano-Árabe*), 179–180, 189, 280
Fez, 7, 63, 91, 136, 293; Andalusian character of, 138; Andalusi music in, 231, 249; Bab Boujloud, 173; in French Protectorate, 14; as "living museum," 11. *See also* Conference of Moroccan Music; Qarawiyyin Mosque
Flamenco: *caña* as early form of, 230; fandango, 42–43; origins of, 230–231; subgenres of, 237–238
Foucault, Michel, 20
1492, events of. *See* Reconquest, Christian
France, 21, 68; al-Andalus territory in, 91; Catalan-speaking areas of, 131; colonial competition with Spain, 138–139, 159, 168–169, 184; imperialist ambitions of, 70; Occitan languages in, 124; al-Saffar in, 83, 84; Spanish Republicans associated with, 168. *See also* Colonialism, French
Franco, Francisco, 9, 11, 119; in Bertuchi painting, 223, 224; Catalan nationalism assaulted by, 140; *Caudillo* title of, 179; depicted as defender of Islam, 152, 193; as editor of *Revista de tropas coloniales*, 134, 223; hajj sponsored by, 26–27, 142–143, 152, 201; international isolation of Franco regime, 171; interview with Amin al-Rihani (1939), 181, 197–199; Moroccan nationalism supported by, 175;

Franco, Francisco *(continued)*
National Catholicism and, 143–147; promise to found Arabic library, 189–190; al-Rahuni and, 147, 156; reception in Seville for returning hajj pilgrims, 157–163, *160;* in Rif War, 134, 147; victory in Spanish Civil War, 279

Francoism, 12, 26, 130, 303–304n30; Andalusi culture promoted by, 28; "Arabization" policy, 174, 185, 269; *convivencia* idea and, 151; "Hispano-Arab culture" concept and, 27, 168, 207; Infante's *andalucista* discourse appropriated by, 130; "renaissance" trope in lexicon of, 178; viewed in historical scholarship, 13

French Protectorate, 14, 138, 184, 196; Arslan barred from entering, 254, 255; Conservatory of Moroccan Music, 246; efforts to divide Arabs and Berbers, 155, 254–255; end of (1956), 17; Franco's effort to undermine authority of, 156; "Hispano-Moorish" style in arts and, 172–173; Moroccan art showcased in exhibitions, 218–219; official establishment (1912), 68; political repression in, 200–201; Service of Indigenous Arts (Service des Arts Indigènes), 219, 234. *See also* Berber *dahir;* Colonialism, French; Lyautey, Louis Hubert

Gaceta de África, La (newspaper), 221
Galicia, 124
Galician language, 123
Gallego Burín, Antonio, 228
Gannun, ʿAbd Allah, 179–180, 265, 279–280
García Barriuso, Patrocinio, 28, 211, 232–233; at Conference of Moroccan Music in Fez, 235, *236,* 237–240; Hasani Conservatory of Moroccan Music and, 248; Moroccan musicians criticized by, 245–246; on regional versions of *nūba* repertoire, 243–244; Spanish-French colonial rivalry and, 243. *See also Música hispano-musulmana en Marruecos, La*

García Figueras, Tomás, 12, 138, 170, 174, 182, 190; colonial education policy in Morocco and, 175–176; "Hispano-Arab culture" project and, 177; "Hispano-Muslim" music and, 240, 242–243; on Spain as transitional Euro-African country, 177–178; on "spiritual empire of al-Andalus," 196; trope of "renaissance" and, 178

García Gómez, Emilio, 262, 263, 264

Garden of the Alhambra, The (Bertuchi painting, 1904), 214

Geertz, Clifford, 78

General Franco Institute for Hispano-Arab Studies, 27, 138, 143, 234, 240, 269; books published by, 190–191; definition of Hispano-Arab culture and, 170–180; *Discursos* pamphlet published by, 182, *183;* Moroccan scholars at, 280; renaissance trope and, 242; *Titwan* journal and, 278–279

Ghanmiya, Ahmad, 182
Ghassani, al-, 171
Ghazzal, al-, 171
Ghurghiz, Mount, 1
Gibraltar (Jabal Ṭāriq), 86
Gibraltar, Strait of, 1, 4, 37, 86, 120, 284; brotherhood discourse and, 71–72; Iberian Peninsula on both sides of, 134; Mediterranean discourses and, 24
Gil Benumeya, Rodolfo, 11, 133–140, 225–226; on Andalucía as neither Orient nor Occident, 134

Glasser, Jonathan, 231
Gómez Jordana, Francisco, 232
Gómez-Rivas, Camilo, 10
Goode, Joshua, 130
Got, Antonio, 218
Granada, 27, 33, 135, 250; Abencerraje, 41, 53; Albayzín neighborhood, 58; in Andalucía region, 120; Andalusi music and, 231, 244; *cármenes* of, 224, 225; Christian reconquest (1492), 3, 4, 6, 39, 83; Corral del Carbón, 227–229; cultural transmission to modern Morocco, 211; Islamic heritage sites in, 294; as "the Jerusalem of the West," 40; literary representations of Muslim past, 49; Moroccan businesses named after, 7; Morocco House (Bayt al-Maghrib), 262; nostalgia for, 51–52; School of Arabic Studies, 262–263; seen in Tetouan, 53–54, 243; Tetouan as daughter of, 71, 268; wandering heritage of, 66; Zegri clan of, 41, 42. *See also* Alhambra; Nasrid dynasty
Guadalete, battle of (711), 47
Guadix, 33, 45
Guattari, Félix, 123
Guerras civiles de Granada (Pérez de Hita), 51
Gutiérrez Lescura, José, 212, 215, 217

Ha'ik, al-, 240, 244–245
Hajj (pilgrimage to Mecca), 26–27, 35, 117, 193; Franco's sponsorship of, 142–143; reception in Seville for returning pilgrims, 157–163, *160*; sea voyage on Spanish ships, 152–156; travel narratives and, 145; "Village of Hajj Franco," 201
Hajj, Muhammad al-, 258
Harraq, Muhammad al-, 83

Harrison, Olivia C., 19
Hasani Conservatory of Moroccan Music, 246–249
Hassan, Waïl, 181
Hassan II, king of Morocco, 277, 291, 292–293, 295, 297
Hay, John Drummond, 68
Haykal, Muhammad Husayn, 164
Hespéris (French colonial journal), 172, 283
Himmish, Bin Salim, 7
Hispanidad (Hispanicity), 217
Hispanisms, 84–85, 103–104, 105
Hispano-Arab culture, 18, 27, 328–329n2; as alternative to French colonialism, 168, 173, 175; *convivencia* and, 167, 178; General Franco Institute and, 170–180; as integral part of Spanish culture, 173; as justification for Spanish colonialism in Morocco, 143, 167; origins of, 170; "renaissance" of, 188, 190; al-Rihani's *Morocco* and, 192–205
Hispano-Arab Institute of Culture, 171
Hispano-Moroccan Music Conservatory, 211, 230, 277
Historia de la Cruzada española [*History of the Spanish Crusade*] (c. 1939–1943), 224
Historia de los bandos de Zegríes y Abencerrajes (Pérez de Hita, 1595), 41, 55
History of Tetouan. See *Tarikh Titwan* [*History of Tetouan*] (Dawud)
Hourani, Albert, 163
Al-Hulal al-sundusiyya fi al-akhbar wa-l-athar al-andalusiyya (Arslan, 1936–1939), 252, 253, 264, 266, 267
Al-Hurriyya [*Freedom*] (newspaper), 174, 246

I Am al-Andalus (al-Sabbagh, 1999), 8, 281
Iberian Peninsula, 25, 32, 50, 113, 294; migration of Andalusi culture from, 6, 10, 297; Morocco's historical relationship with, 81, 84; multiplicity of cultural and linguistic identities in, 122; Muslim invasion (711), 86; Muslim rule in, 21–22, 47
Iberian studies, 122
Ibero-American Exhibition (Seville, 1929), Morocco Pavilion, 212, 215, 217, 221
Ibn al-Amin, ʿAbd al-Salam, 248
Ibn al-Khatib, 10, 87, 88, 89–90, 120
Ibn al-Murahhal, 87, 88–89, 90, 91, 101
Ibn al-Tayyib, 81
Ibn ʿArabi, 193, 195
Ibn Battuta, 145
Ibn Jubayr, 145
Ibn Malik, 84
Ibn Raysun, ʿAbd al-Salam, 85, 87, 114
Ibn Rushd (Averroes), 75, 170–171, 178–179; *Kitab al-kulliyyat*, 190
Ibn Tawit, Muhammad, 269, 279, 280, 283–285
Ibn Zaydun, 91
Ibo Alfaro, Manuel, 37
Ideal andaluz, El [*The Andalusian Ideal*] (Infante, 1915), 121, 125, 126, 127–128, 133
IHEM [Institut des hautes études marocaines] (Institute for Advanced Moroccan Studies), 172, 173, 283
Imperial Economic Conference (Paris, 1935), 219
Imperialism, European, 80, 251, 266
Infante, Blas, 26, 116–121, 125, 138, 141, 213; Catalan nationalism repudiated by, 127–130, 139–140; death of, 130; as "Father of the Andalusian Fatherland," 116, 119, 130, 230; influence on Gil Benumeya, 135, 136, 140; *Motamid*, 116, 117–118; on origins of flamenco, 230–231; racial and cultural mixing defended by, 126–128
International Competition of Popular Song and Dance (Madrid, 1949), 249
Iraq, 192
Irbouh, Hamid, 220
Isabel I (the Catholic), 39, 47, 255
Isabel II, 39
Islam, 19, 27, 40, 66; Berbers and, 201; conflict with Christianity in literary representation, 95–96, 98; Europe/the West in binary opposition to, 21, 22; five pillars of, 143; Hispano-Arab culture concept and, 169; Islamic reform movements, 254; Orientalist scholarship and, 21; peaceful coexistence with Christianity, 197; representation of conflict with Christianity, 76; Spain's transhistorical struggle against, 47. *See also* Muslims
Islam, Moroccan, 11, 14, 136, 137, 154
Italy, 21, 131, 145
ʿIyad b. Musa, Abu al-Fadl, 89–90

Jaén (Jayyan), 83, 84, 97
Jayyusi, Salma Khadra, 80
Jews, 4, 131, 139; *convivencia* ("coexistence") and, 8, 119; expulsion of, 46
Jihad, 104, 106, 107, 108
Journey to Mecca (al-Rahuni, 1941), 27

Kaʿba (Mecca), 118, 147, 151, 152–153; Franco's hajj pilgrimage ship in role of, 154; Mosque of Cordoba compared to, 162

Kattani, al-, 80
Khalil's Summary (Mukhtasar Khalil), 84
Khattabi, 'Abd al-Karim al-, 116
Khizanat al-Dawla al-'Alawiyya (archive of 'Alawi dynasty), 289, 291
Kunnash Afaylal ("Afaylal's Notebook"), 79, 80–81, 85, 90, 314–315n19; chronicle of Spanish-Moroccan War, 81, 106; difficulty of categorizing, 81; on encounter with Christians, 87–88; on music, 114
Kunnash al-Ha'ik, 233
Kutubiyya Mosque (Marrakesh), 149, 289

LaCapra, Dominick, 112
Lakhdar, Kamal, 292
Larache, 138, 181
Larrea Palacín, Arcadio de, 248
Larrocha, José de, 214
League of Moroccan Scholars, 280
League of Nations, 254
Lebanon, 19, 28, 190, 204
Levant, 18, 21, 93, 163, 204, 205, 252
Lévi-Provençal, Evariste, 172
Leyendas de África [*Legends of Africa*] (Ros de Olano), 39
Liberal Party, 200
Liberals, Spanish, 120
Libya, 145, 155
Literature, Andalusi, 10, 83, 89, 91
Literature, Arabic, 92, 163, 164, 166, 180; Eurocentric notions of literature and, 80; "golden age" and decline of, 79–80; *rihla* (travelogue) tradition, 145
Literature, Eurocentric notion of, 80, 81, 144

Literature, Moroccan, 6, 7, 79, 80, 81, 164–165, 279
Literature, Spanish, 51, 67
Lyautey, Louis Hubert, 172–173, 219

Ma'arri, al-, 253
Madinat al-Zahra' (Cordoba), 206
Madrid, 19, 122, 227, 249; Egyptian Institute of Islamic Studies, 283; School of Arabic Studies, 283
Maghrib, the, 10, 18, 89, 113, 137, 188, 192
Al-Maghrib al-Aqsa [*Morocco*] (al-Rihani, 1940), 27, 181, 192–205; Berber influence in al-Andalus downplayed in, 188; Hispano-Arab culture concept and, 192
Mahdiyya Press, 256, 279
"Mahometan," 65–66
Mallette, Karla, 21
Al-Manar (newspaper and publisher), 251–252, 266–267
Mansur, Ya'qub al-, 149, 289
Manzari, Abu al-Hasan 'Ali al-, 3–4, 271, 275; mausoleum of, 1–5, 2, 3, 12, 110, 288, 297, 298; original tomb of, 5, 6
Maqqari, Ahmad b. Muhammad al-, 89, 90
Marrakesh, 14, 118, 149, 289, 293
Marruecos andaluz [*Andalusian Morocco*] (Gil Benumeya, 1942), 135, 139
Marruecos: La acción de España en el Norte de África [*Morocco: Spain's Action in North Africa*] (García Figueras, 1939), 175, 176–177
Martínez Sánchez, José, 30, 33
Martin-Márquez, Susan, 22, 35, 42, 124
Mashriq, the, 192, 256
Mateo Dieste, Josep Lluís, 156

394 INDEX

Mauritania (journal), 234
Mauritania, border with, 17
Mecca, pilgrimage to. *See* Hajj; Ka'ba
Medinaceli, Duchess of, 32, 64
Medinaceli, Duke of, 33
Mediterranean region, 23–25, 169, 186, 307n71, 307n76
Meknes, 51, 84
Melilla, 17, 181
Middle East, 2, 19
Monarchy / royal family, Moroccan, 8, 14, 29, 289–297
"Moor," 35, 39, 48, 66; as ambiguous term, 132–133; as category of Spanish imagination, 33; "Christian Moors," 226; "Moor's last sigh," 52, 54
Moriscos (crypto-Muslims), 59, 233, 239, 304n31; Andalusi music and, 245; expulsion of, 46, 136, 244; resistance to Christian rule, 33, 43, 45. *See also* Alpujarras Rebellion
Moroccan history, 2, 12, 38; "Andalus-centric" narrative of, 6, 28, 115, 135, 265, 268–269; Andalusi literary conventions and, 113; beyond the state, 103; Mediterranean studies and, 23; ongoing revision of, 13
Moroccan League ("Defenders of the Truth"), 252, 256
Moroccan nationalism, 2, 5, 168, 288; Andalusi identity and, 8; Andalusi music and, 246–249; Arab-Berber unity and, 202; Berber *dahir* protested by, 254–255; colonial period depicted in historiography of, 13–14; cultural transmission narrative appropriated by, 250, 278; Franco's encouragement of, 9; Hassan Minaret and, 291; intellectuals, 28; "lost paradise" metaphor abandoned by, 268; promoted by Francoists, 169; repressed in French Protectorate, 200–201; Spanish colonialist ideas coopted by, 270
Moroccan studies, 103
Morocco, 26, 76, 88, 120, 252; Andalus-centric view of, 268–269; Andalusi heritage and identity of, 6–9, 59, 141, 281, 287–288, 292–293; constitution of, 8; indemnity paid after war with Spain, 68; independence (1956), 13, 17, 18, 280, 289; Mashriq in relation to, 192, 256
Morocco (al-Rihani, 1940). *See al-Maghrib al-Aqsa* [*Morocco*] (al-Rihani, 1940)
Morocco House (Bayt al-Maghrib, Cairo), 171, 262, 280
Motamid (Infante, 1920), 116, 117–118, 133
Al Motamid (journal), 138
Mubarak, Sidi al-, 85, 86
Muhammad I, 88
Muhammad IV, 84, 103
Muhammad V, king of Morocco, 291
Muhammad V (Nasrid ruler), 89, 296
Muhammad V Mausoleum (Rabat), 291–297
Muhammad VI, 289, 297
Mulay 'Abd al-Salam, tomb of, 76, 84
Mulay al-'Abbas, 32, 54–55, 64; abandonment of Tetouan to the Spanish, 111; Alarcón dressed as, 54; as leader of Moroccan army, 67, 103, 109
Mulay al-Hasan, 179, 246; Franco and, 156, 182; School of Arabic Studies in Granada and, 262; Spanish Civil War and, 146, 153
Mulay al-Hasan Institute (Instituto "Muley el Hasan"), 171, 180, 278, 279, 280

INDEX 395

Mulay al-Mahdi, Caliph, 208, 214–215
Mulay al-Yazid, Sultan, 86
Mulay Zaydan, 186, 187
Mundo ilustrado (magazine), 226, 229
Muntañola, Pere, 129
Murcia, 11, 97, 193, 194–195
Music, Andalusi, 5, 12, 114–115, 276–277, 348n16; centrality to Hispano-Arab culture, 207; "echoes" of al-Andalus trope, 232; Festival of Andalusi Music, 7; *gharnāṭī* repertoire, 235, 237, 238; Moroccan nationalism and, 247–250; paired with crafts in exhibitions, 229–230; revival under colonial rule, 28, 114, 158–159, 230–246; Spanish–French colonial rivalry and, 235, 237, 239–240, 242–243. See also *Nūba* repertoire
Música hispano-musulmana en Marruecos, La [*Hispano-Muslim Music in Morocco*] (García Barriuso, 1941), 234, 240, 241, 242–246
Muslims, 9, 25, 32; in Afaylal's chronicle of Spanish-Moroccan War, 102–103, 105, 108–109; conflict with Christians in al-Andalus, 92–93; *convivencia* ("coexistence") and, 8, 119; European discourses about, 21. See also Islam
Muʿtamid, al- (Ibn ʿAbbad), 17, 91, 116, 117–118, 119, 138, 149, 159
Muza (fictional figure), 55, 57
Myrtle and Myrrh (al-Rihani, 1905), 180

Nacionalitat catalana, La [*Catalan Nationality*] (Prat de la Riba, 1906), 123–124
Naciri, Said, 7
Nafh al-tib (al-Maqqari), 89
Nahḍa, the, 80, 164

Nasiri, al-Makki al-, 37, 68, 174, 201, 270
Nasrid dynasty, 88, 89, 227, 237, 271, 275, 294; Andalusi music and, 240; in historical imaginary of Hispano-Arabism, 168; Islamic architecture and, 296; motto of, 125, 281, 282, 283, 287, 295; Romantic representation of, 54. See also Granada
Nation Arabe, La (journal), 254, 255, 257, 258, 264
Nietzsche, Friedrich, 78
Ni Oriente, ni Occidente [*Neither Orient nor Occident*] (Gil Benumeya, c. 1930), 134
North Africa, 2, 19, 238; Andalusi migration to, 60; Berbers as indigenous people of, 10; expansion of Islam into, 220; Mediterranean perspective and, 25; Spain's historical connection to, 9, 21–22
North African Muslim Students Association, 252–253
"Notes for a Study of Andalusian Regionalism" (De las Cagigas), 125–126
Nouba de Ochchâk (Chottin, 1931), 235
Novela morisca (literary genre), 51–52
Nūba repertoire, 158, 159, 232–234, 237, 239, 245; loss of suites from, 245–246; *Nubat al-Isbahan*, 114, 248; *Nubat al-ʿushshaq*, 158–159; regional variants of, 243–244; Spanish–French colonial rivalry and, 243. See also Music, Andalusi
Al-Nubugh al-maghribi fi al-adab al-ʿarabi [*Moroccan Genius in Arabic Literature*] (Gannun, 1938), 279, 346n118

O'Donnell, Leopoldo, 37, 54, 55, 67
Orientalism, 19–22, 33, 44–45, 262; essentialist views of the Orient, 58, 61; ontological instability of, 169; Paul Geuthner bookshop (Paris), 253; photography, 35; in Romantic literature, 40, 45; space and time in literature of, 44; in Spanish fiction, 38
Orientalism (Said, 1978), 19, 20, 21
Ortiz de Villajos, Cándido G., 228, 229

Palestine, 74, 76, 132
Pan-Arab nation, 28
Pan-Islamism, 144, 264
Pardo Bazán, Emilia, 33
Paronomasia, 95, 96–97, 108, 111
Party of Moroccan Unity (*Hizb al-wahda al-maghribiyya*), 174, 200
Party of National Reform (*Hizb al-islah al-watani*), 174, 200
Paso del Estrecho [*Crossing the Straits*] (Bertuchi painting, 1938), 223, 224
Pedro I, 149, 159, 296
Pérez de Hita, Ginéz, 41, 49, 51, 55
Pérez Vera, Cristóbal, 190
Philip II, 46
Philip III, 46
Philology, 78
Píñar, 3
Poetics (Aristotle), 75, 314n9
Poetry, Andalusi, 86, 88, 90; adapted to new cultural context, 95; al-Maqqari and preservation of 89; water imagery in, 98
Poetry, Arabic, 91; classical ode, 94, 95; elegiac tradition, 95, 97; in pre-Islamic Arabia, 98
Portugal, 85, 122
Postcolonial studies, 19

Prat de la Riba, Enric, 123–126, 129
Pyrenees, as border of Europe, 21, 121, 139

Qabbani, Nizar, 75
Qarawiyyin Mosque (Fez), 83, 165, 256, 257
Qasr al-Kabir, al- (Alcazarquivir), 90, 102, 137, 318n76
Qur'an and Qur'anic citations, 146, 148, 163, 186, 314n1; Alcázar of Seville associated with, 161; on arrival of pilgrims to the Ka'ba, 153; on Battle of Uhud, 150; in camp of Moroccan army, 109, 110; description of heavenly paradise, 98; memorization of Qur'an, 63; Moroccan literary tradition and, 165–166; Arabic as language of Qur'an, 204; story of Joseph, 74

Rabat, 7, 90, 136; Andalusian character of, 138; as capital of French Protectorate, 14, 288; Conservatory of Moroccan Music, 235; Hassan Minaret, 29, 149, 289, 290, 291–292, 296; as "living museum," 11; Moroccan nationalists in, 256; Muhammad V mausoleum complex, 291–297; Royal Archive, 265
Race: Andalusian nationalism and, 125–126; brotherhood discourse and, 71; Francoist conception of, 130; scientific racism, 124, 128
Rahuni, Ahmad al-, 27, 63, 142, 193; Francoist discourse and, 145–146, 157; in between master narratives, 163–166. *See also al-Rihla al-makkiyya* [*Journey to Mecca*]

INDEX   397

Reconquest, Christian, 3, 4, 6, 10, 54, 70, 91, 100–101; Andalusi emigration resulting from, 136, 273–276; Catalonia associated with, 129; last Muslim territories to fall, 45; parallels with Spanish occupation of Tetouan, 77; Spanish colonialism compared to, 94; Spanish-Moroccan War as continuation of, 25, 36, 37, 38–39, 47
Regionalism, 125, 127–128
Renan, Ernest, 21
Repetition (anaphora), 95, 96–97, 111
Republicans, Spanish, 26, 117, 186–187; *convivencia* idea and, 151; as "godless communists," 146; viewed in historical scholarship, 13. *See also* Spain, Second Republic of
Resina, Joan Ramon, 122–123
"Return to Philology, The" (Said), 78
Revista de la Raza, La (magazine), 134
Revista de tropas coloniales (magazine), 134, 215. See also *África* (journal)
Ricard, Prosper, 219–223, 234, 243
Rida, Muhammad Rashid, 252
Al-Rif (newspaper), 175, 258, 330n26
Rifi, Ahmad b. 'Ali al-, 50, 86
Rif War (1921–1927), 116, 134, 147, 215
Rihani, Amin al-, 27, 171; as cultural translator, 192; Franco interviewed by, 197–199; Franco's government praised by, 199–200; Hispano-Arab culture concept and, 193–194, 203–205; in Morocco and Spain, 180–192; on neo-Arab ("Hispano-Arab") architecture, 205–207; superiority of Spanish over French colonialism argued by, 200–203
Al-Rihla al-makkiyya [Journey to Mecca] (al-Rahuni), 143–144, 152, 157, 161–166, 170

Rinaldy, Aníbal, 214, 224
Rodríguez de la Borbolla y Camoyán, José, 140–141
Romanticism, European, 40, 45, 49, 51
Ronda, 117
Ros de Olano, Antonio, 39
Rundi, al-, 91, 92, 95, 96–98, 100–101, 110, 318n69

Sabbagh, Muhammad al-, 7–8, 281
Sabt (descendant of prophet Noah), 87, 89
Sacks, Jeffrey, 81
Saffar, Muhammad al-, 83–84
Sahara desert, 17, 305n47
Said, Edward, 19, 20–21, 45, 78
Saint, Lucien, 255
Salafiyya movement, 254
Salé, 90, 186, 234
Salwat al-anfas (al-Kattani, 1887), 80
Sarghini, Muhammad al-, 213
Saudi Arabia, 145, 154, 155, 180
School of Indigenous Arts [Escuela de Artes Indígenes] (Tetouan), 138, 220, 224–225, 227, 228, 335n11; Francoist officials' visit to, 209, *210*, 211; tile mosaics, 287
Scott, Joan, 113
Serrano Suñer, Ramón, 208–209, *210*, 211
Seville, 19, 91, 116; Alcázar, 50, 149–150, 151, 159, 296; in Andalucía region, 120; Andalusi music and, 231; Christian conquest (1248), 149, 244; Franco's reception of Moroccan hajj pilgrims in, 152, 157–163, *160;* La Giralda, 56–57, 125, 148–149, 150, 151, 289; Ibero-American Exhibition (1929), Morocco Pavilion, 212, 215, 217, 221; Islamic heritage sites in, 294; Mosque

Seville *(continued)*
    of Yaʿqub al-Mansur, 149; public homage to Infante (1999), 140; al-Rahuni in, 147–150; as rebel stronghold in civil war, 147; Tetouan as Seville in Afaylal's elegy, 92–101
Shaqundi, al-, 10
Sharif, Muhammad al-, 12
Shawdri, Muhammad al-, 232–233
Shawqi, Ahmad, 75, 101
Shurbi family, 63
Sidi Ifni, 14
Sierra Nevada, 43, 44, 52, 53, 56
Société l'Andaloussia ensemble, 235, 238–239
Spain, 66, 88; ambiguous cultural location of, 35; Andalusi heritage shared with Morocco, 7, 27, 42, 196; Castilian language and culture privileged in, 122; colonial competition with France, 138–139, 159, 168–169, 184; as crossroads of East and West, 199; democratic transition (1970s), 213; Hapsburg period, 69–70; Islamic heritage sites in, 261–262, 267; liminal position in Europe, 21–22; loss of last American colonies (1898), 46; Mecca juxtaposed with, 162; Muslim heritage, 67; Orientalist philology in, 21; peripheral nationalisms in, 121–130; post-Franco, 26, 119, 213; reorientation toward Africa, 121; scholarship on Hispano-Arab cultural relations, 18; as transitional Euro-African country, 177–178
Spain, Second Republic of, 122, 123, 128, 132, 143; as "anti-Spain" in Francoist discourse, 242; Franco's overthrow of, 9; Moroccan nationalists and, 263. *See also* Republicans, Spanish

Spanish Civil War, 5, 9, 26, 117, 141; Franco's sponsorship of hajj and, 142–143; historical scholarship on Spain and, 13; Infante killed during, 130; internationalization of, 152, 153; Moroccan nationalism and, 9; Moroccan troops in rebel (Francoist) army, 135, 146, 185, 193, 209; Muslim world and, 156; official Francoist account of, 224; Republican attack on Ceuta, 153; Spanish colonial policy in Morocco and, 174; "Uprising" (*Alzamiento*) as commencement of, 208; victory of rebel (Francoist) forces in, 199, 223, 279
Spanish language, 84–85, 103
Spanish-Moroccan War (1859–1860), 8, 30, 76, 214; Afaylal's chronicle of, 78, 79, 81, 84, 101, 102–113, 115; Alarcón's account of, 43; as beginning of Spanish colonialism in Morocco, 35–36; as continuation of Christian Reconquest, 25, 36, 37, 38–39, 47, 93; eyewitnesses to, 49; legacy of, 67–73; origins of, 36–37; as War of Africa in Spanish historiography, 37–38, 61; as War of Tetouan in Moroccan historiography, 37
Spanish Protectorate, 1, 7, 116, 156, 200, 248; Academy of Arabic and Berber, 170; Andalusians in, 138; Council for Historic and Artistic Monuments, 232; Delegation of Education and Culture, 283; end of (1956), 17; Festival of the Hispano-Arab Book (*Fiesta del Libro Hispano-Árabe*), 280; Francoist intellectuals in, 133–134; Hasani Institute for Moroccan Music, 246; maps of, 15,

16; Moroccan government under, 146; Moroccan nationalism and, 169, 255; northern and southern zones, 14; official establishment (1912), 68; preservation of Moroccan crafts and, 222; al-Rihani's visit to, 171, 181, 182; as savior of Andalusi heritage, 12; School of Carpets, 220; Spanish Civil War and, 153; union with greater Muslim world, 178. *See also* Colonialism, Spanish

Sufism, 76, 81, 83, 155, 165, 193; Andalusi music and, 247

Syria, 76, 192

Tamuda (Spanish colonial journal), 283

Tangier, 7, 14, 29, 69, 179, 209; Arslan in, 254, 255; at Moroccan independence, 280; Moroccan nationalists in, 254; Pension Palace, 286–287, *288*; Spanish Legation, 285; Spanish Post and Telegraph Office, 285–286

Tangier Street (Bertuchi painting), 214

Tarikh Titwan [*History of Tetouan*] (Dawud), 5, 265–266, 268; on cultural practices inherited from al-Andalus, 276–277; "lost paradise" idea and, 270, 277–278; map of al-Andalus and Morocco, 271, *272*, *273*; *Mukhtasar tarikh Titwan* (*Summary of the History of Tetouan*), 269, 270

Tariq b. Ziyad, 86

Tazi, Muhammad al-, 257, 260

Tejado, Gabino, 37–38

Tetouan, 7, 73, 136, 250, 298; Ahliyya School, 274, 280; Andalusi music in, 231, 239, 244–245, 249; architecture of, 12; Arslan in, 28, 257–260, *260*, 280; Bab al-'Uqla, 281; as capital of Spanish Protectorate, 1, 14, 142; cemetery, 1–2, *2*, *3*, *4*, 56, 58; Cemetery Gate (Bab al-Maqabir), 1, 56, 110; as continuation of Muslim Granada, 25, 36, 243, 281; Cordoba resurrected in, 195; as cultural capital of northern Morocco, 4; current struggles (2010s), 297–298; as "daughter of Granada and Fez," 71, 268, 275; Dawud Library, 79; "dove" epithet for, 102; elegy for, 76–77; Ensanche (Spanish colonial annex), 1, 212; General Library, 91; Granada seen in, 53–54; Hispano-Moroccan Music Conservatory, 211, 230, 277; legacy of Spanish-Moroccan War and, 67–73; as "living museum," 11; Medina (old city), 1, 7, 212; Mellah (Jewish quarter), 212; Moroccan nationalists in, 256, 258–260, *260*; Mosque of al-Saqiya al-Fawqiyya, 83; "neo-Arab" architecture in, 205–207; Qasba Mosque, 83; rebuilding of, 3; al-Rihani in, 181; School of Fine Arts, 213, 281; School of Indigenous Arts, 138, 209, *210*, 211; Seville seen in, 92–101; Spanish occupation of, 69, 76–77, 90, 95, 113; Tangier Gate (Bab Tanja), 218; Tower of Geleli (Burj al-Qalalin), 53. *See also* School of Indigenous Arts [Escuela de Artes Indígenes]

Tetouan, Battle of (1860), 54, 111

Tetouan School (artistic movement), 213–214

"Thick reading," 78

Titwan ["Tetouan"] (journal), 269, 278–281, 282, 283–285, 294

Toledo, Alcázar of, 208

Torres Balbás, Leopoldo, 262
Tourism, 7, 119, 215, *216*, 226, 302n19
Tribaq, Ahmad, 7
Truth about the Tablada Plot and the Free State of Andalucía, The (Infante, 1931), 128
Tunis, 231
Tunisia, 238, 252
Turkey, 24
Turris, ʿAbd al-Khaliq al-, 5, 28, 257–258; Francoist colonial regime and, 270; Hasani Conservatory of Moroccan Music and, 246–247; mausoleum of, 1–2, *2*, *3*, 12, 288, 298; party and newspaper led by, 174

Uhud, Battle of (c. 625), 150
Umayyad caliphate (Cordoba), 50, 92, 133, 150, 274; Andalusi music and, 237, 240; *convivencia* ("coexistence") as characteristic of, 127; Gil Benumeya's admiration for, 135–136; Hispano-Arab culture concept and, 195; in historical imaginary of Hispano-Arabism, 168; Madinat al-Zahraʾ gardens, 206
ʿ*Umdat al-rawin fi tarikh Tittawin* [*The Foundational Narrators of Tetouan's History*] (al-Rahuni), 63, 142

Valencia, 131, 227, 244
Verdad sobre el complot de Tablada y el estado libre de Andalucía, La (Infante, 1931), 128
Vo Toan, 291, 293–296

Wad Ras, Battle of (1860), 67, 70
Al-Wafi fi nazm al-qawafi (al-Rundi), 90–91
Wazzani, al-Tuhami al-, 164–165, 175, 181, 258, 270, 281
Wazzani, Ibrahim al-, 200
Why Did Muslims Fall Behind while Others Made Progress? [*Li-madha taʾakhkhara al-muslimun wa-limadha taqaddama ghayruhum?*] (Arslan, 1930), 266

Yamama, Zarqa al-, 93, 318n74
Yusuf I, 89

Zaghlul, Saʿd, 256
Al-Zawiya (al-Wazzani, 1942), 165, 330n26
Zaydan, Jurji, 203, 334n127
Zaynab (Haykal, 1913), 164
Zegri clan, 41, 42
Zionism, *andalucismo* compared to, 131
Zorrilla, José, 40

Printed in the USA
CPSIA information can be obtained
at www.ICGtesting.com
LVHW092246250224
772789LV00018B/164/J

9 780674 980327